THE CRITICAL HERITAGE SERIES

GENERAL EDITOR: B. C. SOUTHAM, M.A., B.LITT. (OXON.)
Formerly Department of English, Westfield College, University of London

For list of books in the series see back endpaper.

MARK TWAIN

THE CRITICAL HERITAGE

Edited by
FREDERICK ANDERSON
Editor of the Mark Twain Papers, University of California, Berkeley

with the assistance of
KENNETH M. SANDERSON

LONDON: ROUTLEDGE & KEGAN PAUL

First published 1971
by Routledge and Kegan Paul Ltd
Broadway House, 68–74 Carter Lane,
London EC4V 5EL
© *Frederick Anderson 1971*
No part of this book may be reproduced in
any form without permission from the
publisher, except for the quotation of
brief passages in criticism

ISBN 0 7100 7084 5

Printed in Great Britain
by Butler & Tanner Ltd, Frome and London

General Editor's Preface

The reception given to a writer by his contemporaries and near-contemporaries is evidence of considerable value to the student of literature. On one side, we learn a great deal about the state of criticism at large and in particular about the development of critical attitudes towards a single writer; at the same time, through private comments in letters, journals or marginalia, we gain an insight upon the tastes and literary thought of individual readers of the period. Evidence of this kind helps us to understand the writer's historical situation, the nature of his immediate reading-public, and his response to these pressures.

The separate volumes in *The Critical Heritage Series* present a record of this early criticism. Clearly, for many of the highly-productive and lengthily-reviewed nineteenth- and twentieth-century writers, there exists an enormous body of material; and in these cases the volume editors have made a selection of the most important views, significant for their intrinsic critical worth or for their representative quality—perhaps even registering incomprehension!

For earlier writers, notably pre-eighteenth century, the materials are much scarcer and the historical period has been extended, sometimes far beyond the writer's lifetime, in order to show the inception and growth of critical views which were initially slow to appear.

In each volume the documents are headed by an Introduction, discussing the material assembled and relating the early stages of the author's reception to what we have come to identify as the critical tradition. The volumes will make available much material which would otherwise be difficult of access and it is hoped that the modern reader will be thereby helped towards an informed understanding of the ways in which literature has been read and judged.

B.C.S.

Contents

CONTENTS

A Tramp Abroad (1880)

The Prince and the Pauper (1881)

Life on the Mississippi (1883)

The Adventures of Huckleberry Finn (1884-5)

A Connecticut Yankee in King Arthur's Court (1889)

The Tragedy of Pudd'nhead Wilson (1894)

Personal Recollections of Joan of Arc (1896)

Following the Equator or *More Tramps Abroad* (1897)

CONTENTS

Preface

In order to present a balanced sense of transatlantic response to Mark Twain's writings, reviews have been selected in approximately equal numbers from British and American journals with emphasis upon books most likely to elicit the strongest expression of national opinion.

The names of anonymous reviewers have been supplied, with explanation for attribution, whenever evidence supported conjecture. The widest possible choice has been made of critical points of view expressed throughout the span of Mark Twain's literary life. It is inevitable that the novels with an English setting aroused a special interest in English critics and these are therefore represented somewhat more fully. American reviewers rather surprisingly neglected to comment on *Adventures of Huckleberry Finn* at the time of its publication so that relatively little space has been allotted to that work in this volume, despite the massive concentration of critical attention in recent years.

Reviews are presented in chronological order to give some sense of the evolution of Mark Twain's literary reputation during his lifetime. In a very few instances this principle has been rejected to allow a retrospective consideration to appear in the context most apt to be useful to the reader.

The literary distinction of the criticism published here is uneven. Much of it was prepared for commercial and ephemeral journals and was motivated by moral, social or regional prejudice. Commentaries on the author's life and times pervade the reviews of his works. If in some sense this approach might appear to be an adulteration of the critical process, it must also be recognized as a valid approach to the unusual interinvolvement of the man and the writer. Mark Twain wrote most successfully when he remained within the matrix of Samuel Clemens' life. The relevance of 'the myth of Antaeus' was implicit in reviews throughout much of Clemens' life, explicit in a commentary in *Dial* (No. 80) at the time of his death and a truism of subsequent criticism.

Acknowledgments

My chief debt for assistance in the preparation of this volume is to Kenneth M. Sanderson whose patient and thorough search for reviews is in part recognized by the appearance of his name on the title-page. Both Robert H. Hirst and Michael B. Frank made valuable suggestions for which I am properly grateful.

Note on the Text

The reviews collected in this volume are reprinted as they originally appeared with no attempt to correct their writers' errors. Only errors which were obviously typographical in origin have been silently emended. Long quotations from Mark Twain's writings have been dropped to conserve space, but in each instance sufficient information has been supplied to identify the passage.

Chronological Table

1835   Born in Florida, Missouri.

1848–57 Worked as a printer.

1857–61 Apprentice and licensed pilot on the Mississippi.

1862–6   Reporter and writer for various Nevada and California newspapers and magazines.

1865   'Jim Smiley and his Jumping Frog' published in *Saturday Press*, New York.

1866–9   Newspaper correspondent from the Sandwich Islands, New York, and the *Quaker City* excursion through the Mediterranean to the Holy Land (June–November 1867); lecture tours.

1867   *The Celebrated Jumping Frog of Calaveras County, And other Sketches.*

1869   *The Innocents Abroad* (English title: *The New Pilgrim's Progress*; English publication, October 1870).

1870   Became editor of the Buffalo (New York) *Express*; married Olivia Langdon.

1871   Built house in Hartford, Connecticut; lecture tours.

1872   *Roughing It*; first English lecture tour.

1874   *The Gilded Age* (with Charles Dudley Warner); second English lecture tour.

1874   *The Gilded Age* ('Colonel Sellers') dramatized and first produced.

1875   *Sketches, New and Old.*

1876   *The Adventures of Tom Sawyer.*

1878–9   Travelled in Germany, Switzerland and Italy.

1880   *A Tramp Abroad.*

1882   *The Prince and the Pauper.*

1882   *The Stolen White Elephant Etc.*

1883   *Life on the Mississippi.*

1884–5   Extended lecture tour with George Washington Cable.

1885   *The Adventures of Huckleberry Finn* (English publication, December 1884).

1889   *A Connecticut Yankee in King Arthur's Court* (English title: *A Yankee at the Court of King Arthur*).

1891-5   Lived in Germany, France and Italy.

1892   *The American Claimant.*

1893   *The £1,000,000 Bank-Note and Other New Stories.*

1894   *Tom Sawyer Abroad.*

1894   *The Tragedy of Pudd'nhead Wilson.*

1895-6   Lecture tour through New Zealand, Australia, India and South Africa.

1896   *Personal Recollections of Joan of Arc.*

1897   *Following the Equator* (English title: *More Tramps Abroad*).

1897-1900   Lived in Vienna and London.

1899   'Collected Editions' published.

1900   *The Man That Corrupted Hadleyburg.*

1901   Litt.D. from Yale.

1902   LL.D. from the University of Missouri.

1903-4   Residence in Italy.

1907   Litt.D. from Oxford.

1909   *Is Shakespeare Dead?*

1910   Died near Redding, Connecticut.

Introduction

Mark Twain's contemporary critics were uneasy in the presence of the Western humour, the high spirits and the vernacular language which characterized much of Mark Twain's most effective work. Even American critics were reluctant to accept as enduring literature humorous writing which broke away from the gentle irony of the New England writers to whom they were accustomed. In an age when piety and the reinforcement of conventional virtues were expected literary concerns, reviewers wanted the 'moral purpose' of humour to be clearly evident. The urbane wit and sentiment which prevailed at Oliver Wendell Holmes' breakfast-table and over his Bostonian tea-cups was far more comfortable than the horse-play and frontier yarns which amused men in smoky Western saloons. But most critics in the United States, England and throughout Europe did come to accept Mark Twain on his own terms even if almost always with reservations. Mark Twain was not uninterested in what reviewers might say, but his chosen subjects and style show no change as a result of criticism. He educated the critics in his purposes rather than accepting their instruction on the proper subjects for literature.

'It is a mark of the democratic independence of America that she has betrayed a singular indifference to the appraisal of her literature at the hands of foreign criticism', Archibald Henderson wrote in 1910 (No. 86). Henderson continued that 'the case of Mark Twain is a literary phenomenon which imposes upon criticism, peculiarly upon American criticism, the distinct obligation of tracing the steps in his unhalting climb to an eminence completely international in character'. The climb may have been unhalting, but it was certainly not without obstacles. On the other hand, unlike Henry James' and, far more dramatically, Herman Melville's, the author's reputation did not reach a peak from which it declined during his lifetime.

The reviews collected here show degrees of approval from the beginning of Mark Twain's career with critical reservations persisting to the end. Much of this ambivalence resulted from the uneven quality of Mark Twain's writing. Much of it resulted from critical irresolution when confronted by work which did not meet the assumed standards of the reading public.

<h1 style="text-align:center">I</h1>

THE CRITICS' PREMISES

Contemporary readers, the author and potential literary historians compose the audience to whom a book's reviewer may address himself. Our interest in the reviewer depends upon the extent to which he affected the sale of a book, influenced the author's literary development or preserved a record of the values of his period.

In the case of Mark Twain's critics, there was relatively little opportunity to influence the reader's decision to buy a book, since throughout most of Mark Twain's career the initial sales of his books were made in advance of publication by subscription purchase. Mark Twain was explicit in his view of the limited area of a critic's influence. The success with which reviewers recorded the intellectual climate of the literate public is demonstrated repeatedly in this volume. We have therefore a substantial view of the literary establishment whose good opinion Mark Twain alternately sought and rejected.

It was difficult for reviewers to award unqualified praise to Mark Twain's writings about the frontier in an age when 'refined', 'delicate', 'generous', 'kindly' and 'worthy' were the terms most often chosen to express critical approval. In at least one case when approval was registered—and this was as late as 1899—it was with a phrase gratifying to the Victorians but astonishing to the modern sense of Mark Twain's value. William Archer concluded his warm praise of *Huckleberry Finn* with the accolade that Mark Twain was the ' "sacred poet" of the Mississippi' (*America To-Day*, pp. 212–13). Before Mark Twain achieved acceptance on these terms he had been repeatedly attacked for scoffing at 'sacred' things and, in the *Melbourne Review* in 1885 among other places, because his humour failed to meet the obligation of 'enforcing morality and exposing vice and folly'. Without an overt statement of moral purpose, humour could not be accepted as literature. Commentary on Mark Twain's writing reveals that the critic enforced the social standards of his time far more frequently than he allowed himself the luxury of discovery or demanded of himself the courage of an independent and exclusively literary judgment.

Despite their persistent anonymity only a rare reviewer chose or dared to commit himself to anything except the most conservative attitude towards a writer who mocked social conventions in language not always expected in the parlour.

II

SUBSCRIPTION BOOK PUBLICATION

Perhaps even more than by their conventional timidity Mark Twain's critics (and potential critics) were discouraged from reviewing his books by the method he chose for publication. Subscription book publication in the second half of the nineteenth century in the United States was regarded by critics and sophisticated readers with scorn. The English subscription publisher offered major novels by standard writers in weekly or monthly instalments at a cheap price. The American publisher of subscription books commonly provided gaudy volumes of little literary worth at high prices. Before publication, a corps of salesmen took 'prospectuses' containing specimen pages and sample bindings of the forthcoming volume from house to house. Aggressive sales techniques, the convenience of purchase at home and the promise of physically impressive volumes led to enormous sales. This large audience bought books for display without regard to their literary content or critical endorsement. Nearly 70,000 copies of *Innocents Abroad*, Mark Twain's first book sold by this means, were distributed within a year of publication. Within the first three months of publication *Roughing It* and *The Gilded Age* each sold approximately 40,000 copies.

William Dean Howells, in 'The Man of Letters as a Man of Business', said in *Scribner's* (October 1893):

At one time there seemed a probability of the author's gains by subscription publication, and one very well-known American author prospered fabulously in that way. The percentage offered by the subscription houses was only about half as much as that paid by the trade, but the sales were so much greater that the author could very well afford to take it. . . . No book of literary quality was made to go by subscription except Mr. Clemens's books, and I think these went because the subscription public never knew what good literature they were.

Mark Twain's exploitation of an audience not much inclined to read is made evident by the inclusion in the salesman's prospectus for *A Tramp*

Abroad of a Cleveland *Herald* comment: 'The illustrations are full of quaint humor, and without reading a line of the text these alone will secure the sale of the book.'

Howells described the reaction to subscription salesmen:

In the cities and large towns he is voted a bore and a nuisance; . . . he is a hissing and a by-word, a proverb of the undesirable. But in the smaller towns and in the country, where people have all the time there is . . . the book agent is not only tolerated, but welcomed; not only asked to sit down on a specially dusted chair, but bidden draw it up to the table when overtaken by dinner in the midst of his eloquence.

George Ade has given an immediate and persuasive account of the provincial community's response to the book agent and his wares (see Appendix B) in which he also makes clear the unique acceptance of Mark Twain's volumes. The books' weight, size, quantity of illustrations and generous embellishments of gilt, stamped design and leather bindings figured prominently in the salesman's appeal to an audience which preferred the appearance of quality over its sometimes uncomfortable if inconspicuous presence. The impressive if meretricious presentation established prices for Clemens' books which ranged, according to binding and gilt decoration, from $3.50 to $8.00. A 'Notice to the Public' on the last page of the first edition of *Tom Sawyer* attempted a rebuttal to charges that subscription books 'are higher in price than those of equal value sold at book stores'. Engravings, paper and printing costs were said to justify subscription prices 'and as through our Agents we sell ten times more of our books than do the trade publishers, we can afford a better book for a given sum'. The prices charged for Mark Twain's books certainly did not restrain their sales or the author's profits. Upon occasion Mark Twain defended his use of this medium as a means of reaching 'the masses', an aim which he undeniably achieved.

The flurry of reviews and retrospective examinations of his work which accompanied the appearance of the collected editions in 1899 in part resulted from his escaping the stigma of the shoddy subscription volume by achieving the reassuring prestige of a collected edition presented in attractive form.

III

THE AUTHOR'S VIEW OF CRITICS

The majority of Mark Twain's readers may not have been much concerned about the professional critics' opinions. Mark Twain may have been willing to risk critical disapproval or disinterest by exploiting a somewhat disreputable publishing medium for personal profit and to reach a mass audience. He may have made little compromise in choice of subject and style to win critical approval. But the author was certainly aware of the power critics possessed and expressed his views of it both ironically and with serious concern.

When Edwin Forrest, near the end of an honourable theatrical career, was scheduled to appear in San Francisco in 1866, Mark Twain, still a newspaperman himself, ironically admonished Forrest about the prejudices of newspaper reviewers. 'Our critics will make you sing a lively tune. They will soon let you know that your giant reputation cannot protect you on this coast.' Mark Twain mordantly anticipated a review the actor should expect:

Mr. Forrest has evidently mistaken the character of this people. We will charitably suppose that this is the case at any rate. We make no inquiry as to what kind of people he has been in the habit of playing before, but we simply inform him that he is now in the midst of a refined and cultivated community, and one which will not tolerate such indelicate allusions as were made use of in the play of *Othello* last night. If he would not play to empty benches, this must not be repeated.

The mock review was followed by advice which would be relevant when Mark Twain later met the same kind of attack. 'They always come the "refined and cultivated" dodge on a new actor—look out for it, Mr. Forrest, and do not let it floor you. The boys know enough that it is one of the most effective shots that can be fired at a stranger.' The 'shots' fired by American critics in the East and by English critics at the Western stranger are amply recorded in the reviews that follow. The first Eastern critic to comment sympathetically about the serious purpose of the frontier humorist was William Dean Howells. His perceptive praise was published and affirmed in the literary establishment's chief journal, the *Atlantic Monthly* (for examples see Nos. 4, 11, 13, 15). Tempered approval was subsequently expressed by more conservative reviewers, but Mark Twain was impatient and expressed his impatience to Howells: 'The longer I live, the clearer I perceive how unmatchable, how unapproachable a compliment one pays when he says of a man "he has the courage [to utter] his convictions". Haven't you had reviewers *talk* Alps to you, & then print potato hills?' Mark Twain's anxiety about the discrepancy between private acclaim and public statement persisted even as late as 1907 when he commented in response to a speech by William Lyon Phelps (see No. 75), 'when a man like Phelps speaks, the world gives attention. Some day I hope to meet him and thank him for his courage for saying those things out in public. Custom is, to think a handsome thing in private but tame it down in the utterance.'

Clemens did not always demonstrate such concern for critical opinions of his works. His apparent disinterest was expressed at least twice in reference to *The Gilded Age* (a book which did not receive critical approval): on 5 January 1874 he wrote to his friend, the Reverend Joseph Twichell, 'My interest in a book ceases with the printing of it', and on 4 September he wrote to another friend, Dr. John Brown. 'My interest in my works dies a sudden and violent death when the work is done.'

Although Mark Twain employed newspaper clipping services, he preserved primarily copies of his public interviews and speeches rather than reviews of his books. When he did collect literary reviews, he seems usually to have intended them for use in advertising. For example, he printed excerpts from thirty-nine reviews of *Innocents Abroad* in the Buffalo *Express* at the time he was a publisher and editor of that journal.

Two kinds of criticism did arouse Mark Twain's professional interest: personal attacks and criticism which disparaged a book for not being what its author had never intended. An extreme example of Clemens' sensitivity to 'personal attack' is illustrated by his response to reports that Whitelaw Reid had been criticizing him in the pages of the New York *Tribune*. He gleefully prepared to launch a counter-offensive intended to destroy Reid's personal and public reputation. This misguided effort fortunately proved abortive for, as Clemens reported to Howells on 28 January 1882, a search of the *Tribune* files produced only four items in two months which could be construed to be uncomplimentary. Among these were 'adverse criticism of P. & P. from an enraged idiot in the London *Athenaeum*' and 'a remark of the *Tribune's* about refusal of Canadian copyright, not complimentary, but not necessarily malicious—& of course adverse criticism which is not malicious is a thing which none but fools irritate themselves about'.

Clemens continued this explicit and sensible definition of his attitude towards criticism by noting that 'the whole offense boiled down, amounts to just this: *one* uncourteous remark of the *Tribune* about my *book*—not me—between Nov. 1 & Dec. 20; & a couple of foreign criticisms (of my *writings*, not me,) between Nov. 1 & Jan. 26! If I can't stand that amount of friction, I certainly need reconstruction.' The author of the *Athenaeum* review, who was in fact not very perceptive about American humour, is dismissed as 'an enraged idiot' and since Clemens could discover no malice on Reid's part, he sensibly dropped the whole matter.

When Clemens legitimately felt he was ill-used by critics he did defend himself. In October 1870, the London *Saturday Review* (No. 8) published an unfriendly account of *Innocents Abroad* which Clemens soon heard about. He promptly published a burlesque in the December *Galaxy* magazine which converted the English journal's criticism into ridiculous terms. The following month Clemens claimed in the *Galaxy* that his 'review', which had been accepted as genuine by Ambrose Bierce among other American writers, was written before he saw the original *Saturday Review* article. Now that he had seen the actual review, Clemens 'found it to be vulgar, awkwardly written, ill-natured, and entirely serious and in earnest'. When Clemens reprinted his burlesque in *Sketches, New and Old*, he added that 'the reader barely needs to be told that the above is not a conscientious reproduction of the *Saturday Review's* article. It is only a burlesque of it. The original review is very readable, and would be inserted here but for the fact that it is marred by grammatical lapses and inelegancies of speech, which cannot, with propriety, be placed before a refined audience.' The humorous content of both characterizations of the English criticism is conveyed in very similar terms: 'vulgar' and 'awkwardly written' become 'grammatical lapses and inelegancies of speech'. When Clemens accused the vastly respectable *Saturday Review* of altogether improbable faults, he phrased his rebuttal in the language of his critic whose reading of *Innocents Abroad*—'entirely serious and in earnest'—had led the reviewer to impugn Mark Twain's taste and skill by identifying the author with his fictional protagonist. In his dislike for the American bumpkin, the reviewer had failed to perceive that only an objective and skilful author could so effectively present the type. This failure to perceive the author's motive called forth Mark Twain's elaborate response.

One more examination of a skirmish between author and critic, this time when attack took the form of censorship, further reveals Mark Twain's complicated reaction to criticism.

Despite generous advance publicity for *Huckleberry Finn*, in the form of the author's readings from the forthcoming book during an extensive lecture tour, the book's publication attracted little formal critical notice. The rejection of the book for the Concord, Massachusetts, Library did lead to a good deal of newspaper publicity, but did not stimulate serious literary consideration although it is reputed to have increased the sale of the volume.

On 17 March 1885, the Boston *Transcript* reported:

The Concord (Mass.) Public Library committee has decided to exclude Mark Twain's latest book from the library. One member of the committee says that, while he does not wish to call it immoral, he thinks it contains but little humor, and that of a very coarse type. He regards it as the veriest trash. The librarian and the other members of the committee entertain similar views, characterizing it as rough, coarse, and inelegant, the whole book being more suited to the slums than to intelligent, respectable people.

Far from discouraged by this turn of events, Clemens wrote the next day to Charles L. Webster, his publisher:

The Committee of the Public Library of Concord, Mass., have given us a rattling tip-top puff which will go into every paper in the country. They have expelled Huck from their library as 'trash & suitable only for the slums.' That will sell 25,000 copies for us, sure.

The Springfield *Republican*, whose editor had long been antagonistic to Clemens, joined the attack with vigour, observing that Clemens' satire 'in certain of his works degenerates into a gross trifling with every fine feeling. The trouble with Mr. Clemens is that he has no reliable sense of propriety.' The attack concluded by commenting of 'these Huckleberry Finn stories' that 'their moral level is low, and their perusal cannot be anything less than harmful'.

After a week of criticism in the *Republican* and other newspapers, Clemens gained an unexpected but welcome position from which to reply when the Concord Free Trade Club offered him an honorary membership. In his letter of acceptance, which was immediately published in the newspapers, Clemens claimed that the ban had 'doubled' the sales of *Huckleberry Finn* and that 'it will cause the purchasers of the book to read it, out of curiosity, instead of merely intending to do so after the usual way of the world & library committees; & then they will discover, to my great advantage & their own indignant disappointment, that there is nothing objectionable in the book, after all.'

When the *Transcript* printed excerpts from Clemens' Free Trade Club letter (4 April 1885), it omitted the defence against the charge of impropriety, and it also printed a paragraph from the Boston *Advertiser* accusing Mark Twain of 'that spirit of irreverence which, as we are often and truly told, is the great fault in American character'. The *Advertiser* expanded its attack, 'for we are unwilling to believe that his impudent intimation that a larger sale and larger profits are a satisfactory recompense to him for the unfavorable judgment of honest critics is a true indication of the standard by which he measures success in literature'.

Clemens decided to exploit these criticisms commercially, and the same day he wrote to Webster, 'The *Advertiser* and the *Republican* still go for me daily. All right, we may as well get the benefit of such advertising as can be drawn from it.' Clemens composed a 'Prefatory Remark' to be inserted in future printings of *Huckleberry Finn* with instructions for its immediate release: 'Huckleberry Finn is not an imaginary person. He still lives; or rather, *they* still live; for Huckleberry Finn is two persons in one—namely, the author's two uncles, the present editors of the Boston *Advertiser* and the Springfield *Republican*.' Mark Twain claimed the only difference between Huck and his 'originals' was that 'this boy's language has been toned down and softened, here and there, in deference to the taste of a more modern and fastidious day'. The 'Prefatory Remark' is perfunctory, humorous grumbling and lacks the sense of real grievance found in the letter to the Free Trade Club. Shortly thereafter Clemens wrote Webster, 'Livy forbids the "Prefatory Remark"—therefore, put it in the fire.'

However, the initial ban on *Huckleberry Finn* rankled, and Clemens made one more effort to strike back. He had been invited to address a Cornell alumni meeting and apparently intended to use the opportunity to enlarge on his grievances against the Concord Library Committee. Howells wrote to him on 20 April, 'On second thoughts I am against that Cornell speech of yours. That Concord Library Committee is game too small for you, and you can't stir it up without seeming to care more than you ought for it. You have done enough.' Apparently Clemens agreed, for we hear no more about the matter. In addition to his confidence that attack would lead to careful reading of his work, the one constant element of Clemens' response was an attempt to turn it to commercial advantage.

Mark Twain's responses to criticism are thus seen to be complex: recognition that a public figure must expect adverse public comment, assumed indifference to critical evaluation, counter-attack, and frustration when public praise did not match private enthusiasm. In his zealous, if erratic, search for the approval which he thought was eluding him, Mark Twain largely ignored the reassurance he sought. For the reviewers were neither as consistently obtuse nor unkind as the author seemed to think.

Innocents Abroad was unsparing in its attack on both the American barbarian's pious hypocrisies and the pompous and stately institutions of Europe. Many American and English reviewers recognized this serious purpose although they often deplored the 'frivolity' of its presentation. For this, as for the succeeding books, critics offered Mark Twain the serious honour which he sought but in terms too tempered to provide him the gratification he craved.

IV

THE COURSE OF CRITICAL OPINION

One posthumous critic of Mark Twain's works, H. L. Mencken in 1913 (No. 88), saw the course of critical opinion of Mark Twain's books as a consistent progress through the various stages of grace from scorn, indifference, toleration, apologetic praise to 'hearty praise' by the time of the author's death. Mencken foresaw 'unqualified enthusiasm' as the impending critical response to Mark Twain's works.

From a perspective well over half a century longer than Mencken's, we can see that although critical interest in his writings has been sustained, neither Mark Twain's critical nor popular readers regard his works with unqualified enthusiasm. Several of the books the author and his contemporaries accepted with the greatest confidence of enduring worth are little read. Other, 'lesser' works are the foundation for the remarkable and persistent affection accorded the writer. But unqualified enthusiasm cannot be applied to any of the books. *Huckleberry Finn* is as widely read and discussed as any American novel but few major works by any writer are regarded with more reservations about their author's final success.

Nor does the evidence sustain in detail Mencken's summary of the even progress of critical acceptance. Mark Twain as a public personage did rapidly attain public favour and finally adulation but reservation and even hostility towards his writing persisted.

Henry Harland (No. 68) as late as 1899 comprehensively condemned the contents of *Innocents Abroad* for 'vulgarity', 'ignorance', 'narrowness', 'provincialism', but above all for its 'colossal irreverence'. His own provincialism is ironically revealed by his concluding attack on Mark Twain's use of American rather than English spellings.

By reference to the 'suave literary graces' and 'honeyed verse' of 'other national humorists like Aristophanes, Cervantes, Molière or Swift', an unsigned review in the *Critic* (No. 55) in 1895 attacks Mark Twain's style. The American writer, it is claimed, cannot achieve the 'exquisite literary form' of Aristophanes whose choral interludes are composed of 'wonderful bird-rhythms and wasp melodies and cloud-architecture, so to speak'.

The *Academy* critic (No. 58) records in 1897 that 'a generation bred up on Mr. Ruskin was left gasping by the impudence of this American, who declined to put on fine phrases and tread delicately just because he had exchanged his own country for an older'. The reviewer anxiously and clumsily involves himself in associative guilt in order to emphasize Mark Twain's creative freedom: 'He is so unburdened by sentiment or reverence—and most of us have too much of both.'

The next year Theodore de Laguna (No. 66) defended Mark Twain from charges of having 'done more for the debasing of the English language than any other recent influence' by commenting that his style 'is a return to the living source of all inspiration and power,— the genius of the spoken language'.

A less generous defender, David Masters in the *Chautauquan* for September 1897 (No. 59), saw the structure of Mark Twain's career as an effort 'to obliterate the memories' of *Innocents Abroad* by 'the purpose and seriousness of his work in his later publications'. Masters supports this attributed purpose by citing Mark Twain's 'steady improvement in his style and facility of expression'.

The distrust with which Victorians regarded any assault on the worthy traditions is summarized by Hiram Stanley in 1898 (No. 65) when he advances and counters the recurrent charge against Mark Twain that 'to many refined people he may seem the vulgar buffoon, entirely unrespectful, unconventional, irreverent; but this aspect is but his surface aspect. He reverences what is essentially worthy of reverence.'

Critics found it difficult to reconcile humour and the quality of reverence which they found so essential. In fact, American humour could scarcely be considered even respectable. On 27 September 1883 *The Nation* published an article on the subject by Arthur G. Sedgwick which was written in response to an announcement that Mark Twain and William Dean Howells 'were going to bring out a book on "American humour" ' (published in 1888 as *Mark Twain's Library of Humor*). Sedgwick quoted a rather lofty judgment from the New York *Tribune*:

We are inclined to think that the queer article which is popularly supposed to be 'American humor' has been exalted overmuch. It is often anything but humor; sometimes it is broad farce—the caper of a clown; and not seldom it is a coarse trifling with things which ought to be sacred—a trifling which implies laughter only by its unexpectedness rather than by any amusing quality. Of this kind of wit Mark Twain has proved himself a master.

This curious conglomeration of assumptions about wit and humour and the proprieties was endorsed and extended by Sedgwick, 'the "American humor" which now goes by the name, and has attracted such world-wide notoriety, is not, properly speaking, literary humor at all . . . . It was begun by Artemus Ward, and has been perpetuated by a long line of jesters, funny men, clowns, or whatever they may be called. . . .'

Reviewers were moved frequently to comment that American humour was a unique phenomenon of varying merit. But it was generally agreed that Mark Twain's position, although integral, was pre-eminent within the 'movement', as Grant Allen (*Fortnightly Review*, 1 August 1888) described it:

. . . Artemus Ward, Josh Billings, and Orpheus C. Kerr being practically his only considerable rivals in the European market. But whoever knows the daily talk and the daily newspapers of Western America knows that embryo Mark Twains grow in Illinois on every bush, and that the raw material of the *Innocents Abroad* resounds nightly, like the voice of the derringer, through every saloon in Iowa and Montana. A large style of cheap and effective homicidal humour, based mainly on exaggeration and grotesque incongruities, flourishes everywhere on the borderlands of American civilization.

V

MARK TWAIN'S VIEW OF THE HUMORIST

Mark Twain's own efforts at definition and distinction of his role as a humorist betray the accuracy of a comment he made for his autobiographical dictation on 28 March 1907: 'Humor is a subject which has never had much interest for me. This is why I have never examined it, nor written about it nor used it as a topic for a speech. A hundred times it has been offered me as a topic of these past forty years, but in no case has it attracted me.' Less than a year before, on 31 July 1906, also for his 'autobiography', in discussing a recently issued anthology of American humorists Mark Twain noted that the volume

reveals the surprising fact that within the compass of these forty years wherein I have been playing professional humorist before the public, I have had for company seventy-eight other American humorists. Each and every one of the seventy-eight rose in my time, became conspicuous and popular, and by and by vanished. . . . Why have they perished? Because they were merely humorists. Humorists of the 'mere' sort cannot survive. Humor is only a fragrance, a decoration. . . . Humor must not professedly teach, and it must not professedly preach, but it must do both if it would live forever.

By forever, I mean thirty years. . . . I have always preached. That is why I have lasted thirty years. If the humor came of its own accord and uninvited, I have allowed it a place in my sermon, but I was not writing the sermon for the sake of the humor.

In 'How to Tell a Story', first published in 1895, Mark Twain made an extended attempt at description of the disciplines of humour which serves in many ways as an answer to questions raised by his critics:

There are several kinds of stories, but only one difficult kind—the humorous. I will talk mainly about that one. The humorous story is American, the comic story is English, the witty story is French. The humorous story depends for its effect upon the *manner* of the telling; the comic story and the witty story upon the *matter*.

The humorous story may be spun out to great length, and may wander around as much as it pleases, and arrive nowhere in particular; but the comic and witty stories must be brief and end with a point. The humorous story bubbles gently along, the others burst.

The humorous story is strictly a work of art—high and delicate art—and only an artist can tell it; but no art is necessary in telling the comic and the witty story; anybody can do it. The art of telling a humorous story—understand, I mean by word of mouth, not print—was created in America and has remained at home.

Despite his emphasis on the oral presentation of what Mark Twain considers the uniquely American quality of the humorous story, the substance of his remarks does apply to the written version and was central to his recording of the material.

Mark Twain had not always considered the humorous story to be 'high and delicate art' and his conception of his role as a writer had not been easily established.

VI

THE AUTHOR IDENTIFIES HIS AUDIENCE

The favourable comment which followed Mark Twain's introduction to a national audience with the publication of 'Jim Smiley and his Jumping Frog' brought this scornful response in 1866: 'To think that, after writing many an article a man might be excused for thinking tolerably good', he wrote to his mother and sister from San Francisco, 'those New York people should single out a villainous backwoods sketch to compliment me on!' His mock-modesty continues in this letter as he states, 'though I am generally placed at the head of my breed of scribblers in this part of the country, the place properly belongs to Bret Harte, I think, although he denies it along with the rest!' At the age of thirty, Mark Twain, behind a very thin veil of disdain, made sure his family became aware of the promise of his success if only at this time in the role of a newspaperman.

Four years later the author of the immensely popular *Innocents Abroad*, an international traveller, syndicated newspaper correspondent and co-proprietor of an Eastern newspaper, again wrote modestly of his respect for Bret Harte. Mark Twain declared that Harte had 'trimmed and trained and schooled me patiently until he changed me from an awkward utterer of coarse grotesquenesses to a writer of paragraphs and chapters that have found a certain favor in the eyes of even some of the very decentest people of the land'. His correspondent was Thomas Bailey Aldrich, who was already a member of the polite society of Boston writers. Mark Twain's acknowledgment of debt to Harte's training is generous (even if the choice of vocabulary brings the success of that training into question) but the modesty of 'a certain favor' from the author of a book which sold 70,000 copies within a year of its publication is not entirely convincing.

As the years moved on, Mark Twain realized that his readers were from a 'popular' rather than a 'literary' audience. 'My books are water; those of the great geniuses are wine. Everybody drinks water', Mark Twain wrote in his notebook in May 1886.

The metaphor appealed to him so much that he repeated it to Howells on 15 February 1887. By that time Mark Twain's acceptance of the nature of his audience appears reasoned and secure:

I haven't as good an opinion of my work as you hold of it, but I've always done what I could to secure & enlarge my good opinion of it. I've always said to myself, 'Everybody reads it, & that's something—it surely isn't pernicious, or the most respectable people would get pretty tired of it.' And when a critic said by implication that it wasn't high & fine, through the remark 'High & fine literature is wine,' I retorted (confidentially to myself,) 'Yes, high & fine literature is wine, & mine is only water; but everybody likes water.'

Mark Twain's conception of his democratic appeal persisted and was expressed even more decidedly to Andrew Lang (see Appendix A) in defence of *A Connecticut Yankee*:

Indeed I have been misjudged, from the very first. I have never tried in even one single little instance, to help cultivate the cultivated classes. I was not equipped for it, either by native gifts or training. And I never had any ambition in that direction, but always hunted for bigger game—the masses. I have seldom deliberately tried to instruct them, but have done my best to entertain them.

In addition to this revelation of his conception of his limited role as a writer, what is perhaps of most remarkable interest is his conclusion that 'My audience is dumb, it has no voice in print, and so I cannot know whether I have won its approbation or only got its censure.'

The pathos of this statement is considerably diminished by reference to fact. The approbation of Mark Twain's supposedly 'dumb audience' had by 1890 been made repeatedly evident to him in the most tangible possible form: the sustained and very profitable sales of his books. Their verbal approval of his writing was evident in the thousands of letters he received, and often saved. It was expressed only slightly less directly by the enormously enthusiastic crowds who attended his public readings.

VII

USES OF CRITICISM

The letter to Lang was not the only instance of Mark Twain's appeal for critical sympathy. In order to confound his critics Mark Twain was frank in seeking early reviews which would be favourable in the hope that successive reviewers would adopt the attitude first established. With no apparent conflict of conscience, William Dean Howells willingly and more than once entered into collusion with the author. Well in advance of the publication of *Tom Sawyer*, Howells proposed that Mark Twain give him 'a hint when it is to be out, and I'll start the sheep to jumping in the right places'. The offer was eagerly accepted, 'I mean to see to it that your review of it shall have plenty of time to appear before the other notices.' In this case it certainly did, for Howells' review, based on an advance reading of the manuscript, was printed in the May 1876 issue of the *Atlantic* although the American edition of the book was not issued until mid-December of that year. Howells cheerfully dismissed the incongruity caused by the book publisher's delay with a casual 'I rather like the fun of the thing'.

But there were serious implications to this procedure, for as Mark Twain had said in commenting on Howells' review of *Sketches, New and Old* in 1875, 'Yours is the recognized critical Court of Last Resort in this country; from its decision there is no appeal.'

In the same letter of 19 October 1875 Clemens expanded upon his attitude towards most critics:

The newspaper praises bestowed upon the *Innocents Abroad* were large & generous, but I hadn't *confidence* in the critical judgment of the parties who furnished them. *You* know how that is, yourself, from reading the newspaper notices of your own books. They gratify a body, but they always leave a small pang behind in the shape of a fear that the critic's good words could not safely be depended upon as *authority*.

Disillusionment about their critical perception and authority did not prevent Clemens from attempting to use even the newspaper reviewers to his own advantage. Before publication of *The Gilded Age* he wrote to Whitelaw Reid (22 April 1873) concerning a proposed review in the New York *Tribune*:

I want the *Tribune* to say it *right* & say it powerful—& then I will answer for the consequences. The consequences will be that all other papers will *follow suit* —which you know, as well as I do. And then our game is made & our venture launched with a fair wind instead of a baffling one.

Few reviews of *The Gilded Age* appeared, however, despite the *Tribune's* satisfactory comments and fewer still were complimentary. It is not the success of these or the many other stratagems employed by Clemens to attract favourable reviews that is at issue. His assumption of critical corruption, irresponsibility or incompetence must inevitably have determined the degree to which Clemens could dismiss the unfavourable responses of his contemporaries.

His real lack of respect for the literary critic's function is evident in a comment he wrote to Howells on 22 September 1889:

As a rule a critic's dissent merely enrages, & so does no good; but by the new art which you use, your dissent must be as welcome as your approval, & as valuable. I do not know what the secret of it is, unless it is your attitude—man courteously reasoning with man & brother, in place of the worn & wearisome critical attitude of all this long time—superior being lecturing a boy.

Since by 1889 Mark Twain had written and published virtually all of his important work, it is clear that he thought critical commentary had had little influence on him and objective evidence does not dispute this, Certainly the development of his work was little changed by what his contemporaries had to say of it in print.

Mark Twain is quoted as having said, about January 1906, 'A critic never made or killed a book or a play. It has always been the people who have been the final judges—it is their opinion which does the job—they are the final arbiters' (S. J. Woolf, *Drawn from Life*, New York, 1932, p. 13). The statement is ambiguous (and conceivably apocryphal) since we cannot tell whether Mark Twain is concerned here with successful sales or the literary survival of worthy books. But his contempt for the critic is clear in either case. While his own creative impulses or the successful sales of a book would lead him to return to characters and themes in subsequent volumes, it is very difficult to identify any review's influence on the style or content of Mark Twain's work.

One reason for the critics' failure to have any effective influence on Mark Twain's writing may have been their general inability to recognize his unique quality. Archibald Henderson's summary statement published in the December 1910 issue of the *North American Review* (No. 86) documents critical imperception: 'Upon her writers who have exhibited derivative genius—Irving, Hawthorne, Emerson, Longfellow —American criticism has lavished the most extravagant eulogiums.' In contrast, the three writers Henderson identified as the product of an American cultural tradition—Poe, Whitman, Mark Twain—'still await their final and just deserts at the hands of critical opinion in their own land'.

VIII

POSTHUMOUS CRITICAL APPRAISAL

Immediately after Mark Twain's death in 1910 several retrospective accounts of his work appeared. William Dean Howells published *My Mark Twain*, a moving account of an enduring professional friendship, whose value cannot be overstated. The revolutionary decade which followed produced two major reviews in 1913 by John Macy and H. L. Mencken which are included in this volume (Nos. 87 and 88). Albert Bigelow Paine's massive but over-protective biography appeared in 1912, his controversial edition of *The Mysterious Stranger* in 1916 and a carefully bowdlerized edition of Mark Twain's letters in 1917. It was not until 1920 that a major attack on this sentimental myth-making appeared.

Van Wyck Brooks' *The Ordeal of Mark Twain* attempted to prove that the limitations of crude frontier origins compounded by frustrating social and emotional pressures exerted by his wife and friends had restrained Mark Twain from realizing his inherent genius. In tone and purpose Brooks represented the genteel view that underlay critical distaste for Mark Twain's 'vulgarity' in his lifetime. Brooks' facts were often wrong or incomplete, his assumptions frequently irrelevant, but he effectively demanded that Mark Twain's literary position be impartially assessed.

Bernard DeVoto took the challenge and in 1932 published *Mark Twain's America*. He saw the strengths of Mark Twain's works as a product of the frontier influences which Brooks had deplored. This engrossing if chauvinistic study of cultural history did not adequately define the degrees of the writer's success and failure and, with some irony, each critic drifted towards the other's views. Brooks in 1933 published an important revision of the *Ordeal* and DeVoto presented a far less sanguine view in the essays, especially 'The Symbols of Despair', collected in 1942 in *Mark Twain at Work*.

As he had eluded Brooks and DeVoto, Mark Twain continues to elude exact critical appraisal. Academic critics and literary historians have interpreted the symbols and pursued the sources, they have discussed Mark Twain's influence and analysed his role among his contemporaries, but they end more often with biography than literary criticism. Despite critical confusion, Mark Twain's works retain an audience on very nearly every level of literary sophistication and political persuasion. In his diversity Mark Twain evidently continues to express the diverse views of opposing regional and national cultures.

THE INNOCENTS ABROAD
or THE NEW PILGRIM'S PROGRESS

September 1869

1. Unsigned review, *Nation*

2 September 1869, ix, 194–5

Mr. Samuel L. Clemens, who is known to many of us, and ought to be known to all of us, as Mark Twain, was one of the passengers on the *Quaker City* when she took her ill-assorted party of excursionists to Europe and the East, and he has just given us, in a thick book of more than six hundred pages, a record of the tour. It might better have been a thinner book, for there is some dead wood in it, as there has to be in all books which are sold by book-agents and are not to be bought in stores. The rural-district reader likes to see that he has got his money's worth even more than he likes wood-engravings. At least, such is the faith in Hartford; and no man ever saw a book-agent with a small volume in his hand.

But if some of the book is needless, none of it is really poor, and much of it very good. Mr. Clemens's plan of delivering an unvarnished tale, of giving just his own impressions of what he saw, at once made his work sure of some real value as well as much freshness, and his book is one to be commended merely as a book of travels. But, of course, the 'American humor' is the great thing. It is not in the light of a traveller that one regards a gentleman who when during his wanderings in the Holy Land he comes upon the 'tomb of Adam,' which the monks exhibit, thus gives utterance to a natural burst of sentiment:

[quotes ch. 53 'The tomb of Adam!' to 'eternal gain'.]

All the prominent characteristics of our peculiar school of humorists —their audacity, their extravagance and exaggeration—Mr. Clemens displays in fulness in the course of his ramblings, and he has some merits which belong to his individual self, and which make him a very agreeable companion when he is at ease and natural—which is not always; for as he pads so, we must make free to tell him, does he sometimes grimace, and is professionally a humorist as he was professionally a book-maker. It will be a just punishment for him to reflect that no doubt many a farmer will read all his jokes—the good ones as well as these bad ones we are speaking to him about—with profound gravity and unshaking belief in them as so much serious log-book.

There is, besides those we have mentioned, another characteristic of 'American humor,' which consists in a certain sort of what may be called fatuousness. When the man in the stage-coach, riding along with 'the great moral showman' without knowing him, kept on telling him, 'some of Artemus Ward's jokes,' and at the end of each one of them punched his companion in the side and said, 'What a damned fool the fellow is!' he was not the worst critic that Artemus ever had. Nearly all his jokes have in them a display of mental helplessness—not to say imbecility—a drifting along of the mind from one topic to another, suggested but not really connected, topic, and are largely dependent upon this for their humorous effect. The same thing may be seen—though not nearly so unmixed nor so often—in the efforts of Mr. Josh Billings. The humor in the Nasby Papers consists rather in Mr. Locke's conception of the low, 'dough-face' Democrat than in anything strictly humorous that is said or done by him after he is made, and the Cross-roads pastor and postmaster gives no exhibition of the trait mentioned. But the author of *The Innocents Abroad* has some of it—though something of what he has is acquired and imitative, we should say—and may be taken to be rather more nearly Artemus Ward's successor in this line than either of the other humorists to whom we have referred.

2. Unsigned review, *Packard's Monthly*

October 1869, ii, 318–19

The Innocents Abroad; or, The New Pilgrim's Progress, is the title of Mark Twain's latest appearance between covers. The book is a ponderous one, containing over 650 pages, splendidly illustrated, and produced in the best style of art by the American Publishing Company, of Hartford. No ordinary 'notice' can do justice to this work. In the language of many others, 'it must be seen (and read) to be appreciated.' It is a curious account of the famous Quaker City pleasure trip to the Mediterranean and the Holy Land, which was conceived by and executed under command of Captain Duncan, in the summer of 1867. There were many intelligent sight-seers among 'the innocents;' but few, we are inclined to believe, who got as much out of the trip as did the author of this book. Mark Twain is a born journalist, besides being at the present time first among American humorists. It is, indeed, doubtful if he has ever had an equal; he certainly has not had in his line—that of dry, self-contained, unobtrusive and pervading fun. There is no glare in his emanations—no blinding coruscations of wit, which, flashing suddenly upon you, as suddenly go out, leaving you in darkness and uncertainty; no apparent striving after sharp effects; no digging in poor soil for poorer puns. What is said is most naturally said, and if there is humor in it, it is because the writer could not express it otherwise. Whatever may be the quality of the wine which fills your glass, you never feel that it is being drawn from an empty cask, or that its flavor is at all dependent upon the abundance of its supply. When Mr. Beecher was reprimanded for saying so many funny things in the pulpit, he replied, 'Oh, but if you only knew the number of funny things I do not say!' And this is the impression left upon the reader of Mark Twain. Whatever good things he may choose to fasten with his pen, one cannot but feel that his best things are yet untold. There is one species of poor wit that Mark has not yet found it necessary to attempt, and we trust he never will, and that is poor orthography and worse grammar. It is not to be denied that a telling point may sometimes be made by a violent assault upon the barriers of 'good English.' Artemus Ward achieved some glory in this field; and his literary successor, Josh Billings, sometimes unearths a nugget; but the game thus far has not been worth the candle, and we doubt if it ever will be. At all events, Mark Twain has no such weak necessity, and we are glad of it. Some portions of the book are devoted to correct, unexaggerated descriptions of the country, and matters requiring historical accuracy; but there is no pretence, other than of a humorous and extravagant account of a memorable voyage. There will be those who will see in the descriptions of the Holy Land a conspicuous lack of reverence for sacred associations, and the contrast between this and ordinary guide-books will not need to be pointed out; but the artistic and effectual disposal of the romantic tales of tourists, which have enveloped these scenes with a mysterious beauty and awe not to be penetrated or approached, will be at least satisfactory to the matter-of-fact reader.

Here is his quiet style of getting down from a high state of mental exhilaration to every-day considerations:

[quotes ch. 47 'At noon we took' to ' "one can hold me!" ']

3. Unsigned review, Buffalo *Express*

16 October 1869

At this time Clemens was part owner of the Buffalo *Express*, and this review may be by his associate, J. N. Larned. The 'supplementary sheet' is dated 9 October 1869 and presents, whole or in part, reviews from forty-five American newspapers selected 'from some twelve hundred complimentary notices of the book which have appeared in the several sections of the Union'.

If any book of late years has so generally interested the press of the country and received so extensive and favorable an introduction to the public as has Mark Twain's *Innocents Abroad*, since its appearance, we fail to remember the instance. We gave to our readers last week, in a supplementary sheet, some specimens of the notices we have found in our exchanges. Numerous as were the excerpts here collected, they represent but a fraction of what have fallen under our observation, and the notable fact is, that, instead of the mere mention so commonly accorded to a new book, almost every journal has given it an unusually elaborate review, written not in a simple spirit of courtesy, but evidently with an inspiration of interest excited by reading the work. The truth is, we believe, that no one of an ordinary disposition of mind can dip into the volume without being snared by a curious fascination. It is so different from any narrative of travel that ever was written before. The mere tickle of an ever pervading humor is not all that makes it delightful, but that humor is like an atmosphere, in which the old world scenes that so many tourists and travellers have led us into, take on a new and altogether novel appearance, so that we follow our droll excursionist from place to place as eagerly as though we had never been carried to them by any narrative before. It would be a great mistake to suppose that the book is just a big package of Mark Twain's jokes, to be read with laughter, and for the sake of laughter. It is the panorama of Europe and the Holy Land as they were seen by one who went abroad with no illusions; who carried about with him a shrewd pair of American eyes, and used them to get his own impressions of things, as they actually presented themselves, not as he had been taught to expect them; who bore with him, moreover, as acute an appreciation of sham and humbug as his sense of the humorous and ludicrous was keen. What he saw he tells, and we believe there is more true description in his book than in any other of the kind that we have read. What is to be told soberly he tells soberly, and with all the admiration or reverence that is due to the subject. But he does like to wash off false colors, to scrape away putty and varnish, to stick a pin into venerable moss grown shams—and it is a perpetual delight to his reader to see him do it in his droll, dry way. We have yet to find the person who could open the book and willingly lay it down again, for, certainly, it is not often that more or livelier entertainment can be had in the same compass. The work has been published by the American Publishing Company, at Hartford, and is sold by agents who canvass for subscriptions.

4. William Dean Howells: unsigned review, *Atlantic*

December 1869, xxiv, 764-6

William Dean Howells (1837–1920), novelist and critic, was an editor of the *Atlantic* at this time. Clemens first met him upon calling at the *Atlantic* offices to thank James T. Fields, the editor, for this anonymous review. The headnote of the review records 'Samuel S. Clements' as the author of the book.

The character of American humor, and its want of resemblance to the humor of Kamtschatka and Patagonia,—will the reader forgive us if we fail to set down here the thoughts suggested by these fresh and apposite topics? Will he credit us with a self-denial proportioned to the vastness of Mr. Clements's very amusing book, if we spare to state why he is so droll, or—which is as much to the purpose—why we do not know? This reticence will leave us very little to say by way of analysis; and, indeed, there is very little to say of *The Innocents Abroad* which is not of the most obvious and easy description. The idea of a steamer-load of Americans going on a prolonged picnic to Europe and the Holy Land is itself almost sufficiently delightful, and it is perhaps praise enough for the author to add that it suffers nothing from his handling. If one considers the fun of making a volume of six hundred octavo pages upon this subject, in compliance with one of the main conditions of a subscription book's success, bigness namely, one has a tolerably fair piece of humor, without troubling Mr. Clements further. It is out of the bounty and abundance of his own nature that he is as amusing in the execution as in the conception of his work. And it is always good-humored humor, too, that he lavishes on his reader, and even in its impudence it is charming; we do not remember where it is indulged at the cost of the weak or helpless side, or where it is insolent, with all its sauciness and irreverence. The standard shams of travel which everybody sees through suffer possibly more than they ought, but not so much as they might; and one readily forgives the harsh treatment of them in consideration of the novel piece of justice done on such a traveller as suffers under the pseudonyme of Grimes. It is impossible also that the quality of humor should not sometimes be strained in the course of so long a narrative; but the wonder is rather in the fact that it is strained so seldom.

Mr. Clements gets a good deal of his fun out of his fellow-passengers, whom he makes us know pretty well, whether he presents them some-what caricatured, as in the case of the 'Oracle' of the ship, or carefully and exactly done, as in the case of such a shrewd, droll, business-like, sensible, kindly type of the American young man as 'Dan.' We must say also that the artist who has so copiously illustrated the volume has nearly always helped the author in the portraiture of his fellow-passengers, instead of hurting him, which is saying a good deal for an artist; in fact, we may go further and apply the commendation to all the illustrations; and this in spite of the variety of figures in which the same persons are represented, and the artist's tendency to show the characters on mules where the author says they rode horseback.

Of course the instructive portions of Mr. Clements's book are of a general rather than particular character, and the reader gets as travel very little besides series of personal adventures and impressions; he is taught next to nothing about the population of the cities and the character of the rocks in the different localities. Yet the man who can be honest enough to let himself see the realities of human life every-where, or who has only seen Americans as they are abroad, has not travelled in vain and is far from a useless guide. The very young American who told the English officers that a couple of our gunboats could come and knock Gibraltar into the Mediterranean Sea; the American who at a French restaurant 'talked very loudly and coarsely, and laughed boisterously, where all others were so quiet and well behaved,' and who ordered 'wine, sir!' adding, to raise admiration in a country where wine is as much a matter of course as soup, 'I never dine without wine, sir'; the American who had to be addressed several times as Gordon, being so accustomed to hear the name pronounced Gorrdong, and who had forgotten most English words during a three months' sojourn in Paris; the Americans who pitilessly made a three days' journey in Palestine within two days, cruelly overworking the poor beasts they rode, and overtaxing the strength of their com-rades, in order not to break the Sabbath; the American Pilgrims who travelled half round the world to be able to take a sail on the Sea of

Galilee, and then missed their sole opportunity because they required the boatman to take them for one napoleon when he wanted two;— these are all Americans who are painted to peculiar advantage by Mr. Clements, and who will be easily recognized by such as have had the good fortune to meet them abroad.

The didactic, however, is not Mr. Clements's prevailing mood, nor his best, by any means. The greater part of his book is in the vein of irony, which, with a delicious impudence, he attributes to Saint Luke, declaring that Luke, 'in speaking of the winding 'street, called Straight' in Damascus, 'is careful not to commit himself; he does not say it is the street which *is* straight, but the "street which is *called* Straight." It is a fine piece of irony; it is the only facetious remark in the Bible, I believe.' At Tiberias our author saw the women who wear their dowry in their head-dresses of coins. 'Most of these maidens were not wealthy, but some few have been kindly dealt with by fortune. I saw heiresses there, worth, in their own right,—worth, well, I suppose I might venture to say as much as nine dollars and a half. But such cases are rare. When you come across one of these, she naturally puts on airs.' He thinks the owner of the horse 'Jericho,' on which he travelled towards Jerusalem, 'had a wrong opinion about him. He had an idea that he was one of those fiery, untamed, steeds, but he is not of that character. I know the Arab had this idea, because when he brought the horse out for inspection in Beirout, he kept jerking at the bridle and shouting in Arabic, "Ho! will you? Do you want to run away, you ferocious beast, and break your neck?" when all the time the horse was not doing anything in the world, and only looked like he wanted to lean up against something and think. Whenever he is not shying at things or reaching after a fly, he wants to do that yet. How it would surprise his owner to know this!' In this vein of ironical drollery is that now celebrated passage in which Mr. Clements states that he was affected to tears on coming, a stranger in a strange land, upon the grave of a blood-relation,—the tomb of Adam; but that passage is somewhat more studied in tone than most parts of the book, which are written with a very successful approach in style to colloquial drolling. As Mr. Clements writes of his experiences, we imagine he would talk of them; and very amusing talk it would be: often not at all fine in matter or manner, but full of touches of humor, —which if not delicate are nearly always easy,—and having a base of excellent sense and good feeling. There is an amount of pure human nature in the book, that rarely gets into literature; the depths of our poor unregeneracy—dubious even of the blissfulness of bliss—are sounded by such a simple confession as Mr. Clements makes in telling of his visit to the Emperor of Russia: 'I would as soon have thought of being cheerful in Abraham's bosom as in the palace of an Emperor.' Almost any topic, and any event of the author's past life, he finds pertinent to the story of European and Oriental travel, and if the reader finds it impertinent, he does not find it the less amusing. The effect is dependent in so great degree upon this continuous incoherence, that no chosen passage can illustrate the spirit of the whole, while the passage itself loses half in separation from the context. Nevertheless, here is part of the account given by Mr. Clements of the Pilgrims' excursion to the river Jordan, over roads supposed to be infested by Bedouins; and the reader who does not think it droll as it stands can go to our author for the rest.

[quotes ch. 55 'I think we must' to 'the lead again', and 'We were moping' to 'their rashness.']

Under his *nom de plume* of Mark Twain, Mr. Clements is well known to the very large world of newspaper-readers; and this book ought to secure him something better than the uncertain standing of a popular favorite. It is no business of ours to fix his rank among the humorists California has given us, but we think he is, in an entirely different way from all the others, quite worthy of the company of the best.

5. 'Tom Folio':
review, Boston *Daily Evening Transcript*

15 December 1869, 1

This reviewer, writing under a pseudonym, directly follows the lead set by Howells (No. 4). Thomas Fuller (1608–61), English divine, historian and prolific author, published *A Pisgah-sight of Palestine* in 1650.

MARK TWAIN'S NEW BOOK. What would the great old romantic voyagers and travellers, the heroes of Hackluyt and Purchas, say of the monster Yankee picnic to Europe and the Holy Land? I think that if those worthies were to get hold of a copy of Mark Twain's account of the excursion, there would be laughter in Elysium. At any rate, I can hardly believe it possible for an earthly reader—unless, indeed, like Charles Lamb's Scotchman, he is joke-proof—to peruse Twain's new book, *The Innocents Abroad*, without 'laughing consumedly.' The work, however, though rich in joke and jest is not, like Gilbert à Becket's dreary comic histories, a merely funny book. On the contrary, it is a very full and matter-of-fact record of travel in Europe and the East, delightfully flavored with humor and plentifully spiced with wit. Addison's sober citizen complained that there were too many plums and no suet in his pudding, but no one can say that Twain's literary pudding is wanting in suet or too full of plums.

Our author is not one of the 'one-eyed travellers,' mentioned by Whateley, who see 'a great deal of some particular class of objects, and are blind to all others,' but a shrewd, quick-witted person, who travelled with his eyes very wide open, and saw things as they were, not as they have been described by poets and romancers. It is not, however, so much for its new, truthful and pleasant pictures of Old-World places and people, as for the delicious wit and humor scattered so freely up and down the book, that one praises and prizes *The Innocents Abroad*. And it is such good humor, too, most of it, and with all its freedom and riot, touching gently and lovingly all serious things.

31

I have been reading Fuller's *Pisgah Sight of Palestine*, and derived no little amusement by comparing his descriptions of the Holy Land with Mark Twain's. Fuller, though as pious and reverent as a saint, was a rare wit and humorist, and his book on Palestine is brimming over with merry quibbles and jocular humor. Although some of Mark Twain's levities might have displeased the witty old divine, I think that he would have laughed loud and long at the passage concerning the tomb of Adam.

The Innocents Abroad is issued by the American Publishing Company of Hartford, and is sold only by subscription. The Boston agents are George M. Smith & Co., No. 6 Tremont street.

6. Bret Harte:
unsigned review, *Overland Monthly*

January 1870, iv, 100–1

Bret Harte (1836–1902), writer of short stories, was the editor of the *Overland Monthly* in San Francisco and a friend of Clemens at this time.

Six hundred and fifty pages of open and declared fun—very strongly accented with wood-cuts at that—might go far toward frightening the fastidious reader. But the Hartford publishers, we imagine, do not print for the fastidious reader, nor do traveling book agents sell much to that rarely occurring man, who prefers to find books rather than let them find *him*. So that, unless he has already made 'Mark Twain's' acquaintance through the press, he will not probably meet him until, belated in the rural districts, he takes from the parlor table of a country farm-house an illustrated Bible, Greeley's *American Conflict*, Mr. Parton's apocryphal *Biographies*, successively and listlessly, and so

comes at last upon 'Mark Twain's' *Innocents* like a joyous revelation
—an Indian spring in an alkaline literary desert. For the book has that
intrinsic worth of bigness and durability which commends itself to the
rural economist, who likes to get a material return for his money. It is
about the size of *The Family Physician*, for which it will doubtless be
often mistaken—with great advantage to the patient.

The entire six hundred and fifty pages are devoted to an account of
the 'steamship *Quaker City's* excursion to Europe and the Holy Land,'
with a description of certain famous localities of which a great many
six hundred and fifty pages have been, at various times, written by
various tourists. Yet there is hardly a line of Mr. Clemens' account that
is not readable; and none the less, certainly, from the fact that he pokes
fun at other tourists, and that the reader becomes dimly conscious that
Mr. Clemens' fellow-passengers would have probably estopped this
gentle satirist from going with them could they have forecast his book.
The very title—*The Innocents Abroad*—is a suggestive hint of the lawlessness and audacity in which the trip is treated. We shall not stop
to question the propriety of his feature: it is only just to Mr. Clemens
to say, that the best satirists have generally found their quarry in the
circle in which they moved, and among their best friends; but we
contend that if he has, by this act, choked off and prevented the
enthusiastic chronicling of the voyage by any of his fellow-passengers,
who may have been sentimentally inclined, he is entitled to the consideration of a suffering world; and it shall stand in extenuation of
some mannerism that is only slang, some skepticism that lacks the
cultivation which only makes skepticism tolerable, and some sentiment that is only rhetoric.

And so, with an irreverence for his fellow-pilgrims which was
equaled only by his scorn for what they admired, this hilarious image-
breaker started upon his mission. The situation was felicitous, the
conditions perfect for the indulgence of an humor that seems to have
had very little moral or æsthetic limitation. The whole affair was a
huge practical joke, of which not the least amusing feature was the
fact that 'Mark Twain' had embarked in it. Before the *Quaker City*
reached Fayal, the first stopping-place, he had worked himself into
a grotesque rage at every thing and every body. In this mock assumption of a righteous indignation, lies, we think, the real power of the
book, and the decided originality of Mr. Clemens' humor. It enables
him to say his most deliberately funny things with all the haste and
exaggeration of rage; it gives him an opportunity to invent such

epithets as 'animated outrage,' and 'spider-legged gorilla,' and apply them, with no sense of personal responsibility on the part of reader or writer. And the rage is always ludicrously disproportionate to the cause. It is 'Mr. Boythorn,' without his politeness, or his cheerful intervals. For, when 'Mark Twain' is not simulating indignation, he is *really* sentimental. He shows it in fine writing—in really admirable rhetoric, vigorous and picturesque—but too apt, at times, to suggest the lecturing attitude, or the reporter's flourish. Yet it is so much better than what one had any right to expect, and is such an agreeable relief to long passages of extravagant humor, that the reader is very apt to overlook the real fact, that it is often quite as extravagant.

Yet, with all his independence, 'Mark Twain' seems to have followed his guide and guide-books with a simple, unconscious fidelity. He was quite content to see only that which every body else sees, even if he was not content to see it with the same eyes. His record contains no new facts or features of the countries visited. He has always his own criticism, his own comments, his own protests, but always concerning the same old facts. Either from lack of time or desire, he never stepped out of the tread-mill round of 'sights.' His remarks might have been penciled on the margins of Murray. This is undoubtedly a good way to correct the enthusiasm or misstatements of other tourists; but is, perhaps, hardly the best method of getting at the truth for one's self. As a conscientious, painstaking traveler, 'Mark Twain,' we fear, is not to be commended. But that his book would have been as amusing, if he had been, is a matter of doubt.

Most of the criticism is just in spirit, although extravagant, and often too positive in style. But it should be remembered that the style itself is a professional exaggeration, and that the irascible pilgrim, 'Mark Twain,' is a very eccentric creation of Mr. Clemens'. We can, perhaps, no more fairly hold Mr. Clemens responsible for 'Mark Twain's' irreverence than we could have held the late Mr. Charles F. Browne to account for 'Artemus Ward's' meanness and humbuggery. There may be a question of taste in Mr. Clemens permitting such a man as 'Mark Twain' to go to the Holy Land at all; but we contend that such a traveler would be more likely to report its external aspect truthfully than a man of larger reverence. And are there not Lamar-tines, Primes, and unnumbered sentimental and pious pilgrims to offset these losel skeptics—or, as our author would say, such 'animated out-rages'—as Ross Browne, Swift, 'Mark Twain,' *et al.*

To subject Mr. Clemens to any of those delicate tests by which we are supposed to detect the true humorist, might not be either fair or convincing. He has caught, with great appreciation and skill, that ungathered humor and extravagance which belong to pioneer communities—which have been current in bar-rooms, on railways, and in stages—and which sometimes get crudely into literature, as 'a fellow out West says.' A good deal of this is that picturesque Western talk which we call 'slang,' in default of a better term for inchoate epigram. His characters speak naturally, and in their own tongue. If he has not that balance of pathos which we deem essential to complete humor, he has something very like it in that serious eloquence to which we have before alluded. Like all materialists, he is an honest hater of all cant—except, of course, the cant of materialism—which, it is presumed, is perfectly right and proper. To conclude: after a perusal of this volume, we see no reason for withholding the opinion we entertained before taking it up, that Mr. Clemens deserves to rank foremost among Western humorists; and, in California, above his only rival, 'John Phœnix,' whose fun, though more cultivated and spontaneous, lacked the sincere purpose and larger intent of 'Mark Twain's.'

7. Unsigned review, *Athenaeum*

24 September 1870, no. 2239, 395–6

This unperceptive review is of the pirated English edition published by John Camden Hotten. Edward P. Hingston visited Nevada in 1863 as lecture agent for Artemus Ward and in the introduction to this volume describes his visit to the office of the Virginia City *Territorial Enterprise* to meet Mark Twain.

But for the Introduction to this book, we should have little difficulty in assigning it its proper place in literature. We should say at once that the author was draping himself in the garb of one of those typical Yankee tourists of whom we hear so often, and whom we do meet occasionally,—the tourists who 'do' Europe in six weeks,—whose comment on Venice is that they do not care much for those old towns, and on the Venus de' Medici that they do not like them stone gals. If we thought at all about the name on the title-page, we should put it down as a pseudonym, though the probability is that we should not think about it. Anyhow, we should come to the conclusion that Mark Twain, whoever he might be, had hit off the oddities of some of his countrymen very well; that many of his remarks were amusing, and almost witty; and that he was certainly not such a fool as he tried to look. But when Mr. Hingston tells us seriously that Mark Twain is really the pseudonym of the sub-editor of a daily paper in a Western city a few months old, that he is a flower of the wilderness, a thoroughly untravelled American applying the standard of Nevada to historical Europe, we are fairly puzzled. We can readily believe that the writer of this book is ignorant of many of those things which would be familiar to an English tourist. His remark that 'Raphael, Angelo, Canova—giants like these gave birth to the designs' of the statues on the Cathedral at Milan, is not much more than the hasty generalization of one who takes his facts from guides and guide-books. The statement that 'Raphael pictured such infernal villains as Catherine de' Medici seated in heaven and conversing familiarly with the Virgin Mary and the angels,' may surprise those who remember that Catherine de' Medici was only born one year before the death of Raphael. Again, we are told that Raphael is buried in Santa Croce, instead of in the Pantheon; but we may conclude from this that in Mark Twain's opinion every great artist should be buried in several places, just as each relic of a saint is multiplied. We owe this suggestion to what Mark Twain says of an important fellow-passenger calling himself Commissioner of the United States of America to Europe, Asia, and Africa. The comment on this 'titular avalanche' is, 'to my thinking, when the United States considered it necessary to send a dignitary of that tonnage across the ocean, it would be in better taste and safer to take him apart and cart him over in sections in several ships.'

In all these mistakes there is nothing unnatural. Most men who are not learned, and who do not take the precaution of using books of reference before they speak, may fall into the same errors. The only thing that characterizes Mark Twain is the reckless manner in which he makes his assertions. The greater his blunder, the more assurance there is in his language. Thus he says, without the slightest reserve, that the Emperor of the French 'kept his faithful watch and walked his weary beat as a common policeman of London,' as if the special constable of 1848 had been Z 264. Yet it is not till we get beyond the mistakes that we light on the genuine untravelled American. It is significant of him that he does not commit himself to facts of his own, because he is sceptical as to the existence of everything. He listens gravely to the guide's stories, and then asks some question which reduces them to an absurdity. He finds everybody else admiring a picture, and that is enough to set him against it. By putting a number of exaggerations together he deprives any little grain of truth of its value. This is the man who, in the present volume, remarks that the Italians spell a word Vinci and pronounce it Vinchy, adding calmly, 'foreigners always spell better than they pronounce.' He, too, when shown the writing of Christopher Columbus, observes, 'Why, I have seen boys in America only fourteen years old that could write better than that. You mustn't think you can impose on us because we are strangers. We are not fools by a good deal. If you have got any specimens of penmanship of real merit, trot them out, and if you haven't, drive on!' There are a good many comments on pictures from the same point of view. Take this on the characters of Sacred Art:—'When we see a monk sitting on a rock, looking tranquilly up to heaven, with a human skull beside him and without other baggage, we know that is St.

Jerome; because we know that he always went flying light in the matter of baggage. When we see a party looking tranquilly up to heaven, unconscious that his body is shot through and through with arrows, we know that that is St. Sebastian. When we see other monks looking tranquilly up to heaven, *but having no trade-mark*, we always ask who those parties are.' Another question on which the untravelled American is worth hearing is the ubiquity of guides, with their constant repetition of legends and their unceasing exaggeration. At Gibraltar one story was dinned into the tourist's ear, till at last he exclaimed to the narrator, 'Sir, I am a helpless orphan in a foreign land; have pity on me.' One supposed safeguard against invention is that a guide 'would hardly try so hazardous an experiment as the telling of a falsehood when it is all he can do to speak the truth in English without getting the lock-jaw.' But even this seems to have failed in Rome, if we may judge from the following tirade against the mythical being to whom the guides give the name of Michael Angelo:—

[quotes ch. 27 'In this connexion' to 'was dead'.]

This last touch is exactly characteristic of the untravelled American. In other places, however, the exaggeration to which Mark Twain gives way shows that he is consciously acting a part. We do not like him any the worse for that, and without the preface we should have been easily reconciled to his eccentricities. His incidental remarks about things in general are sufficiently humorous to ensure his book a hearing, though they have the misfortune to contradict Mr. Hingston's theory. The genuine Yankee tourist would never sneer at one of his fellow countrymen for ignorance of French manners and assumption of native superiority. When Mark Twain finds an American proclaiming his nationality in this offensive way—'I am a freeborn sovereign, Sir, an American, Sir, and I want everybody to know it'—he adds, 'the fellow did not mention that he was a lineal descendant of Balaam's ass, but everybody knew that without his telling it.' Does this come under the rule of *Quis tulerit Gracchos?*★ We think not. In our opinion Mark Twain is merely showing the prevalence of the faults which he satirizes. He wishes to remind us that, whether we take Mr. Hingston's view or the more natural one, he is not the only untravelled American in his party, and that he is always on the look-out for incidents which may serve his purpose. In this respect Mark Twain's travels remind us of *The Book of Snobs*, where the fancy picture of the author wholly eclipsed his characters.

★'Who shall endure the Gracchi.'

8. Unsigned review, *Saturday Review*

8 October 1870, xxx, 467–8

Clemens was so intrigued with this long, unsmiling review that he wrote one of his own, ostensibly even more serious and pontifical, which he attributed without warning to the *Saturday Review* and published in *Galaxy* (December 1870), an American magazine for which he was then writing a monthly column. Ambrose Bierce, among others, accepted the burlesque review as genuine and commented on it in the San Francisco *News Letter* (28 November 1870), stating that 'the average English critic is a dumb beast of dense cuticular rhinocerosity'.

Every traveller on the Continent has met the American tourist, and formed some opinion of his merits. We do not speak of that variety of American who comes over to spend five or six years in Europe, and finds himself rather more at home on the Parisian boulevards than on the New York Broadway. Nor do we refer to the Americans who have been too highly cultivated to obtrude their national peculiarities upon us in any disagreeable form. There is no pleasanter acquaintance than the gentleman, or still more the lady, of this class who has just enough American flavour to be amusingly original. But, besides these types, the United States are kind enough to provide us with a vast number of travellers corresponding in refinement and intelligence to Mr. Cook's tourists. They are the people who do Europe in six weeks, and throw in the Holy Land and Egypt to fill up their spare time. They are gloriously ignorant of any language but their own, supremely contemptuous of every country that had no interest in the Declaration of Independence, and occasionally, it must be admitted, as offensive as the worst kind of Cockney tourist, whilst even less inclined to hide their light under a bushel. Comparing them with the most nearly analogous class of British travellers, it is rather hard to determine which should have the preference. The American is generally the noisier and more actively disagreeable, but, on the other hand, he often partly redeems his absurdity by a certain naïveté and half-conscious humour. He is often laughing in his sleeve at his own preposterous brags, and does not take himself quite so seriously as his British rival. He is vulgar, and even ostentatiously and atrociously vulgar; but the vulgarity is mixed with a real shrewdness which rescues it from simple insipidity. We laugh at him, and we would rather not have too much of his company; but we do not feel altogether safe in despising him. We may save ourselves the trouble of any further attempts at description by quoting a few illustrative passages from the book before us. Mr. Mark Twain, as the author chooses to call himself, is a Californian humourist after the fashion of Artemus Ward. He came to Europe on a grand excursion trip, and describes his impressions of France and Italy in the true tourist style. He parades his utter ignorance of Continental languages and manners, and expresses his very original judgments on various wonders of art and nature with a praiseworthy frankness. We are sometimes left in doubt whether he is speaking in all sincerity, or whether he is having a sly laugh at himself and his readers. To do him justice, however, we must observe that he has a strong tinge of the peculiar national humour; and, though not equal to the best performers on the same instrument, manages to be an amusing representative of his class. The dry joke, which apes seriousness, is a favourite device of his countrymen; and Mr. Mark Twain is of course not as simple as he affects to be. We merely say this to guard ourselves against the imputation of taking a professional jester seriously; but, whether he speaks in downright earnest or with a half-concealed twinkle of the eye, his remarks will serve equally well as an illustration of the genuine unmistakable convictions of many of his countrymen.

Without further preface we will quote some of Mr. Twain's remarks upon foreign countries. And, first of all, he exhibits that charming ignorance of all languages but English which is so common amongst his fellows. French newspapers, he tells us, 'have a strange fashion of telling a perfectly straight story till you get to the "nub" of it, and then a word drops in that no man can translate, and that story is ruined.' He is seriously aggrieved by the names of places, and says that the nearest approach which anybody can make to the true pronunciation of Dijon is 'demijohn.' The spelling is not much assistance under such circumstances. Speaking of a certain distinguished artist, he observes, 'they spell it Vinci, and pronounce it Vinchy; foreigners always spell better than they pronounce.' Gentlemen who

labour under this difficulty of communicating with the natives naturally fall into the hands of guides, and Mr. Twain and his friends appear
to have suffered terribly from the persons whom they hired to take
them to the sights of foreign towns. Their system on arriving at any
large place was to engage a *valet de place*, whom they always called
'Ferguson,' to save the trouble of pronouncing a new name, and were
carried about as helpless victims to such places as he preferred, besides
having to swallow his stories. They took a characteristic revenge,
which appears to have afforded them immense satisfaction. The way to
bully your guide is to affect a profound ignorance—if you have not got
it naturally—and a stony indifference to his information. They therefore
told off a gentleman called the Doctor, to ask questions of the said guide,
because he could 'look more like an inspired idiot, and throw more
imbecility into the tone of his voice, than any man that lives. It comes
natural to him.' Thus, for example, it was assumed that as Americans
they would take a special interest in an autograph letter of Columbus.
The Doctor, after asking some irrelevant questions, pronounced it the
worst specimen of handwriting he ever saw, and added, 'If you have
got any specimens of penmanship of real merit, trot them out; and,
if you haven't, drive on.' The guide, we are told, was 'considerably
shaken up.' On the same principle, when shown an Egyptian monument, the Doctor asked indignantly, 'What is the use of imposing your
vile secondhand carcases on us? If you've got a nice fresh corpse, fetch
him out! or, by George, we'll brain you.' The most irritating question
you can put to such a guide is to ask concerning any distinguished
character to whom he refers—such, for example, as Columbus or
Michael Angelo—'Is he dead?' And this seems to have met with such
success that Mr. Twain scarcely restrained his companions from putting
the inquiry to a monk in a Capuchin convent, who showed them some
of the personal remains of his predecessors.

We may imagine the temper in which some of the remarkable
sights of the Old World would be contemplated under such circumstances. Mr. Twain, indeed, was much impressed by the cathedral at
Milan. The bill for mere workmanship, he says, 'foots up six hundred
and eighty-four millions of francs, thus far (considerably over a
hundred millions of dollars), and it is estimated that it will take a
hundred and twenty years yet to finish the cathedral.' When he gets
to St. Peter's, however, he declares that it did not look nearly so large
as the capitol at Washington, and certainly not a twentieth part
as beautiful from the outside. Even natural wonders are generally

surpassed by their rivals in the United States. The Lake of Como, for example, is pronounced to be very inferior to Lake Tahoe. In clearness it is not to be compared to it. 'I speak,' he says, 'of the north shore of Lake Tahoe, where we can count the scales on a trout at a depth of 180 feet.' Mr. Twain, however, feels constrained to add, 'I have tried to get this statement off at par here, but with no success; so I have been obliged to negotiate it at fifty per cent. discount.' Tahoe, we may explain in passing, for the benefit of philological readers, is Indian for grasshopper soup—so, at least, Mr. Twain believes. The objects, however, against which Mr. Twain feels a special indignation, to which he tells us he is bound to give vent in spite of the remonstrances of his friends, are pictures by the old masters. The old masters irritate him incessantly; and the apparent reason of his objection is characteristic. 'Wherever you find a Raphael, a Rubens, a Michael Angelo, &c.,' he says, 'you find artists copying them, and the copies are always the handsomest. Maybe the originals were handsome when they were new, but they are not now.' He 'harbours no animosity' against the deluded persons who think otherwise; but he regards them as about as wise as men who should stand opposite a desert of charred stumps and say, What a noble forest! Michael Angelo appears to have been a special annoyance to him. 'I never felt so fervently thankful,' he exclaims, 'so soothed, so tranquil, so filled with a blessed peace, as I did yesterday, when I learnt that Michael Angelo was dead.' One would rather like to know how many of Mr. Cook's tourists share this feeling in their hearts, if they only dared to avow their ignorance with an equally touching frankness. Mr. Twain took his revenge by asking the wretched 'Ferguson' of the moment, whenever he came to a 'statoo brunzo' (Italian for a bronze statue), or an Egyptian obelisk, or the Forum or any other work of art, ancient or modern, whether it too was by Michael Angelo; thus at any rate making somebody else share in his tortures. In presence of the ancients he generally indulges in facetiousness of a rather low order. He goes, for example, to some amphitheatre and tries to realize the scene which it once presented. His most vivid picture is that of a Roman youth, who took 'some other fellow's young lady' to a gladiatorial show and amused her and himself during the acts by 'approaching the cage and stirring up the martyrs with his whalebone cane.' But, to say the truth, Mr. Twain here verges upon buffoonery. Once or twice he is driven to what is happily described in the heading of the page as 'general execration.' Here, for example, is a burst of patriotic eloquence. 'O, sons of classic

Italy, is the spirit of enterprise, of self-reliance, of noble endeavour
utterly dead within ye? Curse your indolent worthlessness, why don't
you rob your Church?' And he is very great on occasion in explaining
the many advantages of a free and independent Republic as compared
with a land groaning under priestly dominion and grovelling superstition. That notion of robbing the Church occurs to him very forcibly
at intervals, and he seems to think that, so far as the plan has been
carried out, it is the best chance for Italy.

Perhaps we have persuaded our readers by this time that Mr. Twain
is a very offensive specimen of the vulgarest kind of Yankee. And yet,
to say the truth, we have a kind of liking for him. There is a frankness
and originality about his remarks which is pleasanter than the mere
repetition of stale raptures; and his fun, if not very refined, is often
tolerable in its way. In short, his pages may be turned over with
amusement, as exhibiting more or less consciously a very lively portrait
of the uncultivated American tourist, who may be more obtrusive and
misjudging, but is not quite so stupidly unobservant as our native
product. We should not choose either of them for our companions
on a visit to a church or a picture-gallery, but we should expect most
amusement from the Yankee as long as we could stand him.

9. William Ward: 'American Humorists', Macon (Mississippi) *Beacon*

14 May 1870, 2

Ward was editor of the *Beacon*. J[ohn] Ross Browne (1821–75), traveller and author, wrote *Yusef, or, A Journey of the Frangi: A Crusade in the East* (1853), a travel book. The *Beacon* article closes with praise for the poetry of John G. Saxe.

Within the last thirty years a series of humorous writers have made their appearance, at intervals, each of whom seems to have selected some speciality as a basis upon which he might attain an ephemeral popularity. These specialties have been the different dialects, or, rather provincialisms, which are prevalent in different sections of our country, though a few of them have adopted as a basis the flexibility of our language and its adaptability to antithesis and exaggeration. Of all these, there are only two whose popularity will be permanent—one of the earliest and one of the latest—Washington Irving and 'Mark Twain'—because they have none of these adventitious elements of humor upon which the others depend for popularity, but weave their subtle webs in the unadulterated English.

[discusses briefly twelve American humorists.]

But, since Irving, no humorist in prose has laid the foundation of a permanent fame, except it be Mark Twain, and this, as in the case of Irving, is because he is a pure writer. Aside from the subtle mirth that lurks through his compositions, the grace and finish of his more didactic and descriptive sentences indicate more than mediocrity, though much of his writing has a dash of Bulwer in it. Compare his description of the Sphinx in the *Innocents Abroad* with Bulwer's in the *Last Days of Pompeii*, and we are struck with the similarity of the two passages; there are the same ideas, clothed in the same fine rhetoric, and we cannot but think that the former is an imitation of the latter.

At the same time he confesses that it is a good one, which in itself is high praise. The book is a refinement, an improvement, on Ross Brown's lacking the grotesque features of Yu-self, and more in accordance with the culture of the period.

ROUGHING IT or
THE INNOCENTS AT HOME

February 1872

10. Unsigned review, Manchester *Guardian*

6 March 1872, 7

After discussing *Roughing It*, the reviewer deals with Edward Eggleston's *The Hoosier Schoolmaster*. The column is entitled 'Uncivilised America'.

These two works have been issued by Messrs. Routledge as part of a series of American Humorists. We have coupled them because they both depict, though in a very different style and manner, phases of American frontier life. The main portion of *Roughing It* is an account of the author's experiences among the silver miners in Nevada, and very rough both the experiences and the miners seem to have been, though of course a certain allowance must be made for exaggeration. The life and people are much the same as those that form the subject of Bret Harte's tales; but whereas he has shown a poetical and imaginative spirit, has represented inner life and character, and shown how the tender flower of sentiment or emotion may be found to spring among the rude and unlovely surroundings of a diggers' camp, our author has contented himself with dwelling on the outside of things and simply describing manners and customs.

The frenzied lust for gain and universal spirit of gambling that seizes on a population on the discovery of the existence of precious metals in their soil has before now been depicted in literature. Most people probably have read Mr. Charles Reade's description of the Australian goldfields in *Never too Late to Mend*, and, *mutatis mutandis*, it would hold equally good for California or the diamond miners of the Cape. There is little that is local about the picture, the phenomena exhibited are unfortunately common to all times and places. However, our author gives a lively account of the vicissitudes and perils of a miner's life, and of the strange and weird scenery of the Nevada territory, and there is always a certain fascination in the record of experiences so remote from our own. Illustrating the credulity which always seems to be engendered by any form of gambling, whether it is rouge et noir, stock jobbing, or silver mining, he tells a story of a certain gold mine of fabulous wealth supposed to exist among the mountains. One man alone believed himself to possess the secret, which had been communicated to him by the original discoverer, and was always vainly endeavouring to find the locality. Just as he hunted for the mine, so the population hunted him, till he was compelled to go about in secret:—

[quotes ch. 37 'Every now' to 'go back home'.]

A large part of *Roughing It* is devoted to the account of the journey by the already obsolete overland coach. And here our author treads on much the same ground as Artemus Ward in *Among the Mormons*, though his experiences were of a somewhat different character. He does not shine in comparison, as his humour, such as it is, is immeasurably inferior, though of the same school, depending on ludicrous exaggeration and quaint unexpectedness of comparison. Artemus amused us by his genuine fun and originality; but if there is one thing more than another that is spoilt by mannerism it is humour, and if the mannerism of an individual is offensive, the mannerism of a school is insufferable. Mark Twain, too, often falls into the slang of transatlantic journalism, and displays also its characteristic inability to distinguish between the picturesque and the grotesque.

11. William Dean Howells:
unsigned review, *Atlantic*

June 1872, xxix, 754-5

With this second review Howells took his first tentative step towards acclaiming Clemens as something more than a humorist, a theme he was to amplify in all his subsequent critical writing on the man and his work.

We can fancy the reader of Mr. Clemens's book finding at the end of it (and its six hundred pages of fun are none too many) that, while he has been merely enjoying himself, as he supposes, he has been surreptitiously acquiring a better idea of the flush times in Nevada, and of the adventurous life generally of the recent West, than he could possibly have got elsewhere. The grotesque exaggeration and broad irony with which the life is described are conjecturably the truest colors that could have been used, for all existence there must have looked like an extravagant joke, the humor of which was only deepened by its nether-side of tragedy. The plan of the book is very simple indeed, for it is merely the personal history of Mr. Clemens during a certain number of years, in which he crossed the Plains in the overland stage to Carson City, to be private secretary to the Secretary of Nevada; took the silver-mining fever, and with a friend struck 'a blind lead' worth millions; lost it by failing to comply with the mining laws; became local reporter to a Virginia City newspaper; went to San Francisco and suffered extreme poverty in the cause of abstract literature and elegant leisure; was sent to the Sandwich Islands as newspaper correspondent; returned to California, and began lecturing and that career of humorist, which we should all be sorry to have ended. The 'moral' which the author draws from the whole is: 'If you are of any account, stay at home and make your way by faithful diligence; but if you are of "no account," go away from home, and then you will *have* to work, whether you want to or not.'

A thousand anecdotes, relevant and irrelevant, embroider the work;

excursions and digressions of all kinds are the very woof of it, as it were; everything far-fetched or near at hand is interwoven, and yet the complex is a sort of 'harmony of colors' which is not less than triumphant. The stage-drivers and desperadoes of the Plains; the Mormons and their city; the capital of Nevada, and its government and people; the mines and miners; the social, speculative, and financial life of Virginia City; the climate and characteristics of San Francisco; the amusing and startling traits of Sandwich Island civilization,— appear in kaleidoscopic succession. Probably an encyclopædia could not be constructed from the book; the work of a human being, it is not unbrokenly nor infallibly funny; nor is it to be always praised for all the literary virtues; but it is singularly entertaining, and its humor is always amiable, manly, and generous.

12. Unsigned review, *Overland Monthly*

June 1872, viii, 580–1

Although Bret Harte had reviewed *The Innocents Abroad* for the *Overland Monthly*, he was by this time in New York, and the present reviewer has not been identified.

This is a goodly volume, of nearly six hundred pages; and if mirth is indeed one of the best of medicines, as we have somewhere read—we think in *Hall's Journal of Health*, an unimpeachable authority— *Roughing It* should have a place in every sick-room, and be the invalid's cherished companion. In taking Mr. Clemens' jokes, however, for hygienic purposes, it behooves the patient to exercise great caution in regard to the strength of the dose, if we may judge of the power of the medicine from its effects upon a hungry camel, which once, at the head-waters of the Jordan, made an experiment upon the author's overcoat as an article of diet. The overcoat was left lying upon the ground while the travelers were pitching their tents, and the camel, having contemplated it for awhile with a critical eye, seemed to come to the conclusion that it must be a new edible. But we will let the author tell the story, in his own inimitable way:

[quotes ch. 3 'He put his' to 'loosened his teeth'.]

However, it was not our author's jokes, powerful as were their effects, but one of his statements of facts—one of the mildest and gentlest, he declares, that he ever laid before a trusting public—that proved fatal to the sensitive animal, and caused him to 'fall over as stiff as a carpenter's work-bench, and die a death of indescribable agony.'

This species of humor is certainly grotesque, and hardily extravagant. But it is also genuine, and thoroughly enjoyable. In the same vein, and finer still, is the sketch of the *coyote*, his appearance and characteristics, in which the writer has managed (as he often does) to convey an accurate and graphic picture, while apparently indulging— or rather rioting—in the drollest and most fantastic exaggeration. The episode of Mrs. Beazely and her son, or the Erikson and Greeley correspondence, which has been extensively reproduced in the newspapers, though based upon a well-worn theme, is set in such a quaint, half-pathetic frame-work of narrative as makes it quite fresh and ineffably comic. On almost every page of the volume this vein of broad, robust humor crops out. It is not fine and pensive, like Irving's. It is not artificial, or based upon any literary model, and does not depend for its effect upon elaboration or word-cobbling. Its specific character is its spontaneity and naturalness, together with an underlying element of sturdy honesty and rugged sense, antagonistic to sentimentality and shams. The fun with which the volume overflows more copiously than any previous book of the author's, is not mere fun. It constantly does the work of satire, though in a spirit more genial than that of most satirists; and constantly evinces keen insight and shrewd observation. The preface contains a facetious apology for the circumstance that the book embodies a good deal of information, especially concerning the rise, growth, and culmination of the silver-mining fever in Nevada. The apology is scarcely needed, for though the twenty-odd chapters which deal with that remarkable episode do, in fact, contain a vast amount of information, it is served up in such a style that the reader absorbs it without effort, and becomes unconsciously instructed, while dreaming only of entertainment—as students at German universities are said to become learned in metaphysics, not by much 'poring over miserable books,' but by loquacious discussions, in hours of recreation, over their lager and meerschaums.

As Irving stands, without dispute, at the head of American classic humorists, so the precedence in the unclassical school must be conceded to Mark Twain. About him there is nothing classic, bookish, or conventional, any more than there is about a buffalo or a grizzly. His genius is characterized by the breadth, and ruggedness, and audacity of the West; and, wherever he was born, or wherever he may abide, the Great West claims him as her intellectual offspring. Artemus Ward, Doesticks, and Orpheus C. Kerr, who have been the favorite purveyors of mirth for the Eastern people, were timid navigators, who hugged the shore of plausibility, and would have trembled at the thought of launching out into the mid-ocean of wild, preposterous invention and sublime exaggeration, as Mark Twain does, in such episodes as Bemis' buffalo adventure, and 'Riding the Avalanche,' where, after picturing the unfortunate tourist as 'riding into eternity on the back of a raging and tossing avalanche,' he concludes with the remark, 'This is all very well, but let us not be carried away by excitement, but ask calmly, how does this person feel about it in his cooler moments next day, with six or seven thousand feet of snow on the top of him?'

It would be a great misapprehension, however, to conceive of *Roughing It* as merely a book of grotesque humor and rollicking fun. It abounds in fresh descriptions of natural scenery, some of which, especially in the overland stage-ride, are remarkably graphic and vigorous. The writer's talent for clear, impressive narrative, too, is illustrated in the chapters devoted to the terrible story of the desperado, Slade, which has as intense an interest as any thing in the wildest sensational novel of the day.

Of the three hundred wood-cuts that illustrate the volume we can say nothing complimentary, from an artistic point of view. But some of them are spirited, and many of them suggestive. Crude as they are in design, and coarse in execution, they have afforded us much amusement; and the majority of readers would, we are sure, regret to dispense with them.

SKETCHES, NEW AND OLD

July 1875

13. William Dean Howells: unsigned review, *Atlantic*

December 1875, xxxvi, 749–51

On 19 October 1875 Howells wrote Clemens about this review, 'You can imagine the difficulty of noticing a book of short sketches; it's like noticing a library' (*Mark Twain–Howells Letters*, p. 103).

It is easy to say that these new and old sketches by Mr. Clemens are of varying merit; but which, honest reader, would you leave out of the book? There is none but saves itself either by its humor or by the sound sense which it is based on, so that if one came to reject the flimsiest trifle, one would find it on consideration rather too good to throw away. In reading the book, you go through a critical process imaginably very like the author's in editing it; about certain things there can be no question from the first, and you end by accepting all, while you feel that any one else may have his proper doubts about some of the sketches.

The characteristic traits of our friend—he is the friend of mankind —are all here; here is the fine, forecasting humor, starting so far back from its effect that one, knowing some joke must be coming, feels that nothing less than a prophetic instinct can sustain the humorist in its development; here is the burlesque, that seems such plain and simple fun at first, doubling and turning upon itself till you wonder why Mr. Clemens has ever been left out of the list of our *subtile* humorists; here is that peculiar extravagance of statement which we share with all sufficiently elbow-roomed, unneighbored people, but which our

English cousins are so good as to consider the distinguishing mark of American humor; here is the incorruptible right-mindedness that always warms the heart to this wit; here is the 'dryness,' the 'breadth,' —all the things that so weary us in the praises of him and that so take us with delight in the reading of him. But there is another quality in this book which we fancy we shall hereafter associate more and more with our familiar impressions of him, and that is a growing seriousness of meaning in the apparently unmoralized drolling, which must result from the humorist's second thought of political and social absurdities. It came to Dickens, but the character of his genius was too intensely theatrical to let him make anything but rather poor melodrama of it; to Thackeray, whom our humorists at their best are all alike, it came too, and would not suffer him to leave anything, however, grotesque, merely laughed at. We shall be disappointed if in Mr. Clemens's case it finds only some desultory expression, like 'Lionizing Murderers' and 'A New Crime,' though there could not be more effective irony than these sketches so far as they go. The first is a very characteristic bit of the humorist's art; and the reader is not so much troubled to find where the laugh comes in as to find where it goes out —for ten to one he is in a sober mind when he is done. The other is more direct satire, but is quite as subtle in its way of presenting those cases in which murderers have been found opportunely insane and acquitted, and gravely sandwiching amongst them instances in which obviously mad people have been hanged by the same admirable system.

Nothing more final has been thought of on the subject of a great public, statutory wrong, than Mark Twain's petition to Congress asking that all property shall be held during the period of forty-two years, or for just so long as an author is permitted to claim copyright in his book. The whole sense and justice applicable to the matter are enforced in this ironical prayer, and there is no argument that could stand against it. If property in houses or lands—which a man may get by dishonest trickery, or usury, or hard rapacity—were in danger of ceasing after forty-two years, the whole virtuous community would rouse itself to perpetuate the author's right to the product of his brain, and no griping bidder at tax-sales but would demand the protection of literature by indefinite copyright. The difficulty is, to condition the safety of real estate in this way; but Mark Twain's petition is a move in the right direction.

We should be sorry to give our readers the impression that they are unconsciously to imbibe political and social wisdom from every page of Mr. Clemens's new book, when we merely wished to point out one of his tendencies. Though there is nearly always sense in his nonsense, yet he is master of the art of pure drolling. The grotesque cannot go further than in that 'Mediæval Romance' of his, where he is obliged to abandon his hero or heroine at the most critical moment, simply because he can see no way to get him or her out of the difficulty; and there is a delicious novelty in that 'Ghost Story,' where the unhappy spectre of the Cardiff giant is mortified to find that he has been haunting a plaster cast of himself in New York, while his stone original was lying in Albany. The Experiences of the McWilliamses with the Membranous Croup is a bit of *genre* romance, which must read like an abuse of confidence to every husband and father. These are amongst the new sketches, though none of them have staled by custom, and the old sketches are to be called so merely for contradistinction's sake. 'How I once edited an Agricultural Paper,' 'About Barbers,' 'Cannibalism in the Cars,' 'The Undertaker's Chat,' 'The Scriptural Panoramist,' 'To raise Poultry,' 'A Visit to Niagara,' are all familiar favorites, which, when we have read them we wish merely to have the high privilege of immediately reading over again. We must not leave the famous 'Jumping Frog' out of their honorable and pleasant company; it is here in a new effect, first as the 'Jumping Frog' in Mark Twain's original English, then in the French of the *Revue des deux Mondes*, and then in his literal version of the French, which he gives that the reader may see how his frog has been made to appear 'to the distorted French eye.'

But by far the most perfect piece of work in the book is 'A True Story,' which resulted, we remember, in some confusion of the average critical mind, when it was first published in these pages a little more than one year ago. It is simply the story an old black cook tells of how her children were all sold away from her, and how after twenty years she found her youngest boy again. The shyness of an enlightened and independent press respecting this history was something extremely amusing to see, and we could fancy it a spectacle of delightful interest to the author, if it had not had such disheartening features. Mostly the story was described in the notices of the magazine as a humorous sketch by Mark Twain; sometimes it was mentioned as a paper apparently out of the author's usual line; again it was handled non-committally as one of Mark Twain's extravagances. Evidently the critical mind feared a lurking joke. Not above two or three notices out of hundreds recognized 'A True Story' for what it was, namely, a study of character as true as life itself, strong, tender, and most movingly pathetic in its perfect fidelity to the tragic fact. We beg the reader to turn to it again in this book. We can assure him that he has a great surprise and a strong emotion in store for him. The rugged truth of the sketch leaves all other stories of slave life infinitely far behind, and reveals a gift in the author for the simple dramatic report of reality which we have seen equaled in no other American writer.

14. Matthew Freke Turner: 'Artemus Ward and the Humourists of America', *New Quarterly Magazine*

April 1876, no. 11, 208–12

Turner omits mention of *The Innocents Abroad* or *Roughing It*. He was probably using as a text for review a collection entitled *Eye Openers*, published by Ward, Lock and Tyler in 1875—which, in turn, was a reprint of Hotten's 1871 piracy of the same title. Ward, Lock and Tyler published the *New Quarterly Magazine*.

Of the American writers who have more or less imitated the manner of Mr. Charles Brown, and attained some sort of place in public estimation, I shall notice but two—two only of them, in my opinion, deserving any kind of public criticism—Bret Harte, and the gentleman known to the reading public as Mark Twain. Among the crowd of self-constituted satirists of the day in the United States, only these two gentlemen have shown any distinctive manner as well as original power in their mode of exposing the follies and absurdities of the public. Of these two living authors I, of course, forbear to give any biographical details, further than to say that both are comparatively young men, and that both have seen much of the new and wilder societies of the so-called Pacific Slope, of California, and the adjacent states and territories. The better known and the most read of the two is probably Mark Twain. His popularity at this moment, both in America and this country, is, I should imagine, greater than was ever Mr. Brown's, at least during his lifetime.

There is no mistake at all about Mark Twain's cleverness, but his fun does not appeal to one as does that of Artemus Ward; it is drier, harder, less to the point, and not nearly so fresh and racy. It is a great deal more diffuse; Mark Twain will take a page to bring his jest home —Artemus Ward will do it in a line, in a phrase, in the misspelling of a single word. There is, perhaps, a little too much of the professional jester about Mark Twain. He takes his pen in hand to write a funny paper: his jokes are often forced and far-fetched. Artemus Ward never seems to seek for a jest; his jokes come spontaneously, as if by accident. He does not seem to be aware of them till the reader laughs; then he stops and laughs too, or else he stops gravely to point out a peculiarly recondite joke, and, as it were, to label it. Mark Twain's humour is drier; he follows the old rule that Charles Lamb disapproves—he never laughs at his own jokes.

A common form that his humour takes is to treat a subject from an entirely extravagant point of view, and yet to write with most perfect moderation and propriety of language; and, be it observed, Mark Twain's English, when he does not purposely introduce colloquial Yankeeisms, is excellent. Of this kind of humour is his 'Cannibalism in the Cars.' Perhaps no happier combination of the ghastly and the humorous has been made since Swift's famous proposition about cooking babies. The paper is too long, and the humour a trifle, perhaps, too grim for quotation.

There is one sort of fun much employed by Mark Twain; against which I strongly protest. It is where he turns solemn or sacred subjects into ridicule. It may be a tempting resource to a professional jester, in search of a subject, to exercise his wits upon topics which only require to be treated with levity to make some light-brained people laugh; but it is quite unworthy of such a writer as Mark Twain. The excuse is sometimes made that Americans have not our insular regard for the proprieties, and that it is one phase of the Puritan spirit of our New England cousins to speak very plainly of sacred subjects. If plain speaking means profanity of the kind which Mark Twain indulges in, I beg to disabuse those who believe in such an excuse. I should very strongly advise a traveller to America to refrain from any levity of speech on such topics, in any respectable drawing-room of Boston or New York. There are as many well-dressed rowdies in London, Manchester and Liverpool, as in the cities of New England, and I apprehend that these are the readers with whom Mark Twain's sins against decency find favour. At any rate, I counsel Mark Twain, if he is anxious for the suffrages of decent readers, in his own and this country, to leave profanity alone.

Of the same low type of humour is the account of 'The Killing of Julius Cæsar,' in the style of a Western newspaper describing the result of a 'difficulty in a bar-room:'—

As the result of that affray, it is our painful duty, as public journalists, to record the death of one of our most esteemed citizens—a man whose name is known wherever this paper circulates, and whose fame it has been our pleasure and our privilege to extend, and also to protect from the tongue of slander and falsehood, to the best of our poor ability. We refer to Mr. J. Cæsar.

This is surely very poor indeed. The idea is no better a one than would occur to a used-up Western Editor, and the execution is as low and vulgar as well can be. Still worse, and almost entirely destitute of fun, is the Biblical story of Joseph, told as the frequenter of a bar-room might tell it to his pot companions, over his Bourbon whisky or Lager beer.

Not a bit better are the parodies. When will jesters understand that parodies and travesties of works of true merit are the very poorest forms that wit or humour can take? The best of such parodies ever written are not superlatively good, and the second-rate ones are absolutely insupportable; to say nothing of the impertinence of a man's attempting to make better work than his own ridiculous, and to bring it down to his own level. To burlesque what is in itself contemptible, and yet popular, is, of course, another matter.

A good and well deserved jest underlies the mock *Advice to Little Girls*, written after the fashion of certain 'goody' guides of youth:—

[quotes 'Advice for Good Little Girls', 'Good little girls' to 'ruin and disaster'.]

Mark Twain might write the famous line of Mademoiselle Thérèsa's song on his title page,—

Rien n'est sacré pour un sapeur.

He is a veritable literary 'sapper,' and does not hold at all with the

Sunday-school books, which tell us how the good little boy got his reward, and the wicked little boy came to a bad end. This is his story of the bad little boy who didn't come to grief:—

[quotes 'Once there was' to 'got over it'.]

And the sequel of it all was that Jim is now 'the wickedest scoundrel in his native village, and is universally respected, and belongs to the Legislature.'

It will be seen that Mark Twain is, by no means, a genial, kindly humourist, like his predecessor, Artemus Ward; that, though he hits the same blots, his mode of attack is altogether different.

Mark Twain is a jester, and very little more. When he is not on the trail of some joke, he is apt to be insufferably tedious. Herein, I apprehend, lies the difference between a breaker of jests and a true humourist; between our Dickenses and Thackerays, our Sternes and Goldsmiths, and such men as Hook and the younger Coleman.

15. William Dean Howells: unsigned review, *Atlantic*

May 1876, xxxvii, 621–2

Howells reviewed *Tom Sawyer* from proof sheets, and due to manufacturing delays the review appeared six months before the book was published. When Clemens saw Howells' review he wrote him on 3 April 1876, 'It is a splendid notice, & will embolden weak-kneed journalistic admirers to speak out, & will modify or shut up the unfriendly' (*Mark Twain–Howells Letters*, p. 128).

William Mumford Baker's *Carter Quarterman* was published in 1876. Thomas Bailey Aldrich's *Story of a Bad Boy* appeared in 1870, and Thomas Hughes' *Tom Brown's School Days* had been reissued in 1876 by James R. Osgood, who would publish a book by Mark Twain the following year as well as several subsequent volumes by him.

Mr. Aldrich has studied the life of A Bad Boy as the pleasant reprobate led it in a quiet old New England town twenty-five or thirty years ago, where in spite of the natural outlawry of boyhood he was more or less part of a settled order of things, and was hemmed in, to some measure, by the traditions of an established civilization. Mr. Clemens, on the contrary, has taken the boy of the Southwest for the hero of his new book, and has presented him with a fidelity to circumstance which loses no charm by being realistic in the highest degree, and which gives incomparably the best picture of life in that region as yet known to fiction. The town where Tom Sawyer was born and brought up is some such idle, shabby little Mississippi River town as Mr. Clemens has so well described in his piloting reminiscences, but Tom belongs to the better sort of people in it, and has been bred to fear God and dread the Sunday-school according to the strictest rite of the faiths that have characterized all the respectability of the West. His subjection in these respects does not so deeply affect his inherent tendencies but that he makes himself a beloved burden to the poor, tender-hearted old aunt who brings him up with his orphan brother and sister, and struggles vainly with his manifold sins, actual and imaginary. The limitations of his transgressions are nicely and artistically traced. He is mischievous, but not vicious; he is ready for almost any depredation that involves the danger and honor of adventure, but profanity he knows may provoke a thunderbolt upon the heart of the blasphemer, and he almost never swears; he resorts to any stratagem to keep out of school, but he is not a downright liar, except upon terms of after shame and remorse that make his falsehood bitter to him. He is cruel, as all children are, but chiefly because he is ignorant; he is not mean, but there are very definite bounds to his generosity; and his courage is the Indian sort, full of prudence and mindful of retreat as one of the conditions of prolonged hostilities. In a word, he is a boy, and merely and exactly an ordinary boy on the moral side. What makes him delightful to the reader is that on the imaginative side he is very much more, and though every boy has wild and fantastic dreams, this boy cannot rest till he has somehow realized them. Till he has actually run off with two other boys in the character of buccaneer, and lived for a week on an island in the Mississippi, he has lived in vain; and this passage is but the prelude to more thrilling adventures, in which he finds hidden treasures, traces the bandits to their cave, and is himself lost in its recesses. The local material and the incidents with which his career is worked up are excellent, and throughout there is scrupulous regard for the boy's point of view in reference to his surroundings and himself, which shows how rapidly Mr. Clemens has grown as an artist. We do not remember anything in which this propriety is violated, and its preservation adds immensely to the grown-up reader's satisfaction in the amusing and exciting story. There is a boy's love-affair, but it is never treated otherwise than as a boy's love-affair. When the half-breed has murdered the young doctor, Tom and his friend, Huckleberry Finn, are really, in their boyish terror and super-stition, going to let the poor old town-drunkard be hanged for the crime, till the terror of that becomes unendurable. The story is a wonderful study of the boy-mind, which inhabits a world quite distinct from that in which he is bodily present with his elders, and in this lies its great charm and its universality, for boy-nature, however human nature varies, is the same everywhere.

The tale is very dramatically wrought, and the subordinate characters are treated with the same graphic force that sets Tom alive before us. The worthless vagabond, Huck Finn, is entirely delightful throughout, and in his promised reform his identity is respected: he will lead a decent life in order that he may one day be thought worthy to become a member of that gang of robbers which Tom is to organize. Tom's aunt is excellent, with her kind heart's sorrow and secret pride in Tom; and so is his sister Mary, one of those good girls who are born to usefulness and charity and forbearance and unvarying rectitude. Many village people and local notables are introduced in well-conceived character; the whole little town lives in the reader's sense, with its religiousness, its lawlessness, its droll social distinctions, its civilization qualified by its slave-holding, and its traditions of the wilder West which has passed away. The picture will be instructive to those who have fancied the whole Southwest a sort of vast Pike County, and have not conceived of a sober and serious and orderly contrast to the sort of life that has come to represent the Southwest in literature. Mr. William M. Baker gives a notion of this in his stories, and Mr. Clemens has again enforced the fact here, in a book full of entertaining character, and of the greatest artistic sincerity.

Tom Brown and Tom Bailey are, among boys in books, alone deserving to be named with Tom Sawyer.

16. Moncure D. Conway: unsigned review, London *Examiner*

17 June 1876, pp. 687-8

Moncure Daniel Conway (1832-1907), an American clergyman, biographer, novelist, and writer of liberal pamphlets, served as pastor to a Unitarian congregation in England (1864-84, 1892-7) and acted informally as Clemens' literary agent in London in the 1870s. At this time Conway was also the London correspondent for the Cincinnati *Commercial*. He wrote another, longer review of *Tom Sawyer* which appeared in that newspaper on 26 June 1876. In it he conjectured about the effect on English children, raised by English standards, of the picture of childhood freedom painted in *Tom Sawyer*.

This newest work of Mark Twain increases the difficulty of assigning that author a literary *habitat*. 'American humorist' has for some time been recognised as too vague a label to attach to a writer whose 'Jumping Frog' and other early sketches have been reduced to mere fragments and ventures by such productions as *The Innocents Abroad* and *The New Pilgrim's Progress*, in which, while the humour is still fresh, there is present an equal art in graphic description of natural scenery, and a fine sense of what is genuinely impressive in the grandeurs of the past. Those who have travelled with Mark Twain with some curiosity to observe the effect of the ancient world interpreted by a very shrewd eye, fresh from the newest outcome of civilisation, may have expected to find antiquity turned into a solemn joke, but they can hardly have failed to discover a fine discrimination present at each step in the path of the 'new pilgrim;' while he sheds tears of a kind hardly relished by the superstitious or sentimental over the supposed grave of his deceased parent Adam, he can 'listen deep' when any true theme from the buried world reaches his ear. Without being pathetic he is sympathetic, and there is also an innate refinement in his genius felt in every subject it selects and in its treatment of it. *Tom*

Sawyer carries us to an altogether novel region, and along with these characteristics displays a somewhat puzzling variety of abilities. There is something almost stately in the simplicity with which he invites us to turn our attention to the affairs of some boys and girls growing up on the far frontiers of American civilisation. With the Eastern Question upon us, and crowned heads arrayed on the political stage, it may be with some surprise that we find our interest demanded in sundry Western questions that are solving themselves through a *dramatis personæ* of humble folk whose complications occur in a St. Petersburg situated on the Missouri river. Our manager, we feel quite sure, would not for a moment allow us to consider that any other St. Petersburg is of equal importance to that for which he claims our attention. What is the deposition, death, or enthronement of a Sultan compared with the tragical death of 'Injun Joe,' the murderer, accidentally buried and entombed in the cavern where his stolen treasures are hid? There he was found.

[quotes ch. 33 'The poor unfortunate' to 'rival it'.]

In such writing as this we seem to be reading some classic fable, such as the Persian Sâdi might point with his moral, 'Set not your heart on things that are transitory; the Tigris will run through Bagdat after the race of Caliphs is extinct.' Nor is this feeling of the dignity of his subject absent when the author is describing the most amusing incidents. Indeed, a great deal of Mark Twain's humour consists in the serious—or even at times severe—style in which he narrates his stories and pourtrays his scenes, as one who feels that the universal laws are playing through the very slightest of them. The following is a scene in which the principal actors are a dog, a boy, and a beetle, the place being the chapel:—

[quotes ch. 5 'The minister gave' to 'carry it off'.]

The scene we have selected is not so laughable, perhaps, as some others in the volume, but it indicates very well the kind of art in which Mark Twain is pre-eminent in our time. Every movement of boy, beetle, and poodle, is described not merely with precision, but with a subtle sense of meaning in every movement. Everything is alive, and every face physiognomical. From a novel so replete with good things, and one so full of significance, as it brings before us what we can feel is the real spirit of home life in the far West, there is no possibility of obtaining extracts which will convey to the reader any idea of the purport of the book. The scenes and characters cannot be really seen apart from their grouping and environment. The book will no doubt be a great favourite with boys, for whom it must in good part have been intended; but next to boys we should say that it might be most prized by philosophers and poets. The interior life, the everyday experiences, of a small village on the confines of civilisation and in the direction of its advance, may appear, antecedently, to supply but thin material for a romance; but still it is at just that same little pioneer point that humanity is growing with the greatest freedom, and unfolding some of its unprescribed tendencies. We can, indeed, hardly imagine a more felicitous task for a man of genius to have accomplished than to have seized the salient, picturesque, droll, and at the same time most significant features of human life, as he has himself lived it and witnessed it, in a region where it is continually modified in relation to new circumstances. The chief fault of the story is its brevity, and it will, we doubt not, be widely and thoroughly enjoyed by young and old for its fun and its philosophy.

17. Unsigned review, *Athenaeum*

24 June 1876, no. 2539, 851

Apparently this reviewer's knowledge of Mark Twain's works before *Tom Sawyer* is limited to volumes like the pirated collection called *Screamers*, published by Hotten in 1871 and reprinted by Ward, Lock and Tyler in 1875. He seems not to have read either *The Innocents Abroad* or *Roughing It*.

The name of Mark Twain is known throughout the length and breadth of England. Wherever there is a railway-station with a bookstall his jokes are household words. Those whose usual range in literature does not extend beyond the sporting newspapers, the *Racing Calendar*, and the *Diseases of Dogs*, have allowed him a place with Artemus Ward alongside of the handful of books which forms their library. For ourselves, we cannot dissociate him from the railway-station, and his jokes always rise in our mind with a background of Brown & Polson's Corn Flour and Taylor's system of removing furniture. We have read *The Adventures of Tom Sawyer* with different surroundings, and still have been made to laugh; and that ought to be taken as high praise. Indeed, the earlier part of the book is, to our thinking, the most amusing thing Mark Twain has written. The humour is not always uproarious, but it is always genuine and sometimes almost pathetic, and it is only now and then that the heartiness of a laugh is spoilt by one of those pieces of self-consciousness which are such common blots on Mark Twain's other books. *The Adventures of Tom Sawyer* is an attempt in a new direction. It is consecutive, and much longer than the former books, and as it is not put forward as a mere collection of *Screamers*, we laugh more easily, and find some relief in being able to relax the conventional grin expected from the reader of the little volumes of railway humour. The present book is not, and does not pretend to be a novel, in the ordinary sense of the word; it is not even a story, for that presupposes a climax and a finish; nor is it a mere boys' book of adventures. In the Preface the author says, 'Although my book is intended mainly for the entertainment of boys and girls, I hope it will not be shunned by men and women on that account, for part of my plan has been to try pleasantly to remind adults of what they once were themselves, and of how they felt and thought and talked, and what queer enterprises they sometimes engaged in.' Questions of intention are always difficult to decide. The book will amuse grown-up people in the way that humorous books written for children have amused before, but (perhaps fortunately) it does not seem to us calculated to carry out the intention here expressed. With regard to the style, of course there are plenty of slang words and racy expressions, which are quite in place in the conversations, but it is just a question whether it would not have been as well if the remainder of the book had not been written more uniformly in English.

18. Unsigned review, London *Times*

28 August 1876, 4

Just preceding this review, the critic discusses Charlotte M. Yonge's *The Three Brides*.

Mark Twain belongs to a somewhat different school of writers from Miss Yonge, and *Tom Sawyer* is a characteristic production of his genius. We recognize the germ of it in the stories of the good and bad little boys, which went some way towards making their author's popularity. *Tom Sawyer*, as we are told in the Preface, is intended primarily for the amusement of children, but it is hoped that 'it will not be shunned by men and women on that account, for part of my plan has been to try pleasantly to remind adults of what they once were themselves.' How far Master Sawyer's eccentric experiences may come home in that way to American citizens we cannot pretend to say. To our English notions, Tom appears to have been a portentous phenomenon, and his eventful career exhibits an unprecedented precocity. His conceptions were as romantic as their execution was audacious. Holding all sedentary occupations in aversion, his cast of thought was as original as his quaint felicity of picturesque expression. We are very sure there are no such boys in this country, and even in the States it may be supposed that the breed has been dying out, for fully more than a generation has gone by since Tom was the glory and plague of his native village on the Mississippi. His remarkable talent for mischief would have made him an intolerable thorn in the flesh of the aunt who acted as a mother to him had it not been that his pranks and misconduct endeared him to that much-enduring woman. 'Cuteness' is scarcely the word for Tom's ingrained artfulness. Take, by way of example, one of his earliest achievements. He is caught by his aunt in some flagrant delict, and condemned to whitewash the fence that runs in front of her cottage. Tom had planned to make one of a swimming party, and, what is more, he knows that he will be jeered by his playmates, and contempt is intolerable to his soaring spirit. So, when he sees Ben

66

Rogers, whose satire he stands most in dread of, come puffing along the road, personating a high-pressure steamer, Tom buckles himself to his task with a will. He is so absorbed, in fact, in artistic enthusiasm that Ben's ribald mockery falls on unheeding ears, and Tom has actually to be twitched by the jacket before he turns to recognize his friend. Ere long Ben, who was bound for the river, is begging and praying to be permitted to have a turn with the brush. Tom is slow to be persuaded; had it been the back fence it might have been different, but his aunt is awful particular about this front one—

Ben, I'd like to, honest injun; but Aunt Polly—well, Jim wanted to do it, but she wouldn't let him. Sid wanted to do it, but she wouldn't let Sid. Now, don't you see how I'm fixed? If you was to tackle this fence and anything was to happen to it.

The result is that Tom, as an immense favour, trades the privilege of a few minutes' painting for an apple. Each of the other boys, as he comes up in Ben's wake, makes a similar deal on his own account. Tom amasses a wealth of miscellaneous treasure, which he subsequently barters for a sufficiency of tickets of merit at the Sunday school to entitle him to walk off with the honours for which meritorious children have been toiling; while his aunt, to her intense surprise, finds her fence covered with several coatings of whitewash, and goes into raptures over Tom's capacity for work on the rare occasions when he chooses to apply himself. But, though anything but a bookish boy, Tom had paid considerable attention to literature of an eccentric kind, and, indeed, his knowledge of men and things was very much taken from his favourite authors. He runs away with a couple of comrades to follow the calling of pirates on an island of the Mississippi, the grand inducement being 'that you don't have to get up mornings, and you don't have to go to school and wash and all that blame foolishness.' After some days, when the trio are bored and half-starved and rather frightened, Tom plans a melo-dramatic return, and the missing ones emerge from the disused gallery of the church and present themselves to the congregation of weeping mourners, just as the clergyman's moving eloquence is dwelling on the virtues of the dear departed. Afterwards Tom, who 'all along has been wanting to be a robber,' but has never been able to find the indispensable cave, stumbles on the very thing to suit him. So he carries off a devoted follower who has been hardened for an outlaw's life by the habit of living on scraps and sleeping in empty hogsheads—Republican freedom from class prejudices seems to have been a marked feature among the boys of the Transatlantic St. Petersburg. He teaches Huck his duties as they are flying from the society of their kind out of the accumulated stores of his own erudition. 'Who'll we rob?' asks Huck. 'Oh,' most anybody —waylay people; that's mostly the way.' 'And kill them?' 'No, not always. Hide them in the cave till they can raise a ransom. You make them raise all they can off o' their friends, and after you've kept them a year, if it ain't raised, then you kill them. That's the general way, Only you don't kill the women; you shut up the women, but you don't kill them. They're always beautiful and rich and awfully scared. You take their watches and things, but you always take off your hat and talk polite. There ain't everybody as polite as robbers; you'll see that in any book. Well, the women get to loving you; and after they've been in the cave a week or two weeks they stop crying, and after that you couldn't get them to leave. If you drove them out they'd turn right round and come back. It's so in all the books.' In the course of their researches in the cavern they come on what Tom pronounces 'an awful snug place for orgies.' 'What's orgies?' inquires Huck. 'I dunno,' says Tom very frankly; 'but robbers always have orgies, and of course we've got to have them too.'

We fear these elegant extracts give but a faint idea of the drollery in which the book abounds; for the fact is that the best part of the fun lies in the ludicrous individuality of Tom himself, with whom we have been gradually growing familiar. But we should say that a perusal of *Tom Sawyer* is as fair a test as one could suggest of anybody's appreciation of the humorous. The drollery is often grotesque and extravagant, and there is at least as much in the queer Americanizing of the language as in the ideas it expresses. Practical people who pride themselves on strong common sense will have no patience with such vulgar trifling. But those who are alive to the pleasure of relaxing from serious thought and grave occupation will catch themselves smiling over every page and exploding outright over some of the choicer passages.

19. Unsigned review, New York *Times*

13 January 1877, 3

This reviewer's objection to the violence in *Tom Sawyer* is not unlike Robert Bridges's comment on *Huckleberry Finn* (No. 36) eight years later. *The History of Sandford and Merton*, by Thomas Day, appeared in three volumes, 1783–9. *The Tales of Peter Parley about America* (1827) was the first of more than one hundred moralistic children's books published by Samuel G. Goodrich (1793–1860).

Shades of the venerable Mr. Day, of the instructive Mrs. Barbauld, of the persuasive Miss Edgeworth! Had you the power of sitting today beside the reviewer's desk, and were called upon to pass judgment on the books written and printed for the boys and girls of today, would you not have groaned and moaned over their perusal? If such superlatively good children as Harry and Lucy could have existed, or even such nondescript prigs as Sandford and Merton had abnormal being, this other question presents itself to our mind: 'How would these precious children have enjoyed Mark Twain's *Tom Sawyer*?' In all books written for the amusement of children there are two distinct phases of appreciation. What the parent thinks of the book is one thing; what the child thinks of it is another. It is fortunate when both parent and child agree in their conclusions. Such double appreciation may, in most instances, simply be one in regard to the fitness of the book on the part of the parent. A course of reading entirely devoted to juvenile works must be to an adult a tax on time and patience. It is only once in many years that such a charming book as *Little Alice in Wonderland* is produced, which old and young could read with thorough enjoyment. If, thirty years ago, *Tom Sawyer* had been placed in a careful father's hands to read, the probabilities would have been that he would have hesitated before giving the book to his boy—not that Mr. Clemens' book is exceptional in character, or differs in the least, save in its cleverness, from a host of similar books on like topics which are universally read by children today. It is the judgment of the book-givers which has undoubtedly undergone a change, while youthful minds, being free from warp, twist, or dogma, have remained ever the same.

Returning then to these purely intellectual monstrosities, mostly the pen-and-ink offspring of authors and authoresses who never had any real flesh and blood creations of their own, there can be no doubt that had Sandford or Merton ever for a single moment dipped inside of *Tom Sawyer's* pages, astronomy and physics, with all the musty old farrago of Greek and Latin history, would have been thrown to the dogs. Despite tasseled caps, starched collars, and all the proprieties, these children would have laughed uproariously over Tom Sawyer's 'cat and the pain-killer,' and certain new ideas might have had birth in their brains. Perhaps had these children actually lived in our times, Sandford might have been a Western steam-boat captain, or Merton a fillibuster. *Tom Sawyer* is likely to inculcate the idea that there are certain lofty aspirations which Plutarch never ascribed to his more prosaic heroes. Books for children in former bygone periods were mostly constructed in one monotonous key. A child was supposed to be a vessel which was to be constantly filled up. Facts and morals had to be taken like bitter draughts or acrid pills. In order that they should be absorbed like medicines it was perhaps a kindly thinker who disguised these facts and morals. The real education swallowed in those doses by the children we are inclined to think was in small proportion to the quantity administered. Was it not good old Peter Parley who in this country first broke loose from conventional trammels, and made American children truly happy? We have certainly gone far beyond Mr. Goodrich's manner. There has come an amount of ugly realism into children's story-books, the advantages of which we are very much in doubt about.

Now, it is perfectly true that many boys do not adopt drawing-room manners. Perhaps it is better that little paragons—pocket Crichtons—are so rare. Still, courage, frankness, truthfulness, and self-reliance are to be inculcated in our lads. Since association is everything, it is not desirable that in real life we should familiarize our children with those of their age who are lawless or dare-devils. Granting that the natural is the true, and the true is the best, and that we may describe things as they are for adult readers, it is proper that we should discriminate a great deal more as to the choice of subjects in books intended for children. Today a majority of the heroes in such books have longings to be pirates, want to run away with vessels, and millions of our American boys read and delight in such stories. In olden times the *Pirate's Own Book* with its death's-head and crossbones on the back, had no concealment about it. It is true, edition after edition was sold. There it was. You saw it palpably. There was no disguise about it. If a father or mother objected to their child's reading the *Pirate's Own Book*, a pair of tongs and a convenient fireplace ended the whole matter. Today the trouble is: that there is a decidedly sanguinary tendency in juvenile books. No matter how innocent, quiet, or tame may be the title of a child's book, there is no guarantee that the volume your curly-headed little boy may be devouring may not contain a series of adventures recalling Capt. Kidd's horrors. In the short preface of *Tom Sawyer*, Mr. Clemens writes, 'Although my book is intended mainly for the entertainment of boys and girls, I hope it will not be shunned by men and women on that account.' We have before expressed the idea that a truly clever child's book is one in which both the man and the boy can find pleasure. No child's book can be perfectly acceptable otherwise. Is *Tom Sawyer* amusing? It is incomparably so. It is the story of a Western boy, born and bred on the banks of one of the big rivers, and there is exactly that wild village life which has schooled many a man to self-reliance and energy. Mr. Clemens has a remarkable memory for those peculiarities of American boy-talk which the grown man may have forgotten, but which return to him not unpleasantly when once the proper key is sounded. There is one scene of a quarrel, with a dialogue, between Tom and a city boy which is perfect of its kind. Certain chapters in Tom's life, where his love for the schoolgirls is told, make us believe that for an urchin who had just lost his milk-teeth the affections out West have an awakening even earlier than in Oriental climes. In fact, Tom is a preternaturally precocious urchin. One admirable character in the book, and touched with the hand of a master, is that of Huckleberry Finn. There is a reality about this boy which is striking. An honest old aunt, who adores her scapegrace nephew, is a homely picture worked with exceeding grace. Mr. Clemens must have had just such a lovable old aunt. An ugly murder in the book, over-minutely described and too fully illustrated, which Tom and Huck see, of course, in a graveyard, leads, somehow or other, to the discovery of a cave, in which treasures are concealed, and to which Tom and Huck fall heirs. There is no cant about Mr. Clemens. A description of a Sunday-school in *Tom Sawyer* is true to the letter. Matters are not told as they are fancied to be, but as they actually are.

If Mr. Clemens has been wanting in continuity in his longer sketches, and that sustained inventive power necessary in dovetailing incidents, Tom, as a story, though slightly disjointed, has this defect less apparent. As a humorist, Mr. Clemens has a great deal of fun in him, of the true American kind, which crops out all over the book. Mr. Clemens has an audience both here and in England, and doubtless his friends across the water will re-echo 'the hearty laughs which the reading of *Tom Sawyer* will cause on this side of the world'. We are rather inclined to treat books intended for boys and girls, written by men of accredited talent and reputation, in a serious manner. Early impressions are the lasting ones. It is exactly such a clever book as *Tom Sawyer* which is sure to leave its stamp on younger minds. We like, then, the true boyish fun of Tom and Huck, and have a foible for the mischief these children engage in. We have not the least objection that rough boys be the heroes of a story-book. Restless spirits of energy only require judicious training in order to bring them into proper use. In the books to be placed into children's hands for purposes of recreation, we have a preference for those of a milder type than *Tom Sawyer*. Excitements derived from reading should be administered with a certain degree of circumspection. A sprinkling of salt in mental food is both natural and wholesome; any cravings for the contents of the castors, the cayenne and the mustard, by children, should not be gratified. With less, then, of Injun Joe and 'revenge,' and 'slitting women's ears,' and the shadow of the gallows, which throws an unnecessarily sinister tinge over the story, (if the book really is intended for boys and girls) we should have liked *Tom Sawyer* better.

March 1880

20. William Ernest Henley: unsigned review, *Athenaeum*

24 April 1880, no. 2739, 529–30

William Ernest Henley (1849–1903), essayist and playwright, appears to be the author of this review. A fragment of a letter, lacking both heading and signature, which is now in the Huntington Library (HM 722), contains the phrase, 'I have just written a crackling review of [Mark Twain] in the *Athenaeum*,' and comments particularly on the blue jay. The handwriting is almost certainly Henley's. Henley may also be the author of three other reviews in this collection (see Nos. 31, 34, and 47).

A new book by the American humourist who calls himself Mark Twain is sure to find readers; more than that, it is sure to deserve them. Mr. Clemens, in truth, is the most successful and original wag of his day; he has a keen, sure sense of character and uncommon skill in presenting it dramatically; and he is also an admirable story-teller, with the anecdotic instinct and habit in perfection, and with a power of episodic narrative that is scarcely equalled, if at all, by Mr. Charles Reade himself. He has seen men and cities, has looked with a shrewd and liberal eye on many modes of life, and has always something apt and pointed to say of everything; finally, he shares with Walt Whitman the honour of being the most strictly American writer of what is called American literature. Of all, or almost all, the many poets, novelists, essayists, philosophers, historians, and such like notables (orators excepted) America has produced, the origins are plainly European. The New World is responsible but for their bodies and souls; artistically they are the Old World's offspring, and the Old World's only. This one is a nursling of France, that one of Spain, that other of England and Germany, and so on. To take but the instances that are most familiar, it is not easy to imagine an Irving guiltless of Goldsmith and Addison; or a Longfellow innocent of Goethe and Heine, of the 'Romancero' and the 'Commedia,' of the Northern saga-men and the song-smiths of the South; or an Emerson anterior to Carlyle; or a prae-Miltonic 'Thanatopsis'; or an uncultured and un-eclectic Henry James. But Mark Twain is American pure and simple. To the eastern mother-land he owes but the rudiments, the ground-work, already archaic and obsolete to him, of the speech he has to write; in his turn of art, his literary methods and aims, his intellectual habit and temper, he is as distinctly national as the fourth of July itself.

No doubt in Mark Twain there is something too much of the ab-stract reporter as American needs and usages have modified and finished that interesting entity; no doubt there is something too much of the professional jester. He is immoderately given to 'layin' around' after matter for paragraphs, with the manner and air of a smart ignoramus, not unconscious of his defects, but rejoicing in them and preferring them. Again, it is impossible for him to be serious for more than two minutes at once about anything. Do what he will, the old vocation is sure to get the better of him. He has cracked jokes and told comic stories till the use of applause has come to be second nature, and the world, unless it be laughing at him, is a poor, tame, uninteresting monster. Luckily he is in his way a literary artist of exceptional skill, so that, his vices notwithstanding, he is not often offensive and hardly ever tedious. Sooth to say, he might be both more frequently than he is, and yet find grace with everybody. Usually the professional joker is but a dull rascal after all. Seriously to set to work to be funny is to become stale, flat, and unprofitable forthwith; and it is not Sam and Mr. Bob Sawyer who are the sport of *Pickwick*, but Tony Weller and Ben Allen. It is the peculiarity of Mark Twain that, while he is always bent on being funny—deliberately and determinedly funny—he almost always succeeds in his intent. He has a certain dry, imaginative extra-vagance of fun that is neither more nor less than a literary intoxicant, so irresistible is its operation and so overwhelming its effect.

His new book, *A Tramp Abroad*, is the record of a walking tour through certain parts of Europe. No one who knows Mark Twain will be surprised that the walking tour was got through every how but on foot. Of uniform excellence *A Tramp Abroad* is not; but it is very vigorously and picturesquely written throughout; it contains some of the writer's happiest work; it is a worthy sequel to books of such uncommon point and freshness as *Roughing It* and *The Innocents at Home*. In the second chapter Mark Twain is already at work, and at his best and brightest, too, as those who read his adventure with a raven will feel. This adventure reminds him of Jim Baker's theory of animal linguistics, and particularly of that theory in connexion with the blue jay:—

[quotes ch. 2 ' "There's more" ' to ' "that's all".']

Then, on the top of this incomparable statement, Jim Baker being still the speaker, comes the story of a blue jay who lighted on a hole in the roof of a log hut, and began trying to fill it up with acorns. Of course the acorns all fell into the hut, and the hole remained unstopped, and the operator mystified and exhausted. He was very much overcome indeed; in Jim Baker's own words,—

He just had strength enough to crawl up on to the comb, and lean his back agin the chimbly, and then he collected his impressions, and begun to free his mind. I see in a second that what I had mistook for profanity in the mines was only just the rudiments, as you may say.

How the matter ended it would be unfair to say. The fun and tenderness of the conception, of which no living man but Mark Twain is capable, its grace and fantasy and slyness, the wonderful feeling for animals that is manifest in every line, make of all this episode of Jim Baker and his jays a piece of work that is not only delightful as mere reading, but also of a high degree of merit as literature. It is the best thing in the book, though the book is full of good things, and contains passages and episodes—as, for instance, the sleepless night, the excellent burlesque on the literature of Alpine adventure, the appendix on the German language, the laborious ant, the veterinary student, the young and sportive American lady, the steamboat bore, the ascent of the Rigi, and others—that, as has been said already, are equal to the funniest of those that have gone before. For the rest, the traveller's experiences were extremely varied. He watched with interest the process of duelling as it is maintained at Heidelberg, and had afterwards the honour to act as second to M. Gambetta in that memorable combat with M. de Fourtou. He studied art, and painted gorgeous pictures that were mistaken for the works of Turner; and one good result of his studies is that he now understands Mr. Ruskin. He discovered a new writer of most gaudy English, a certain L. W. Garnharm, B.A., of whose work he gives some specimens, and produced a very creditable translation of Heine's famous 'Ich weiss nicht was soll es bedeuten.' After making a successful ascent of the Neckar on a raft, he was ill advised enough on the return voyage to try and pilot the structure through Heidelberg bridge himself.

[quotes ch. 19 'We went tearing along' to 'and solitude'.]

With which pleasant piece of fooling we shall take our leave of Mark Twain and his most excellent book. Only let his next be as good, and his peculiar public may vaunt their fortune against that of the admirers of any other living prose writer, English or American.

21. Unsigned review, *Saturday Review*

17 April 1880, xlix, 514–15

The tone of this review and its knowledgeable references to mountain climbing and 'well-known books about Alpine climbing' make it possible this review was written by Sir Leslie Stephen, who was an ardent climber and at this time editor of the *Alpine Journal* as well as a contributor to the *Saturday Review*.

Mr. Mark Twain started for Europe in March 1878, with the intention of course of writing a book about what he did and saw. The result is the two volumes called *A Tramp Abroad*; and the first fault which a person who reads through the two volumes will probably be inclined to find with them is that they are two instead of one. On the other hand, nobody but a reviewer would dream of reading straight through the volumes. They are things to be taken for a spell and then laid down again until another idle half-hour is ready to be filled up. This would perhaps make a sufficient general answer to the reviewer's complaint;

but it will not account for the carelessness with which, in the English edition, a good deal of matter which is obviously out of place is retained in the second volume. It may be interesting to some American readers to have put before them extracts from exceedingly well-known books about Alpine climbing; but it can hardly be interesting to any English readers. There is something not altogether unpleasing in the simplicity with which the author waxes enthusiastic about the 'imposing Alpine mass' of the Rigi; but one may have too much of that sort of thing. Besides, calling the Rigi by this grandiloquent name leaves the writer rather at a loss what to say about the Matterhorn. He gets out of it with some ingenuity by the help of such phrases as 'colossal wedge,' 'sky-cleaving monolith,' and 'Napoleon of the mountain world.' In speaking of the Matterhorn, by the way, Mr. Twain constantly refers to 'Lord Douglas,' although in one of the extracts above referred to the title occurs more than once, and is of course correctly given. However, if there are certain parts of Mr. Twain's volumes which are dull (and there is one story of an imaginary expedition the dulness of which, relieved by a very few bright touches, is monstrous and overwhelming), there are also plenty of passages, stories, bits of observation, scraps of character and conversation, and so forth, which are delightfully bright and clever. And a practised reader can always skip the dull parts.

One of the most pleasing instances of Mr. Twain's powers is found very early in the book. He wandered into the beautiful Heidelberg woods, and was standing in meditation beneath the pine-trees. A raven croaked. He looked up and saw the bird observing him, and felt as a man feels who finds that a stranger has been secretly watching him. 'I eyed the raven and the raven eyed me. Nothing was said during some seconds. Then the bird stepped a little way along his limb to get a better point of observation, lifted his wings, stuck his head far down below his shoulders toward me, and croaked again—a croak with a distinctly insulting expression about it. If he had spoken in English, he could not have said any more plainly than he did say in raven, "Well, what do *you* want here?"' This was bad enough, especially as Mr. Twain's refusal to bandy words with a raven only encouraged the adversary to the use of what was evidently the most horrible language. But when, not content with this, the raven called to another raven, and the two together discussed Mr. Mark Twain with the most complete freedom, he felt that there was nothing for it but flight, and he was probably right. This incident reminds him of Jim Baker, a simple-hearted, middle-aged miner who lived all alone in a corner of California, and had studied the beasts and birds around him so closely that he got, as he said, to understand everything they said. He found that some animals have a very limited language, and are unable to use any adornments of speech, while others have a fine and ready command of brilliant words and phrases, which they enjoy exhibiting. After long and careful consideration he had settled that the blue-jays were the best talkers he had found among birds and beasts:—

[quotes ch. 2 ' "There's more" ' to ' "about some blue-jays".']

The 'perfectly true fact' occupies the next chapter, and is well worth reading. To tell it in any words but those of Jim Baker would be to spoil it.

The author has naturally a good deal to say about the Heidelberg students, and he devotes considerable space to the duels of the Corps-Students, those curious encounters which take place at the Hirsch-Gasse, and which have been more than once briefly described in these columns. Mr. Twain seems to have been fortunate or unfortunate in seeing, on the day when he visited this place, a succession of unusually ghastly duels, and his impression of the whole proceedings was a good deal more serious than we should have expected. However, no doubt most of these duels do look ugly enough, and possibly Mr. Twain has deliberately heightened his description, for the sake of contrast to the very amusing skit upon a French duel which follows his serious account of the Hirsch-Gasse and its occupants. In some particulars this account is curiously incorrect. Mr. Mark Twain describes the schläger as 'quite heavy.' He has not noted that it is a weapon absolutely useless except for the artificial student-duelling, and, as he has given so much space to these unique and somewhat barbaric contests, it is a pity that it did not occur to him to try to throw some light on the origin of the schläger, that curious blade which resembles a sharp-edged harlequin's bat made in steel and fitted with a solid claymore-like hilt. So lately as in Crabb Robinson's time the student duels were fought with small swords, fitted with a button not on, but near, the point, so as to avoid the chance of a fatal wound, while admitting a visible and tangible puncture. How the altogether abnormal arm now in use was developed we have never been able to discover, in spite of many inquiries. That there is science in its employment there is no doubt; but the one fact that the heavily-padded right arm is constantly brought into requisition in the fashion of a shield to receive the adversary's blows, will show at once how useless, except indeed as a kind of corollary to backsword play, the science is. Mr. Twain dwells, by no means unjustly, on the endurance exhibited by Corps-Students in taking, without any signs of pain, cuts on the face, which always look ugly, must be considerably painful, and may, if neglected, be highly dangerous. The contrast between this endurance and the rule of the game which stops a duel for the slightest scratch on the hand caused by the flexible blade making its way inside the hilt opposed to it is curious. Mr. Twain, in connexion with the student-duels, informs his readers that a Corps-Student's wearing a riband across his breast indicates that he has fought three decisive duels and is 'free'—that is, can refuse all but serious duels without reproach. As a matter of fact, it signifies that he has ceased to be a *fuchs*, or freshman, and, having become a *bursch*, or full member of the corps, has more fighting on his hands than he had before. We may note in passing that a *fuchs* in a duel wears a cap which gives some slight protection to the head, while a *bursch* fights bareheaded.

From his French duel the author goes on to the theatre at Mannheim, where he heard *Lohengrin*, as to which he has some astoundingly stupid would-be-humorous remarks to make. What he says, however, of the considerate behaviour of members of German audiences in never disturbing their companions is both true and well worth attention. Apparently his account of a raft journey is genuine, and some of the bits of description in connexion with this have truth and vigour. The truth and humour of his account of his getting lost at dead of night in the dark in his own bed-room can perhaps be only appreciated by people who have gone through the same experience, and for the sake of the world at large it is to be hoped that such people are few. In the course of his journeys Mr. Twain fell in with a wonderful guide-book written from the German a long time ago by an Englishman. Of this it is only fair to leave Mr. Twain to expound the humours, but we cannot resist giving a few quotations from a rival production which was presented to him under the title *Catalogue of Pictures in the old Pinacotek* (at Munich). Among the descriptions are:—

Portrait of a young man. A long while this picture was thought to be Bindi Altoviti's portrait; now somebody will again have it to be the self-portrait of Raphael.

Susan bathing, surprised by the two old men. In the background is the lapidation of the condemned.

A larder with greens and dead game animated by a cook-maid and two kitchen-boys.

And the work contains this warning:—

It is not permitted to make use of the work in question to a publication of the same contents as well as to the pirated edition of it.

Some of the best things in the book are to be found, where they are placed with a probably conscious air of pedantry, in the appendices at the end of the second volume. For instance, in an Appendix on the German language, we have this practical illustration of some of its difficulties:—

[quotes appendix D 'Tale of the Fishwife' to 'in Spots'.]

Mr. Twain's volumes are, to quote a pantomime clown's phrase, very 'loose and careless,' and he has sometimes reached intense dulness in the desire to be funny. He is perhaps more irritating, however—and it may be added offensive—when he writes seriously, as in the chapter on 'Indecent License in Art,' concerning things of which he evidently has no sort of comprehension. But, we repeat, to people who know how to skip, and how to read, if they do read them, such passages as the one referred to without feeling annoyed, the book is sure to furnish a good deal of genuine amusement.

22. William Dean Howells: unsigned review, *Atlantic*

May 1880, xlv, 686–8

On 22 March 1880 Howells wrote to tell Mark Twain that Mrs. Howells declared *A Tramp Abroad* was 'the wittiest book she ever read, and I say there is *sense* enough in it for ten books. That is the idea which my review will try to fracture the average numbscull with' (*Mark Twain–Howells Letters*, p. 293). Both Clemens and his wife wrote Howells to express their gratitude for the tone of his review.

In the natural disgust of a creative mind for the following that vulgarizes and cheapens its work, Mr. Tennyson spoke in parable concerning his verse:

> Most can raise the flower now,
>   For all have got the seed.
> And some are pretty enough,
>   And some are poor indeed;
> And now again the people
>   Call it but a weed.

But this bad effect is to the final loss of the rash critic rather than the poet, who necessarily survives imitation, and appeals to posterity as singly as if nobody had tried to ape him; while those who rejected him, along with his copyists, have meantime thrown away a great pleasure. Just at present some of us are in danger of doing ourselves a like damage. 'Thieves from over the wall' have got the seed of a certain drollery, which sprouts and flourishes plentifully in every newspaper, until the thought of American Humor is becoming terrible; and sober-minded people are beginning to have serious question whether we are not in danger of degenerating into a nation of wits. But we ought to take courage from observing, as we may, that this plentiful crop of humor is not racy of the original soil; that in short the thieves from over the wall were not also able to steal Mr. Clemens's garden-plot.

His humor springs from a certain intensity of common sense, a passionate love of justice, and a generous scorn of what is petty and mean; and it is these qualities which his 'school' have not been able to convey. They have never been more conspicuous than in this last book of his, to which they may be said to give its sole coherence. It may be claiming more than a humorist could wish to assert that he is always in earnest; but this strikes us as the paradoxical charm of Mr. Clemens's best humor. Its wildest extravagance is the break and fling from a deep feeling, a wrath with some folly which disquiets him worse than other men, a personal hatred for some humbug or pretension that embitters him beyond anything but laughter. It must be because he is intolerably weary of the twaddle of pedestrianizing that he conceives the notion of a tramp through Europe, which he operates by means of express trains, steamboats, and private carriages, with the help of an agent and a courier; it is because he has a real loathing, otherwise inexpressible, for Alp-climbing, that he imagines an ascent of the Riffelberg, with 'half a mile of men and mules' tied together by rope. One sees that affectations do not first strike him as ludicrous, merely, but as detestable. He laughs, certainly, at an abuse, at ill manners, at conceit, at cruelty, and you must laugh with him; but if you enter into the very spirit of his humor, you feel that if he could set these things right there would be very little laughing. At the bottom of his heart he has often the grimness of a reformer; his wit is turned by preference not upon human nature, not upon droll situations and things abstractly ludicrous, but upon matters that are out of joint, that are unfair or unnecessarily ignoble, and cry out to his love of justice for discipline. Much of the fun is at his own cost where he boldly attempts to grapple with some hoary abuse, and gets worsted by it, as in his verbal contest with the girl at the medicinal springs in Baden, who returns 'that beggar's answer' of half Europe, 'What you please,' to his ten-times-repeated demand of 'How much?' and gets the last word. But it is plain that if he had his way there would be a fixed price for those waters very suddenly, and without regard to the public amusement, or regret for lost opportunities of humorous writing.

It is not Mr. Clemens's business in Europe to find fault, or to contrast things there with things here, to the perpetual disadvantage of that continent; but sometimes he lets homesickness and his disillusion speak. This book has not the fresh frolicsomeness of the *Innocents Abroad*; it is Europe revisited, and seen through eyes saddened by much experience of *tables d'hôte*, old masters, and traveling Americans,—whom, by the way, Mr. Clemens advises not to travel too long at a time in Europe, lest they lose national feeling and become traveled Americans. Nevertheless, if we have been saying anything about the book, or about the sources of Mr. Clemens's humor, to lead the reader to suppose that it is not immensely amusing, we have done it a great wrong. It is delicious, whether you open it at the sojourn in Heidelberg, or the voyage down the Neckar on a raft, or the mountaineering in Switzerland, or the excursion beyond Alps into Italy. The method is that discursive method which Mark Twain has led us to expect of him. The story of a man who had a claim against the United States government is not impertinent to the bridge across the river Reuss; the remembered tricks played upon a printer's devil in Missouri are the natural concomitants of a walk to Oppenau. The writer has always the unexpected at his command, in small things as well as great: the story of the raft journey on the Neckar is full of these surprises; it is wholly charming. If there is too much of anything, it is that ponderous and multitudinous ascent of the Riffelberg; there is probably too much of that, and we would rather have another appendix in its place. The appendices are all admirable; especially those on the German language and the German newspapers, which get no more sarcasm than they deserve.

One should not rely upon all statements of the narrative, but its spirit is the truth, and it honestly breathes American travel in Europe as a large minority of our forty millions know it. The material is inexhaustible in the mere Americans themselves, and they are rightful prey. Their effect upon Mr. Clemens has been to make him like them best at home; and no doubt most of them will agree with him that 'to be condemned to live as the average European family lives would make life a pretty heavy burden to the average American family.' This is the sober conclusion which he reaches at last, and it is unquestionable, like the vastly greater part of the conclusions at which he arrives throughout. His opinions are no longer the opinions of the Western American newly amused and disgusted at the European difference, but the Western American's impressions on being a second time confronted with things he has had time to think over. This is the serious undercurrent of the book, to which we find ourselves reverting from its obvious comicality. We have, indeed, so great an interest in Mr. Clemens's likes and dislikes, and so great respect for his preferences generally, that we are loath to let the book go to our readers without again wishing them to share these feelings. There is no danger that they will not laugh enough over it; that is an affair which will take care of itself; but there is a possibility that they may not think enough over it. Every account of European travel, or European life, by a writer who is worth reading for any reason, is something for our reflection and possible instruction; and in this delightful work of a man of most original and characteristic genius 'the average American' will find much to enlighten as well as amuse him, much to comfort and stay him in such Americanism as is worth having, and nothing to flatter him in a mistaken national vanity or a stupid national prejudice.

THE PRINCE AND THE PAUPER

December 1881

23. H. H. Boyesen: unsigned review, *Atlantic*

December 1881, xlviii, 843–5

Hjalmar Hjorth Boyesen (1848–95), a Norwegian-born novelist, critic, and professor of German at Cornell (1874–80) and Columbia (1880–95), was a friend and protégé of William Dean Howells. The title of this review is 'Mark Twain's New Departure'.

Clemens wrote to Boyesen that he 'was mightily delighted' with the review and commented that *The Prince and the Pauper* was an unusual experiment

for I went for the bulk of the profits, and so published the volume at my own expense, opening with an edition of 25,000 copies, for the manufacture of which I paid $17,500. . . . I find myself a fine success, as a publisher; and literally the new departure is a great deal better received than I had any right to hope for. [11 January 1882.]

Inclination to forsake the field of assured success, and seek distinction in untried paths, has shown itself a controlling impulse in many an artistic mind. Examples are most frequent, probably, amongst actors, whose eagerness to shine in unexpected situations, and to demonstrate merits apart from those by which they have achieved prominence, is a common characteristic. For reasons sufficiently obvious, these efforts of theatrical aspiration are seldom satisfactory; nor would they be likely to win applause, even if based upon sound judgment and sustained by positive ability. The actor, as a rule, must be content with fame in a single branch of his vocation, unless he is prepared to undertake a fresh career in regions where his person and his precedents are unknown. In other arts ambition is subject to no such restraints. If the

85

power of versatility exists, it is fairly sure of recognition. A Doré may desert the narrower channel of his early fortune, and enlarge his fame in proportion to the breadth of his spreading canvas. Rossini, with a reputation founded upon dozens of dazzling comic operas, could not rest, in his old age, until he had produced a solemn mass which might stand beside the grave works of more majestic composers. Scott, after securing eminence enough to content his modest nature through the exercise of one gift, built himself secretly a higher renown by means of another. Bulwer's less brilliant light shone with a still greater variety of rays. The 'deed' may not in all cases be equal to the 'attempt,' but the evidences of determined endeavor to establish this sort of manifold claim upon public attention and regard have always been abundant, and will be as long as the imagination of men can be turned to creative account.

The publication of Mark Twain's new story, *The Prince and the Pauper*, supplies a rather striking instance in point,—or, at least, supplies material for illustration of the tendency of writers whose position is fixed and prosperous to give their faculties a new and unexpected range, and strive for a totally different order of production from any previously accomplished. It would be impertinent to pronounce too confidently upon the author's motive, but what he has done is, in one particular, plain to every comprehension. He has written a book which no reader, not even a critical expert, would think of attributing to him, if his name were withheld from the title-page. There is nothing in its purpose, its method, or its style of treatment that corresponds with any of the numerous works by the same hand. It is no doubt possible to find certain terms of phraseology, here and there, which belong to Mark Twain, and characteristically convey his peculiar ideas; but these are few, and would pass unnoticed as means of identification, although we recognize their familiarity readily enough, when we are already aware from whom they come. It is also possible to recall episodical passages in his earlier volumes—quaint legends and antique fantasies—which seem to be animated by a spirit similar to that of the present tale; but these, again, would have suggested nothing as to the origin of *The Prince and the Pauper*, if it had appeared anonymously. So far as Mark Twain is concerned, the story is an entirely new departure; so much so as to make it appear inappropriate to reckon it among that writer's works. It is indisputably by Clemens; it does not seem to be by Twain,—certainly not by the Twain we have known for a dozen or more years as the boisterous and rollicking humorist, whose chief function has been to diffuse hilarity throughout English-reading communities and make himself synonymous with mirth in its most demonstrative forms. Humor, in quite sufficient proportion, this tale does assuredly contain; but it is a humor growing freely and spontaneously out of the situations represented,—a sympathetic element, which appeals sometimes shrewdly, sometimes sweetly, to the senses, and is never intrusive or unduly prominent; sometimes, indeed, a humor so tender and subdued as to surprise those who are under its spell with doubts whether smiles or tears shall be summoned to express the passing emotion.

The book is not only a novelty of Mark Twain's handiwork; it is in some respects a novelty in romance. It is not easy to place it in any distinct classification. It lacks the essential features of a novel, and while principally about children, is by no means a tale exclusively for children, although the young may have their full share in the enjoyment of it. The subject is so absolutely simple that to know it beforehand deprives the reader of none of the pleasure he has a right to expect. There is no pretense of a formal plot, and all the charm is owing to the sincerity, the delicacy, and the true feeling with which the story is told. Two little boys (one a bright figure in history, the other a gem of fiction; the former King Edward the Sixth of England, the latter a pauper vagrant) accidentally exchange stations at the age of about twelve years, and each remains for several days in his strangely altered condition. A strong resemblance between the two, coöperating with accidents of time and place, makes it possible for the substitution to remain undetected. The sharply contrasting adventures of the pair constitute the whole tale. The incident of the exchange is the sole point that would seem to be hazardous for the narrator; but whether the skill is conscious or not, whether that particular passage gets its truthfulness from the author's own sense of its validity, or is carefully elaborated with a view to the reader's beguilement, it certainly presents no difficulty as it stands. The rest follows naturally and ingenuously. There is no strain upon credulity, for the characters come and go, live and breathe, suffer and rejoice, in an atmosphere of perfect reality, and with a vivid identity rarely to be found in fictions set in mediaeval days. The same life-like verisimilitude that is manifest in many pages of Scott, and throughout Reade's Cloister and the Hearth, glows in every chapter of this briefer chronicle of a real prince's fancied griefs and perils. To preserve an illusion so consistently, it would seem that the author's own faith in the beings of his creation must have been firm, from beginning to end of their recorded career. Unless the teller of a story believes it all himself, for the time, he can hardly impress such conviction as he does in this case upon the mind of the reader.

However skillful in invention a writer may be, it is certain that his work loses nothing of effect from a studious harmonization with the period in which it is placed. In *The Prince and the Pauper* this requirement has been scrupulously observed. The details are not made obtrusive, and the 'local color' is never laid on with excess; but the spirit of the age preceding that of Elizabeth is maintained with just the proper degree of art to avoid the appearance of artfulness. Critical examination shows that no inconsiderable labor has been given to the preservation of this air of authenticity; but the idea that the results of research are inflicted with malice aforethought is the last that would occur to any reader. On the other hand, if irrelevant phrases may be once or twice detected, their employment is obviously intentional,— the indulgence of some passing whim, the incongruity of which, it is taken for granted, will be excused for the sake of its fun. Such might easily be spared, no doubt, though they do no serious harm. It is in every way satisfactory to observe that the material accessories are brought into view with an accuracy which coherently supports the veracity of the narrative. Dresses, scenery, architecture, manners and customs, suffer no deviation from historical propriety. It would be a pity if our trust in the existence of the little pair of heroes, or of the well-proportioned figures that accompany them, were to be shaken by short-comings in these respects. But there is no danger. The big-hearted protector of guileless childhood is as palpable to our senses as to the grateful touch of the prince's accolade. The one soft spot in the hard old monarch's nature reveals itself to our apprehension as clearly as to the privileged eyes of the courtiers at Westminster. The burly ruffian of the gutters, the patient, sore-afflicted mother, the gracious damsels of pure estate and breeding, the motley vagabonds of the highway, the crafty and disciplined councilors of the realm, the mad ascetic, and the varied throng of participants in the busy scenes portrayed,—all these take to themselves the shape and substance of genuine humanity, and stamp themselves on our perceptions as creatures too vital and real to be credited to fable land. We go beyond the author's cautious proposition in the prefatory lines, that the story '*could* have happened:' we are sure that it ought to have happened, and we willingly believe it did happen.

It will be interesting to watch for the popular estimate of this fascinating book. Of the judgment of qualified criticism there can be little question. That it will be accorded a rank far above any of the author's previous productions is a matter of course. It has qualities of excellence which he has so long held in reserve that their revelation now will naturally cause surprise. Undoubtedly, the plan upon which most of his works have been framed called for neither symmetry, nor synthetic development, nor any of the finer devices of composition. Generally speaking, they served their purpose, without the least reference to the manner in which they were thrown together. They stood, and stand, at the head of all the genuine successes of modern comic writing; but, notwithstanding the frequent flashes of power that give them vigor, the felicities of characterization that brighten them, the pathos that chastens them, and no one can say how many other manifestations of cleverness, they remain the most heterogeneous accumulations of ill-assorted material that ever defied the laws of literature, and kept the public contentedly captive for half a score of years. Now the same public is called upon to welcome its old favorite in a new guise,—as the author of a tale ingenious in conception, pure and humane in purpose, artistic in method, and, with barely a flaw, refined in execution.

24. E. Purcell: review, *Academy*

24 December 1881, xx, 469

This review may be by Edmund Sheridan Purcell (1824–99), a Catholic journalist, editor of the *Westminster Gazette* (1866–78), and author of the frank and controversial *Life of Cardinal Manning* (1895).

Those who have discovered wit, wisdom, and good taste in Mark Twain's previous works will laugh beforehand at even an historical romance from his pen. But whether we were expected to laugh or cry we could not quite make out—on the whole, the volume seemed to be written *au grand sérieux*—but, at all events, we did neither. Against the happy thought which forms the backbone of the tale, we must really protest. A street Arab, one Tom, is supposed to have changed clothes with Edward VI. during Henry's last illness, to have played the part of a royal Christopher Sly, and reigned with much distinction till the real Edward, after dreadfully low adventures, steps forward at the coronation and claims his own. And this is intended for 'young people of all ages.' Mr. Clemens will permit us to point out that, if the young Britisher has once passed the age when such historical heresies must either be prohibited or extirpated by the rod, he will infallibly fall to criticising, and probably even to making fun at, instead of with, Mark Twain. Victor Hugo's veiled Wapentake, or Court of Arches, that synod of the English Church, is not more astounding than this picture of Reformation times—a misty atmosphere of Scott's chivalry in which floats all the flunkeyism, aristocratic oppression, and so forth, of all or any later period, as revealed to Columbia's stern eye. It is not worth while to multiply instances; let the absurd description of the young King's *levée* in chap. xviii. suffice, where the author exaggerates something he must have read somewhere about the ceremonies of the bedchamber introduced by Louis XIV. There is no excuse for this libel on the English Court. The list of thirteen officials, ending with the Primate, through whose hands the royal hose pass is concocted with peculiar clumsiness. Not even Cranmer would have stooped to hand the King's breeches, no matter how heavy the pockets felt. Foxe's classical work has apparently been consulted; burnings and boilings are done full justice to, and the general Protestant tone would be highly satisfactory were it not that the author is always fidgeting about certain 'Blue Laws of Connecticut.' From the Appendix (which, in its quotations from Hume, Mr. Timbs, and the erudite Dr. Trumbull, author of a Defence of the said Blue Laws, is quite a curiosity) we gather that this ponderous fantasia on English history is intended to show up British barbarism, and so, by contrast, to whitewash this embarrassing Blue business, which, in a solemn last general note in italics and capitals, he calls '*the first* SWEEPING DEPARTURE FROM JUDICIAL ATROCITY *which the "civilised" world had seen,*' and '*this humane and kindly Blue-Law Code.*' And why? Because our laws had 123 capital crimes, and the Blue Laws only fourteen. What those fourteen were he does not say. We think we can guess. The book is full of pictures in the spirited, florid old style. These will amuse the children. Naturally, the plot has suggested several comical situations, some of which are amusingly dwelt on; while a few smart sayings relieve the monotony of a prolix work singularly deficient in literary merit.

25. Unsigned review, *Athenaeum*

24 December 1881, no. 2826, 849

In his letter to Howells of 28 January 1882 Clemens called this reviewer 'an enraged idiot' (*Mark Twain–Howells Letters*, p. 388).

To the innumerable admirers of *Roughing It* and *A Tramp Abroad*, *The Prince and the Pauper* is likely to prove a heavy disappointment. The author, a noted representative of American humour, has essayed to achieve a serious book. The consequences are at once disastrous and amazing. The volume, which deals with England in the days of

Edward VI., and is announced as 'A Tale for Young People of all Ages', is only to be described as some four hundred pages of careful tediousness, mitigated by occasional flashes of unintentional and unconscious fun. Thus Mr. Clements, who has evidently been reading history, and is anxious about local colour, not only makes a point of quoting documents, and parading authorities, and being fearfully in earnest, but does so with a look of gravity and an evident sense of responsibility that are really delicious. On the whole, however, of Mr. Clements's many jokes, *The Prince and the Pauper* is incomparably the flattest and worst. To this, as a general reflection, it may be added that if to convert a brilliant and engaging humourist into a dull and painful romancer be necessarily a function of the study of history, it cannot be too steadily discouraged. Messrs. Chatto & Windus are the publishers.

26. Unsigned review, *Century Magazine*

March 1882, xxiii, 783–4

The use of H. H. Boyesen's phrase 'new departure' (from the *Atlantic* review, No. 23) in quotation marks indicates that the *Century* writer has seen that piece and apparently assumes his readers have also. The tone and substance here presents almost a negative image of the review published in the *Atlantic* three months earlier.

In his new book, Mark Twain has so far divested himself of his usual literary habit, that the reader is inclined now and then, as he follows the quaint story, to turn back to the title page in the expectation of finding that the famous humorist and satirist has been writing, incognito, as Mr. Clemens. *The Prince and the Pauper* is a curious mixture of fact and fancy.

[gives plot summary]

In many respects, *The Prince and the Pauper* is a remarkable book; it is certainly effective as a story, though it is spun-out almost to tediousness. It appears also to be overweighted with purpose. The least interesting part of the story, and that which as a whole is not essential to the main narrative, proceeds from the author's purpose to vindicate the 'humane and kindly' character of the Blue-Laws of Connecticut. Another purpose or effect of the story is to satirize kingcraft. This is cleverly done. The quiet satire, the ingenuity of the plot, and the clever development of the thoughts and motives of the Prince and the Pauper, in their changed circumstances, form the main interest of the story.

So far as it was the author's purpose to produce a work of art after the old models, and to prove that the humorous story-teller and ingenious homely philosopher, Mark Twain, can be a literary purist, a scholar, and an antiquary, we do not think his 'new departure' is a conspicuous success. It was not necessary for the author to prop his literary reputation with archaic English and a somewhat conventional manner. His recent humorous writings abound in passages of great excellence as serious compositions, and his serious, nervous style is the natural expression of an acute mind, that in its most fanciful moods is seldom superficial in its view. Indeed, it is because Mark Twain is a satirist, and in a measure a true philosopher, that his broadly humorous books and speeches have met with wide and permanent popular favor.

Considered as a work of art, *The Prince and the Pauper* is open to criticism. The author has taken great pains to be 'early English,' as they say in *Patience*, and his mild attempt to be aesthetic is almost necessarily artificial. In the conversation of the story, he attempts to reproduce the idiom of the time of Henry VIII., and the effort is well sustained. But the descriptive parts in which (if we may take the style of the preface as the key-note of his purpose) he also intended to keep the flavor of 'early English,' are a mixture of old and modern idiom, and the artistic unity of the work is frequently disturbed by quotations from old writers, and by the use of an occasional Americanism. Some of the fun sprinkled through the story grates on the ear. In speaking of the king's 'taster,' whose duty it was to make sure that poison had not been put into the royal food, the author wonders 'why they did not use a dog or a plumber.' At his first royal meal, the Pauper drinks out of the finger-bowl. There is an air of antiquity about this bit of fun, but is it 'early English'? A strangely obscure allusion appears on page 45. Here the reader is informed that the Prince 'snatched up and put away *an article of national importance.*' Five chapters farther on, it transpires that the great seal cannot be found, and at the end of the story the Prince proves his identity by remembering where he hid it. It will probably occur to few readers that the phrase 'an article of national importance' is a synonym for 'great seal'.

27. John Nichol on Mark Twain

1882

Extract from *American Literature: An Historical Sketch, 1620–1880* (Edinburgh, 1882), pp. 425–32.

John Nichol (1833–94), critic, lecturer and poet, was professor of English literature at the University of Glasgow.

The Americans are perhaps the gravest people in the world: therefore their notion of Humour—generally, as we have indicated, a superficial one—is of something contrary to real life. Their conception of wit is, like that of the pseudo-metaphysical poets, justly decried by Dr. Johnson. They laugh of malice prepense; and in, as well as out of the pulpit are apt to flaunt their eccentricities, and confound the genial glow of genuine comedy with the 'flat, stale, and unprofitable' mounte-bankeries of the farce. The master of this degenerate style is a writer to whom it is hard to do neither more nor less than justice: his success is, relatively, so far in advance of his deserts, that we have to resist the temptation to depreciate his really great, though, as seems to me, often misused ability. He has aimed at and attained an enormous popularity. It is probable that, to the lower class of British Philistines, American prose is, at this day, represented not so much by Irving, Emerson, or Hawthorne, as by 'Mark Twain,' who has done perhaps more than any other living writer to lower the literary tone of English speaking people. The most conspicuous intellectual trait of Mr. CLEMENS seems to me an almost preternatural shrewdness, thinly veiled under an assumption of simplicity. He knows perfectly what he is about, and is

able to turn every incident or circumstance to his advantage. He pre-
fixes a recent paper, 'The Idle Excursion', with the remark, 'All the
journeyings I have done had been purely in the way of business. The
pleasant May weather suggested a novelty, a trip for pure recreation,
the bread and butter element left out:' but he writes seventy pages
about the trip; and so provides for the element ostentatiously neglected.
Of the alarming tribe of recent American cynics he is the most genuine.
He hates humbug and cant, and nothing delights him more than to
run a tilt at copy-book texts. It goes without saying that his 'bad little
boy,' will prosper, and his 'good little boy' come to grief; or that he
will give an absurd turn to the story of Washington and the cherry-
tree. Romance and sentiment, in either continent, fare equally at his
hands: 'Old masters' at Milan, Florence, and Rome are served in the
same manner as the journalists in Tennessee; he writes his text to the
sketch of a weazened hag perched on the summit of the Loreley Rock;
makes a grimace at the Pyramids; puts his finger to his nose among the
Alps; and, as it were, turning the statues in the Louvre, the Uffizi, and
the Vatican, upside down, inspects their legs. But, if his scepticism is
intense, his morality is truculent: he visits the tomb of Abelard, and
pronounces a blessing on his semi-assassins; and his blushes are blent
with curses over Regent Street. Mark Twain's attraction is due in
great measure to his freshness: he is not an imitator; he does not rely
on books—though his writings evince a more than average culture:
he is a parodist of his own experience, to which he holds up a mirror,
like one of the round balls in German gardens.

> Life's a jest, and all things show it;
> I thought so once, and now I know it,

is the refrain of his philosophy. His satire, unlike that of 'Billings,' is
conveyed not so much in dogmatic sentences as in often dramatic
narrative, *e.g.* in all that relates to his Western real or imagined
adventures, among which 'How I Edited an Agricultural Paper' is the
most savage attack on newspapers I have anywhere seen. He is, however, capable of condensation, as in the following—one of the keenest
of the sarcasms that rely on the favourite Transatlantic figure, hyperbole. It is an editor's 'answer to an inquiry from the coming man'—

Young Author.—Yes, Agassiz does recommend authors to eat fish, because
the phosphorus in it makes brains. So far you are correct. But I cannot help
you to a decision about the amount you need to eat—at least, not with certainty. If the specimen composition you send is about your usual average, I

should judge that perhaps a couple of whales would be all you would want for the present. Not the largest kind; but simply good, middling-sized whales.

One of this writer's most successful tricks is to say exactly the opposite of what he means; another is an assumption of modesty, and habit of pretending to laugh at himself. Unsophisticated people are consoled for their own stupidity by the reflection that so brilliant a person had a distant relation who was hanged, and that he himself has been so often duped: (*e.g.* by Artemus Ward, by his watchmaker, by the Limerick Indians at Niagara), and has made such a bad map of Paris. The initiated will incline to find a more genuine leaf from the author's autobiography in *My First Literary Venture*. Mr. Clemens's satire is often trenchant, seldom fine: it wants the background of good humour which softens that of Mr. Browne. It is more vicious, without any of the grandeur which elevates the malignity of Swift—an author to whom America has produced no proximate parallel. His Western sketches are vivid—we doubt not veracious—and may be useful as deterrents to heedless intending emigrants. His simpler narratives are among his best, and give free play to the remarkable observing powers which stand him in good stead in his records of European travel. Of the two series of those—for *The New Pilgrim's Progress* is but a continuation of *The Innocents Abroad*—the *Tramp Abroad* is in some respects the best. It is more to the point, less ambitious than its predecessors, and its irreverences are less jarring. 'Mark Twain,' who seems quite out of place in the Desert and on the Sea of Galilee, is at home on the Righi Railroad, as the looker-on at a German students' duel, and a moral lounger at Baden-Baden. The Riffelberg is his altitude; we can scarce imagine him risking the Riffelhorn. The *Tramp* is, on the whole, an excellent guide-book, illustrated by jokes and cuts excluded from the dry dignity of Murray or Baedecker, and with almost as precise practical information as the last. Many travellers from England, as well as America, will be grateful to Mr. Clemens for his thoroughly reliable information as to the *douceurs* legitimately due to the porter, boots, and chambermaid of German hotels, for periods of residence ranging from one day to six months. The most amusing part of this book is in the Appendices, especially those on the use of the Heidelberg Tun, and on 'the awful German language.' The following gives expression to common griefs:—

[quotes extracts Appendix D 'I translate this' to '*Kinderbewahrungsaustalten*'.]

After more of the same reasonable remonstrance he winds up with suggestions for reform, all, except perhaps the last, more or less practical.

[quotes extracts Appendix D 'In the first' to 'thirty years'.]

In common with graver writers, Mark Twain is in danger of rapaciously mining out his vein of ore. His last volume might have marred, but could never have made, a reputation. *The Stolen White Elephant* is a satire on detectives, in which it is hard to detect a chance to smile; *Punch, Brothers, Punch*, is a joke at which we can only once laugh; *The Decay of Lying*, an evidence of the decay of invention; *Crime in Connecticut*, a lame travesty of Edgar Poe's *William Wilson*. The Nemesis of persistent parody is that, like the cultivation of the tobacco plant, it exhausts the soil. The successful writer of burlesques seldom succeeds in anything else. Mr. Clemens' most ardent admirers cannot read his *Pauper and Prince*. There is something almost ineffably pathetic in his own half-unconscious forecast of his own literary lot in one of the earliest of his books, *The Mississippi Pilot*, where his keen eye and quick wit, as yet undimmed by the strain of a professional jester, are displayed to their best advantage,—where the puns spring up naturally as the foam-bells on the great stream itself. The space given to the following extract is justified by the fact that it is an unintentional, but weighty, apologue of the whole tribe in whose ranks the author has elected to enlist himself,—as we consider, unhappily, for the passage gives evidence of far higher capacities. He is speaking of the acquired instincts, the second nature of the pilot:—

[quotes extracts ch. 9 'The face of' to 'learning his trade?']

'De te fabula narratur.' Who would have thought that the writer of this fine description and eloquent parable, elsewhere in his pages unequalled, would have fallen into the very trap, error, and sin against which he warns his readers! The 'father of waters' is 'an image of the mighty world;' the trained pilot, the hardened doctor, is the professional humorist, who has lost the power of seeing the beauty of the universe, because he has come to regard it as a mere text-book for his sadly incessant and ultimately wearisome jests. The price we have to pay for always making others laugh is never being able to admire, seldom even to laugh heartily ourselves. Not only Lear's Fool, but his whole kith and kin, have been, if among the wisest, also among the most melancholy of men.

28. William Dean Howells: 'Mark Twain', *Century Magazine*

September 1882, xxiv, 780–3

This article was the first substantial consideration of Clemens' literary career. The first third of the piece, which is not printed here, consists of a discursive account of Clemens' life.

In 1867, Mr. Clemens made in the *Quaker City* the excursion to Europe and the East which he has commemorated in *The Innocents Abroad*. Shortly after his return he married, and placed himself at Buffalo, where he bought an interest in one of the city newspapers; later he came to Hartford, where he has since remained, except for the two years spent in a second visit to Europe. The incidents of this visit he has characteristically used in *A Tramp Abroad*; and in fact, I believe the only book of Mr. Clemens's which is not largely autobiographical, is the *The Prince and the Pauper*: the scene being laid in England, in the early part of the sixteenth century, the difficulties presented to a nineteenth century autobiographer were insurmountable.

The habit of putting his own life, not merely in its results but in its processes, into his books, is only one phase of the frankness of Mr. Clemens's humorous attitude. The transparent disguise of the pseudonym once granted him, he asks the reader to grant him nothing else. In this, he differs wholly from most other American humorists, who have all found some sort of dramatization of their personality desirable if not necessary. Charles F. Browne, 'delicious' as he was when he dealt with us directly, preferred the disguise of 'Artemus Ward' the showman; Mr. Locke likes to figure as 'Petroleum V. Nasby,' the cross-roads politician; Mr. Shaw chooses to masquerade as the saturnine philosopher 'Josh Billings'; and each of these humorists appeals to the grotesqueness of misspelling to help out his fun. It was for Mr. Clemens to reconcile the public to humor which contented itself with the established absurdities of English orthography; and I am inclined to attribute to the example of his immense success, the humane spirit which characterized our recent popular humor. There is still sufficient flippancy and brutality in it; but there is no longer the stupid and monkeyish cruelty of motive and intention which once disgraced and insulted us. Except the political humorists, like Mr. Lowell—if there were any like him—the American humorists formerly chose the wrong in public matters; they were on the side of slavery, of drunkenness, and of irreligion; the friends of civilization were their prey; their spirit was thoroughly vulgar and base. Before 'John Phoenix,' there was scarcely any American humorist—not of the distinctly literary sort—with whom one could smile and keep one's self-respect. The great Artemus himself was not guiltless; but the most popular humorist who ever lived has not to accuse himself, so far as I can remember, of having written anything to make one morally ashamed of liking him. One can readily make one's strictures: there is often more than a suggestion of forcing in his humor; sometimes it tends to horseplay; sometimes the extravagance overleaps itself, and falls flat on the other side; but I cannot remember that in Mr. Clemens's books I have ever been asked to join him in laughing at any good or really fine thing. But I do not mean to leave him with this negative praise; I mean to say of him that as Shakspere, according to Mr. Lowell's saying, was the first to make poetry all poetical, Mark Twain was the first to make humor all humorous. He has not only added more in bulk to the style of harmless pleasures than any other humorist; but more in the spirit that is easily and wholly enjoyable. There is nothing lost in literary attitude, in labored dictionary funning, in affected quaintness, in dreary dramatization, in artificial 'dialect'; Mark Twain's humor is as simple in form and as direct as the statesmanship of Lincoln or the generalship of Grant.

When I think how purely and wholly American it is, I am a little puzzled at its universal acceptance. We are doubtless the most thoroughly homogeneous people that ever existed as a great nation. There is such a parity in the experiences of Americans that Mark Twain or Artemus Ward appeals as unerringly to the consciousness of our fifty millions as Goldoni appealed to that of his hundred thousand Venetians. In one phrase, we have somehow all 'been there'; in fact, generally, and in sympathy almost certainly, we have been there. In another generation or two, perhaps, it will be wholly different; but as yet the average American is the man who has risen; he has known poverty, and privation, and low conditions; he has very often known squalor; and now, in his prosperity, he regards the past with a sort of large, pitying amusement; he is not the least ashamed of it; he does not feel that it characterizes him any more than the future does. Our humor springs from this multiform American experience of life, and securely addresses itself— in reminiscence, in phrase, in its whole material—to the intelligence bred of like experience. It is not of a class for a class; it does not employ itself with the absurdities of a tailor as a tailor; its conventions, if it has any, are all new, and of American make. When it mentions hash we smile because we have each somehow known the cheap boarding-house or restaurant; when it alludes to putting up stoves in the fall, each of us feels the grime and rust of the pipes on his hands; the intro-duction of the lightning-rod man, or the book-agent, establishes our brotherhood with the humorist at once. But how is it with the vast English-speaking world outside of these States, to which hash, and stove-pipes, and lightning-rod men and book-agents are as strange as lords and ladies, dungeon-keeps and battlements are to us? Why, in fine, should an English chief-justice keep Mark Twain's books always at hand? Why should Darwin have gone to them for rest and refresh-ment at midnight when spent with scientific research?

I suppose that Mark Twain transcends all other American humorists in the universal qualities. He deals very little with the pathetic, which he nevertheless knows very well how to manage, as he has shown, notably in the true story of the old slave-mother; but there is a poetic lift in his work, even when he permits you to recognize it only as something satirized. There is always the touch of nature, the presence of a sincere and frank manliness in what he says, the companionship of a spirit which is at once delightfully open and deliciously shrewd. Elsewhere I have tried to persuade the reader that his humor is at its best the foamy break of the strong tide of earnestness in him. But it would be limiting him unjustly to describe him as a satirist; and it is hardly practicable to establish him in people's minds as a moralist; he has made them laugh too long; they will not believe him serious; they think some joke is always intended. This is the penalty, as Dr. Holmes has pointed out, of making one's first success as a humorist. There was a paper of Mark Twain's printed in the *Atlantic Monthly* some years ago and called, 'The Facts concerning the late Carnival of Crime in Connecticut,' which ought to have won popular recognition of the ethical intelligence which underlies his humor. It was, of course, funny; but under the fun it was an impassioned study of the human conscience. Hawthorne or Bunyan might have been proud to imagine that power-ful allegory which had a grotesque force far beyond either of them. It had been read before a literary club in Hartford; a reverend gentleman had offered the author his pulpit for the next Sunday if he would give it as a homily there. Yet it quite failed of the response I had hoped for it, and I shall not insist here upon Mark Twain as a moralist; though I warn the reader that if he leaves out of the account an indignant sense of right and wrong, a scorn of all affectation and pretense, an ardent hate of meanness and injustice, he will come indefinitely short of knowing Mark Twain.

His powers as a story-teller were evident in hundreds of brief sketches before he proved them in *Tom Sawyer* and *The Prince and the Pauper*. Both of these books, aside from the strength of characterization, are fascinating as mere narratives, and I can think of no writer living who has in higher degree the art of interesting his reader from the first word. This is a far rarer gift than we imagine, and I shall not call it a subordinate charm in Mark Twain's books, rich as they otherwise are. I have already had my say about *Tom Sawyer*, whose only fault is an excess of reality in portraying the character and conditions of southwestern boyhood as it was forty years ago, and which is full of that poetic sympathy with nature and human nature which I always find in Mark Twain. *The Prince and the Pauper* has particularly interested me for the same qualities which, in a study of the past, we call romantic, but which alone can realize the past for us. Occasionally the archaic diction gives way and lets us down hard upon the American parlance of the nineteenth century; but mainly the illusion is admirably sustained, and the tale is to be valued not only in itself, but as an earnest of what Mr. Clemens might do in fiction when he has fairly done with autobiography in its various forms. His invention is of the good old sort, like De Foe's more than that of any other English writer, and like that of the Spanish picturesque novelists, Mendoza and the rest; it flows easily from incident to incident, and does not deepen into situation. In the romance it operates as lightly and unfatiguingly as his memory in the realistic story.

His books abound in passages of dramatic characterization, and he is, as the reader knows, the author of the most successful American play. I believe Mr. Clemens has never claimed the reconstruction of Colonel Sellers for the stage; but he nevertheless made the play, for whatever is good in it came bodily from his share of the novel of *The Gilded Age*. It is a play which succeeds by virtue of the main personage, and this personage, from first to last, is quite outside of the dramatic action, which sometimes serves, and sometimes does not serve the purpose of presenting Colonel Sellers. Where the drama fails, Sellers rises superior and takes the floor; and we forget the rest. Mr. Raymond conceived the character wonderfully well, and he plays it with an art that ranks him to that extent with the great actors; but he has in nowise 'created' it. If any one 'created' Colonel Sellers, it was Mark Twain, as the curious reader may see on turning again to the novel; but I suspect that Colonel Sellers was never created, except as other men are; that he was found somewhere and transferred, living, to the book.

I prefer to speak of Mr. Clemens's artistic qualities because it is to these that his humor will owe its perpetuity. All fashions change, and nothing more wholly and quickly than the fashion of fun; as any one may see by turning back to what amused people in the last generation; that stuff is terrible. As Europe becomes more and more the playground of Americans, and every scene and association becomes insipidly familiar, the jokes about the old masters and the legends will no longer be droll to us. Neither shall we care for the huge Californian mirth, when the surprise of the picturesquely mixed civilization and barbarism of the Pacific coast has quite died away; and Mark Twain would pass with the conditions that have made him intelligible, if he were not an artist of uncommon power as well as a humorist. He portrays and interprets real types, not only with exquisite appreciation and sympathy, but with a force and truth of drawing that makes them permanent. Artemus Ward was very funny, that can never be denied; but it must be owned that the figure of the literary showman is as wholly factitious as his spelling; the conception is one that has to be constantly humored by the reader. But the innumerable characters sketched by Mark Twain are actualities, however caricatured,—and, usually, they are not so very much caricatured. He has brought back the expression of Western humor to sympathy with the same orthography of John Phoenix; but Mark Twain is vastly more original in form. Derby was weighed upon by literary tradition; he was 'academic' at times, but Mr. Clemens is never 'academic.' There is no drawing from casts; in his work evidently the life has everywhere been studied: and it is his apparent unconsciousness of any other way of saying a thing except the natural way that makes his books so restful and refreshing. Our little nervous literary sensibilities may suffer from his extravagance, or from other traits of his manner, but we have not to beat our breasts at the dread apparition of Dickens's or Thackeray's hand in his page. He is far too honest and sincere a soul for that; and where he is obliged to force a piece of humor to its climax—as sometimes happens—he does not call in his neighbors to help; he does it himself, and is probably sorry that he had to do it.

I suppose that even in so slight and informal a study as this, something like an 'analysis' of our author's humor is expected. But I much prefer not to make it. I have observed that analyses of humor are apt to leave one rather serious, and to result in an entire volatilization of the humor. If the prevailing spirit of Mark Twain's humor is not a sort of good-natured self-satire, in which the reader may see his own absurdities reflected, I scarcely should be able to determine it.

29. Thomas Sergeant Perry: 'An American on American Humour', *St. James's Gazette*

5 July 1883, vii, 5–6

Thomas Sergeant Perry (1845–1928) was on the staff of the *North American Review* (1872–7), and taught at Harvard (1868–72, 1877–1882) and at the University of Keiogijiku in Japan (1898–1901). He was a close friend of Howells and of William and Henry James.

This article bears the dateline 'Boston, June, 1883'.

H. R. Haweis wrote *American Humorists* (London, 1883).

One is perhaps safe in saying that American humour has been quite as successful in promoting discussion as in arousing laughter; those writers who are for ever trying to define the distinctions between wit and humour ask for no greater range of subject than an examination of the humour native to America. Mr. Haweis has published a volume of artless prattle on American humourists, and we occasionally come across a stray Yankee in an English novel who makes on American readers very much the same impression of verisimilitude that the performance of the *Pinafore* might make on a very serious sailor.

In general we feel that those who discuss the matter are most entertaining when they are quoting; yet it may be that there is a meaning in American humour which is not sure to be detected if one looks only at its irreverence and somewhat monotonous insistence on two or three lines of thought. Let us take a single well-known man, Mark Twain, and see if there is any real significance in his amusing writings. In the first place, his prominence implies the existence of a large constituency behind him; he is by no means a single representative of humour in a humourless land. There are numberless Mark Twains in America—duller, feebler, more wearisome, but thinking in the same way. Wherever half a dozen Americans meet, miniature repetitions of him are to be found. In every steamboat and car, in every street crowd, one may overhear the same girding spirit, shrouded in apparent gloom, giving an acrid tone to whatever is under discussion. There is the same well-understood exaggeration of what is minute and diminution of everything great which is the shibboleth of American humour, the same keen insight into pretended impulses before which zeal as well as affectation shrivels like the petal of a flower at the touch of an acid.

This unsmiling seriousness, this rigid chaining of every quality but irony, is well understood in America. Moments of silence have the effect of epigrams; and a handful of men will sit about a red-hot stove in a country 'store' uttering remarks which would sound dull enough to a listening foreigner, but which convey to the men themselves infinite suggestions of delight. To a stranger in America this apparent vacuity of the conversation is ominous of imperceptible satire; there is doubtless some very subtle derision attacking him. A foreigner may well be puzzled by what seems to be our seriousness: it is often the mark of an intense humorous joy. We are a nation of conspirators against the expression of the emotions. We are Nihilists in the face of inherited prepossessions.

This is obviously an extravagant statement. What I mean to say is this: Mark Twain is the representative of what is really a national trait, and this trait is a good part of what America is contributing to the thought of the world, and, intellectually, perhaps its greatest part. This vulgarizing denigrating spirit finds its expression in the life and literature of the new democracy. It is not the mere arid buffoonery of a few merry-andrews; it is as important in its way as the loud roystering hilarity of Rabelais or as Molière's wit—as important, that is to say, to the historian. After all, when we rid our minds of the notion that literature is a manufactured product, and perceive that it is really humanity speaking, just as politics is humanity governing, then a manifestation that belongs to a whole large country assumes serious importance. The political career of America is certainly worth study: it is of the nature of an unfolding enacted prophecy for the rest of the civilized world; and in American humour it is easy to detect one side of its spirit.

In many respects the significance of America is this: that it is a reaction against Europe; not necessarily an actively hostile reaction, and certainly not a wholly independent reaction, since in development there can be no absolute breach of continuity, but rather an evolution of what Europe contains or has contained. The absence of a State Church, of an aristocracy, the rule of universal suffrage—all of which were the result of earlier theories—are but outward signs of one great animating spirit which is continually making itself felt in the growth of the country, and is obviously the core of democracy: the importance, namely, of the people, of the present, by the side of which all traces of aristocracy, of the past, are valueless. 'You have the past,' an American would say; 'we are seizing the present, and we mean to have the future.'

The political aspect of this spirit is sufficiently familiar; but what is literature except the expression of the same spirit that we see in politics? We recognize this fact very clearly when we read mediæval literature; when we see chivalry reflected in the old romances and vulgar life in the *fabliaux*; when we see the majestic energy of contemporary life glowing in the Elizabethan dramatists and the narrowing graces of their better-educated contemporaries; when we hear the first dull mutterings of the French Revolution in the literature of the last century. Is our own time, then, the only exception to this rule? This has never been proved.

If it is not an exception, it may be worth while to examine briefly Mark Twain's writings; and if we do this, the first thing that strikes us is the familiar irreverence. What is his *Innocents Abroad* but a full account of the raw unregenerate American before the antiquities of Europe and the East? What is the state of mind of that American but contempt for what he sees, and infinite self-satisfaction? His taste is, according to our conventional notions, as raw as that of a savage listening to a symphony; but it must be remembered that Mark Twain belongs to a huge, civilized, prosperous, growing race whose political development is far advanced, and laughing at him is as idle as laughing with him.

The spirit that animates him is the spirit of the present democracy, which is at war with all the literary conventions that we have inherited from the civilization of Rome. His contemptuous writing forebodes a coming change. Our modern literature, we must never forget, is, like European society, built upon aristocratic conventions. Mediæval literature was more nearly a national literature, the property of the whole people. With the Renaissance literature became almost exclusively the possession of a learned class: such, at least, it ultimately became; and the result is well known. As Dr. Gustav Koerting has put it in his admirable book—*Petrarca's Leben und Werke* (Leipzig, 1870), pp. 522 *et seq.*—there was a people formed within the people: the cultivated formed a separate caste among the great mass of the uncultivated; and the consequence of this is that we have, as he says, two distinct races, growing side by side, educated differently, with divergent, often opposing aims, interests, beliefs, and in general with no further comprehension of each other than the Shah of Persia has of Racine's plays.

For more than a hundred years the tendency of literature has been towards the destruction of these divergences. The extravagantly aristocratic framework which grew up under what is called French influence has been swept away with the political condition it expressed. In the early Romanticism fresh vigour was drawn from the soil; but that second Renaissance began—as changes often begin—under the lead of admiration for what was picturesque. It was at first in great measure a literary revival: at least, it became that when writers found more satisfactory models. One set of exotics took the place of another. Yet the safe seclusion of what Koerting calls the hot-house has been broken. At the end of the last century some of the writers left the north door open, and the blast froze the feeble plants. The ballads, Ossian, Burns's songs overgrew the juiceless shrubs that had long been admired; although there were for a time some who detected a fragrance in what the others regarded as withered twigs.

The 'cold wave' that comes from America freezes even the flowers under the securest cover, like our north-west wind; and Mark Twain is doing in one way what Walt Whitman is doing in another. These two men are fellow workers—one with a mystical seriousness, the other with a chilling contempt—in the task of destroying conventions. The humorous writer benumbs all our familiar enthusiasms. In his eyes the past is but a ridiculous mummy; the present a mass of absurd affectations: a glittering chromo-lithograph is far superior to a battered statue or a crumbling fresco. This is the destructive spirit, and one which appeals to millions of respectable, busy, energetic inhabitants of a great country. One may travel miles and miles among a people who find in Mark Twain the best expression of their beliefs and feelings. There is a thin varnish of European cultivation on the seashore, and here and there in the inland towns; but any one who will read the incredible Sunday papers or the less formal congressional debates, who listens to the people talking, will become aware of its insignificance and of the bulk at least of the new rawness.

If we may be pardoned for mentioning Walt Whitman in a paper nominally upon American humour, we may see in his poems and in his *Specimen Days and Collect* the constructive part of this spirit. Like every new utterance, the book abounds with crudities, and with the egotism that necessarily goes to the composition of a fanatic or reformer. In his discussion of literary matters we see what often precedes literary performance—an urgent call for it. He demands 'a new-founded literature not merely to copy and reflect existing surfaces, or pander to what is called taste—not only to amuse, pass away time, celebrate the beautiful, the refined, the past, or exhibit technical, rhythmic, or grammatical dexterity—but a literature underlying life, religions, consistent with science, handling the elements and forces with competent power, teaching and training men,' etc. This is a statement that is open to criticism, but it expresses definite dissatisfaction with recognizable literary methods—a spirit with which the book abounds.

It is far from just or sufficient to call America vulgar; this is no more a complete definition than it would be to call Rabelais coarse. The great mass of life is vulgar and coarse, if one chooses to use these words. But the historian knows no adjectives of praise or blame; he sees simply what is done. What is doing here cannot be kept within our shores: 'le monde s'américanise;' and it is not by a mere accidental coincidence that, when American novelists are writing about the vulgar life they see, Zola and his school are drawing the great seething mass that have hitherto been but objects of a pleased romantic interest. Where are his conventions? Everything that is done for the first time is done confusedly, awkwardly: when the sterling coin is worn so smooth that it serves for counters, there must be a new issue; and this issue we are now having.

The outlook for letters is not necessarily dark because it is novel, and one may be excused for hoping that literature may be the better for the destruction of conventionalities. Obstinate conservation will tend to secure a wiser compromise; but the change is unavoidable, and in the study of the change it will be important to see how much of it is indicated by the apparently idle talk of the American humourists. For one thing, they succeed in ridding the world of a great many prejudices; and a prejudice that is once banished is not apt to return.

30. Lafcadio Hearn: review, New Orleans *Times-Democrat*

30 May 1883

Lafcadio Hearn (1850–1904) is best known for his writings on Japan. From 1869 to 1887 he wrote for newspapers in the Mississippi valley, first in Cincinnati, Ohio, and then in New Orleans. This review was reprinted in Lafcadio Hearn, *Essays on American Literature*, edited by Sanki Ichikawa (Tokyo, 1929).

The appendix mentioned consists of a sequence of three letters to the New Orleans *Times-Democrat* about the experiences of the *Susie B.*, a steamer sent by the newspaper to assist the evacuation of flooded parts of the Mississippi delta in March 1882.

Life on the Mississippi,—Mark Twain's new production, is a large volume of more than six hundred pages,—much resembling in form the famous *Innocents Abroad*, and *Roughing It*. Like those highly successful books, *Life on the Mississippi* has been illustrated with humorous engravings, the spirit of which will be appreciated by all familiar with the picturesque features of American river-life. A number of the early chapters are already familiar to readers of the *Atlantic*,—having been contributed to that periodical several years ago; but their interest has been greatly augmented, and their verisimilitude emphasized, by the drawings which now accompany them. The past and present types of steamboatmen are portrayed with a certain rough and lively humor in thorough keeping with the text.

Notwithstanding its lively spirit of fun, the volume is a more serious creation by far than *The Innocents Abroad*; and in some respects seems to us the most solid book that Mark Twain has written. Certainly the first two hundred and fifty pages possess a large historical value; and will be referred to in future years as trustworthy paintings of manners, customs, and social phases which have already been much changed, and will doubtless, before another generation, belong altogether to the past. But in addition to reminiscences of the old-time river-life, and the curious multitude of incidents and amusing experiences, one finds that the author has taken pains to collect and set forth almost every important fact connected with the Mississippi River—historical or geographical. These positive data rather gain than lose in weight by their humorous presentation; and it may safely be said that many persons who may read the opening chapters will obtain from them a better knowledge of what the Mississippi is, than they could gain by laborious study of physical geographies. When one finds upon page 25 the statement that *'nearly the whole of that one thousand three hundred miles of old Mississippi River which La Salle floated down in his canoe, two hundred years ago, is good solid dry land now'*—one gains a juster idea of the river's eccentricities than the perusal of many volumes of solid and statistical reports could give. Within less than five pages an astonishing variety of information is given in similarly compressed shape;—the whole natural history of the river, (its importance, its fickleness, its capacities of construction) is presented in a brief series of ingeniously epitomized paragraphs which, once read, will not easily be forgotten.

The most delightful part of the book is included in the autobiographical chapters—in the history of the author's early experience as a pilot's apprentice. These pages are full of laughing vividness, and paint the brighter side of old-fashioned river-life with such a delicate exaggeration of saliencies as that by which the peculiarities of English habits fifty years ago are perpetuated for us by the early artists of *Punch*. But there is a kernel of curious fact in every richly-flavored incident of humor. Here the book is absolutely unique;—it contains the only realistic history of piloting on the Mississippi in existence, and written by perhaps the only author of the century whose genius is thoroughly adapted to the subject treated. Indeed, one must have followed for years some peculiar river-calling in order to comprehend what steamboat life is, and appreciate its various presentations of tragedy, comedy, and poetry—to all of which we find ample justice done in the book before us. It is the sum of the experience of years; and no little art has been shown in selecting specimens from such a range of memoirs. The old-time flatboatmen and raftsmen—so famous in Mississippi River history—are capitally drawn; and we have a rare sketch of the lordly pilots of ante-bellum days, who drew their $250 or more per month, and were idolized by the fair of numberless little river-towns. Not less interesting is the brief history of the Pilots' Association in those days—an imperious monopoly which sustained many furious campaigns against steamboat owners, and almost invariably won the fight at last by dint of certain ingenious devices pleasantly recounted in Chapter XV.

Mark Twain's humor being of the most typically American sort, and rich in that imaginative quality which an ingenious foreign critic has compared to 'sheet lightning, flashing over half a world at once,' has won him that literary reputation in Europe formerly held by Artemus Ward. Ward is now old-fashioned; Twain occupies a far larger transatlantic position. His stories have been widely translated; and within the past six months we have seen as many of his sketches 'done into French,' for the Paris *Figaro*. Much of the dialectic fun was necessarily lost in the transmutation; but otherwise the comic element survived admirably in the French—a language especially well suited to the exaggerations of American humor. We fancy that the present work will have a larger success in Europe than its illustrated predecessors; for it is more novel in its character, and even more thoroughly American in its fun, and withal, more historically valuable. Others have described the frontier life sketched in *Roughing It*, and the days of '49; but no other has ever touched the subject of Mississippi life except in ballads or brief stories.

The last three hundred pages are devoted to the Mississippi Life of to-day as compared with that of before the war;—they represent the result of the author's Southern trip during the last inundation. This part of his history opens with the recital of a pleasant personal adventure, in which the author attempted to play *incognito* with an old pilot too sharp to be caught, who tells a wonderful yarn about a dredge-boat, which he calls by another name:—

[quotes ch. 24 ' "An alligator boat?" ' to ' "aground on alligators." ']

Finally, after a most interesting history of 'alligator pilots,' Mark Twain's mask is torn off, and he is put to the wheel in expiation of his attempt at mystification. He finds that even after twenty-one years he has not forgotten how to manage a steamboat; but the river has so changed in the long interval that portions of its ante-bellum geography are no longer recognizable. He wants to go ashore subsequently, and so informs the captain:—

[quotes ch. 32 ' "Go ashore where?" ' to ' "into the Mississippi!" ']

This spirit of fun never flags, even to the end of the book; but every page of humor is underlaid by some solid truth, often more or less grim, and bearing important witness for one side of that now vastly agitated subject—The Mississippi River Question. Here the reader will find a startling account of the changes of the Mississippi since the era of our civil war.

We have already published extracts from the chapter on New Orleans; but the author has given a great deal more space to our city and its features than the aforesaid extracts would suggest. Here and there he pokes some sharp fun at New Orleans' peculiarities,—especially regarding funerals and undertakers; but there is no malice in the satire and nobody is badly hurt. Some pleasant reminiscences of his visit appear,—his acquaintance with George W. Cable and others; and *The Times-Democrat* must acknowledge the handsome compliments paid to it throughout the volume, besides the republication in the appendix of Mr. Whitney's correspondence during the relief trip of the *Susie B.* in March 1882.

The work is published by James R. Osgood & Co., of Boston.

31. Unsigned review, *Athenaeum*

2 June 1883, no. 2901, 694–5

On comparison of the tone and style of this review with William Ernest Henley's review of *Tramp Abroad* (No. 20), it seems not unlikely that Henley is the author here. Henley was a free-lance critic for several periodicals, including the *Athenaeum*, during the 1880s.

'Old Times on the Mississippi' (not 'Old Days' as mentioned here) had been printed as a series of articles in the *Atlantic* (January to June and August 1875). Belford Bros., Toronto, had published a pirated version in book form in 1876. Ward, Lock and Tyler produced a reprint of the piracy in London in 1877, titled *The Mississippi Pilot*.

Mr. Clemens's new book is a disappointment. To begin with, it has a vulgar red cover, it is cumbered with a quantity of illustrations of the cheapest and least suggestive American type, its lines are ungraceful; so that, coming as it does in an age of *Parchment Libraries* and *Petites Bibliothèques Elzéviriennes*, and *Éditions Jouaust*, it appears at once anomalous and offensive, and prejudices its readers against it as a book even before they get seriously to work upon it as literature. Nor is this the only thing that may be said against it. On examination its best part turns out to be years old—to be, in fact, a reprint of the vigorous and pleasant set of sketches published as 'Old Days on the Mississippi.' They are excellent, as we all know; they are in some ways the author's best work; but they are already ancient history. What is even more to the point, perhaps, they are vastly superior to their present environment. There is plenty of drollery, of American humour, in the new chapters; there is some good writing; not a little of the matter is interesting and novel; but they have none of the freshness and force of their predecessors. In his trials and triumphs as a Mississippi pilot Mr. Clemens had an admirable subject, and handled it with the greatest gusto imaginable. You feel as you read that what is written is the outcome of years of experience, is a record of memories mellow with age and instinct with the cheerful vitality that comes of retrospection; that the writer has thoroughly enjoyed his work; and that the production of his book has made him sincerely happy. From the new chapters the impression received is very different. Mr. Clemens as a Mississippi tourist is not to be compared with Mr. Clemens as a Mississippi pilot. His experiences seem all brand-new; his impressions are not remarkably profound; he is rather glib than abundant, rather restless than vivacious, rather forced and ambitious than easy and successful; his humour is too often strained, his narrative has too often the flavour of mere 'copy,' his cleverness has too often a likeness to that of the brilliant bagman. As he appears in 'Old Days on the Mississippi' he is the Mark Twain of *Roughing It* and the *Innocents at Home*; as he appears in the record of his cruise he is more or less the Mark Twain of the *New Pilgrim's Progress*, and certain chapters in the *Tramp Abroad*, and that dreadful book in which he tells the story of his impressions of the continent of Europe. In the one set of works, that is to say, he is fresh, vigorous, irresistibly amusing; in the other, he is merely parading his own vulgarity, and talking of things from the point of view of the professional American humourist. The contrast, as they know who are learned in Mark Twain, is discomforting in the extreme.

His opening chapter is a good example of the vices of his new method. Part of it he has got from books, and part of it—a very little part—is touched with his own experience. He begins it with geographical statistics, and tells us how the Mississippi is 4,300 miles long; how it discharges three times as much water as the St. Lawrence, and 338 times as much as the Thames; how it drains an area of forty-five degrees of longitude; how it discharges 406,000,000 tons of mud per annum into the Gulf of Mexico, and all the rest of it. The information is valuable no doubt; but in a book of this sort it is, on the whole, superfluous, and it certainly suggests the matter of an American lecture. In the next few pages Mr. Clemens picks himself up a little, and talks of the Mississippi's eccentricities: how it is given to the practice of 'cut offs,' how it is always changing its locality by 'moving bodily *side ways*,' how in thirty years it has increased the size of Prophet's Island from 1,500 to 2,000 acres, and how in more instances than one 'it has shortened itself thirty miles at a single jump.' After this he becomes a mere compiler. It is as though he were ashamed of having jested, and were determined to show that on occasion he can be as serious as any one else. In this respect his second chapter is even more disappointing than his first.

But afterwards, for a dozen or fifteen chapters, we have to deal with 'Old Days on the Mississippi,' and we come in contact with Mark Twain at his best. They treat of a time when steamboating was a great industry, and along some thousands of miles of water-way the pilot was a creature of a superior race—a privileged and impeccable being. Here is Mr. Clemens's description of the advent of a steamboat at Hannibal:—

[quotes ch. 4 'The town drunkard' to 'skids once more'.]

He goes on to tell how the steamboat men and boys were heroes to the long-shore boys and men; how 'now and then we had a hope that if we lived and were good, God would permit us to be pirates, . . . but the ambition to be a steamboatman always remained'; how, in course of time, disgusted and exasperated by the airs of boys upon steamboats, he ran away, and presently became apprentice to a pilot; how for a time he rejoiced and was glad, and how for a time he despaired and was wretched; how he had to learn the great river bit by bit, mark by mark, feature by feature, accident by accident, backwards and for-wards, by day and night, in all its innumerable details; how in due course he became a pilot, and what manner of men the pilots, his con-temporaries, were; how they talked, and how they worked, and how they earned tremendous wages, and how they towered above created things; of the feats they did, and the oaths they swore, and the airs they gave themselves; and how, at last, the war came and stopped their work, and broke up their corporation, and gave the river over to tugs and the shores to locomotives, and put an end to the Golden Age of steamboating, and took the heroic quality from piloting as completely as though it had never existed. He is on a level with his argument throughout. As we have said, he writes as one who enjoys his work. His fun is natural and spontaneous, his dialogue is everywhere admir-able, and in certain places—in telling, for instance, how his master, Mr. Bixby, carried his boat past Hat Island in the teeth of darkness and a falling tide and the opinion of all the pilots aboard—he shows such a mastery of narrative, such a power of story-telling pure and simple, as is within the reach of few contemporaries or none.

When, years afterwards, Mr. Clemens returned to the river and revisited the scene of his former triumphs, he found that things had suffered a change that is almost indescribable. This change it is which is the matter of his new chapters. In itself it is of uncommon interest; but it has reacted on the writer's spirits, and though his account of it is easily read, it is not easily remembered. It is not that Mr. Clemens is found wanting either in sincerity or in ingenuity. On the contrary, he describes what he sees with point and propriety, he is anxiously funny, and he makes original remarks with immense application; he is responsible for certain pages on the mournful influence of Walter Scott and his share in the production of the peculiar 'chivalry' of the Southern States, which are monuments of misplaced and unhappy ambition. But his heart is not in his work. What is good in it deals with the past—is for the most part as though omitted from 'Old Days on the Mississippi.' The rest is mere reporting, and we cannot but regret that it was not published separately, and that the older and better matter was not left to take care of itself.

32. Robert Brown: review, *Academy*

28 July 1883, xxiv, 58

The author of this review is probably Robert Brown (1842–95), a Scottish naturalist and geographer who took part in expeditions to Greenland, Alaska, Vancouver Island and other places. Most of his books on science and geography were written for a popular audience.

This pleasantly written and profusely illustrated volume is an English reprint of an American book the first portion of which appeared several years ago. It describes, with all the dry humour and often graphic power of Mr. Clemens, his experiences as an apprentice-pilot on board the great steamers plying between New Orleans and St. Louis in the far-away days to which the Southerner refers so sadly as 'befo' the wah.' The second section, which forms a sequel to the first, narrates a visit to the old scenes twenty-one years after the author had left 'the river.' The result is a singularly interesting work, though probably the earlier chapters will prove of most lasting value, for the later ones are more personal, and often needlessly padded with anecdotes and reminiscences which, however diverting, have a very remote, if any, connexion with the narrative.

The fun in Mr. Clemens' *Tramps Abroad* is frequently forced, and sometimes quite unsuited to the subject in hand. His American experiences have rarely this fault; the writer seems to feel the ground he is treading more secure, and his broad pleasantry is in better keeping with raftsmen, back-woods settlers, and gold-diggers than with monks, mountains, kings, cathedrals, and other sanctities of old-fashioned Europe. The description of the Mississippi, its steam-boat captains, mates, and pilots, the broad-horns and their rough crews, the ague-shaken settlers roosting on fences while the 'river was out,' and the ways of the great valley of the vast American river as they existed before the war are in his best style. Half-a-century ago, the Mississippi Valley was the favourite field for English tourists; for in times where Concord coaches over corduroy roads were the only means of penetrating the continent, the river and its tributaries, covered with palatial steamers, were among the easiest highways through the centre of the United States, or its then farthest civilised boundaries. Marryat, Mrs. Trollope, Basil Hall—all the little army of literary visitors—have much to say about the Mississippi. Later travellers scarcely ever mention it, for they are so eager to rush West that, except where they catch a glimpse of it and the Missouri on their rapid run for the Rocky Mountains, the Father of Waters is strange to their note-books. The railways, in like manner, ruined the old steam-boating times, and humbled the pride of pilots—whose pride was the pride of kings—and even made the captains and mates regard ordinary passengers as of the same flesh and blood with themselves. The rise, decline, and fall of these potentates is told with admirable effect; and, leaving out of account a little characteristic exaggeration here and there, with minute fidelity. Now and then, an expert in American *facetiae* will detect a very old friend, disguised for the occasion; but these familiar faces in no way detract from the freshness of a volume which does not contain a dull page.

The book is indeed the best account of social life on the Mississippi with which we are acquainted. But it possesses an additional merit which possibly the author may disclaim—it embodies a clear and, take it all in all, very accurate account of the physical features of the river, its shiftings, and general vagaries. Specialists will, of course, turn to Humphrey and Abbot's stern tomes, or to the Reports of the Commission which is fast making piloting on the Mississippi as prosaic and easy as it is on the Elbe or the Thames; but less exigent people, whose thirst for knowledge is quenched with something less than quartos, may safely take 'Mark Twain' for their guide. The illustrations are rough, but graphic; and the book is altogether so good that we regret to see that the ardour which is lavished in scarlet and gold is unequal to the production of an index.

33. Unsigned review, *Graphic*

1 September 1883, xxviii, 231

This curiously self-contradictory review does represent a persistent reluctance by critics to admit that what they enjoyed of Mark Twain's writing also possessed merit.

'Mark Twain,' in the earlier chapters of his new book, *Life on the Mississippi* (Chatto and Windus), gives such an admirable specimen of his powers as a serious writer of history, that one is almost tempted to wish that, for this occasion only, he would lay aside altogether his funny style, or at least subordinate it to purposes of serious literary work. But the old Adam cannot long be subdued. Mr. Clemens soon slips into his accustomed style; and almost before the reader is aware that he has changed from the graphic to the grotesque, he is deep in sketches of life and character in all of which the great river forms the background. Pilot's exploits, and the misfortunes of pilot's 'cubs,' river superstitions and river romances, tales of hard drinking, hard fighting, and hard swearing—these are the materials of which the book is made up. Sometimes the quaint humour is varied by some grisly tale of murder and revenge, such as 'A Thumb-Print, and What Came of It,' a peculiarly horrible story of a night-watchman in a German morgue. That *Life on the Mississippi* will be as popular as the books by which 'Mark Twain's' name was made is not likely. Nevertheless it is well worth reading.

THE ADVENTURES OF
HUCKLEBERRY FINN

1884-5

34. Unsigned review, *Athenaeum*

27 December 1884, no. 2983, 855

The language and critical point of view of this piece suggest that
this, like the *Athenaeum* review of *Life on the Mississippi* (No. 31),
may be by William Ernest Henley (see No. 20).

For some time past Mr. Clemens has been carried away by the ambition of seriousness and fine writing. In *Huckleberry Finn* he returns
to his right mind, and is again the Mark Twain of old time. It is such
a book as he, and he only, could have written. It is meant for boys;
but there are few men (we should hope) who, once they take it up,
will not delight in it. It forms a companion or sequel, to *Tom Sawyer*.
Huckleberry Finn, as everybody knows, is one of Tom's closest friends;
and the present volume is a record of the adventures which befell him
soon after the event which made him a person of property and brought
Tom Sawyer's story to a becoming conclusion. They are of the most
surprising and delightful kind imaginable, and in the course of them
we fall in with a number of types of character of singular freshness and
novelty, besides being schooled in half a dozen extraordinary dialects
—the Pike County dialect in all its forms, the dialect of the Missouri
negro, and 'the extremest form of the backwoods South-Western
dialect,' to wit. Huckleberry, it may be noted, is stolen by his disreputable father, to escape from whom he contrives an appearance of
robbery and murder in the paternal hut, goes off in a canoe, watches
from afar the townsfolk hunting for his dead body, and encounters
a runaway negro—Miss Watson's Jim—an old particular friend of Tom
Sawyer and himself. With Jim he goes south down the river, and is the

hero of such scrapes and experiences as make your mouth water (if you have ever been a boy) to read of them. We do not purpose to tell a single one; it would be unfair to author and reader alike. We shall content ourselves with repeating that the book is Mark Twain at his best, and remarking that Jim and Huckleberry are real creations, and the worthy peers of the illustrious Tom Sawyer.

35. Brander Matthews: unsigned review, *Saturday Review*

31 January 1885, lix, 153–4

Brander Matthews (1852–1929) wrote plays, fiction and criticism and was a professor of literature and, subsequently, of dramatic literature at Columbia (1892–1924). G. P. R. James (1799–1860) wrote many historical romances, of which the first was *Richelieu* (1829). F. Anstey (Thomas Anstey Guthrie) (1856–1934) was a member of the staff of *Punch* (1887–1930) and a prolific novelist. George Washington Cable (1844–1925) wrote several novels set in Louisiana. Joel Chandler Harris (1848–1908) had just begun to write the *Uncle Remus* stories which he continued to produce for the rest of his life.

The boy of to-day is fortunate indeed, and, of a truth, he is to be congratulated. While the boy of yesterday had to stay his stomach with the unconscious humour of *Sandford and Merton*, the boy of to-day may get his fill of fun and of romance and of adventure in *Treasure Island* and in *Tom Brown* and in *Tom Sawyer*, and now in a sequel to *Tom Sawyer*, wherein Tom himself appears in the very nick of time, like a young god from the machine. Sequels of stories which have been widely popular are not a little risky. *Huckleberry Finn* is a sharp exception to this general rule. Although it is a sequel, it is quite as worthy of wide popularity as *Tom Sawyer*. An American critic once neatly declared that the late G. P. R. James hit the bull's-eye of success with his first shot, and that for ever thereafter he went on firing through the same hole. Now this is just what Mark Twain has not done. *Huckleberry Finn* is not an attempt to do *Tom Sawyer* over again. It is a story quite as unlike its predecessor as it is like. Although Huck Finn appeared first in the earlier book, and although Tom Sawyer reappears in the later, the scenes and the characters are otherwise wholly different. Above all, the atmosphere of the story is different. *Tom Sawyer* was a tale of boyish adventure in a village in Missouri, on the Mississippi river, and it was told by the author. *Huckleberry Finn* is autobiographic; it is a tale of boyish adventure along the Mississippi river told as it appeared to Huck Finn. There is not in *Huckleberry Finn* any one scene quite as funny as those in which Tom Sawyer gets his friends to white-wash the fence for him, and then uses the spoils thereby acquired to attain the highest situation of the Sunday school the next morning. Nor is there any distinction quite as thrilling as that awful moment in the cave when the boy and the girl are lost in the darkness, and when Tom Sawyer suddenly sees a human hand bearing a light, and then finds that the hand is the hand of Indian Joe, his one mortal enemy; we have always thought that the vision of the hand in the cave in *Tom Sawyer* is one of the very finest things in the literature of adventure since Robinson Crusoe first saw a single footprint in the sand of the seashore. But though *Huckleberry Finn* may not quite reach these two highest points of *Tom Sawyer*, we incline to the opinion that the general level of the later story is perhaps higher than that of the earlier. For one thing, the skill with which the character of Huck Finn is maintained is marvellous. We see everything through his eyes—and they are his eyes and not a pair of Mark Twain's spectacles. And the comments on what he sees are his comments—the comments of an ignorant, superstitious, sharp, healthy boy, brought up as Huck Finn had been brought up; they are not speeches put into his mouth by the author. One of the most artistic things in the book—and that Mark Twain is a literary artist of a very high order all who have considered his later writings critically cannot but confess—one of the most artistic things in *Huckleberry Finn* is the sober self-restraint with which Mr. Clemens lets Huck Finn set down, without any comment at all, scenes which would have afforded the ordinary writer matter for endless moral and political and sociological disquisition. We refer particularly to the account of the Grangerford–Shepherdson feud, and of the

shooting of Boggs by Colonel Sherburn. Here are two incidents of the
rough old life of the South-Western States, and of the Mississippi
Valley forty or fifty years ago, of the old life which is now rapidly
passing away under the influence of advancing civilization and increasing commercial prosperity, but which has not wholly disappeared even
yet, although a slow revolution in public sentiment is taking place.
The Grangerford–Shepherdson feud is a vendetta as deadly as any
Corsican could wish, yet the parties to it were honest, brave, sincere,
good Christian people, probably people of deep religious sentiment.
Not the less we see them taking their guns to church, and, when
occasion serves, joining in what is little better than a general massacre.
The killing of Boggs by Colonel Sherburn is told with equal sobriety
and truth; and the later scene in which Colonel Sherburn cows and
lashes the mob which has set out to lynch him is one of the most
vigorous bits of writing Mark Twain has done.

In *Tom Sawyer* we saw Huckleberry Finn from the outside; in the
present volume we see him from the inside. He is almost as much
a delight to any one who has been a boy as was Tom Sawyer. But only
he or she who has been a boy can truly enjoy this record of his adventures, and of his sentiments and of his sayings. Old maids of either sex
will wholly fail to understand him or to like him, or to see his significance and his value. Like Tom Sawyer, Huck Finn is a genuine boy;
he is neither a girl in boy's clothes like many of the modern heroes of
juvenile fiction, nor is he a 'little man,' a full-grown man cut down;
he is a boy, just a boy, only a boy. And his ways and modes of thought
are boyish. As Mr. F. Anstey understands the English boy, and especially the English boy of the middle classes, so Mark Twain understands
the American boy, and especially the American boy of the Mississippi
Valley of forty or fifty years ago. The contrast between Tom Sawyer,
who is the child of respectable parents, decently brought up, and
Huckleberry Finn, who is the child of the town drunkard, not brought
up at all, is made distinct by a hundred artistic touches, not the least
natural of which is Huck's constant reference to Tom as his ideal of
what a boy should be. When Huck escapes from the cabin where his
drunken and worthless father had confined him, carefully manufacturing a mass of very circumstantial evidence to prove his own murder
by robbers, he cannot help saying, 'I did wish Tom Sawyer was there.
I knowed he would take an interest in this kind of business, and throw
in the fancy touches. Nobody could spread himself like Tom Sawyer
in such a thing as that.' Both boys have their full share of boyish

imagination; and Tom Sawyer, being given to books, lets his imagination run on robbers and pirates and genies, with a perfect understanding with himself that, if you want to get fun out of this life, you must never hesitate to make believe very hard; and, with Tom's youth and health, he never finds it hard to make believe and to be a pirate at will, or to summon an attendant spirit, or to rescue a prisoner from the deepest dungeon 'neath the castle moat. But in Huck this imagination has turned to superstition; he is a walking repository of the juvenile folklore of the Mississippi Valley—a folklore partly traditional among the white settlers, but largely influenced by intimate association with the negroes. When Huck was in his room at night all by himself waiting for the signal Tom Sawyer was to give him at midnight, he felt so lonesome he wished he was dead:—

[quotes ch. 1 'the stars was shining' to 'killed a spider.']

And, again, later in the story, not at night this time, but in broad daylight, Huck walks along a road:—

When I got there it was all still and Sunday-like, and hot and sunshiny—the hands was gone to the fields; and there was them kind of faint dronings of bugs and flies in the air that makes it seem so lonesome and like everybody's dead and gone; and if a breeze fans along and quivers the leaves, it makes you feel mournful, because you feel like it's spirits whispering—spirits that's been dead ever so many years—and you always think they're talking about *you*. As a general thing it makes a body wish *he* was dead, too, and done with it all.

Now, none of these sentiments are appropriate to Tom Sawyer, who had none of the feeling for nature which Huck Finn had caught during his numberless days and nights in the open air. Nor could Tom Sawyer either have seen or set down this instantaneous photograph of a summer storm:—

[quotes ch. 9 'It would get' to 'deal, you know'.]

The romantic side of Tom Sawyer is shown in most delightfully humorous fashion in the account of his difficult devices to aid in the easy escape of Jim, a runaway negro. Jim is an admirably drawn character. There have been not a few fine and firm portraits of negroes in recent American fiction, of which Mr. Cable's Bras-Coupé in the *Grandissimes* is perhaps the most vigorous, and Mr. Harris's Mingo and Uncle Remus and Blue Dave are the most gentle. Jim is worthy to rank with these; and the essential simplicity and kindliness and generosity of the Southern negro have never been better shown than here by Mark Twain. Nor are Tom Sawyer and Huck Finn and Jim the only fresh and original figures in Mr. Clemens's new book; on the contrary, there is scarcely a character of the many introduced who does not impress the reader at once as true to life—and therefore as new, for life is so varied that a portrait from life is sure to be as good as new. That Mr. Clemens draws from life, and yet lifts his work from the domain of the photograph to the region of art, is evident to any one who will give his work the honest attention which it deserves. Mr. John T. Raymond, the American comedian, who performs the character of Colonel Sellers to perfection, is wont to say that there is scarcely a town in the West and South-West where some man did not claim to be the original of the character. And as Mark Twain made Colonel Sellers, so has he made the chief players in the present drama of boyish adventure; they are taken from life, no doubt, but they are so aptly chosen and so broadly drawn that they are quite as typical as they are actual. They have one great charm, all of them—they are not written about and about; they are not described and dissected and analysed; they appear and play their parts and disappear; and yet they leave a sharp impression of indubitable vitality and individuality. No one, we venture to say, who reads this book will readily forget the Duke and the King, a pair of as pleasant 'confidence operators' as one may meet in a day's journey, who leave the story in the most appropriate fashion, being clothed in tar and feathers and ridden on a rail. Of the more broadly humorous passages—and they abound—we have not left ourselves space to speak; they are to the full as funny as in any of Mark Twain's other books; and, perhaps, in no other book has the humourist shown so much artistic restraint, for there is in *Huckleberry Finn* no mere 'comic copy,' no straining after effect; one might almost say that there is no waste word in it. Nor have we left ourselves room to do more than say a good word for the illustrations, which, although slight and unpretending, are far better than those to be found in most of Mark Twain's books. For one thing, they actually illustrate—and this is a rare quality in illustrations nowadays. They give the reader a distinct idea of the Duke and the King, of Jim and of Colonel Sherburn, of the Shepherdsons and the Grangerfords. They are all by one artist, Mr. E. W. Kemble, hitherto known to us only as the illustrator of the *Thompson Street Poker Club*, an amusing romance of highly-coloured life in New York.

36. Robert Bridges: unsigned review, *Life*

26 February 1885, v. 119

Robert Bridges (1858–1941), literary critic of the comic weekly, *Life*, usually signed his columns 'Droch'. Although this review, entitled 'Mark Twain's Blood-Curdling Humor', is unsigned, 'Droch' commented favourably a few weeks later on the Concord Library Committee's action of removing *Huckleberry Finn* from the library in *Life* (9 April 1885), v, 202. Bridges was on the staff of the New York *Evening Post* (1881–7) and later served as assistant editor (1887–1914) and editor (1914–30) of *Scribner's Magazine*. He was a literary adviser and director of Charles Scribner's Sons until 1939.

Mark Twain is a humorist or nothing. He is well aware of this fact himself, for he prefaces the *Adventures of Huckleberry Finn* with a brief notice, warning persons in search of a moral, motive or plot that they are liable to be prosecuted, banished or shot. This is a nice little artifice to scare off the critics—a kind of 'trespassers on these grounds will be dealt with according to law.'

However, as there is no penalty attached, we organized a search expedition for the humorous qualities of this book with the following hilarious results:

A very refined and delicate piece of narration by Huck Finn, describing his venerable and dilapidated 'pap' as afflicted with delirium tremens, rolling over and over, 'kicking things every which way,' and 'saying there was devils ahold of him.' This chapter is especially suited to amuse the children on long, rainy afternoons.

An elevating and laughable description of how Huck killed a pig, smeared its blood on an axe and mixed in a little of his own hair, and then ran off, setting up a job on the old man and the community, and leading them to believe him murdered. This little joke can be repeated by any smart boy for the amusement of his fond parents.

A graphic and romantic tale of a Southern family feud, which resulted in an elopement and from six to eight choice corpses.

A polite version of the 'Giascutus' story, in which a nude man, striped with the colors of the rainbow, is exhibited as 'The King's Camelopard; or, The Royal Nonesuch.' This is a good chapter for lenten parlor entertainments and church festivals.

A side-splitting account of a funeral, enlivened by a 'sick melo-deum,' a 'long-legged undertaker,' and a rat episode in the cellar.

37. Unsigned article, 'Modern Comic Literature', *Saturday Review*

7 March 1885, lix, 301

In response to a discursive and ill-argued attack on the vulgarity of 'modern' humour in the *Melbourne Review* (January 1885, x, 94–100), the *Saturday Review* critic cited, among others, Mark Twain's works as possessing popular appeal and elevated quality. When he forwarded the *Saturday Review* article to Mark Twain, Brander Matthews conjectured 'that it is the work of . . . Mr. Andrew Lang' (18 March 1885).

No doubt in some books of 'American Humour' colossal exaggeration makes part of the fun. No doubt there is a plentiful lack of good taste in *The Innocents Abroad*. But no critic worthy of the name can deny to MARK TWAIN at his best the essential qualities of wit and humour. He has, when quite himself, a lower kind of SYDNEY SMITH's wonderful airy high spirits which lift him buoyantly into a kind of Laputa, a place whence he sees all the mad humours of men. He has, when he likes, tenderness and melancholy, and an extraordinary sense of human limitations and contradictions. The struggles of conscience of HUCKLE-BERRY FINN about betraying the runaway negro have poetry and pathos blent in their humour. Only a great humorist could have made 'HUCK' give his own unvarnished account of the splendour and terror of a night of storm on the Mississippi, and of the coming of dawn. A mere buffoon could not have imagined the passage, a less finished humorist would have made HUCK 'talk fine' like Mr. CLARK RUSSELL'S sailors in their high flown descriptive tootle. In MARK TWAIN the world has a humorist at once wild and tender, a humorist who is yearly ripening and mellowing. But our Australian censor calls him 'the burlesquing and painfully artificial MARK TWAIN.' Yes, there are men so great that nothing can please them, not even the miraculous observation, sympathy, and wit of the passage on the credulous blue jay, or the high spirits of the philological remarks on the German language, or the unrivalled adventure of the Celebrated Mexican Plug, or the story of editing an agricultural newspaper by a literary amateur.

38. Thomas Sergeant Perry: review, *Century Magazine*

May 1885, xxx, 171–2

In this, the earliest substantial American criticism of *Huckleberry Finn*, the question of the novel's contrived conclusion is first raised.

Mark Twain's *Tom Sawyer* is an interesting record of boyish adventure; but, amusing as it is, it may yet be fair to ask whether its most marked fault is not too strong adherence to conventional literary models? A glance at the book certainly does not confirm this opinion, but those who recall the precocious affection of Tom Sawyer, at the age when he is losing his first teeth, for a little girl whom he has seen once or twice, will confess that the modern novel exercises a very great influence. What is best in the book, what one remembers, is the light we get into the boy's heart. The romantic devotion to the little girl, the terrible adventures with murderers and in huge caves, have the air of concessions to jaded readers. But when Tom gives the cat Pain-Killer, is restless in church, and is recklessly and eternally deceiving his aunt, we are on firm ground—the author is doing sincere work.

This later book, *Huckleberry Finn*, has the great advantage of being written in autobiographical form. This secures a unity in the narration that is most valuable; every scene is given, not described; and the result is a vivid picture of Western life forty or fifty years ago. While *Tom Sawyer* is scarcely more than an apparently fortuitous collection of incidents, and its thread is one that has to do with murders, this story has a more intelligible plot. Huckleberry, its immortal hero, runs away from his worthless father, and floats down the Mississippi on a raft, in company with Jim, a runaway negro. This plot gives great opportunity for varying incidents. The travelers spend some time on an island; they outwit every one they meet; they acquire full knowledge of the hideous fringe of civilization that then adorned that valley; and the book is a most valuable record of an important part of our motley American civilization.

What makes it valuable is the evident truthfulness of the narrative, and where this is lacking and its place is taken by ingenious invention, the book suffers. What is inimitable, however, is the reflection of the whole varied series of adventures in the mind of the young scapegrace of a hero. His undying fertility of invention, his courage, his manliness in every trial, are an incarnation of the better side of the ruffianism that is one result of the independence of Americans, just as hypocrisy is one result of the English respect for civilization. The total absence of morbidness in the book—for the *mal du siècle* has not yet reached Arkansas—gives it a genuine charm; and it is interesting to notice the art with which this is brought out. The best instance is perhaps to be found in the account of the feud between the Shepherdsons and the Grangerfords, which is described only as it would appear to a semi-civilized boy of fourteen, without the slightest condemnation or surprise,—either of which would be bad art,—and yet nothing more vivid can be imagined. That is the way that a story is best told, by telling it, and letting it go to the reader unaccompanied by sign-posts or directions how he shall understand it and profit by it. Life teaches its lessons by implication, not by didactic preaching; and literature is at its best when it is an imitation of life and not an excuse for instruction.

As to the humor of Mark Twain, it is scarcely necessary to speak. It lends vividness to every page. The little touch in *Tom Sawyer*, page

105, where, after the murder of which Tom was an eye-witness, it seemed 'that his school-mates would never get done holding inquests on dead cats and thus keeping the trouble present to his mind,' and that in the account of the spidery six-armed girl of Emmeline's picture in *Huckleberry Finn*, are in the author's happiest vein. Another admirable instance is to be seen in Huckleberry Finn's mixed feelings about rescuing Jim, the negro, from slavery. His perverted views regarding the unholiness of his actions are most instructive and amusing. It is possible to feel, however, that the fun in the long account of Tom Sawyer's artificial imitation of escapes from prison is somewhat forced; everywhere simplicity is a good rule, and while the account of the Southern *vendetta* is a masterpiece, the caricature of books of adventure leaves us cold. In one we have a bit of life; in the other Mark Twain is demolishing something that has no place in the book.

Yet the story is capital reading, and the reason of its great superiority to *Tom Sawyer* is that it is, for the most part, a consistent whole. If Mark Twain would follow his hero through manhood, he would condense a side of American life that, in a few years, will have to be delved out of newspapers, government reports, county histories, and misleading traditions by unsympathetic sociologists.

39. Andrew Lang: 'The Art of Mark Twain', *Illustrated London News*

14 February 1891, 222

Andrew Lang (1844–1912), a Scottish journalist, anthropologist, authority on folklore and fairy tales, a Greek scholar and translator, a poet, novelist and historian, was a prolific contributor to newspapers and periodicals.

This article is apparently Lang's response to Clemens' request for support in the face of adverse criticism (see Introduction, p. 15). Subsequently the *Critic* reprinted these comments in two parts (7 March 1891, xviii, 130, and 25 July 1891, xix, 45–6).

The duty of self-examination is frequently urged upon us by moralists. No doubt we should self-examine our minds as well as our conduct now and then, especially when we have passed the age in which we are constantly examined by other people. When I attempt to conduct this delicate inquiry I am puzzled and alarmed at finding that I am losing Culture. I am backsliding, I have not final perseverance, unless indeed it is Culture that is backsliding and getting on to the wrong lines. For I ought to be cultured: it is my own fault if I have not got Culture.

I have been educated till I nearly dropped; I have lived with the earliest Apostles of Culture, in the days when Chippendale was first a name to conjure with, and Japanese art came in like a raging lion, and Ronsard was the favourite poet, and Mr. William Morris was a poet too, and blue and green were the only wear, and the name of Paradise was Camelot. To be sure, I cannot say that I took all this quite seriously, but 'we too have played' at it, and know all about it. Generally speaking, I have kept up with Culture. I can talk (if desired) about Sainte-Beuve, and Mérimée, and Félicien Rops; I could rhyme 'Ballades,' when they were 'in,' and knew what a *pantoom* was. I am acquainted with the scholia on the Venetus A. I have a pretty taste in

Greek gems. I have got beyond the stage of thinking Mr. Cobden Sanderson a greater binder than Bauzonnet. With practice I believe I could do an epigram of Meleager's into a bad imitation of a sonnet by Joachim du Bellay, or a sonnet of Bellay's into a bad imitation of a Greek epigram. I could pass an examination in the works of M. Paul Bourget. And yet I have not Culture. My works are but a tinkling brass, because I have not Culture. For Culture has got into new regions where I cannot enter, and, what is perhaps worse, I find myself delighting in a great many things which are under the ban of Culture.

This is a dreadful position, which makes a man feel like one of those Liberal politicians who are always 'sitting on the fence,' and who follow their party, if follow it they do, with the reluctant acquiescence of the prophet's donkey. Not that I *do* follow it. I cannot rave with pleasure over Tolstoï, especially as he admits that 'The Kreutzer Sonata' is not 'only his fun' but a kind of Manifesto. I have tried Hartmann, and I prefer Plato. I don't like poems by young ladies in which the verses neither scan nor rhyme, and the constructions are all linguistically impossible. I am shaky about Blake, though I am stalwart about Mr. Rudyard Kipling.

This is not the worst of it. Culture has hardly a new idol but I long to hurl things at it. Culture can scarcely burn anything, but I am impelled to sacrifice to that same. I am coming to suspect that the majority of Culture's modern disciples are a mere crowd of very slimly educated people, who have no natural taste or impulse; who do not really know the best things in literature; who have a feverish desire to admire the newest thing, to follow the latest artistic fashion; who prate about 'style' without the faintest acquaintance with the ancient examples of style, in Greek, French, or English; who talk about the classics and criticise the classical critics and poets, without being able to read a line of them in the original. Nothing of the natural man is left in these people; their intellectual equipment is made up of ignorant vanity, and eager desire of novelty, and a yearning to be in the fashion.

Take, for example—and we have been a long time in coming to him—Mark Twain. If you praise him among persons of Culture, they cannot believe that you are serious. They call him a Barbarian. They won't hear of him, they hurry from the subject; they pass by on the other side of the way. Now I do not mean to assert that Mark Twain is 'an impeccable artist,' but he is just as far from being a mere coarse buffoon. Like other people, he has his limitations. Even Mr. Gladstone, *disagree with this point in the essay after discussion* (handwritten)

for instance, does not shine as a Biblical critic, nor Mark Twain as a critic of Italian art nor as a guide to the Holy Land. I have abstained from reading his work on an American at the Court of King Arthur, because here Mark Twain is not, and cannot be, at the proper point of view. He has not the knowledge which would enable him to be a sound critic of the ideal of the Middle Ages. An Arthurian Knight in New York or in Washington would find as much to blame, and justly, as a Yankee at Camelot. Let it be admitted that Mark Twain often and often sins against good taste, that some of his waggeries are mechanical, that his books are full of passages which were only good enough for the corner of a newspaper. Even so, the man who does not 'let a laugh out of him'—like the Gruagach Gaire—at the story of the Old Ram, or of the Mexican Plug, or of the editing of the country newspaper, or of the Blue Jay, or at the lecture on the German language, can hardly have a laugh in him to let out. Chesterfield very gravely warns his son that it is wrong and vulgar to laugh; but the world has agreed to differ from Chesterfield. To 'Homo Ridens' Mark Twain is a benefactor beyond most modern writers, and the Cultured, who do not laugh, are merely to be pitied. But his art is not only that of a maker of the scarce article—mirth. I have no hesitation in saying that Mark Twain is one among the greatest of contemporary makers of fiction. For some reason, which may perhaps be guessed, he has only twice chosen to exercise this art seriously, in *Tom Sawyer* and in *Hucklebury Finn*. The reason, probably, is that old life on the Mississippi is the only form of life in which Mark Twain finds himself so well versed that he can deal with it in seriousness. Again, perhaps his natural and cultivated tendency to extravagance and caricature is only to be checked by working on the profound and candid seriousness of boyhood. These are unlucky limitations, if they really exist, for they have confined him, as a novelist, to a pair of brief works, masterpieces which a fallacious appearance has confounded with boys' books and facetiæ. Of the two, by an unheard-of stroke of luck, the second, the sequel, is by far the better. I can never forget nor be ungrateful for the exquisite pleasure with which I read *Hucklebury Finn* for the first time, years ago. I read it again last night, deserting *Kenilworth* for Huck. I never laid it down till I had finished it. I perused several passages more than once, and rose from it with a higher opinion of its merits than ever.

What is it that we want in a novel? We want a vivid and original picture of life; we want character naturally displayed in action, and if we get the excitement of adventure into the bargain, and that adventure possible and plausible, I so far differ from the newest school of criticism as to think that we have additional cause for gratitude. If, moreover, there is an unstrained sense of humour in the narrator, we have a masterpiece and *Hucklebury Finn* is nothing less. Once more, if the critics are right who think that art should so far imitate nature as to leave things at loose ends, as it were, not pursuing events to their conclusions, even here *Hucklebury Finn* should satisfy them. It is the story of the flight down the Mississippi of a white boy and a runaway slave. The stream takes them through the fringes of life on the riverside; they pass feuds and murders of men, and towns full of homicidal loafers, and are intermingled with the affairs of families, and meet friends whom they would wish to be friends always. But the current carries them on: they leave the murders unavenged, the lovers in full flight; the friends they lose for ever; we do not know, any more than in reality we would know, 'what became of them all.' They do not return, as in novels, and narrate their later adventures.

As to the truth of the life described, the life in little innocent towns, the religion, the Southern lawlessness, the feuds, the lynchings, only persons who have known this changed world can say if it be truly painted, but it looks like the very truth, like an historical document. Already *Hucklebury Finn* is an historical novel, and more valuable, perhaps, to the historian than *Uncle Tom's Cabin*, for it was written without partisanship, and without 'a purpose.' The drawing of character seems to be admirable, unsurpassed in its kind. By putting the tale in the mouth of the chief actor, Huck, Mark Twain was enabled to give it a seriousness not common in his work, and to abstain from comment. Nothing can be more true and more humorous than the narrative of this outcast boy, with a heart naturally good, with a conscience torn between the teachings of his world about slavery and the promptings of his nature. In one point Mark Twain is Homeric, probably without knowing it. In the *Odyssey*, Odysseus frequently tells a false tale about himself, to account for his appearance and position when disguised on his own island. He shows extraordinary fertility and appropriateness of invention, wherein he is equalled by the feigned tales of Hucklebury Finn. The casual characters met on the way are masterly: the woman who detects Huck in a girl's dress; the fighting families of Shepherdson and Grangerford; the homicidal Colonel Sherborne, who cruelly shoots old Boggs, and superbly quells the mob of would-be lynchers; the various old aunts and uncles; the negro Jim; the two wandering impostors; the hateful father of Huck himself.

Then Huck's compliment to Miss Mary Jane, whom he thought of afterwards 'a many and a many million times,' how excellent it is! 'In my opinion she had more sand in her than any girl I ever see; in my opinion she was just full of sand. It sounds like flattery, but it ain't no flattery. And when it comes to beauty—and goodness, too—she lays over them all.' No novel has better touches of natural description; the starlit nights on the great river, the storms, the whole landscape, the sketches of little rotting towns, of the woods, of the cotton-fields, are simple, natural, and visible to the mind's eye. The story, to be sure, ends by lapsing into burlesque, when Tom Sawyer insists on freeing the slave whom he knows to be free already, in a manner accordant with 'the best authorities.' But even the burlesque is redeemed by Tom's real unconscious heroism. There are defects of taste, or passages that to us seem deficient in taste, but the book remains a nearly flawless gem of romance and of humour. The world appreciates it, no doubt, but 'cultured critics' are probably unaware of its singular value. A two-shilling novel by Mark Twain, with an ugly picture on the cover, 'has no show,' as Huck might say, and the great American novel has escaped the eyes of those who watch to see this new planet swim into their ken. And will Mark Twain never write such another? One is enough for him to live by, and for our gratitude, but not enough for our desire.

40. Sir Walter Besant: 'My Favorite Novelist and His Best Book', *Munsey's Magazine*

February 1898, xviii, 659–64

Sir Walter Besant (1836–1901) was a novelist, biographer and critic. This article was one of a series published by *Munsey's Magazine*. Other articles in this series, all having the same title, were contributed by such authors as William Dean Howells, Bret Harte and Arthur Conan Doyle.

I have been invited to write upon my 'Favorite Novel.' Alas, I have so many favorite novels! How can I incur the jealousy of all the others by selecting one as the favorite? Novels are live things; they love admiration; they resent neglect; they hate the preference of others. Like Charles Lamb, who loved every book because it was a book—except the Law List—I love every novel because it is a novel—except those which are not novels, but only shams. I love the novel of adventure; I find the *Three Musketeers* as delightful now as when I sat in a corner, breathless, panting, and followed, all a lifelong holiday, the fortunes of the Immortal Three who were Four. And I love the novel which portrays human life and society, whether it is *Tom Jones*, or *Humphrey Clinker*, or *Nicholas Nickleby*. And I love Charlotte Yonge's gentle girls; and Marryat's anything but gentle sailor; and Lever's swaggering soldier; and Jane Austen, and Maria Edgeworth, and Wilkie Collins, and Charles Reade, and Edgar Allan Poe, and Hawthorne, and Oliver Wendell Holmes—not to speak of living men and women by the score whose works I read with joy.

Of a novel I ask but one thing. 'Seize me,' I say—'seize me and hold me with a grip of steel. Make me deaf and blind to all the world so long as I read in thine enchanted pages. Carry me whither thou wilt. Play on me; do with me what thou wilt, at thine own sweet will. Make me shriek with pain; fill my eyes with tears and my heart with sorrow;

let me laugh aloud, let me bubble over with the joy of silent mirth; let me forget that the earth is full of oppression and wickedness. Only seize me and hold me tight—immovable, rapt, hypnotized; deaf and blind to all the world.'

I confess that unless this condition is fulfilled I cannot read a novel. Many novels I try to read, only to lay them down. A few such I have had to read on occasions—they were rare—when an editor has asked me to review a novel. To me it is more painful than words can tell to read such a book; it is more irksome than any convict's task to write a review of such a book. The only excuse that I will admit from a reviewer who dishonestly pronounces judgment on a book which he has not read is that the novel was one of the kind which cannot be read. If he pleads that excuse, I pity him and pass on. For this reason, also, I am in no hurry to take up any new novel. I like to have it 'tasted' for me first. The tasting enables me to escape the attempt to read a great many new novels. As a rule I buy only those of which other people have already spoken. As a wise man and a philosopher, I take my recommendations not from the critics, but from the other people. Then, if a story possesses the gift of grip, I am ready to forgive all other sins. A novel cannot be really bad, though it may have many faults, if it seizes the reader and holds him spellbound till the last page.

These remarks prepare the way for a selection which is perhaps unexpected. I do not respond to the invitation by taking one of the acknowledged masterpieces; nor shall I worry myself to find something fresh to say about a book which has already been reviewed over and over again. Cervantes, Fielding, Dickens, Thackeray—all these I leave to the professors of literature, and to the critic of the big and serious 'appreciation'—to him who estimates influence, finds out blemishes, and explores the sources. I am only a critic in so far as I really do know the points of a good novelist and something about the art of construction of a novel; and I prefer to apply this knowledge on the present occasion to a work of perhaps humbler pretensions, albeit a work of genius, and a work which will live and will belong to the literature of the language. I speak of one of my favorites; not my single favorite. I love the book for a variety of excellent reasons, but not to the exclusion of other books. It is expected of a well regulated mind that it cannot love more than one woman at a time. This galling restriction applies not to the lover of novels, which, with poetry, are the fair women of literature. One can love then all—yes, all. So catholic is love in literature, so wide is his embrace, so universal; so free from jealousy are his mistresses.

The book which I have selected is Mark Twain's *Huckleberry Finn*. At the outset I observe, and intend to respect, a warning after the title page to the effect that any person who may try to find a motive in the narrative will be prosecuted; that any person who may try to find a moral in it will be banished, and that persons attempting to find a plot will be shot.

Let us repeat this warning. Let us not try to find in *Huckleberry Finn* either motive, moral, or plot.

I lay it down as one of the distinctive characteristics of a good story that it pleases—or rather, seizes—every period of life; that the child, and his elder brother, and his father, and his grandfather, may read it with like enjoyment—not equal enjoyment, because as a man gets older and understands more and more what the world of men and women means, he reads between the lines and sees things which the child cannot see and cannot understand. Very likely, if the painting is true to nature, he sees things which the artist himself could not see or understand. The note of genius is that it suggests so much more than it meant to suggest, and goes so much deeper than the poet himself intended. To discover and to read the superadded letterpress, the invisible part of the printed page, is one of the compensations of age.

The first quality that I claim for this book, then, is that it does appeal to all ages and every age. The boy of twelve reads it with delight beyond his power of words to express; the young man reads it; the old man reads it. The book is a joy to all alike. For my own part, I have read it over and over again, yet always with delight and always finding something new in its pages.

There is no motive in the book; there is no moral; there is no plot. The book is like a panorama in which the characters pass across the stage and do not return. They follow each other with the unexpectedness belonging to a voyage down a river. All happens by chance; the finger of providence—which means the finger of Mark Twain—is nowhere visible. There is no motive; there is no moral; there is no plot. This directing, intervening, meddlesome finger you will find very often in the novel which does not permit itself to be read; it sticks out in the carpenter's novel. You see the thumb—it wants washing—in the novel made by rule. It is nowhere visible in *Huckleberry Finn*.

The book commends itself, to begin with, by the humorous treatment of perfectly serious situations. It is unconsciously humorous, it is humorous because the narrator sees no humor in anything. In some places, when an English boy would have rolled on the floor with laughing, the American boy relates the scene without a smile. Indeed, from beginning to end, there is hardly a smile. Yet, while all the situations lie open for sentiment, for moralizing, or for laughing, the actors are perfectly serious—and perfectly comic.

The reason of the serious nature of the performance is that the narrator is a boy whose experiences of life have not, so far, inclined him to look at things from a humorous point of view. He is the son of a drunken scoundrel, the disgrace and terror of the town.

He said he'd cowhide me till I was black and blue if I didn't raise some money for him. I borrowed three dollars from Judge Thatcher, and pap took it and got drunk and went a-blowing around and cussing and whooping and carrying on; and he kept it up all over town, with a tin pan, till 'most midnight. Then they jailed him; next day they had him before court and jailed him again for a week.

Even the boys in the town spoke of him as 'a man who used to lay drunk with the hogs in the tan yard.' It is with the gravest face that the boy speaks of his father; relates how he took the pledge in presence of the judge—who 'said it was the holiest time on record'—and broke it the next day; and how he had delirium tremens and tried to murder his son. With such a father; with no education; with no religion; living about in the woods; without respect of persons; untruthful whenever it seemed easier to conceal the truth; yielding when necessary; watchful of opportunities; not immoral, but unmoral—the boy starts off to tell his tale of adventure. Writers of fiction, of whom there are now so many, will understand the difficulty of getting inside the brain of that boy, seeing things as he saw them, writing as he would have written, and acting as he would have acted; and presenting to the world a true, faithful, and living *effigies* of that boy. The feat has been accomplished: there is no character in fiction more fully, more faithfully presented than the character of *Huckleberry Finn*. What that character finally appears, when the book is finished, when the glamour dies away, when the figure stands out plainly before us, I will endeavor to portray after touching on some of the points of *Huckleberry's* pilgrimage.

The earlier chapters, with *Tom Sawyer* and the other boys, are hardly worthy to be taken as an introduction to the book. But they are soon got over. The adventures really begin with the boy's life in the cabin where his father has taken him. The man was always drunk, always abusing and threatening the boy, always falling about in his half drunk moments, and cursing.

Down he went in the dirt and rolled there and held his toes; and the cussing he done there laid over anything he had ever done previous. He said so, his own self, afterwards.

Observe the boy's standard as to cursing considered as fine art.

He escapes; he finds a canoe drifting down the river; he gets on board, takes certain steps which will make his father believe that he has been murdered, and paddles down the river to an island. The river is the mighty Mississippi; and now we are on or beside its waters and hear the swirl and the swish as the current rolls past the reeds and sedges of the island and washes the planks of the craft. We see the huge lumber rafts making their slow way with the stream; we hear, with the boy, the voice of the man on board—'Stern oars! Heave her head to stabboard!'

On his desert island the boy, perfectly happy, caught fish and broiled them; found wild strawberries—the *fraises à quatre saisons* which flourish all over the world; and went about exploring his kingdom. It was a glorious time, only it was difficult to get through the day. Presently he found another resident on the island, the runaway 'nigger' *Jim*, whom he knew very well. The white boy was so wild, so uncivilized, that even in a slave holding State he had imbibed no proper feeling as regards runaway slaves. He chummed with *Jim* immediately. The river rises; the island is under water; they live in a cave on a rock which is above the flood; they paddle about in the canoe, either on the river or among the woods; they pick up things that come floating down—among other things part of a lumber raft.

It was lucky they found the raft, because smoke had been seen on the island, and suspicion had arisen about the runaway 'nigger.' They decided to run away from their island and to make for the first point where a fugitive slave would be free. They loaded the raft with all they had; they carried their canoe on board; and in the dead of night they slipped off the island and so down stream. Where they were going to, whither the river would carry them, they never inquired. The book, you see, has no plot, no motive, no moral.

They ran about seven or eight hours every night, the current making four miles an hour. They fished as they slid down the stream. Sometimes they took a swim to keep off sleepiness.

It was a kind of solemn, drifting down the big still river, laying on our backs looking up at the stars, and we didn't feel like talking loud and it wasn't often that we laughed, only a little kind of a low chuckle.

Every night about ten o'clock, the boy went ashore to some village and bought ten or fifteen cents' worth of meal or bacon.

Sometimes I lifted a chicken that wasn't roosting comfortable. Pap always said, 'Take a chicken when you get a chance, because if you don't want him yourself you can easy find somebody that does, and a good deed ain't never forgot.' I never see pap when he didn't want the chicken himself, but that is what he used to say, any way.

In the same way, the boy went into the fields and borrowed a watermelon or a 'mush melon' or a 'punkin' or some new corn. The book, you observe, has no moral.

They then take on board the immortal pair of rogues and vagabonds —the *King* and the *Duke*. Writes the young philosopher:

It didn't take me long to make up my mind that these liars wasn't no kings and dukes at all, but just low down humbugs and frauds. But I never said nothing, never let on; kept it to myself. It's the best way; then you don't have no quarrels and don't get into no trouble.

The chapters with the *King* and the *Duke* are amazing for the sheer impudence of the two rogues and the remarks of the boy. He makes no remonstrance, he affects no indignation; he falls in with every pretense on which his assistance is required, and he watches all the time —watches for the chance to upset their little plans. And such plans! One sells quack medicines; plays and recites; lectures on mesmerism and phrenology; teaches singing and geography at schools for a change; does anything that comes handy. The other preaches temperance, also religion; gets up camp meetings; is a missionary; lays on hands for curing paralysis and the like. Together they agree to get up scenes from Shakspere, especially the balcony scene in *Romeo and Juliet*; to discover water and treasure by means of the divining rod; to dissipate witch spells; to get subscriptions and advertisements for a bogus paper; to continue the preaching, and so on. The great *coup* was the personation of a man in England, brother of a man just deceased. This, in fact, very nearly came off; it would have come off, with a bag of six thousand dollars, but for the boy, who defeats their villainies. How he does this, how the older of the two rogues sells *Jim* for a runaway, how the two rascals, the *King* and the *Duke*, have to ride on a rail, how *Jim* is recovered, is well known by those who have read the book, and can be easily learned by those who have not. It is a book which, to repeat, has no moral. One does not expect the punishment of villainy; yet it is pleasant to catch this last glimpse of the *King* and the *Duke* thus honored by their grateful fellow citizens. This American custom of riding a rogue on a rail is not, as is generally supposed, an invention or a growth of the American people, though they are eminently inventive. It crossed the Atlantic from the old country, where, under the name of 'Riding the Stang'—a rail for the men, a basket for the women—it flourished in certain parts almost down to the present time.

Also, though the book has no moral, one is pleased to find the 'nigger' receiving his freedom at the end. And, although it has no plot, one is delighted to find that *Huckleberry* remains the same at the end as he began at the beginning. That blessed boy, who has told as many lies as there are pages in the book, is left impenitent.

I reckon I got to light out for the Territory ahead of the rest, because Aunt Sally she's going to adopt me and civilize me, and I can't stand it. I been there before.

These are his parting words.

It was fifty years ago. Do you know what happened afterwards? I will tell you. *Huckleberry*, of course, remained not civilized; he went to live with *Jim* on Jackson Island. They had a raft and a canoe; they fished and shot and trapped; they built a log hut. *Tom Sawyer* used to visit them till he was taken away and sent to college and became a lawyer. He is now, as everybody knows, the governor of his State, and may possibly become President. Presently *Jim* died. Then *Huckleberry* was left alone. He still lives on Jackson Island in his log hut. He is now an old man; his beard is as white as that of the veteran fraud, the *King*; he is full of wisdom and wise thoughts; long and lonely nights beneath the stars, watching the endless roll of the Mississippi, have made him wise. Of the world he still knows nothing; of his ancient fibs and tricks he is impenitent.

There is another side of the book. It belongs to the fifties, the old time before the civil war, when the 'institution' was flourishing against all the efforts of the Abolitionists. Without intending it—the book has no motive—the boy restores for us that life in the Southern States. It is now so far off that even those who are old enough to remember it think of it as a kind of dream. Consider how far off it is. There is the elderly maiden lady, full of religion, who tries to teach the boy the way to heaven. She herself is living, she says, so as to go there. She has

one old 'nigger' who has been with her all her life—a faithful servant,
an affectionate creature. This pious woman deliberately proposes to
sell the man—to *sell* him—for the sum of eight hundred dollars, or one
hundred and sixty pounds sterling. Only forty years ago! Yet how far
off! How far off! Is there, anywhere in the Southern States of today,
any living lady who could in cold blood sell an old servant into slavery
among strangers? Then there is the feud between the families of the
Grangerfords and the *Shepherdsons*. They have a feud—do families in the
South have feuds and go shooting each other now? It seems so far off;
so long ago. The *Shepherdsons* and the *Grangerfords* alike are all filled
out with family pride; no descendant of all the kingly houses of Europe
could be prouder of family than these obscure planters. They have no
education; they shoot at each other whenever they meet; they murder
even the boys of either family. It is only a glimpse we catch of them
as we float down the Mississippi, but it belongs to a time so long ago
—so long ago.

There is another glimpse—of a riverside town. It consists of one
street, of stores with awnings in front; loafers in wide straw hats and
neither coat nor waistcoat lie and sit about. They do nothing; they
borrow 'chaws' of tobacco of each other; the street is quite quiet and
empty. Presently some wagons come in from the country, and the
town is animated. It is a kind of market day. Then a drunken man rides
amuck through the town, roaring and threatening. He threatens one
prominent citizen so long that, after a while, the man says he has lost
patience, and shoots the drunkard dead. It is all so long ago, you see.
Or we are at a camp meeting—perhaps those meetings go on still,
somewhere. There are a thousand people present. The meeting is provided with sheds for preaching and sheds for selling watermelons and
lemonade. The young men go barefooted; the girls have sun-bonnets
and linsey woolsey frocks. Some of them listen to the preaching; some
sit out and carry on flirtations of the more elementary. People are
invited to the mourners' bench; they crowd in, on the invitation,
moved by the contagious emotion, weeping, crying, throwing themselves down in the straw. Among them, weeping more bitterly than
the rest, is the wicked old *King*; he has got conviction of sin; he is
broken down; he is on the mourners' bench. He is so contrite that you
may hear his groans above all the rest. He begs permission to speak
to the people; he confesses that he has been a pirate all his life; he is now
repentant; he will be a pirate no more; he will go among his old friends
and convert them. It will be difficult without money, but he will try

—he will try. So they take up a collection for him, and he goes back to the raft, after kissing all the girls, with eighty seven dollars and twenty five cents in his purse. He had also found a three gallon keg of whisky, too, under a wagon. The good old man said, 'Take it all around, it laid over any day he'd ever put in, in the missionary line. Heathens,' he said, 'don't amount to shucks, alongside of pirates, to work a camp meeting with.' There are still, perhaps, country villages and places in the Central States, of which we of England know so little, where the people are simple and unsuspicious, and enjoy a red hot religion; but the world has moved, even for them. There are surely no country places left where such a ridiculous old fraud as the *King* could be believed. It may be objected that the characters are extravagant. Not so. They are all exactly and literally true; they are quite possible in a country so remote and so primitive. Every figure in the book is a type; *Huckleberry* has exaggerated none. We see the life—the dull and vacuous life—of a small township upon the Mississippi forty years ago; so far as I know, it is the only place where we can find that phase of life portrayed.

If the scenes and characters of the book are all life-like and true to nature, still more life-like is the figure of the boy as he stands out, at the end, when we close the volume, self revealed.

He is, to begin with, shrewd. It is a word which may have a good or a bad meaning; in the former sense, I think that shrewdness is a more common characteristic of the American than of the Englishman. I mean that he is more ready to question, to doubt, to examine, to understand. He is far more ready to exercise freedom of thought; far less ready to accept authority. His individuality is more intense; he is one against the world; he is more readily on the defensive. *Huckleberry*, therefore, however it may be with his countrymen at large, is shrewd. He questions everything. For instance, he is told to pray for everything. He tries it; he prays for fish hooks. None come; he worries over the matter a while, and then he concludes to let it go. If he has no religion, however, he has plenty of superstition; he believes all the wonderful things the 'nigger' *Jim* tells him: the ghosts and the signs of bad luck and good luck.

He has an immense natural love for the woods and forests; for the open air; for the great river laden with the rafts forever going down the stream; for the night as much as the day; for the dawn as much as the splendor of the noonday.

[quotes ch. 19 'Not a sound, anywheres' to 'look that way'.]

If he loves the still and solemn night and the woods, he loves also the creatures in the woods—squirrels, turtles, snakes. He is a boy who belongs to the river, which he will never desert. His lies and his thievings and his acquiescence in frauds—to be sure, he was forced—do not affect his nature; he passes through these things and will shake them off and forget them. All his life he will live in the present, which is a part of the nomadic spirit. He will look on without indignation at the things men do around him; but his home will be on Jackson's Island in a log hut, alone, and far from the haunts of men. And he will never grow weary of watching the lumber rafts go by; or of sitting beside the mighty flood; or of watching the day break, and the sun set; or of lying in the shade so long as he can look at the snakes and the turtles or listen while a couple of squirrels 'set on a limb and jabber at him friendly.' Because, you see, there is no moral in this book; and no motive; and no plot.

41. Andrew Lang: Jubilee Ode to Mark Twain

1886

Extract from a column, 'At the Sign of the Ship', *Longman's Magazine* (February 1886), vii, 445–6.
Despite his somewhat strained tribute, no worse than most of the unfortunate genre, Andrew Lang's appraisal of the appropriateness of Mark Twain's settings is succinct and unique.

Mark Twain has reached his fiftieth year, and has been warmly congratulated on his 'Jubilee' by most of the wits of his native land. As the Ettrick Shepherd said to Wordsworth when first they met, 'I'm glad you're so young a man,' so one might observe to Mark, and wish that he were still younger. But his genius is still young, and perhaps never showed so well, with such strength and variety, such veracity and humour, as in his latest book, *Huckleberry Finn*. Persons of extremely fine culture may have no taste for Mark. When he gets among pictures and holy places perhaps we all feel that he is rather an awful being. But on a Mississippi boat, or in a bar-room, or editing (without sufficient technical information) an agricultural journal, or bestriding a Celebrated Mexican Plug, or out silver-mine hunting, or on the track of Indian Joe, Mark is all himself, and the most powerful and diverting writer, I think, of his American contemporaries. Here followeth, rather late, but heartily well meant, a tribute to Mark on his jubilee.

FOR MARK TWAIN.

> A star danced, and under that was *he* born.
> *Much Ado about Nothing.*

To brave Mark Twain, across the sea,
The years have brought his jubilee;
   One hears it half with pain,

That fifty years have passed and gone
Since danced the merry star that shone
   Above the babe, Mark Twain!

How many and many a weary day
When sad enough were we, 'Mark's way'
   (Unlike the Laureate's Mark's)[1]
Has made us laugh until we cried,
And, sinking back exhausted, sighed,
   Like Gargery, *Wot larx!*

We turn his pages, and we see
The Mississippi flowing free;
   We turn again, and grin
O'er all *Tom Sawyer* did and planned,
With him of the Ensanguined Hand,
   With *Huckleberry Finn*!

Spirit of mirth, whose chime of bells
Shakes on his cap, and sweetly swells
   Across the Atlantic main,
Grant that Mark's laughter never die,
That men, through many a century,
   May chuckle o'er Mark Twain!

[1] 'Mark's way', said Mark, and clove him through the brain.

A CONNECTICUT YANKEE IN KING ARTHUR'S COURT

December 1889

42. Sylvester Baxter: unsigned review, Boston Sunday *Herald*

15 December 1889, 17

Sylvester Baxter (1850–1927) wrote for the Boston *Daily Advertiser* (1871–5) and the Boston *Herald* (1879–83, 1887–1905).

Howells sent Clemens a copy of this review the day it appeared. In a letter to Baxter (19 December 1889) Clemens thanked him for the 'admirable' review and for praising Dan Beard's illustrations (quoted in *Mark Twain–Howells Letters*, p. 624).

Of all the extraordinary conceits that have germinated in his fruitful imagination, nothing more delicious has ever occurred to Mark Twain than that of running riot among the legendary times of our ancestral race by placing 'A Connecticut Yankee in King Arthur's Court.' These quoted words form the title of the latest successor to *Innocents Abroad*. Here is a rare field for the unbridled play of fancy, and right bravely has the author used his opportunity. There is a most audacious rollicking around among the dusty bric-a-brac of chivalry—which is not handled at all gently—and a merry tossing about of poetic finery in a way that ruthlessly exposes in their literal ugliness the illusively mantled facts. Of course there is most abundant fun, and Mark Twain's rich humor never coursed more freely than here, where just provocation is never absent. But there is much more than this; the sources of the claims of aristocratic privileges and royal prerogatives that yet linger in the world are so exposed to the full glare of the sun of 19th century common sense, are shown in so ridiculous an aspect, that the work can hardly fail to do yeoman service in destroying the still existing remnants of respect for such pretensions. Through the book there is a steady flowing undercurrent of earnest purpose, and the pages are eloquent with a true American love of freedom, a sympathy with the rights of the common people, and an indignant hatred of oppression of the poor, the lowly and the weak, by the rich, the power-ful and the proud. While much false glamour is dispelled by resolving it into absurdity under the touchstone of truth, the book is marked by real beauty, by a poetry of style worthy of its rich material, with much sympathetic tenderness, as well as frankness of speech. The quaint early English speech is handled with the same artistic skill that characterized the author's facile handling of the stately Elizabethan in that lovely idyll of childhood, *The Prince and the Pauper*, and the constant admixture of a concisely expressive American vernacular thereto makes a contrast of lingual coloring that is unspeakably delightful.

We may fancy that the same matter-of-fact Englishman who seriously reasoned that certain statements in *Innocents Abroad* were preposterously absurd, and could not be based upon fact, might again step forward to break a lance against this book by showing, from historical and philological data, that such a language could not possibly have been spoken in the sixth century, since the English tongue did not exist, and that the use of Norman French names before the conquest is anachronistic in the highest degree! But this is an excursion back into the England of the chronicles, and not of strict chronology, and that eminent ethnologist, Tylor, would undoubtedly perceive with delight the accuracy of scientific perception in the treatment of human nature which marks the book. For, in order to characterize with truth a past period we must make ourselves familiar with some existing state of society that is analogous therewith. Only under such conditions can a faithful historical romance be written, for otherwise the writer cannot fail to modernize his work, and falsify its life with 19th century senti-ments that could not have been known in a previous age. By resorting to the principle that 'distribution in time' is paralleled by 'distribution in space,' we may solve many a problem. So there is a certain aspect of sober truth in this most fanciful tale, and, just as the Connecticut Yankee went back into the days of King Arthur's court, so might he go out into the world today, into Central Asia or Africa, or even into certain spots in this United States of ours, find himself amidst social conditions very similar to those of 1300 years ago, and even work his astonishing 19th century miracles with like result. For it is a fact that, when Frank Hamilton Cushing astounded the Zuni Indians with an acoustic telephone constructed of two tomato cans and a string, they deemed him a magician, and tried him for witchcraft. And, for parallels of the inhumanities which, as we here read of them, seem to have been left far behind us in the track of the centuries, we have but to look with George Kennan into the dungeons of Siberia; and, in our own country, read the records of the investigations into the horrors of the almshouses, jails and lunatic hospitals here in this enlightened commonwealth of Massachusetts so late as the time of Horace Mann, or look to the record of the nameless barbarities of negro slavery alive in the memories of men still young. How the conscience and the sympathies of the world have quickened with the advent of the railway, the steamship and the telegraph! We have, after all, but just passed out across the threshold of the dark ages, and, in view of the few steps we have taken, we can hardly doubt that we are yet to make an infinitely mightier progress into the light of a genuine civilization, putting far behind us the veneered barbarism of the present, that still retains the old standards of conduct and intercourse for our guidance in all 'practical' affairs.

As an instance of the scientific fidelity of this book in its picture of mediaeval society, we may take this from the description of the company at King Arthur's Round Table, around which there was an average of about two dogs to one man, watching for bones:

[quotes ch. 2 'As a rule' to 'white Indians'.]

The following also illustrates an exact perception of the essentially savage traits of such a people: 'Finally it occurred to me all of a sudden that these animals didn't reason; that they never put this and that together; that all their talk showed that they didn't know a discrepancy when they saw it.' Again, when Sir Sagramour le Desirous caught a chance remark of the Yankee applied to some one else and thought it meant for him, and so challenged him to the memorable encounter that took place several years after, and was fought with lariat versus lance, the 'Sir Boss,' as he was called said: 'Whenever one of those people got a thing into his head, there was no getting it out again. I knew that, so I saved my breath, and offered no explanations.' The foregoing characterizations might apply equally well to a tribe of Dakota Indians, to their hardly more civilized foes, the cowboys of the plains, to the mountaineers of Tennessee and Georgia, or even to the savages in our great city slums.

By some strange means, perhaps more marvellous than those by which Edward Bellamy transferred the hero of *Looking Backward* forward to the year 2000, the Yankee is carried back 1300 years in time, and in the record of his adventures affords us another and very instructive sort of *Looking Backward*.

[lengthy plot summary with quotations]

The advance in the art of popular bookmaking in the past two decades is illustrated by the contrast between *Innocents Abroad* and this volume. In illustration, the progress is particularly notable. Even a child of today would turn in contempt from the crude woodcuts of the former to the beautiful pen-and-ink drawings by Dan Beard that adorn the new work. These drawings are graceful, picturesque and thoroughly characteristic of the spirit of the book. Many of them embody instructive allegories, as, for instance, in a cut of Justice, with her scales, one containing the heavy hammer of 'Labor' and the other the baubles of 'Aristocracy,' but the latter made to outweigh the former by means of the string of 'Self-interest,' artfully attached to the toe of 'Law,' who stands by; another, in a similar vein, shows the Justice of the 19th century and Justice of the sixth century standing opposite each other, and simultaneously remarking, 'Sister, your blind is disarranged,' for, with the same manner of string attached to the toe of each, 'Money' is made to outweigh 'Labor' by the former, just as titles are made heavier in the balance by the latter. One little cut shows 'Decorations of Sixth Century Aristocracy' as 'Rewards for all Babes Born Under Specified Conditions,' such as 'Slave Driver,' 'Robber of Unarmed Savages,' 'Robber of Orphans,' 'Absorber of Taxes,' 'Murderer of Rivals,' etc., the whole supported by 'Honi soit qui mal y pense!' Another illustrates the remark of the king concerning a peasant: 'Brother! to dirt like this?' by depicting the three phases of oppression of man by man, first by violence under the sword of royal power, then by the book of 'law,' making man subject to the slave driver's lash, and last, the subjection of the workingman to the millions of the monopolist. A strong and spirited picture of an arrogant slave driver shows in its face the unmistakable portrait of a celebrated American billionaire and stock gambler.

We are so accustomed to regard England of today as 'essentially a republic, with a monarchical head,' that it seems strange that the utterances of this book, so thoroughly in accordance with accepted American ideas, should find any difficulty in obtaining publicity in England, yet so strong is the prejudice there still that its English publisher has cut out some of the best passages, including a portion of the preface, with some persiflage about 'the divine right of kings.'

43. William Dean Howells: unsigned review, *Harper's Magazine*

January 1890, lxxx, 319–21

Howells set the tone for much of the American criticism of *Connecticut Yankee* with this review, but many British critics did not share his opinion, and the *Spectator* (5 April 1890, lxiv, 484) was as disgusted by Howells' 'raptures over this sorry performance' as by the book itself.

In the first part of this 'Editor's Study', Howells praises Philip Gilbert Hamerton's *French and English: A Comparison* (Boston, 1891) as 'an admirable example' of 'the spirit of comity in international criticism'. The *Connecticut Yankee* review begins with a reference to Hamerton's book.

The chapter on Purity will most surprise Anglo-Saxon readers; but the chapter on Caste is of even more interest, and it is of almost unique value both in temper and in substance, for it describes without caricature, in a democratic commonwealth, and on the verge of the twentieth century, an ideal of life entirely stupid, useless, and satisfied, and quite that which Mark Twain has been portraying in his wonder-story of *A Connecticut Yankee at the Court of King Arthur*. Mr. Hamerton's French noble of the year 1890 is the same man essentially as any of that group of knights of the Round Table, who struck Mr. Clemens's delightful hero as white Indians. In his circle, achievement, ability, virtue, would find itself at the same disadvantage, without birth, as in that of Sir Launcelot. When you contemplate him in Mr. Hamerton's clear, passionless page, you feel that after all the Terror was perhaps too brief, and you find yourself sympathizing with all Mr. Clemens's robust approval of the Revolution.

Mr. Clemens, we call him, rather than Mark Twain, because we feel that in this book our arch-humorist imparts more of his personal quality than in anything else he has done. Here he is to the full the humorist, as we know him; but he is very much more, and his strong, indignant, often infuriate hate of injustice, and his love of equality, burn hot through the manifold adventures and experiences of the tale. What he thought about prescriptive right and wrong, we had partly learned in *The Prince and the Pauper*, and in *Huckleberry Finn*, but it is this last book which gives his whole mind. The elastic scheme of the romance allows it to play freely back and forward between the sixth century and the nineteenth century; and often while it is working the reader up to a blasting contempt of monarchy and aristocracy in King Arthur's time, the dates are magically shifted under him, and he is confronted with exactly the same principles in Queen Victoria's time. The delicious satire, the marvellous wit, the wild, free, fantastic humor are the colors of the tapestry, while the texture is a humanity that lives in every fibre. At every moment the scene amuses, but it is all the time an object-lesson in democracy. It makes us glad of our republic and our epoch; but it does not flatter us into a fond content with them; there are passages in which we see that the noble of Arthur's day, who battened on the blood and sweat of his bondmen, is one in essence with the capitalist of Mr. Harrison's day who grows rich on the labor of his underpaid wagemen. Our incomparable humorist, whose sarcasm is so pitiless to the greedy and superstitious clerics of Britain, is in fact of the same spirit and intention as those bishops who, true to their office, wrote the other day from New York to all their churches in the land:

It is a fallacy in social economics, as well as in Christian thinking, to look upon the labor of men and women and children as a commercial commodity, to be bought and sold as an inanimate and irresponsible thing. . . . The heart and soul of a man cannot be bought or hired in any market, and to act as if they were not needed in the doing of the world's vast work is as unchristian as it is unwise.

Mr. Clemens's glimpses of monastic life in Arthur's realm are true enough; and if they are not the whole truth of the matter, one may easily get it in some such book as Mr. Brace's *Gesta Christi*, where the full light of history is thrown upon the transformation of the world, if not the church, under the influence of Christianity. In the mean time, if any one feels that the justice done the churchmen of King Arthur's time is too much of one kind, let him turn to that heart-breaking scene where the brave monk stands with the mother and her babe on the scaffold, and execrates the hideous law which puts her to death for stealing enough to keep her from starving. It is one of many passages in the story where our civilization of to-day sees itself mirrored in the cruel barbarism of the past, the same in principle, and only softened in custom. With shocks of consciousness, one recognizes in such episodes that the laws are still made for the few against the many, and that the preservation of things, not men, is still the ideal of legislation. But we do not wish to leave the reader with the notion that Mr. Clemens's work is otherwise than obliquely serious. Upon the face of it you have a story no more openly didactic than *Don Quixote*, which we found ourselves more than once thinking of, as we read, though always with the sense of the kindlier and truer heart of our time. Never once, we believe, has Mark Twain been funny at the cost of the weak, the unfriended, the helpless; and this is rather more than you can say of Cid Hamet ben Engeli. But the two writers are of the same humorous largeness; and when the Connecticut man rides out at dawn, in a suit of Arthurian armor, and gradually heats up under the mounting sun in what he calls that stove; and a fly gets between the bars of his visor; and he cannot reach his handkerchief in his helmet to wipe the sweat from his streaming face; and at last when he cannot bear it any longer, and dismounts at the side of a brook, and makes the distressed damsel who has been riding behind him take off his helmet, and fill it with water, and pour gallon after gallon down the collar of his wrought-iron cutaway, you have a situation of as huge a grotesqueness as any that Cervantes conceived.

The distressed damsel is the Lady Corisande; he calls her Sandy, and he is troubled in mind at riding about the country with her in that way; for he is not only very doubtful that there is nothing in the castle where she says there are certain princesses imprisoned and persecuted by certain giants, but he feels that it is not quite nice: he is engaged to a young lady in East Hartford, and he finds Sandy a fearful bore at first, though in the end he loves and marries her, finding that he hopelessly antedates the East Hartford young lady by thirteen centuries. How he gets into King Arthur's realm, the author concerns himself as little as any of us do with the mechanism of our dreams. In fact the whole story has the lawless operation of a dream; none of its prodigies are accounted for: they take themselves for granted, and neither explain nor justify themselves. Here he is, that Connecticut man, foreman of one of the shops in Colt's pistol factory, and full to the throat of the invention and the self-satisfaction of the nineteenth century, at the court of the mythic Arthur. He is promptly recognized as a being of extraordinary powers, and becomes the king's right-hand man, with the title of The Boss; but as he has apparently no lineage or blazon, he has no social standing, and the meanest noble has precedence of him, just as would happen in England to-day. The reader may faintly fancy the consequences flowing from this situation, which he will find so vividly fancied for him in the book; but they are simply irreportable. The scheme confesses allegiance to nothing; the incidents, the facts follow as they will. The Boss cannot rest from introducing the apparatus of our time, and he tries to impart its spirit, with a thousand most astonishing effects. He starts a daily paper in Camelot; he torpedoes a holy well; he blows up a party of insolent knights with a dynamite bomb; when he and the king disguise themselves as peasants, in order to learn the real life of the people, and are taken and sold for slaves, and then sent to the gallows for the murder of their master, Launcelot arrives to their rescue with five hundred knights on bicycles. It all ends with the Boss's proclamation of the Republic after Arthur's death, and his destruction of the whole chivalry of England by electricity.

We can give no proper notion of the measureless play of an imagination which has a gigantic jollity in its feats, together with the tenderest sympathy. There are incidents in this wonder-book which wring the heart for what has been of cruelty and wrong in the past, and leave it burning with shame and hate for the conditions which are of like effect in the present. It is one of its magical properties that the fantastic fable of Arthur's far-off time is also too often the sad truth of ours; and the magician who makes us feel in it that we have just begun to know his power, teaches equality and fraternity in every phase of his phantas-magory.

He leaves, to be sure, little of the romance of the olden time, but no one is more alive to the simple, mostly tragic poetry of it; and we do not remember any book which imparts so clear a sense of what was truly heroic in it. With all his scorn of kingcraft, and all his ireful con-tempt of caste, no one yet has been fairer to the nobility of character which they cost so much too much to develop. The mainly ridiculous

Arthur of Mr. Clemens has his moments of being as fine and high as the Arthur of Lord Tennyson; and the keener light which shows his knights and ladies in their childlike simplicity and their innocent coarseness throws all their best qualities into relief. This book is in its last effect the most matter-of-fact narrative, for it is always true to human nature, the only truth possible, the only truth essential, to fiction. The humor of the conception and of the performance is simply immense; but more than ever Mr. Clemens's humor seems the sunny break of his intense conviction. We must all recognize him here as first of those who laugh, not merely because his fun is unrivalled, but because there is a force of right feeling and clear thinking in it that never got into fun before, except in *The Bigelow Papers*. Throughout, the text in all its circumstance and meaning is supplemented by the illustrations of an artist who has entered into the wrath and the pathos as well as the fun of the thing, and made them his own.

This kind of humor, the American kind, the kind employed in the service of democracy, of humanity, began with us a long time ago; in fact Franklin may be said to have torn it with the lightning from the skies. Some time, some such critic as Mr. T. S. Perry (if we ever have another such) will study its evolution in the century of our literature and civilization; but no one need deny himself meanwhile the pleasure we feel in Mr. Clemens's book as its highest development.

44. Desmond O'Brien: review, *Truth*

2 January 1890, xxvii, 25

The column in which this review appears is in the form of a letter to a Mr. Wyndham.

My dear Mr. Wyndham,—It has occurred to a good many prophets since Lord Lytton wrote *The Coming Race*,—

> To dip into the future, far as human eye could see,
> Show the vision of the world, and all the wonders that would be.

but it was reserved, I think, for Mark Twain to put on Hans Andersen's Goloshes of Happiness and go back to the past, carrying with him all the wonders of the present. *A Yankee at the Court of King Arthur* is a bizarre book, full of all kinds of laughable and delightful incongruities —the most striking of its incongruities, however, being unconscious, grim, and disenchanting. For Mark Twain, as he goes on, gets into a fury so ferocious (and natural) with the infernal oppression of the people by the Nobles, the King, and the Church that he passes in a sentence from laughing into raving at the 'good old times'; and, like Macbeth at sight of Banquo's ghost, he 'displaces the mirth' of the feast he had prepared for us. His fooling is admirable and his preaching is admirable, but they are mutually destructive. In every page he preaches pretty much what Richard Rumbold preached two centuries since—'I never could believe that Providence had sent a few men into the world ready booted and spurred to ride, and millions ready saddled and bridled to be ridden'—but Rumbold preached it from the most commanding of pulpits—the scaffold—whereas Mark Twain preaches it from the sawdust of the circus and in the intervals between a couple of jests or a couple of summersaults. But it is thoroughly sound doctrine, and is needed still so sorely in England and Ireland that it is ungracious to grumble at the mode of its delivery. It will reach a larger audience, and, perhaps, strike many of them more by its grotesque presentation than if the preacher wore a less bizarre garb than motley.

Ridentem dicere verum
Quid vetat?

Still, such frightful episodes as that of the woman who was burned to make a fire to warm a slave gang, or that of the hanging of the young mother—wife of the 'pressed' man-o'-war's man—with her baby at her breast (an incident, by the way, Mr. Mark Twain, not of the sixth century, but of the beginning of the nineteenth), freeze the laughter on our lips.

45. Unsigned review, *Speaker*

11 January 1890, i, 49–50

In the first half of this article, which was entitled 'Didactic Humourists', the critic had commented on Lewis Carroll's *Silvie and Bruno*. He appreciated that book's 'suitable nonsense for children' but deplored its 'polemics' and its 'love-story of the most fatuous sentimentality'.

English condemnation of *Connecticut Yankee* was general, but this attack on the illustrations by Dan Beard was most unusual.

Mark Twain is also somewhat affected by the Spirit of his Time, which is didactic; and by the Spirit of his Nation, which is inventive, but not refined. Mr. Lewis Carroll is far beyond Mr. Clemens in points of delicacy and taste; but it may be doubted whether any English author of repute would have tried to win a laugh by an irreverant treatment of the legend of the Holy Grail, as Mr. Clemens has done in *A Yankee at the Court of King Arthur*. It is quite certain that there are few English readers who will care to see the subject begrimed with prime American jests. Mr. Clemens used to be able to make us laugh without resorting to this easy and distressing method; in his last book he fails to make us laugh by any method, even the worst.

But Mr. Clemens is not only dull when he is offensive; he is perhaps even more dull when he is didactic. His views on the peerage, religious tolerance, republics, political economy, and the application of electricity to warfare, may be—some of them are—admirable. But they are out of place in a farcical book: the satire is not fresh; the information is second-hand or inaccurate; and the moral—or immoral, as the case may be—is clumsily enforced and unduly prominent. Tediousness is still further ensured by the length of the book. The joke is a long joke, and the author has not 'gompressed him.' It would be idle to point out that the book is not a sketch of the sixth century; because Mr. Clemens is careful to remove by a prefatory note any such objection. But he must not think that his confession of incompetence will make him seem any the less incompetent to the intelligent reader.

The illustrations to the book are occasionally allegorical, and remind us of the hieroglyphic which is to be found at the beginning of prophetic almanacks. In one of them the root of a tree is marked Religious Intolerence (sic); but the artist spells quite as well as he draws. They are very badly arranged; they seldom occur at the right place; and they break into text, making the task of reading very difficult. The task was hard enough, too, without that. We hope—we may even believe—that we have seen the artist at his worst; we certainly have not seen the author at his best.

Sometimes we think that we shall never see the author at his best again. American humour depended much upon quaint and happy phrase. When these phrases are repeated ad nauseam, their quaintness and happiness seem to disappear. But we have been saddened and depressed by reading two long and humorous books, and are, perhaps unduly inclined to be pessimistic. We had expected to laugh a little; and, instead of that, we have learned much—much that we knew before. And, after all, it must be easy for Mr. Clemens to do better; and we know why it must.

Anti - novee
Readylay
TW.
good see
the
essay !

46. Unsigned review, London *Daily Telegraph*

13 January 1890

The notion that Arthur would find much to criticize if he were to visit the United States in the late nineteenth century was revived briefly, and more moderately, by Andrew Lang (No. 39) a year after this review appeared.

At this holiday season, in books and newspapers, on stage and in drawing-room, the poet and the painter, the author, the actor, and the dramatist compete with one another to bring before young and old scenes and suggestions of beauty, heroism, purity, and truth. One writer is an exception. MARK TWAIN sets himself to show the seamy side of the legendary Round Table of King ARTHUR's time. He depicts all the vices of feudalism—the licentiousness of the nobles, their arrogance and insolence to the middle classes, their neglect of the poor, their hours of gluttony and idleness, varied by raids and brawls and riotous disorders. He describes how a Yankee visiting the Court uses modern inventions, defeats the best warriors, and redresses the wrongs of the poor. It is quite possible that a serious purpose underlies what otherwise seems a vulgar travesty. We have every regard for MARK TWAIN—a writer who has enriched English literature by admirable descriptions of boy life, and who in *The Prince and the Pauper* has given a vivid picture of mediæval times. A book, however, that tries to deface our moral and literary currency by bruising and soiling the image of King ARTHUR, as left to us by legend and consecrated by poetry, is a very unworthy production of the great humourist's pen. No doubt there is one element of wit—incongruity—in bringing a Yankee from Connecticut face to face with feudal knights; but sharp contrast between vulgar facts and antique ideas is not the only thing necessary for humour. If it were, then a travelling Cockney putting a flaming tie round the neck of the 'Apollo Belvidere,' or sticking a clay pipe between the lips of the 'Venus de Medici,' would be a matter-of-fact MARK TWAIN, and as much entitled to respect. Burlesque and travesty are satire brought down to the meanest capacity, and they have their proper province when pretentious falsehoods put on the masks of solemnity and truth. Stilted tragedies, artificial melodramas, unnatural acting, are properly held up to ridicule on the stage or in parodies. The mannerisms of a popular writer like CARLYLE, BROWNING, or even TENNYSON, may, through caricature, be good-humouredly exposed; but an attack on the ideals associated with King ARTHUR is a coarse pandering to that passion for irreverence which is at the basis of a great deal of Yankee wit. To make a jest of facts, phrases, or words—Scriptural, heroic, or legendary—that are held in awe or reverence by other men is the open purpose of every witling on a Western print, who endeavours to follow in the footsteps of ARTEMUS WARD, BRET HARTE, and MARK TWAIN. They may finally be successful enough to destroy their own trade. They now live by shocking decent people who still retain love for the Bible, HOMER, SHAKESPEARE, SCOTT, and TENNYSON; but when they have thoroughly trained a rising generation to respect nothing their irreverence will fall flat.

The stories of King ARTHUR that have come down to us represent in legendary form not any historical fact, but an ideal of kingship and knighthood which had birth in the hearts and aspirations of mediæval men. This was their ideal of what a King amongst his warriors ought to be, and the beautiful image has fired the thoughts and purified the imagination of millions of men and women for many generations. Will this shrine in human souls be destroyed because a Yankee scribe chooses to fling pellets of mud upon the high altar? The instincts of the past and the genius of TENNYSON have consecrated for ever 'the goodliest fellowship of famous knights Whereof this world holds record.' The Round Table is dissolved, but we can still 'delight our souls with talk of knightly deeds,' as they at Camelot in the storied past. We can still apply the image of the ideal knight as a criterion of modern worth. King ARTHUR swore each of his followers to 'reverence his conscience as his King, To ride abroad redressing human wrongs, To speak no slander, no, nor listen to it, To honour his own word as if his GOD'S, To lead sweet lives in purest chastity. To love one maiden only, cleave to her, And worship her by years of noble deeds.' Such an oath presented to a modern Yankee would seem to convey in almost every phrase a covert insult to American institutions. In a land where commercial fraud and industrial adulteration are fine arts we had better omit appeals to 'conscience.' The United States are not likely to 'ride abroad redressing human wrong'—as they never gave a dollar or a man to help Greece, Poland, Hungary, or Italy in their struggles to be free. 'To speak no slander, no, nor listen to it,' would utterly uproot America's free press—based to a great extent on scandalous personalities. Loving one maiden only and cleaving to her must seem too 'high-toned' in the States, where there are many facilities for ready divorce. So far MARK TWAIN is right as a Western iconoclast to pelt with sarcasm ideals which are not included in the Constitution or customs of the United States. Yet, in spite of all that America has done or can do to deface images of self-sacrifice and beauty, there are chosen souls in her own borders who have fulfilled the heroic ideals of the olden time. The Abolitionists of New England encountered great perils when they first set out to redress the great human wrong of negro slavery, and they fought as noble a contest against organised iniquity as any knight of ARTHUR's Court. They faced political obloquy, mob violence, loss of limb, sometimes of life, and the falling away of friends and relatives, because they had inherited the old instinct of knights, to lead lives of duty to their fellow-men. They were jeered and derided by the MARK TWAINS of the day, but their foresight was proved at the end of the war, when the world recognised the two-fold result, 'a nation saved, a race delivered.' What, too, would have been the fate of the Republic if no ideal image of their country shone before the souls of the men who died to save the Union? Coward souls at the North said, 'It will cost much money and many lives to re-conquer the South: let them go; let the Republic break up; what is a country to us?' but a chivalry that came down from British ancestors animated the men who followed GRANT, and they kept to their high purpose until the field was won. Where was MARK TWAIN then? Why did he not satirise the patriotism that would not let a Republic be mutilated? Why did he not sneer at Yankee reverence for a paper Constitution not a hundred years old? Why did he not sing the glories of trade as better than any preservation of the Union or liberation of negro slaves?

Even if we look at the real feudalism idealised in the legends of King ARTHUR, it was not all evil. No doubt there were licentious nobles at all times, and there were great landlords who were occasionally cruel to the peasants in their fields. The change to modern times, however, is not all a gain. A great lord of old held his possessions by 'suit and service'; he was bound to follow his King to the wars. Now he owns his broad lands free of duty, and may live a life of shameful luxury when he likes. The peasant of the olden times was not always in distress. The country was thinly peopled; he had as much land as he wanted; the woods were full of wild game, the streams of fish; except on occasions of rare famine he was fed well. Such a thing as an eviction was unknown, and for one good reason—the lord was not only bound to serve the King, but to bring men for his army; consequently he had an interest in raising on his estates a body of faithful followers. The modern landlord drives his peasants into the towns, where, uncared for by him, they degenerate and die in slums. We must remember, too, that the vices of the past were characteristic of rough times; they were the sins of brutality, not of fraud. A bad knight of the feudal age wronged a maid or widow, and refused redress; but what are the offences of a commercial age? In America and in England, to a lesser extent, financial swindling is elaborately organised. The wicked man of modern times does not couch his lance against the weak or lowly; he sends out a prospectus. In twelve months the widow and orphan are breadless; the promoter and the financier have added another twenty thousand to their stores. Were King ARTHUR to descend in New York to-morrow he would make for Wall-street, where he would find a host of men whose word is as good, and as bad, as their bond —railway schemers who plunder the shareholders of a continent, and are ever intent by every device of falsehood and of plot to deceive each other and to defraud the public. Talk of the inequality of man! King ARTHUR and the meanest menial in his halls were nearer to each other in conditions of life than the tramp in the slums of New York and the ASTORS, VANDERBILTS, and JAY GOULDS who have piled up millions extracted from the pockets of less successful men. The Republic is a 'land of liberty,' yet its commerce, its railways, and its manufactures are in the hands of a few cliques of almost irresponsible capitalists, who control tariffs, markets, and politics in order that they may be enriched, to the disadvantage of the masses. Which, then, is to be most admired—the supremacy of a knight or the success of a financier? Under which King will the Americans serve—the ideal or the real? Will they own allegiance to King ARTHUR or JAY GOULD?

47. Unsigned review, *Scots Observer*

18 January 1890

The *Scots Observer* was edited by William Ernest Henley, who may have been the author of this review (see Nos. 20, 31 and 34).

Memorials of a Southern Planter (Baltimore, 1887) was highly praised by W. E. Gladstone, 'the Sage of Hawarden', in *Nineteenth Century* (December 1889, xxvi, 984-6). His review concludes with the words, 'Let no man say, with this book before him, that the age of chivalry has gone, or that Thomas Dabney was not worthy to sit with Sir Percival at the "table round" of King Arthur.' It was William Dean Howells who in his review of the *Yankee* (No. 43) referred to Mark Twain as 'our arch humorist'. His name has apparently been mysteriously conflated with that of M. A. de Wolfe Howe here. 'Hamibel Chollop' is Hannibal Chollop, an aggressively provincial character, who is strongly prejudiced against England, in *Martin Chuzzlewit*.

Mrs. Smedes' *A Southern Planter* and Mark Twain's new lapse into Ibsenity and the cultus of the thesis, *A Yankee at the Court of King Arthur*, appear about the same time, and both are pretty sure to be widely read in Britain: the latter because Mark Twain is currently believed to have been once a writer of funny books, and the former because the Sage of Hawarden has blessed it. He is not always happy, is the Sage of Hawarden, in his selection of books to dignify with his *imprimatur*, having a natural and peculiar leaning to religious fiction; but in commending *A Southern Planter* to British readers he has done well. Mrs. Smedes' book and Mark Twain's have at first sight little enough in common but their transatlantic origin; but that view is naught. Nothing could be further removed from the blatant frivolity of the Yankee exwag—'our arch-humourist,' as Mr. de Howells styles him in the current *Harper*, not without a hint of unconscious pathos—than the record of a noble life which Mrs. Smedes has written with such simple piety; and had Mr. Clemens been content to write about the court of King Arthur as he wrote about Arkansas and the Mexican Plug no one would have mentioned the two in the same breath.

For in those days Mr. Clemens lived to make the light-hearted laugh; and his life was a success. But he has exhausted his vein, and with faded cap and fools' bells jangled has got bewrayed with seriousness and bedevilled with a purpose. He treats you to a 'lecture' in dispraise of monarchical institutions and religious establishments as the roots of all evil, and in praise of Yankee 'cuteness and Wall Street chicanery as compared to the simple fidelity and devotion of the knightly ideal. The key to this precious piece of apostolics is contained in a frontispiece where the Supreme Yank, the Connecticut man in a state of heroism, the Bagman *in excelsis*, is pictured in the act of tickling the nose of the British Lion with a switch. Now the life of Thomas Dabney—Virginian aristocrat and slave-owner—is an effective commentary on such violent vulgarity. He was full of just those qualities which make the memory of King Arthur fragrant. The mainspring of his life was not the almighty dollar but *noblesse oblige*. Amid the prosperity of his plantation times, as amid the havoc wrought on his and his country's fortunes by the war, his supreme purpose was to fulfil the honourable ideal of a gentleman. Such an ideal is no doubt inconsistent with the democratic notions of the superior Yank; but it is not the least precious heritage in the world's history for all that, and Mr. Clemens stamps himself when he makes the bagman's mistake of bedaubing it with cheap wit. It is the ideal which in English literature animated Sir Roger de Coverley, and Mr. Allworthy, and Colonel Newcome, of whose virtues, indeed, the life of Thomas Dabney was in many ways a realisation. Mrs. Smedes has done her part of the work very well, except that she might have cut down the correspondences with advantage. As for Mark Twain, he has turned didactic, and being ignorant is also misleading and offensive. His method, which was that of Hamibel Chollop, consists in attributing every social, political, and economic evil to the Crown and the Church. That slavery and Protection have flourished under American republican institutions does not hinder the ingenious creature from attributing their existence to monarchy and what he calls the Established Roman Catholic Church. To him that is decorous and just. But then he is a bagman with a thesis, and his notions of justice and decorum are of those that commend themselves to none but renegade Europians—Europians of the stamp of Mr. Andrew Carnegie. To add to all this that Mr. W. de Howells has taken occasion to contrast him and his achievement in bagmanising with Cervantes and *Don Quixote*, somewhat to the disadvantage of the latter, is to begin to pity the poor devil. After all, he knows no better; after all, he is the parent of Huck Finn and Jim the Nigger and the genuine Mexican Plug and the incomparable Blue Jay. What should he do where Arthur first in court began whose proper place is the Capitol, or Tammany Hall, or the shadow of the Saint Louis Bridge? What should he do with a thesis? What he really wants is a wooden nutmeg or a razor-strop.

48. William T. Stead: unsigned review, *Review of Reviews* (London)

February 1890, i, 144–56

William Thomas Stead (1849–1912), founder and editor of the *Review of Reviews*, rose to prominence while editing the *Pall Mall Gazette* (1883–9). Always an iconoclast and crusader, he campaigned, often successfully, against social and political evils which he felt were ignored by government and the press. In 1890, Harold Frederic said that Stead, who had just started the *Review of Reviews*, 'between the years 1884 and 1888 came nearer to governing Great Britain than any other one man in the kingdom' (quoted in Frederic Whyte, *The Life of W. T. Stead*, I, 114).

This review, entitled 'Mark Twain's New Book; A Satirical Attack on English Institutions', was followed by ten full pages of extracts from the book.

In selecting as the Novel of the Month Mark Twain's new story, *A Yankee at the Court of King Arthur*, I am aware that I expose myself to many remonstrances. There is a certain profanation in the subject, and withal a certain dulness in its treatment. It is not a novel; it is a ponderous political pamphlet, and so forth and so forth. Nevertheless, to those who endeavour to understand what the mass of men who speak English are thinking, as opposed to those who merely care about what they think they ought to be thinking, this book of Mark Twain's is one of the most significant of our time. It is notable for its faults quite as much as for its virtues, and for the irreverent audacity of its original conception as much as for the cumbrous and strenuous moralising which makes it at times more like one of Jonathan Edwards' sermons than a mere buoyant and farcical bubbling up of American humour.

Mark Twain is one of the few American authors whose writings are popular throughout the English-speaking world. Our superfine literary men of culture who pooh-pooh the rough rude vigour of the American humorist represent a small clique. Mark Twain gets 'directlier at the heart' of the masses than any of the blue-china set of nimminy-pimminy criticasters. In his own country, if we may judge from the remarks in the January *Harper*, *A Yankee at the Court of King Arthur* has been received with an enthusiasm which it has hitherto failed to evoke on this side of the Atlantic. We read there that

the delicious satire, the marvellous wit, the wild, free, fantastic humour, are the colours of the tapestry, while the texture is a humanity that lives in every fibre. We can give no proper notion of the measureless play of an imagination which has a gigantic jollity in its feats, together with the tenderest sympathy. The humour of the conception and of the performance is simply immense; but more than ever Mr. Clemens's humour seems the sunny break of his intense conviction.

What a contrast this to the frigid condemnation of the *Speaker*: 'In his last book Mr. Clemens fails to make us laugh by any method, even the worst. He is not only dull when he is offensive, but perhaps even more dull when he is didactic.' Yet I make free to say that the vote of the mass of English people would be on the side of the American and against the English critic. For what our critical class has failed to appreciate is that the Education Act has turned out and is turning out millions of readers who are much more like the Americans in their tastes, their ideas, and their sympathies than they are to the English of the cultured, pampered, and privileged classes. The average English-speaking man is the product of the common school in America, of the public elementary school in Britain and Australia. His literary taste is not classical but popular. He prefers Longfellow to Browning, and as a humorist he enjoys Mark Twain more than all the dainty wits whose delicately flavoured quips and cranks delight the boudoir and the drawing-room. This may be most deplorable from the point of view of the supercilious æsthetes, but the fact in all its brutality cannot be too frankly recognised.

Another circumstance which gives significance to the book is the fact that it is the latest among the volumes whereby Americans are revolutionising the old country. The two books which have given the greatest impetus to the social-democratic movement in recent years have both come to us from America. Henry George's land nationalisation theories were scouted by the superfine, but they have gained a firm hold of the public mind. His book has circulated everywhere, and is still circulating. Of another kind, but operating in the same direction, is Edward Bellamy's *Looking Backwards*, which has supplied our people with a clearly written-out apocalypse of the new heaven and the new earth that are to come after the acceptance of the Evangel of Socialism. Mark Twain's book is a third contribution in the same direction. His Yankee is a fierce and furious propagandist of anti-monarchical and aristocratic ideas. Under the veil of sarcasms levelled at King Arthur we see a genial mockery of the British monarchy of to-day, with its Royal grants and all its semi-feudal paraphernalia. Nor is it only at British abuses Mark Twain levels his burly jests. He thwacks the protectionist American as readily as the aristocratic Briton. There is something infinitely significant in the very form of his satire. If there is nothing sacred to a sapper, neither can there be anything sacred to a descendant of the men of the *Mayflower*, who has all the fervour of Mr. Zeal-for-the-Lord-Busy and the confident, complacent assurance of Sam Slick, who dismissed unceremoniously the authority of Plato or Aristotle with the observation that we need not heed what they said as there were no railways in their times. Here is the New England Democrat and Puritan as passionately sympathetic with the common man as the nobles and knights whom he scourges were sympathetic with men of their order, determined to avenge the injustice of centuries and by holding the mirror up to fact to punish the chivalric age by showing how it treated the common man. It is not longer enough to judge systems of to-day by the effect which they have upon Hodge the ploughman and Bottom the weaver; the war must be carried into the enemy's camp, the verdict of history must be reversed, and all our ideals of the past transformed in the light of this new and imperious interrogation.—The labouring man, what did that age or that institution make of him?

Tennyson sang the idyls of the King, and as long as the world lasts Sir Thomas Malory's marvellous old Romance will fill the hearts and imaginations of men with some far-off reflection of the splendours and the glories of that child-like age. But truly he sang 'the old order changeth, giving place to the new,' of which can we have a more notable and even brutal illustration than the apparition of this vulgar Yankee realist, with his telephones and his dynamite, his insufferable slang and his infinite self-conceit, in the midst of King Arthur's Court, applying to all the knighthood of the Round Table the measure of his yard-stick,—the welfare of the common man? It is the supreme assertion of the law of numbers, of the application of the patent arithmetical proposition that ten is more than one, to the problems of politics and of history.

Tennyson himself, in the 'Last Tournament,' supplied a vivid picture, which may well serve as a frontispiece of Mark Twain's vision:—

> Into the hall swaggered, his visage ribbed
> From ear to ear with dog whip-weals, his nose
> Bridge-broken, one eye out and one hand off,
> And one with shattered fingers dangling, lame;
> A churl, to whom indignantly the king,
> 'My churl, for whom Christ died; what evil beast
> Hath drawn his claws athwart thy face? or fiend,
> Man, was it who marr'd heaven's image in thee thus?'

The churl for whom Christ died is the centre of Mark Twain's story, which is a long and a passionate attempt to suggest that the evil beast who marred the visage of the poor wretch was the three-headed chimera of Monarchy, Aristocracy, and Church. There is much strange misreading of history caused by the extent to which Mark Twain has allowed the abuses of institutions to obscure their use.

49. Unsigned review, *Athenaeum*

15 February 1890, no. 3251, 211

A Yankee at the Court of King Arthur, by Mark Twain (Samuel L. Clemens), published by Messrs. Chatto & Windus, is a rather laborious piece of fun with a sort of purpose in it. One of the illustrations, early in the volume, represents a Yankee tickling with a straw the nose of a gigantic statue of a lion, and indicates the general nature of the serious purport of the 525 pages of that very American kind of American humour of which 'Mark Twain' is the chief master. Laughing at British institutions, and showing that the good old times were uncommonly bad times for the people, and that not a few of the historical privileges which still exist do not suit the ideas of the great republic of the West, afford a good deal of harmless amusement and opportunities for very trite comment. It is a mistake to decide that ridicule cast upon the story of Arthur is an offence in any way other than in the matter of taste in jokes. Sir Thomas Malory and Lord Tennyson will survive. Masterpieces will stand any amount of parody. 'The Burial of Sir John Moore' and Gray's 'Elegy' are just as impressive and admirable as if they had not been parodied with all sorts of jocularity and ribaldry scores of times. One may easily read Mark Twain's book without any ill will; but it is a harder task to read it with sustained merriment. By writing so much the author has shown how mechanical his method really is, and, with all respect for the cleverness of the writers of Gaiety burlesques, one doubts if anybody could be amused by reading one of them if it ran to five hundred pages. That is, however, the sort of task which Mark Twain offers to his readers. One may be pardoned for confessing that the task has proved too severe. A trial of several chapters taken at random shows that the author is still as fresh as ever in his racy contrasts between things ancient and modern, and as quaint in his droll expressions. He can raise a laugh once, twice, or even twenty times, but not a thousand.

50. Unsigned review, Boston *Literary World*

15 February 1890, xxi, 52–3

This most unfavourable American review of *Connecticut Yankee* reflects a Bostonian aristocratic tradition as Sylvester Baxter's review in the Boston Sunday *Herald* (No. 42) reflects the American proletarian view.

Mark Twain's latest book, which his publishers have brought out in a handsome volume, seems to us the poorest of all his productions thus far. The conceit of taking a Yankee of this generation of telephones and the electric light back to King Arthur's Court may please some minds, if presented in a story of moderate length, but there can be few who will really enjoy it when long-drawn out to the extent of nearly six hundred pages. Whatever value Mr. Clemens might have incidentally imparted to his burlesque by giving something like a correct picture of the customs of the time in which the mythical King flourished is entirely absent. He has crowded into his picture a great number of episodes illustrating 'ungentle laws and customs' which are historical, indeed; but he says:

> It is not pretended that these laws and customs existed in England in the sixth century; no, it is only pretended that, inasmuch as they existed in the English and other civilizations of far later times, it is safe to consider that it is no libel upon the sixth century to suppose them to have been in practice in that day also. One is quite justified in inferring that wherever one of these laws or customs was lacking in that remote time, its place was competently filled by a worse one.

Mr. Clemens' method of writing history would justify him in picturing the Connecticut of the seventeenth century as afflicted with loose divorce customs and great corruption at the polls—or something worse—simply because these are vices of the nineteenth century! To crowd into a representation of one age the social evils of all its successors known to us, and to omit those special redeeming features of the time which made life tolerable, is a very irrational proceeding.

The serious aim under Mark Twain's travesty is the glorification of American Protestant democracy. The effort fails through the extreme partiality of the procedure. Even a Mark Twain, the persistent teacher of irreverence for great men and great events, should have some little respect left for fair play. Mr. Clemens' previous books have been bad enough in their strong encouragement of one of the worst tendencies in a democratic State, the inclination to sheer flippancy and unmanly irreverence in the face of the natural sanctities of private life and the grand heroisms of human history. But this volume goes much further in its endeavor to belittle a century surrounded with romantic light by men of later times, who thus fell back upon poetry as a slight relief to the hard prose of their actual lot. A buffoon, like the hero of this tale, playing his contemptible tricks where Sir Thomas Malory has trod with a noble teaching of knightly courtesy, and uttering his witless jokes where Tennyson has drawn so many a high moral of true gentleness, is a sorry spectacle. It is not calculated to make a reflecting person proud of a shallow and self-complacent generation which can enjoy such so-called humor.

The one consolation to be derived from this melancholy product of the American mind in the ninth decade of the nineteenth century is that, equally in its serious and in its jesting parts, it must bring about a healthy reaction in some of its admiring readers because it overshoots the mark; because its history is perverse, in its one-sided accumulation of evils; and because its humor will be wearisome in the extreme when its falsity is seen.

When Mr. Clemens relates his Life on the Mississippi with characteristic American exaggeration, we cannot fail to laugh and become friends. But when he prostitutes his humorous gift to the base uses of historical injustice, democratic bigotry, Protestant intolerance, and nineteenth-century vainglory, we must express the very sincere animosity we feel at such a performance. If anything could be less of a credit to our literature than the matter of this book, it certainly is the illustrations which disfigure it. A Protestant of the Protestants himself, the writer of this review cannot refrain from thus freeing his soul in the cause of literary decency when the Roman Catholic Church, that is to say the Christian Church in one of the noblest periods of its history, is thus grossly assailed by the writer and the illustrator of this tiresome travesty.

51. Unsigned review, *Plumas National*

5 July 1890, 2

The *Plumas National* was a newspaper published in Quincy, California, a small town about seventy miles from Virginia City, Nevada, where Mark Twain first became a journalist. This review suggests the light in which *Connecticut Yankee* was seen by one part, at least, of the American reading public. Robert G. Ingersoll (1833–99), a politician and nationally famous orator, was known as 'The Great Agnostic'.

Mark Twain has never written anything brighter and wittier than *A Yankee in King Arthur's Court*, his latest book, which is now issued with all the advantages of illustrations that add zest to the great humorist's fun and satire. The book is as able and original as *The Innocents Abroad* or *Adventures of Huckleberry Finn*, while it bids fair to be fully as popular with the American public as either of these books. It is one long satire on modern England and Englishmen, under the clever guise of an attempt to picture the England of the sixth century and of Arthurian legend. It is said that Mark wrote the story about seven years ago, but about the time he had completed it he paid a visit to England and was received so handsomely that he didn't have the heart to print his bitter satire, that in places reminds one of Swift. Mark Twain has come up from the people. He is American to the backbone, and the assumption of natural superiority by titled English aristocrats and the terrible wrongs inflicted on the working people, evidently galled him beyond endurance. He has taken his revenge in this volume, and a thorough going over it is, for he has mercilessly flayed the follies, vices, cruelties and false pretensions of English royalty and aristocracy.

A mere statement of the plot of the story shows the ample field it gives for 'most excellent fooling.' Mark pretends to find a Connecticut Yankee in London who recalls his experiences in the age of King Arthur. The story is told with great realistic effect, and the extraordinary contrasts of modern slang and archaic speech, of nineteenth-century progress and sixth-century superstition, when developed by a master of the art of humor, are inexpressibly droll. The Yankee is captured by one of the Knights of the Round Table and brought to the court, where he is about to be executed as a curious monster, when he chances to remember that an eclipse occurs on that day. So he adopts the device which Rider Haggard has used with so much effect in his African romances, and threatens to destroy the sun unless he is released. The sun's disk begins to be obscured and before the eclipse is ended he has been made a great noble, Sir Boss, with ample revenue, and the office of chief adviser of the King. Then begin contests with jealous knights and especially bouts of witchcraft with Merlin, in which the famous magician is completely vanquished by modern science.

Mark's picture of the deficiencies of the Arthurian court in little conveniences is very droll. 'No soap, no matches, no looking glass, except a metal one about as powerful as a pail of water, and not a chromo. I had been used to chromos for years and I saw now that without my suspecting it a passion for art had got worked into the fabric of my being and had become a part of me.' And then the make-shifts for light—'a bronze dish half full of boarding-house butter with a blazing rag floating in it was the thing that produced what is regarded as a light.'

And here is the picture of the people of England at the time of King Arthur, which, curiously enough, is as applicable to the great body of Englishmen of to-day as to those of thirteen centuries ago:

[quotes ch. 8 'Well, it was' to 'their own exertions'.]

These extracts give a fair idea of the sarcasm which the author heaps upon England. He is in dead earnest when he gets to tilting at the divine right of kings and aristocrats to make the people slave and sweat blood for them, but he unbends when he deals with chivalry. He has no more reverence for the beautiful legends which Tennyson has embalmed in his *Idyles of the King* than Bob Ingersoll has for St. Peter's or the best works of some of the old masters. Some of his caricature is very funny, as, for instance, this bit about the search for the Holy Grail:

[quotes ch. 9 'The boys all took' to 'but no money'.]

In the last chapters the author puts no bridle on his extravagance, and the book ends in scenes of warfare that will make Haggard green with envy. The illustrations by Dan Beard are full of humor, and bring out the fun of the story. The book is finely printed and bound and lavishly illustrated. For sale by subscription only by A. L. Bancroft & Co., 132 Post Street, sole agents for the coast.

52. H. C. Vedder: article, New York *Examiner*

6 April 1893

Henry C. Vedder (1853–1935), a clergyman, journalist and church historian, served on the staff of the New York *Examiner*, a leading Baptist newspaper, from 1876 to 1894. He was professor of church history at Crozier Theological Seminary from 1895 to 1926.

This article is one of a series on 'Living American Writers', which, after newspaper publication, was issued as *American Writers of To-Day* in 1894.

The immediate and permanent popularity of *Innocents Abroad* is not wonderful; it is a book of even greater merit than the public gave it credit for possessing. It was read and enjoyed for its fun, and though nearly twenty-five years have passed it is still a funny book, whether one reads it now for the first or the forty-first time. But underneath the fun was an earnest purpose that the great mass of readers failed to see at the time, and even yet imperfectly appreciate. This purpose was to tell, not how an American ought to feel on seeing the sights of the Old World, but how he actually does feel if he is honest with himself. From time immemorial, books of travel had been written by Americans purporting to record their experiences, but really telling only what the writers thought they might, could, would, or should have experienced. These are the kind of travellers that are seen everywhere in Europe, Murray or Baedeker constantly in hand and carefully conned, lest they dilate with the wrong emotion—or, what is almost as bad, fail to dilate with the proper emotion at the right instant. For sham emotion, sham love of art, sham adventures, Mark Twain had no tolerance, and he gave these shams no quarter in his book. 'Cervantes smiled Spain's chivalry away' is a fine phrase of Byron's, which, like most of Byron's fine phrases, is not true. What Cervantes did was to 'smile away' the ridiculous romances of chivalry—chivalry had been long dead in his day—the impossible tales of knightly adventure, out-doing the deeds of the doughty Baron Munchausen, that were pro-duced in shoals by the penny-a-liners of his time. Not since this feat of Cervantes has a wholesome burst of merriment cleared the air more effectually, or banished a greater humbug from literature than when *The Innocents Abroad* laughed away the sentimental, the romantic book of travels. Mark Twain, perhaps, erred somewhat on the other side. His bump of reverence must be admitted to be practically non-existent. He sees so clearly the humbug and pretence and superstition beneath things conventionally held to be sacred, that he sometimes fails to see that they are not all sham, and that there is really something sacred there. He was throughout the book too hard-headed, too realistic, too unimpressionable, too frankly Philistine, for entire truth-fulness and good taste; but it was necessary to exaggerate something on this side in order to furnish an antidote to mawkish sentimentality. His lesson would have been less effective if it had not been now and then a trifle bitter to the taste. Since that time travellers have actually dared to tell the truth—or shall we say that they have been afraid to scribble lies so recklessly? Whichever way one looks at the matter, there is no doubt that American literature, so far as it has dealt with Europe and things European, has been more natural, wholesome, and self-respecting since the tour of this shrewd Innocent.

The same earnestness of purpose underlies much else that Mark Twain has written, especially *The Prince and the Pauper*, and *A Yankee at King Arthur's Court*. The careless reader no doubt sees nothing in the first of these books but a capital tale for boys. He cannot help seeing that, for it is a story of absorbing interest, accurate in its historical setting, and told in remarkably good English. In the latter book he will no doubt discover nothing more than rollicking humor and a burlesque of *Morte d'Arthur*. This is to see only what lies on the surface of these volumes, without comprehending their aim or sympathizing with the spirit. Not the old prophet of Chelsea himself was a more honest and inveterate hater of shams than Mark Twain. Much of the glamor and charm of chivalry is as unreal as the tinsel splendors of the stage—to

study history is like going behind the scenes of a theatre, a disenchant-
ment as thorough as it is speedy. *Morte d'Arthur* and Tennyson's *Idylls
of the King* present to the unsophisticated a very beautiful, but a very
shadowy and unsubstantial picture of Britain thirteen centuries ago.
Even in these romances a glimpse of the real sordidness and squalor
and poverty of the people may now and then be caught amid all the
pomp and circumstance of chivalry. Nobody has had the pitiless
courage heretofore to let the full blaze of the sun into these regions
where the lime-light of fancy has had full sway, that we might see
what the berouged heroes and heroines actually are.

But Mark Twain has one quality to which Carlyle never attained.
Joined to his hatred of shams is a hearty and genuine love of liberty.
His books could never have been written by one not born in the
United States. His love of liberty is characteristic in its manifestation.
In a Frenchman it would have found vent in essays on the text of
liberté, fraternité, equalité, but eloquent writing about abstractions is not
the way in which an American finds voice for his sentiments. Mark
Twain's love of liberty is shown unostentatiously, incidentally as it
were, in his sympathy for, and championship of, the down-trodden
and oppressed. He says to us, 'Here, you have been admiring the age of
chivalry; this is what your King Arthur, your spotless Galahad, your
valiant Launcelot made of the common people. Spending their lives
in the righting of imaginary wrongs, they were perpetuating with all
their energy a system of the most frightful cruelty and oppression.
Cease admiring these heroes, and execrate them as they deserve.' This,
to be sure, is a one-sided view, but it is one that we need to take in
endeavoring to comprehend the England of King Arthur. There is no
danger that we shall overlook the romantic and picturesque view while
Malory and Tennyson are read, but it is wholesome for us sometimes
to feel the weight of misery that oppressed all beneath the privileged
classes of England's days of chivalry.

Except in the two books that may be called historic romances, Mark
Twain has been a consistent realist. He was probably as innocent ot
intent to belong to the realistic school when he began writing as
Molière's old gentleman had all his life been of the intent to talk prose.
He was realistic because it came sort o' nateral to him, as a Yankee
would say. His first books were the outcome of his personal experiences. These were many and varied, for few men have knocked about
the world more and viewed life from so many points. Bret Harte has
written of life on the Pacific coast with greater appreciation of its

romantic and picturesque features, but one suspects with considerable less truthfulness in detail. The shady heroes and heroines of Bret Harte's tales are of a quality that suggests an amalgam of Byron and Smollett; they smack strongly of Bowery melodrama. Mark Twain's *Roughing It* is a wholesome book, and as accurate in its details as a photograph, but there is nothing romantic or thrilling about it.

It is in the Mississippi Valley, however, that our author finds himself most at home, not only because his knowledge of it is more comprehensive and minutely accurate, but because it is a more congenial field. Mark Twain understands California, admires it even, but he loves the great river and the folk who dwell alongside it. He is especially happy in his delineation of the boy of this region. If ever any writer understood boy nature in general, from A to izzard, the name of that writer is Mark Twain. He has explored all its depths and shallows, and in his characters of Tom Sawyer and Huckleberry Finn he has given us such a study of the American boy as will be sought in vain elsewhere. He has done more than this: he has given us a faithful picture, painfully realistic in details, of the ante-bellum social condition of the Mississippi Valley. The books, considered from any other point of view, are trash or worse. Their realism redeems them from what would otherwise be utter worthlessness, and gives them a certain value.

One ought also to mention the value of this writer's short stories. He has not done as much work in this line as one wishes he had, in view of the great merit of what he has written. Most of these stories are humorous in their fundamental conception, or have a vein of humor running through them, but they are not, for the most part, boisterously funny. They range in style from the avowedly funny tale of 'The Jumping Frog of Caleveras' to the surface sobriety of 'The £1,000,000 Bank Note.' In the composition of the short story, Mark Twain is so evidently perfecting his art, as to warrant one in hazarding the prediction that much of his best work in future is likely to be done along this line.

Even our English cousins—as a rule, not too lenient in their judgments of kin across the sea—admit that American humor has a distinct flavor. Not only so, they also admit that this flavor is delightful. To their tastes there is something wild and gamy about American humor, a 'tang' that is both a new sensation and a continuous source of enjoyment. British commendation of American humor, however, is not always as discriminating as it is hearty. We must allow Englishmen the praise of having been prompt to appreciate the humor of Artemus

Ward; but of late years they seem impervious to American humor, except of one type—that which depends for its effect on exaggeration. Exaggeration is, no doubt, one legitimate species of humor. The essence of humor lies in the perception of incongruity, and the effect of incongruity may be produced by exaggeration. This is the more effectively done if the style is 'dry'; the writer must give no sign, until the very end (if even there), that he does not take himself seriously; the narrator must not by a tone of voice or change of facial expression betray any lack of exact veracity in his tale, or the effect is measurably lost. Mark Twain has frequently shown himself to be master of this style of humor. He can invent the most tremendous absurdities, and tell them with such an air of seriousness as must frequently deceive the unwary.

But this is not, as English readers mistakably imagine, the best type of American humor in general, or even the humor in which Mark Twain reaches his highest level. Exaggeration is comparatively cheap humor. Anybody can lie, and the kind of Mark Twain's humor most admired abroad is simply the lie of circumstance minus the intent to deceive. It is morally innocuous, therefore, but it is bad art. No doubt it is frequently successful in provoking laughter, but the quality of humor is not to be gauged by the loudness of the hearers' guffaws. The most delightful fun is that which at most provokes no more than a quiet smile, but is susceptible of repeated enjoyment when the most hilarious joke has become a 'chestnut.' To borrow a metaphor from science, humor is the electricity of literature, but in its finest manifestation it is not static but dynamic. The permanent charm of humorous writing is generally in inverse ratio to its power to incite boisterous merriment when first read. The joker who gives one a pain in the side soon induces 'that tired feeling' that is fatal to continued interest. It is Mark Twain's misfortune at present to be appreciated abroad mainly for that which is ephemeral in his writings. His broad humanity, his gift of seeing far below the surface of life, his subtle comprehension of human nature, and his realistic method, are but dimly apprehended by those Britons who go off in convulsions of laughter the moment his name is mentioned. A false standard of what is truly 'American' has been set up abroad, and only what conforms to that standard wins admiration. For that reason British readers have gone wild over Bret Harte and Joaquin Miller, while they neglected Bryant and Holmes, and for a time even Lowell, on the ground that the latter were 'really more English than American, you know.' Their own countrymen have a juster notion of the relative standing of American authors. In the case of Mark Twain they do not believe that he is rated too high by foreign critics and readers, but that his true merits are very imperfectly comprehended.

THE TRAGEDY OF PUDD'NHEAD WILSON

December 1894

53. William Livingston Alden: unsigned review, *Idler*

August 1894, vi, 222–3

William Livingston Alden (1837–1908) served on the editorial staff of the New York *Times* (1865–85) and was American consul-general in Rome (1885–9). He was Paris correspondent for the New York *Herald* (1890–3) and in 1893 he became literary correspondent in London for the New York *Times*.

Puddenhead Wilson, Mark Twain's latest story, is the work of a novelist, rather than of a 'funny man.' There is plenty of humour in it of the genuine Mark Twain brand, but it is as a carefully painted picture of life in a Mississippi town in the days of slavery that its chief merit lies. In point of construction it is much the best story that Mark Twain has written, and of men and women in the book at least four are undeniably creations, and not one of them is overdrawn or caricatured, as are some of the most popular of the author's lay figures. There is but one false note in the picture, and that is the introduction of the two alleged Italian noblemen. These two young men are as little like Italians as they are like Apaches. When challenged to fight a duel, one of them, having the choice of weapons, chooses revolvers instead of swords. This incident alone is sufficient to show how little Italian blood there is in Mark Twain's Italians. But this is a small blemish, and if Mark Twain, in his future novels, can maintain the proportion of only two lay figures to four living characters, he will do better than most novelists. The extracts from 'Puddenhead Wilson's Almanac,' which are prefixed to each chapter of the book, simply 'pizon us for more,' to use Huck Finn's forcible metaphor. Let us hope that a complete edition of that unrivalled almanac will be issued at no distant day.

54. Unsigned review, *Athenaeum*

19 January 1895, no. 3508, 83–4

The best thing in *Pudd'nhead Wilson*, by Mark Twain (Chatto & Windus), is the picture of the negro slave Roxana, the cause of all the trouble which gives scope to Mr. Wilson's ingenious discovery about finger-marks. Her gusts of passion or of despair, her vanity, her motherly love, and the glimpses of nobler feelings that are occasionally seen in her elementary code of morals, make her very human, and create a sympathy for her in spite of her unscrupulous actions. But hers is the only character that is really striking. Her son is a poor creature, as he is meant to be, but he does not arrest the reader with the same unmistakable reality: his actions are what might be expected, but his conversations, especially with Wilson and the Twins, seem artificial and forced. Wilson, the nominal hero, appears to most advantage in the extracts from his calendar which head the chapters, but as a personage he is rather too shadowy for a hero. And what has to be said about the book must be chiefly about the individuals in it, for the story in itself is not much credit to Mark Twain's skill as a novelist. The idea of the change of babies is happy, and the final trial scene is a good piece of effect; but the story at times rambles on in an almost incomprehensible way. Why drag in, for example, all the business about the election, which is quite irrelevant? and the Twins altogether seem to have very little *raison d'être* in the book. Of course there are some funny things in the story—it would not be by Mark Twain if there were not—but the humour of the preface might very well be spared; it is in bad taste. Still, if the preface be skipped the book well repays reading just for the really excellent picture of Roxana.

55. Unsigned review, *Critic*

11 May 1895, xxvi, 338–9

The literary critic is often puzzled how to classify the intellectual phenomena that come within his ken. His business is of course primarily with *literature*. A work may be infinitely amusing, it may abound even with flashes and touches of genius, and yet the form in which it comes into the world may be so crude, so coarse, so erring from the ways of true classicism, so offensive to immemorial canons of taste, that the critic, in spite of his enjoyment and wonder, puts it reluctantly down in the category of unclassifiable literary things—only to take it up and enjoy it again!

Of such is *Pudd'nhead Wilson*, and, for that matter, Mark Twain in general. The author is a signal example of sheer genius, without training or culture in the university sense, setting forth to conquer the world with laughter whether it will or no, and to get himself thereby acknowledged to be the typical writer of the West. He is the most successful of a class of American humorists whose impulse to write off their rush of animal spirits is irresistible, and who snatch at the first pen within reach as the conductor of their animal electricity. If we look at other national humorists, like Aristophanes, Cervantes, Molière or Swift, we find their humor expressed in an exquisite literary form, in which a certain polish tempers the extravagance, and annoying metrical (or it may be imaginative) difficulties have been overcome. What wonderful bird-rhythms and wasp melodies and cloud-architecture, so to speak, emerge from the marvellous choral interludes of the Greek comedian; what suave literary graces enclose the gaunt outlines of Don Quixote; in what honeyed verse are Alceste and Tartuffe entangled, and what new, nervous, powerful prose describes the adventures of Gulliver! When we turn our eyes westward we encounter Judge Haliburton, Hosea Biglow, Uncle Remus, Mark Twain —an absolutely new *genre* distinct from what we had previously studied in the line of originalities. The one accomplished artist among these is Lowell, whose university traditions were very strong and controlled his bubbling humor. The others are pure 'naturalists'—men of instinctive genius, who have relied on their own conscious strength to produce delight in the reader, irrespective of classicity of form, literary grace or any other of the beloved conventions on which literature as literature has hitherto depended. This is true in a less degree of Uncle Remus than of Judge Haliburton and Mark Twain.

Pudd'nhead Wilson is no exception to the rule. It is a Missouri tale of changelings 'befo' the wah,' admirable in atmosphere, local color and dialect, a drama in its way, full of powerful situations, thrilling even; but it cannot be called in any sense *literature*. In it Mark Twain's brightness and grotesqueness and funniness revel and sparkle, and in the absurd extravaganza, 'Those Extraordinary Twins,' all these comicalities reach the buffoon point; one is amused and laughs unrestrainedly but then the irksome question comes up: What *is* this? is it literature? is Mr. Clemens a 'writer' at all? must he not after all be described as an admirable after-dinner storyteller—humorous, imaginative, dramatic, like Dickens—who in an evil moment, urged by admiring friends, has put pen to paper and written down his stories? Adapted to the stage and played by Frank Mayo, the thing has met with immediate success.

PERSONAL RECOLLECTIONS OF JOAN OF ARC

May 1896

56. William Peterfield Trent: review, *Bookman* (New York)

May 1896, iii, 207–10

William Peterfield Trent (1862–1939) was a professor, first of history and then of English, at the University of the South, Sewanee, Tennessee (1888–1900). Subsequently he taught at Barnard College and the graduate school of Columbia University (1900–27). He was an editor of the *Cambridge History of American Literature* (1917–21) and author of several books on American literature.

This review was entitled 'Mark Twain as an Historical Novelist'. Charles Francis Richardson's *American Literature, 1607–1885*, was published in 1886. The passage from which Trent takes a phrase is quoted more fully by William Lyon Phelps (No. 75). Matthews' essay is No. 35.

Some years since, I amused myself during a railway journey between Providence and New York by watching a man in front of me read *The Adventures of Tom Sawyer* steadily for an hour without once cracking a smile or giving a chuckle. Even a slow reader must in that time have got to the inimitable scene in which Tom gets his chums to whitewash the fence and pay him for the privilege of being allowed to do it, so I felt warranted in concluding that the saturnine stranger in front of me was a prodigy who had never known the pleasure of a hearty laugh and never been a boy. Perhaps, however, he had previously read Professor Charles F. Richardson's pathetic advice to Mark Twain and our other humorists to 'make hay while the sun shines,' and had concluded, as a good American Philistine, that, the vogue of these humorists being but temporary, it would be highly improper for a devotee of eternity to concern himself with their works save for the laudable purpose of drawing from them salutary lessons with regard to idleness and want of sobriety and decorous dulness. He had evidently never read Professor Brander Matthews's appreciative essay on 'Mark Twain's Best Story,' or he would have learned that our greatest humorist had already laid up perennial if not eternal treasure in the very book he was then reading so sedately and in its admirable sequel.

Whether Mark Twain himself has taken Professor Richardson's advice seriously to heart and determined to win a permanent place in literature by coming out in the high but to him new rôle of historical novelist, is a point on which I have no definite information; but I suspect that he was thinking more of his favourite heroine, Joan of Arc, than he was of himself when he began the story that we have all been reading of late in the pages of *Harper's Magazine*. Self-consciousness is not a characteristic of Mr. Clemens's art, and, like other great writers, he probably knows deep down in his soul that he will best secure the suffrages of posterity by writing simply and truly about that which he is fullest of and best understands. He also knows probably that the portion of the reading public which treats him as a mere humorist is sadly mistaken, and that he has already done work in fiction that the world will not willingly let die. It is most likely, therefore, that his new rôle of historical novelist has been assumed by the veteran writer for no self-seeking purpose, but simply because he has been caught in the eddies of that enthusiasm for the Maid of Orleans which has been sweeping of late over the literary world.

In attributing a new rôle to Mr. Clemens I have spoken advisedly, for although he has twice before essayed fiction of a historical cast, it is only with the *Personal Recollections of Joan of Arc* that he has challenged criticism as a historical novelist, properly speaking. That juvenile classic, which has charmed many an older reader, *The Prince and the Pauper*, depends for its interest rather upon Mr. Clemens's thorough knowledge of a boy's heart and his power to bring out the pathos inherent in a situation mainly based on the world-old contrast implied in the title of the story than upon the historical environment in which the characters of that story work out their respective destinies. But in a true historical novel the interest depends as much upon the fact that its characters move and live and have their being in an epoch removed from the present as upon the fact that they act, and feel, and think along lines that are universally true for the human race in all times and in all lands. Tested by this criterion, that other of Mr. Clemens's books to which he has given a historical setting, *A Yankee at King Arthur's Court*, falls still farther short of being a historical novel. It is really the work of a humorist, not of a novelist—of a humorist who seeks to gain his effects mainly by the use of violent contrasts, which are as likely to stir up feelings of repugnance in a reader as to move him to hearty and genuine laughter. The satiric purpose, too, of the book removes it still farther from the category of historical fiction, although for some readers, perhaps, this may give it its chief value.

But in the *Personal Recollections of Joan of Arc* we have a deliberate contribution to a class of fiction which, after suffering an eclipse for the space of a generation, has been of late steadily gaining in popular favour. Beginning in *Harper's Magazine* for April, 1895, it has run a course of thirteen months, shrouded in as much mystery as editorial wit could devise and the author's stylistic idiosyncrasies could keep up. Almost immediately critics and general readers alike began to suspect that no one save Mark Twain could be hiding his features behind a mask supposed to represent the countenance of the Sieur Louis de Conte, page and secretary to the martial maid, and this suspicion changed to certainty when they read the elaborate descriptions of the Paladin's powers of lying and of the Sieur Louis's attempt at a poem to the fair Catherine Boucher. But editor and supposititious translator kept their peace, while the artists furnished their excellent illustrations and the public read and enjoyed. Now, however, that the story is finished, the critic's time has arrived, although for any detailed examination one should await the appearance of the unmutilated book.

I do not purpose any elaborate criticism here, but only to start a few questions which must sooner or later be answered. Has Mark Twain at last made Professor Richardson's advice about making hay as superfluous in the eyes of the public at large as it is now in the eyes of Professor Matthews and of all who properly appreciate *Tom Sawyer* and *Huckleberry Finn*? Has he succeeded in writing a great book or even a thoroughly satisfactory historical novel? Has he atoned in part for the wanton injuries done to the noblest woman that ever lived by the English of her time and for the injustice done her memory in dramas which are properly credited to the greatest poet of England

and the world? Has he taken his stand by De Quincey's side as an inspired champion of a still more inspired heroine? These are the important questions that criticism will have to answer with regard to Mr. Clemens and his book, and with all due humility and regret I am compelled to make the confession that it is my opinion that the final answer of criticism will be a reluctant but decided 'No.' Not that a sympathetic reader or critic of the future will think for an instant that Mr. Clemens has not conceived his heroine's greatness in a worthy manner, that he has not told her story in a simple and moving style, that he has not at times set before us in vivid colours scenes of imperishable interest and importance. He has done all this, but it seems to me that he has failed, as many another writer has done ere now, to fuse properly the historic and the purely imaginary or fictive elements of his narrative. He has given us a large piece of mosaic work; first we have a slab of history, then a slab of fiction, and so on, with the history predominating over the fiction. It is true that the historical events that fill so many pages are told with an insight, a verve, a humour that professed historians might well envy; but the fusing process has not taken place, and the history and the fiction are separate, though in juxtaposition. Such was not the method of him who was at once the first and the greatest of historical novelists—that Sir Walter who, whatever certain modern critics may say, grows greater with the years both as a writer and as a man.

There are, I fear, other defects in the *Personal Recollections* that will not escape the attention of the critic, but that require only the slightest notice here. Mr. Clemens has essayed the difficult task of making Joan his chief character, and I rather think that his admiration for her has prevented him from making her really human and alive. It is true that he often presents her to us in her homely peasant's dress and ways, and he not infrequently strikes a note of genuine pathos; but too often he has to content himself with that most disappointing form of description, to wit, exclamatory comment. Yet if Joan does not truly live, hardly any other character can be said to breathe, unless it be Sieur de Conte himself, who is certainly full of high-minded appreciation of his noble mistress, but expresses it in a manner that makes one wonder how he got as far east as Domremy, if, as we are told, the Normans were the Yankees of France. De Conte may not have been a Norman, but his speech bewrayeth him to be a 'Yankee at the Court of Charles VII.' Perhaps, however, I am too sweeping in denying life to the characters who follow the Maid's fortunes. The Paladin, although he is simply a variation of a well-worn type of boaster, does live when he is entrusted with Joan's standard, and when he dies defending it, and La Hire lives both when he curses, which is frequently, and when he prays, which is emphatically seldom.

It would be an ungracious task to indulge in verbal criticism or to endeavour to show that one often detects a lack of imagination in descriptive passages that especially require it. It is not every reader who will object to the close of a paragraph describing Joan's approach to the throne of the disguised Charles, which is couched in the following style: 'They were not expecting this beautiful and honourable tribute to our little country maid.' The lack of *timbre* in the adjectives here employed, the lack of imagination seen in the description of Joan in armour rising aloft like 'a silver statue,' which occurs more than once; the lack of taste, if not of humour, shown in the story of the mad bull's breaking up the funeral procession; the lack of a sense of proportion displayed in the lengthy treatment of the trial, will have little meaning to the reader who reads for amusement simply, but will probably show the critic where one of the chief defects of Mr. Clemens's work lies. It lies, it seems to me, in the fact that Mr. Clemens is not primarily a man of letters. But fortunately for American literature and for the permanent fame of a man whom no one can know without loving and honouring, the creator of Tom Sawyer is something far more than a mere man of letters, even a great one; he is something far more than a mere humorist, even a thoroughly genial and whole-souled one—he is a great writer. Like Balzac himself he can afford to let the critics have their say about his style, in the consciousness that he has understood and expressed the workings of the human heart.

57. Brander Matthews: 'Mark Twain—His Work', *Book Buyer*

January 1897, n.s. xiii, 977–9

This article is a shorter version of what would become Matthews' introduction to the 'Uniform Edition' of Mark Twain's works.

There are many advantages in the growing practice of signing a literary criticism with the name of the writer; and not the least of them is that it permits the writer to praise heartily and abundantly those whom he truly admires, taking on himself all responsibility for his eulogy. I don't know whether or not THE BOOK BUYER would allow me to say anonymously all that it might be quite willing to have me say over my own signature. The wielder of the editorial *we* cannot but take into account average public opinion; it is that indeed he has chiefly to reckon with. But an individual writer, isolated by his own signature, may be a chartered libertine, having full license to say what he pleases. Now, it has long pleased me to think and to say that the average public opinion does not yet rate at its full value the work of the admirable story-teller who is known to all of us as Mark Twain.

The public having once made up its mind about any man's work, does not relish any attempt to force it to unmake this opinion and to remake it. Like other juries, it does not like to be ordered to reconsider its verdict as contrary to the facts of the case. It is always very sluggish in beginning the necessary readjustment, and not only sluggish, but somewhat grudging. Very naturally it cannot help seeing the later works of a popular writer from the point of view it had to take to enjoy his earlier writings. Now, as it happens, the earlier writings of Mark Twain gave little or no promise of the high qualities to be found in certain of his later works. Many of the sketches included in the *Jumping Frog* and most of the account of the *Innocents Abroad* were little more than 'comic copy.' They were very good 'comic copy' indeed, but none the less did they reveal the conventions, the formulas, and the limitations of 'comic copy.'

The Mark Twain these two books disclosed was a shrewd and keen-eyed observer, having broad fun, abundant humor, and exuberant fantasy, and so deficient in reverence for the equator that he treated the ordinary degrees of longitude and latitude without any respect whatever. Properly enough, he was classified promptly as a professional humorist—as a writer whose sole duty it was to make us laugh, and to whom therefore we need never give a second thought after the smile had faded from our faces. In any attempt to take stock of our native literature, Mark Twain was set down as a mere rival of the other pseudonymous fun-makers, John Phoenix, Artemus Ward, and Josh Billings. Even in 1886 Professor Charles F. Richardson, in his solid tomes on *American Literature*, solemnly warned Mark Twain and his fellows that, 'clever as they are, they must make hay while the sun shines,' since 'twenty years hence, unless they chance to enshrine their wit in some higher literary achievement, their unknown successors will be the privileged comedians of the republic.' And yet when this complacent judgment was delivered, Colonel Sellers had already found 'Millions in it!' Tom Sawyer had already reluctantly let the contract for whitewashing his aunt's fence, and Huck Finn had already been a witness of the Shepardson-Grangerford feud. Even in 1886 it might have been possible to perceive that the narrator of the adventures of Colonel Sellers, of Tom Sawyer, and of Huckleberry Finn was to be ranked with the creators of Ichabod Crane and of Hosea Biglow, rather than with the mere fun-makers of the comic papers. Half of Professor Richardson's twenty years have now come and gone; and Mark Twain has since given us *Puddenhead Wilson*, with its sombre figure of Roxy, sold down the river by her own son. He has chosen also to tell reverently and indeed almost devoutly the wonderful story of Joan of Arc. And yet there are not a few readers of his books careless and thoughtless enough to think of him even now as only 'the privileged comedian of the republic.'

The first of our humorists he is still, fortunately for us, with all the qualities we found in his earlier books, but now riper and richer. The *Jumping Frog* and the *Innocents Abroad* did not call forth more laughter than was evoked by later books like *Life on the Mississippi*, *Roughing It*, the *Stolen White Elephant*, and *A Tramp Abroad*. And these later books were in every way better than the earlier books of the same kind: they revealed less effort, a broader outlook on life, a deeper insight into human character; they showed that Mark Twain had learnt how to suggest the pathos that must underlie true humor; they were better written also—indeed, for his purpose, no American author to-day has at his command a style more nervous, more varied, more flexible, or more direct than Mark Twain's. The tale of the Blue Jay (in *A Tramp Abroad*) is as well told as it is full of humor sustained by unstated pathos; and the account of Mark Twain's own training as a cub-pilot (in the earlier chapters of *Life on the Mississippi*) is as vigorous in narrative as it is valuable as a record of a vanished phase of American life.

For these volumes of mingled realism and humor I have a relish as hearty as any reader's; but I must confess that my fondness is less for some other and more fantastic volumes—for *A Connecticut Yankee at King Arthur's Court*, for one, and for *The Prince and the Pauper*. In neither book can Mark Twain give his finer qualities full scope. My liking is still less for *Tom Sawyer Abroad*, in which the admixture of the realistic trio of Tom and Huck and Jim in purely fantastic adventures seems to me unfortunate. And noble and dignified as is the *Joan of Arc*, I do not think that it shows us Mark Twain at his best; although it has many a passage that only he could have written, it is perhaps the least characteristic of his works. Yet it may well be that the certain measure of success he has achieved in handling a subject so lofty and so serious, will help to open the eyes of the public to see the solid merits of his other stories, in which his humor has fuller play and in which his natural gifts are more abundantly displayed.

In *Tom Sawyer*, in *Huckleberry Finn*, and in *Puddenhead Wilson* Mark Twain is something more than 'the privileged comedian of the republic'; he is something very different from this,—something far more important. He is like Cervantes in that he makes us laugh first and think afterwards. Mr. Ormsby, in an essay which accompanies his translation of *Don Quixote*, points out that for a full century after its publication that greatest of novels was enjoyed chiefly as a tale of humorous misadventures, and that three generations had laughed over it before anybody suspected that it was more than a merely funny book. It is perhaps rather with the picaroon romances of Spain that *Huckleberry Finn* is to be compared than with the masterpiece of Cervantes; but I do not think it will be a century or take three generations before we Americans generally discover how great a book *Huckleberry Finn* really is, how keen its vision of character, how close its observation of life, how sound its philosophy, and how it records for us once and for all certain phases of South-western society which it is very important for us to perceive and to understand. The influence of slavery, the prevalence of feuds, conditions and the circumstances that make lynching possible—all these things are set before us clearly and without comment. It is for us to draw our own moral, each for himself, as we do when we see Shakespeare acted.

Huckleberry Finn, in its art, for one thing, and also in its broader range, is superior to *Tom Sawyer* and to *Puddenhead Wilson*, fine as both these are in their several ways. In no book in our language, to my mind, has the boy, simply as a boy, been better realized than in *Tom Sawyer*. In some ways *Puddenhead Wilson* is the most dramatic of Mark Twain's longer stories, and also the most ingenious; like *Tom Sawyer* and *Huckleberry Finn*, it has the full flavor of the Mississippi Valley, in which its author spent his own boyhood, and from contact with the soil of which he always rises reinvigorated. It is by these three stories, and especially by *Huckleberry Finn*, that Mark Twain is likely longest to live in our literature.

It remains for me to say now only that this new library edition of Mark Twain's works is in every way worthy. Six volumes have now appeared—seven, if the *Joan of Arc* be included, which the others match in height at least. They are all seemly tomes, clear in print, broad of page, simple in binding. The *Connecticut Yankee*, the *Prince and the Pauper*, *Life on the Mississippi*, and *Huckleberry Finn*, each fills a volume by itself. In the volume with *Tom Sawyer Abroad* we have 'Tom Sawyer, Detective,' and also the selection of sketches hitherto published under the name of the first of them, the 'Stolen White Elephant'; and, in like manner, the second half of the volume the *American Claimant* contains a score or so of essays and tales.

58. Unsigned article, 'Mark Twain, Benefactor', *Academy*

26 June 1897, li, 653–5

Kipling wrote of his visit with Mark Twain in *Idler* (February 1892, i, 85–7). The account was reprinted in *From Sea to Sea* (New York, 1899). Clemens' version of the meeting may be found in Paine's *Mark Twain: A Biography* (New York, 1912), pp. 880–1.

The anecdote 'Higgins', the first English publication of which was in *Piccadilly Annual*, 1870, has seldom been reprinted.

A few years ago Mr. Kipling called on Mark Twain at Hartford. Afterwards, in an account of his visit, he described the temptation which had beset him to steal the great man's corncob pipe as a relic. It was a nice touch of homage, coming from the man who has done more than any other to carry on the traditions established by the American writers, and in so doing in a large measure to supersede him. These traditions may be briefly described as the wish to set down as bluntly and forcibly as possible whatever one has to say, and the refusal to allow any intermediary between oneself and one's subject. Before Mr. Kipling rose glowing in the East, Mark Twain held the field. He was the ideal of masculine writers. There were no half ways with his readers—either they swore by him through thick and thin or unconditionally they cast him aside. Probably no author has been so little read by women, although, on the other hand, there was hardly a boy in the English-speaking world who would not have bartered his soul for Mark Twain's corncob pipe as a relic. He did just what boys and elemental men like: he came straight to the point; he feared no one; and he esteemed laughter above all the gifts of God.

Thus it was from twenty-five to a dozen years ago. But then, in the early eighties, Mark Twain's old manner became changed. He abandoned his zest in lawless life and the records of his personal impressions in the serious places of the earth, and he turned to satire and romance.

His sorrowing readers had only just perceived the melancholy truth when *Soldiers Three* appeared, in its quiet blue-grey covers, to mark the beginnings of a new sledge-hammer pen and divert their grief. British India won; and to-day Mr. Rudyard Kipling is the ideal masculine writer, and his is the pipe that is coveted by boys and elemental men. He is a finer artist than Mark Twain, his sympathies are wider, his genius is more comprehensive, and yet, when all be said, the fact remains that Mark Twain is his literary progenitor.

On his own ground, despite a huge and generally tiresome band of imitators, American and English, Mark Twain has never been equalled, hardly approached. Mr. Kipling is his son only in manner: in matter the two are wide asunder. Mark Twain is the most objective of writers: Mr. Kipling would penetrate to the innermost man. Mark Twain stands by with alert eye and twitching mouth, setting down in nervous, sinewy sentences whatever strikes him as picturesque, interesting, or humorous. He is catholic: for a good swearer, for a grotesque horse, or for the Sphinx itself he has the same apprehensive glance, the glance of the reporter of genius. It is there that he and Mr. Kipling take hands —they are both superb journalists at bottom, but whereas one adds to his journalistic equipment an extravagant sense of fun, the other is enriched by dramatic power and knowledge of hearts.

Mark Twain at his best is the most bracing companion in the world —he is so amusing and amused, and withal so sane. He is so unburdened by sentiment or reverence—and most of us have too much of both. It was the absence of these qualities which made *The Innocents Abroad* the refreshing book it was. A generation bred up on Mr. Ruskin was left gasping by the impudence of this American, who declined to put on fine phrases and tread delicately just because he had exchanged his own country for an older. It was the first Transatlantic democratic utterance which found its way into the hearing of the mass of English people. Mr. Bret Harte's idylls of the Californian mines had paved the way; but he only described the rough Western diamond —this was the diamond itself, articulate. People who were tired of formal diction and machine-made periods, turned to Mark Twain as thirsty travellers turn to a spring. He gave them a new language, a freer air. He brought the Far West vociferous to our doors. He acquainted us with America's national humour—its extravagance, its carelessness, its unscrupulousness, its daring. He was the first man who had ever laughed in catacombs, the first to connect Michael Angelo with fun.

But Mark Twain did more than this. Not only did he offer broad comic effects and sagacious criticism of life, he passed on to add notable contributions to that mass of data concerning human nature which novelists and dramatists have been accumulating these many centuries. Tom Sawyer has been called the completest boy in fiction, and it would be hard to prove this praise at fault; and Huck Finn is surely immortal. It was said that in some of his poems Nature took the pen from Wordsworth and wrote for him. In *Huckleberry Finn* it may be said that natural man took the pen from Mark Twain and wrote for him. That great book, which is likely to remain the standard picaresque novel of America, is the least trammelled piece of literature in the language. It is worthy to rank with *Gil Blas*.

To neglect Mark Twain's later books is easy, and, one fears, inevitable; but it should be done only with compensating references to those that came before in the great period that culminated with *Huckleberry Finn*. In condemning 'The £1,000,000 Bank Note', and its companion stories, let us recall the perfection of 'yarning' in some of the first collections. Let us especially recall 'Higgins':

'Yes, I remember that anecdote,' the Sunday-school superintendent said, with the old pathos in his voice, and the old sad look in his eyes. 'It was about a simple creature named Higgins, that used to haul rock for old Maltby. When the lamented Judge Bagley tripped and fell down the court-house stairs and broke his neck, it was a great question how to break the news to poor Mrs. Bagley. But finally the body was put in Higgins' waggon, and he was instructed to take it to Mrs. B., but to be very guarded and discreet in his language, and not break the news to her at once, but do it gradually and gently. When Higgins got there with his sad freight he shouted till Mrs. Bagley came to the door.

'Then he said, "Does the Widder Bagley live here?"

' "The *Widow* Bagley? *No*, sir."

' "I'll bet she does. But have it your own way. Well, does *Judge* Bagley live here?"

' "Yes, Judge Bagley lives here."

' "I'll bet he don't. But never mind, it ain't for me to contradict. Is the Judge in?"

' "No, not at present."

' "I jest expected as much. Because, you know—take hold o' suthin', mum, for I'm a-going to make a little communication, and I reckon maybe it'll jar you some. There's been an accident, mum. I've got the old Judge curled up out here in the waggon, and when you see him you'll acknowledge yourself that an inquest is about the only thing that could be a comfort to *him*!" '

In turning without too much regret from the unrealities of *Joan the Maid*, let us remember that its author could once write of the chivalry of the mining camps:

[quotes *Roughing It* ch. 57 'It was a wild' to 'went home satisfied'.]

And voting *A Yankee at the Court of King Arthur* tedious and in bad taste, let us remember the wonderful bombast which Mark Twain puts into the mouths of the two braggarts on board the Mississippi raft, in that chapter of *Huckleberry Finn* which strayed into *Life on the Mississippi*.

[quotes ch. 3 'Then the man' to ' "calamity's a-coming!" ']

Let us judge of a man by his best. Let us remember Scotty Briggs' interview with the minister concerning Buck Fanshawe's funeral, and the story of Jim Blaine's grandfather's old ram, and the great Horace Greeley correspondence, and the jumping frog of Calaveras County, and Tom Sawyer and the whitewashed fence, and the great Granger-ford–Shepherdson feud, and the death of Boggs, and the performance of the King's Cameleopard or Royal Nonsuch, and the contest between the Child of Calamity and the Corpse-maker of Arkansas, and the great duel between Gambetta and Fourtou, and Jim Baker's story of the blue jays, and the taming of a genuine Mexican plug— these are the incomparable passages to associate with the name of Mark Twain.

59. David Masters: 'Mark Twain's Place in Literature', *Chautauquan*

September 1897, xxv, 610–14

As a rule authors who can write anything better than mere humor strive by every means in their power to show the world that they have other and higher gifts than those of the mirth-provoking order. Twain belongs to this class, and of later years he has been striving to obliterate the memories of his first success, the success that made him famous— *The Innocents Abroad*. It is safe to assume that the best things he has written since then have been produced under the spur of a determination to show the world that the court jester can take off his cap and bells and say a striking thing seriously.

The immense reputation attained by his first book has been a heavy handicap to Twain in one sense, and an advantage to him in another. It was a rough-and-tumble sort of book, the worst of all his literary efforts, but probably the most popular, striking the public fancy at a time when it was ready to be amused, and the success of the work was instantaneous and positive, being no doubt an astonishment to authors of more pretentious ambitions, who had burned the midnight oil more assiduously than he, and no doubt with more painstaking effort, only to find themselves, after years of hard work, still unknown quantities in the world of letters.

One can readily surmise after reading Twain's later works that he has been for years past trying with commendable purpose to live down *The Innocents Abroad*. Finding himself in the broad glare of public interest, he set about doing something better than the effort that had first attracted the attention of the country. To realize how admirably he has succeeded, one has but to note the steady improvement in his style and facility of expression, as well as the purpose and seriousness of his work in his later publications.

The public, however, has tenaciously clung to the first impressions formed of the writer, and for this reason has overlooked the fact that there are much more substantial things in his writings than merely humorous conceits. His *Yankee at the Court of King Arthur* is an able argument in favor of free trade, but most of his readers pay but little attention to this fact, as they are not looking for free trade theories in such a place and only devour the fun and frolic of the pages. His *Prince and Pauper* is a book of intense dramatic interest, the details worked out with rare skill, and some of the descriptive work has a dignity of diction hard to surpass.

The idea is often conveyed to us by eastern writers that the atmosphere of the West is in some way detrimental to perfection in literary work, and that the successful writer must of necessity pass his early life in the East, where he can enjoy the environments of colleges and come in contact with a certain sort of civilization not to be found in the West.

There was a time when the people of England did not deem it worthy of admission that an American author could write English, until Washington Irving convinced them of their error. The same spirit now possesses the writers along the Atlantic seaboard, and they persistently decry the literary work done west of the eightieth parallel of longitude.

Let us note for a moment to what extent they have a right to do this. Bret Harte, Eugene Field, Ambrose Bierce, Joaquin Miller, W. C. Morrow, and a dozen others that might be named have shown what the West could do in the line of good writing. Their work is rugged and full of a force and originality that cannot be found outside the surroundings these men have enjoyed. Some of the pens now furnishing the hackwork for the eastern magazines never get beyond a certain monotony, yet they are put forward as the only lights in the literary horizon. They have by constant practice become the masters of commonplace and their long-drawn descriptions of commonplace events are pronounced true to life. No one can dispute their fidelity to the subject treated, but a great artist is one who can reproduce a great subject by bringing out its most striking points, and he need not be a master of technique in order to produce a great painting. The artist who portrays a great battle-scene or depicts the force and movement of a mountain storm may lack the rudimentary training of one who can paint a dead fish so perfectly that it is hard to keep the house cat from pouncing on it, but the picture of the tragedy and the storm will appeal most to our senses, because the soul and imagination of the artist is to some extent infused into the picture and absorbed by the art lover.

Twain, while not a master of literary technique, is above all of his

contemporaries the master of strong description and the art of presenting a picture that glows with a certain light that brings in bold relief
every point that the writer wants the reader to see. To write plainly
and understandingly and make everything vivid and plain to the
reader seems to be the acme of good writing, and in this sort of work
Twain stands preeminent.

Suppose for the sake of argument that Twain had put in his early
days at some eastern college; no doubt that quality of composition
which Mr. Thompson calls 'style' might have been molded differently,
but it would have been at the expense of those characteristics of
originality which now stamp all his writing. With no artificial cultivation, his genius took its own bent, and proved strong enough to tower
into a sturdy tree, in a soil where the more delicately nurtured plant,
first propagated in the city hothouse, would have died.

With the writer of weak individuality and small self-confidence
there is an inevitable tendency to imitate the style of some great writer
of the past, and this inclination soon disposes of its victim. Twain, with
his early poverty and uninviting environments, had but little opportunity to study the works of the standard writers, and was thus saved
from the endeavor to imitate them, had he been so disposed. His
inborn desire to write could not be suppressed and he gave the world
a style of his own, a style which, in spite of its incapacity to satisfy
the eastern critic, would make a great gap in American literature were
all of his books to be suddenly effaced.

Much of the conciseness of his narration is due to his early association with Joseph Goodman and D. E. McCarthy, who first gave him
employment on the *Territorial Enterprise* at Virginia City, Nevada.
These men were the leading newspaper writers of the coast, and were
the faithful disciples of the concise school of writing of which Charles
A. Dana, of the New York *Sun*, is the acknowledged founder. Under
their tuition Twain acquired the art of brevity and clearness in literary
composition, and for this the American public owes them something
of a debt.

The West did something else for Twain: it made him a hater of
sham; for in no place in the world is imposition and fraudulent
pretense so soon measured up and weighed. There men acquire nothing
by hereditary right, and those who came to the country in Twain's
time were all supposed to start alike in the race for preferment.
The pretender soon went to the wall and people who assumed to be
what they were not were held in the most profound contempt. All

through his writings he lays the flail upon all manner of shams, whether in society, politics, or the learned professions, and one has yet to find a line in all his works that defends any principle that is unjust or smacks of humbug. He might quote Omar in speaking of himself:

> Let this one thing for my atonement plead:
> That 'one' for 'two' I never did misread.

In introducing his characters Twain generally indulges in a touch of his characteristic description that in a single paragraph tells the reader just what may be expected of the party introduced. For instance, he introduces a group of loungers in an old Missouri town and speaks of a man who 'pursed his mouth up like the stem end of a ripe tomato' and took a shot at a tumble-bug about six feet away, overwhelming it with a stream of tobacco juice. At once the various members of the group, with an accuracy born of long practice, direct their respective streams of tobacco juice upon the hapless insect and drown it then and there. The narration of this incident, bordering as it does on the vulgar and commonplace, still serves better than anything else imaginable to convey to the reader the sort of people to be met in the succeeding pages of the book, and no amount of introductory writing could more clearly perform this service.

In *Huckleberry Finn*, *Tom Sawyer*, and other works it is claimed that the author gave to the world his own youthful escapades, which sounds probable, but I feel safe in saying that he also drew in the same pages many character sketches which are photographically true to life, for I was personally acquainted with some of their originals.

Prince and Pauper, the most dramatic and the most feelingly written of his works, and probably the one that received the least public appreciation, is a splendid satire on the fuss and flummery of royalty, and contains some of the most dramatic strokes in literature. Tom Canty, of Offal Court, riding at the head of a richly caparisoned host to be crowned king of England, in the midst of the thundering welcome of cannon, is accosted by his mother, and with his head turned giddy with the intoxication of the occasion denies her recognition. For an instant the reader would like to hurl Tom Canty from his steed, but forgives him later on, when, bowed with contrition and a torturing conscience, he says in a dead voice to the duke at his side, 'She was my mother.' This pathetic incident soon yields its hold upon the reader when the great seal of England is discovered only on the bogus young prince's announcing that he has been using it to crack nuts with.

In *A Yankee at the Court of King Arthur* there is another dramatic scene, when the king goes into the pauper's hut and comes out bearing in his arms the poor girl stricken with smallpox. All the poets and romancers who have delighted to clothe chivalry with the glamour of romance and unreality never were able to place a king in a more sublime position than that.

The world has been wont to look at the knights of the Round Table, Sir Launcelot, Merlin, and the enchanted country about Camelot through the poetic spectacles of Tennyson; but Twain, with his hard-headed, practical way of looking at everything, regards chivalry as a humbug, just as Cervantes regarded it, and prods the sham much in the same way, except that his fun is more modern, and he hammers away at game which Cervantes has already killed.

People who read Twain by skipping everything that is not humorous, or by trying to extract a laugh from every paragraph, overlook much that is beautiful or philosophical. Twain can paint a beautiful piece of landscape when he feels disposed. Here is where he tells of his morning ride with Sandy, the irrepressible creature he picked up in Arthur's court:

[quotes ch. 12 'Straight off' to 'into the glare'.]

This does not sound like Twain at all, but seems to have been written by him merely to show the reader what he could do in the way of fine descriptive writing when the mood seized him.

The touch that spoils it is the earliest birds 'turning out and getting down to business.' This, however, was probably thrown in by the author to indicate that while he could pen this sort of descriptions very easily, he really had a very light opinion of them.

There are numberless delightful bits of picturesque landscape in Twain's writing, and clever dashes of color upon which one stumbles in the most unexpected places. If they were all collected and published by themselves as some anonymous writer's work, few would associate them with Twain.

This is because the court jester can never shake off the rôle he has once filled. No matter how wise, eloquent, or serious his utterances may be, they will still be regarded as coming from the jester, and be treated accordingly. Twain has made the American people laugh so much and so long that they can only associate his name with a burst of levity, and thus it comes about that his deep, beautiful, and pathetic things are either overlooked or misconstrued.

A friend of Twain's, a gentleman very close to him, once stated to me that he had every reason to believe that Twain had in contemplation the publication of an anonymous book so unlike anything he had ever written that his own wife would not be able to recognize it. Twain could then enjoy the fun of reading the criticisms, and would doubtless take a hand himself in writing a few of them. Who knows but that he has already placed such a work before the public? That he could do such a thing well, no one will deny, for if there is a writer in America capable of performing a neater feat of literary legerdemain than Twain, he is certainly unknown to the public.

The charge that Twain is neither elegant nor graceful in his writing may be well founded, but he has the happy faculty of writing plainly and with a blunt force that can never be misunderstood, and this pleases the average reader better than an elegance of diction made to conceal poverty of thought. Much of his work was written only for the day and generation in which it was published, and so will pass away, but meanwhile let us hope that his method of utilizing plain Anglo-Saxon will not perish from literature.

60. D. C. Murray: article, *Canadian Magazine*

October 1897, ix, 497–8

David Christie Murray (1847–1907), English novelist and journalist, included these comments in one part of a series on 'My Contemporaries in Fiction' which was published as a book under the same title (London, 1897).

Bret Harte, studying a form of life now extinct, which once (with certain allowances made for the romantic tendency) flourished in the West; Mr. Howells, taking micrographic studies of present-day life in the great centre of American culture; Mr. James, with a clever, weary *persiflage* skimming the face of society in refined cosmopolitan circles; and Miss Wilkins, observing the bitter humours of the Eastern yokel, are none of them distinctively American either in feeling or expression. Mr. Samuel L. Clemens—otherwise Mark Twain—stands in striking contrast to them all. He is not an artist in the sense in which the others are artists, but he is beyond compare the most distinct and individual of contemporary American writers. He started as a mere professional funmaker, and he has not done with funmaking even yet, but he has developed in the course of years into a rough and ready philosopher, and he has written two books which are in their own way unique. Tom Sawyer and Huck Finn are the two best boys in the whole wide range of fiction, the most natural, genuine, and convincing. They belong to their own soil, and could have been born and bred nowhere else, but they are no truer locally than universally. Mark Twain can be eloquent when the fancy takes him, but the medium he employs is the simplest and plainest American English. He thinks like an American, feels like an American, is American blood and bones, heart and head. He is not the exponent of culture, but more than any man of his own day, excepting Walt Whitman, he expresses the sterling, fearless, manly side of a great democracy. Taking it in the main, it is admirable, and even lovable, as he displays it. It has no reverence for things which in themselves are not reverend, and since its point of view is not one from which all things are visible it seems occasionally overbold and crude; but the creed it expresses is manly, and clean, and wholesome, and the man who lives by it is a man to be admired. The point of view may be higher in course of time, and the observer's horizon widened. The limitations of the mind which adopts the present standpoint may be found in *A Yankee at the Court of King Arthur*. Apart from its ethics, the book is a mistake, for a jest which could have been elaborated to tedium in a score of pages is stretched to spread through a bulky volume, and snaps into pieces under that tension.

FOLLOWING THE EQUATOR or
MORE TRAMPS ABROAD

December 1897

61. Unsigned review, *Academy*

11 December 1897, lii, 519–20

Mark Twain's last book of travels was titled in the United States *Following the Equator*; in England, *More Tramps Abroad*.

We lay aside this extensive book (it has 486 pages of small type) with the reflection that Mark Twain is wiser and wittier than ever, but less funny. His power of seeing straight and setting down his opinions in unmistakable sentences is still with him; his asides on men and their ways show, if anything, an increase of shrewdness and a new flavour of cynicism, gained probably in a hard school; his interest in what is interesting is as quick; but the quality for which nine out of every ten persons buy his books—his fun—is not what it was. As a sequel to *A Tramp Abroad*—as the title *More Tramps Abroad* implies it is intended to be—this book is a failure. As a rambling, disordered account of travels in Australasia, India, and South Africa, interspersed with dissertations on government and Thuggism and social problems and life generally, it is a work unusually able and picturesque; for although Mark Twain grows less amusing, he is not to thinking persons, therefore, less attractive. His good sense is so dominant. At the same time, the majority of English readers do not greatly care for the political and serious opinions of an American author to whom they once confidently resorted for laughter. When they wish to be instructed concerning Greater Britain, they prefer that it should be done by an Englishman. Hence Mark Twain's new book is likely to be far more popular in America than in this country.

We do not wish to suggest that there is no fun in its pages. There is a good leavening, but the proportion of fun to hard sense and hard facts is smaller than usual and the quality less high. There is nothing, for example, to bear comparison with the Blue Jays or the Gambetta-Fourtou duel in *A Tramp Abroad*. Mark Twain seems to have lost the inclination to elaborate a joke. The funny passages in *More Tramps Abroad* are hurried, and for the most part are retrospective. But now and then there is an old touch, as in this description of the Australian bell-bird:

The naturalist spoke of the bell-bird, the creature that at short intervals all day rings out its mellow and exquisite peal from the deeps of the forest. It is the favourite and best friend of the weary and thirsty sundowner; for he knows that wherever the bell-bird is there is water, and he goes somewhere else.

Again, an Indian servant with a limited stock of English words led to the following memorable passage:

[quotes ch. 39 ' "How did you get" ' to ' "family, dam good." ']

India also yields the following:

After a while we stopped at a little wooden coop of a station just within the curtain of the sombre jungle—a place with a deep and dense forest of great trees and scrub and vines all about it. The royal Bengal tiger is in great force there, and is very bold and unconventional. From this lonely little station a message once went to the railway manager in Calcutta: 'Tiger eating station-master in front porch; telegraph instructions.'

A book with such good absurdities is not wholly futile. But their infrequency causes sadness that, since he wrote *A Tramp Abroad*, Mark Twain has undergone changes. We regret that he has studied the history of Joan of Arc and dabbled in occult arts; that he has tried his hand at business and failed and grown quite lamentably fond of facts and figures and politics: because the result is that fun has passed into the background of his brain. The loss is ours. Of the stories told in the new book, the following is among the best. It refers to a dis-cussion at *table d'hôte* as to whether the Scotch peasantry pronounced the word 'three'—'three' or 'thraw':

[quotes ch. 5 'The solitary Scot' to 'six of it'.]

After the South African chapters (in the reading of which we do not envy Dr. Jameson) many persons will value most the maxims from Pudd'nhead Wilson's New Calendar. In his early work Mark Twain did not display much epigrammatic ability. He 'spread himself.' Nor does he tend to compactness in the body of this, his latest, book. But at the head of each chapter he has put a little crisp aphorism, usually cynical, almost always true, and often witty. Some are excellent, and are likely to pass into our proverbial wisdom. With the quotation of a few, we take leave of a good-humoured, instructive, entertaining, careless, ill-considered, and rather disappointing book.

[quotes twelve maxims.]

62. Unsigned review, *Speaker*

11 December 1897, xvi, 671

One of the things which 'nobody can deny' is that Mark Twain, at his best, is a 'jolly good fellow.' Unfortunately, the dry Yankee humorist, like less gifted mortals, is not always at his best, and perhaps that circumstance accounts for our disappointment over *More Tramps Abroad*. We took up the book with lively recollections of the *Jumping Frog* and other side-splitting diversions, on the American soil and also in Europe; and, since open confession is good for the soul, we confess to have been slightly bored with much of this latter-day elaborate fooling. What we get is Mark Twain on his travels through India, Ceylon, Australasia, and South Africa, with his comments, often piquant enough, on men and movements. There is much shrewd common-sense in the book, and no lack of saucy opinion, whilst here and there the old wit flashes forth, and genial, even if extravagant, banter. But there are not a few prosy passages, and every now and then the fun is distinctly laboured. The latest of the 'empire-builders,' in the person of the redoubtable Mr. Cecil Rhodes, is made the hero of an ironical appreciation. Mr. Rhodes is described as the marvel of the times, the mystery of the age. Mark Twain is evidently lost in wonder over his strange but fascinating personality. He thinks that Mr. Rhodes has 'beguiled England into buying Charter waste-paper for

Bank of England notes,' and yet 'the ravished still burn incense to him as the Eventual God of Plenty.' Half the world, we are assured, regard the South African statesman as an 'archangel with wings,' whilst the other half is equally persuaded that he is 'Satan with a tail.' But let us hear the conclusion of the whole matter, especially as it is as pithy and as cynical as anything in the book. 'I admire him, I frankly confess it; and when his time comes—I shall buy a piece of the rope for a keepsake.' Mark Twain's humour is neither at its best nor at its worst in these pages; in other words, he has risen much higher and sunk much lower than is the case in the present instance. But *More Tramps Abroad* is distinctly worth reading, if only for the quick-witted and caustic social judgments which it contains of an unconventional and fearless lecturer on his way through the world.

63. Unsigned review, *Saturday Review*

29 January 1898, lxxxv, 153

Reviewers were quick to comment on the excessive length and dullness of *Following the Equator*, but only the unknown critic for the *Saturday Review* pointed out that a cause for this was Mark Twain's ill-advised introduction of extraneous matter not his own.

The veteran jester, attired 'in cosmic guise,' again makes his appearance before an admiring world, with his best bow, his whitest hand, and his wink. For Mark Twain has put a girdle round the earth, as he lets you to know in 486 pages—no less. But these are not all his; some—indeed, many—are borrowed from other historians. Whenever the ship draws near the port, and the lead is going on the harbour bar, does our author lug forth the historiographer, asking us to come and sit at his (or her) feet beside Mark Twain, and then we shall know what kind of country we are coming to, and all about it; which, as intelligent, high-toned persons, we naturally like to do. But we don't like it, all the same. If the publishers particularly requested their author to provide a book containing not less than 486 pages, they were acting unwisely; and if they did not, the author might have guessed that we know where we go for history when we want it; and that if we want Mark Twain, we like to get him. Why should we listen to Mrs. Krout on Honolulu, or Captain Wawn on the Kanaka, or Mrs. Praed on Queensland, or the Blue Book on Thuggee?

We care, just now, for none of these things. When we open a book with 'Mark Twain' on the cover, we want to behold the Great American Spirit, tongue in cheek, strolling irresponsibly around the universe. And, between its wads of padding, *More Tramps Abroad* does afford us this spectacle. When he is content to be himself, Mark Twain, as we all know of old, is very good company. But, with years of practice, he has come to be so deft at the manufacture of jests, that he must always be at it; and nothing in the world is more apt to become tedious than long elaborate jokes with all the joints evidently manifest. Thus, the 'Delicately Improper Tale' which was never finished, is quite unamusing, despite its ingenuity. And in the story of Cecil Rhodes and the Shark, the jester misses his tip, because the performance is altogether too ingenious for this world, and because it is too long for its size. But the story of the Mark Twain Club of Corrigan Castle is entertaining; so is the story of the Dog with the gentleman from Baroda and Mr. Augustin Daly's Irishman; and—to select at hazard one more instance from many—so is the description of the view from the mosque in Benares. Read these things once, read them swiftly, and you shall be diverted. And as to reading them more than once—well, why should you? Read, moreover, Chapter XVII. on the Tichborne Case; and especially peruse Chapters LXIX.—LXXI. on the South African business, which make one of the best pieces of smart, insolently irresponsible journalism ever written. For, although Mark Twain may specialise at will upon the artificial joke, his real pursuit in life is journalism. The great journalist—compact of a rare fusion of qualities—will write as much as you please upon any topic under the sun; and—whether you approve it or do not—the result will always be more or less interesting, and often exciting. And of such is Mark Twain.

64. Unsigned review, *Critic*

5 February 1898, xxxii, 89–90

It must be difficult to name Mark Twain's books, but there can be no denying that the present is a good all-round title. It is somewhat inclusive, and covers considerable ground without leaving the writer or reader at sea, besides allowing the widest latitude for observations. The ingenious will leap to the conclusion that *Following the Equator* comprehends a trip around the world in company with the most capable of pilots; and after making the voyage, he will be confirmed in his suspicions, and will also learn that this pilot has not so keen an eye for natural beauties that he overlooks the rocks and snags in the course of civilization.

A larger part of the author's popularity is due to his Americanism. His attitude of mind, from the earliest *Jumping Frog* days, has been a sublimation of the American cast of thought, which can perhaps be best defined by saying that the modern American is the *enfant terrible* of the human family. His clarity of vision is perfect, his frankness of speech is awful—but as wholesome as a thunder-storm. He refuses enthusiasm to shams, faith to superstitions, hearing to bores, acceptance to conventions. He speaks out in meeting, laughs in church, and snores during the lecture. He refuses to 'hush!' if he sees a wrong committed, and cheerfully loads up his sling when Goliath strides forth in full panoply. He opposes a cheese-box on a raft to the ironclad, or sneaks under the leviathan of the deep and torpedoes her to kingdom come. Incidentally, he may object to *The Vicar of Wakefield*, and define a classic as 'a book which people praise and don't read.' But who is so interesting, and who tells so much truth to the square inch? If all spoke with equal sincerity, criticism would be throned in the market-place, instead of begging its bread.

The proportion of the humorous to the serious is about that of the bread to the sack in Falstaff's *menu*. One reads as if traveling with a shrewd, kindly, sincere, and humorous man of the world who has kept only illusions enough to make life really living. The journey around the world was not a necessary scaffolding upon which to build this structure. Mark Twain could have smoked on his front doorstep, and philosophized as acceptably. But the many climes lend variety to the subjects treated, and permit the reformer a wider choice of illustration.

What a range of subjects! and how depressing are these he has elaborated. It is to be hoped that this new volume of Mr. Clemens's reflections will not be bought by those who seek quiet, amusing and relaxing literature to amuse an invalid. Tyranny of man over men, and over woman, lepers and leprosy, slavery, savagery and civilization, the savage insensibility to pain and torture, the extinction of the Tasmanians, convicts in penal settlements, diseases and parasites, woman suffrage, a murderer's confession, the mistakes of missionaries, the cruelties of caste, towers of silence, the plague, the thugs, the suttee, fakirs, women laborers, snake-bites in India, the Sepoy mutiny, mistakes of educators, the Trappists, the war with the Boers—and so on, pass before the reader in gruesome procession.

Mark Twain has reached the terrible frankness of maturity and fame; he tells tales like Bismarck, regardless whom he hits, so long as the blow is deserved. And yet, of humor in the old sense the book is full. Each chapter is headed by one of the 'New Pudd'nhead Wilson Calendar' sentences; and many of these could have been written by no other hand. 'She was not what you would call refined; she was not what you would call unrefined. She was the kind of woman that keeps a parrot,' is worth a hundred pages of statistics. 'The English are mentioned in the Bible. Blessed are the Meek for they shall inherit the Earth,' and 'There are no people who are quite so vulgar as the over-refined ones,' are other fair specimens of a form of wit that had no exact forerunner. It is not Artemus Ward, or Voltaire, or Rochefoucauld, or Sydney Smith—or any one but Mark Twain.

With less of broad farce, this latest book has more wit, and more literary value, than any other volume of the author's work. Toward the end there is a delicious discussion of the Jameson raid that for sustained irony is perfect. It is hard to compare extracts from a new book with those that have become familiar. The novelty of a first impression counts for much, and the keenest witticism is blunted by repetition. Of equal merit is the summing-up of Cecil Rhodes, with its final illuminating sentence:—'I admire him, I frankly confess it. And when his time comes, I shall buy a piece of the rope for a keepsake.'

In another field we learn the writer's power of description. Turn to his acute and sound criticism of the Taj Mahal and of its appreciators, and read on through his descriptive sketch of an American ice-storm. Ruskin could do no better, though he would have posed more. There is a refreshing absence of the 'chestnut' element; books meant to be 'funny' resort to old stories, as unscrupulous divines to printed sermons, or mediæval authors to plagiarism—under a sort of poetic license. Of the illustrations, charity will say nothing—excepting the reproduced half-tones, which are documents only. The frontispiece is an excellent photograph of the author, seated alone, with the new-born but immortal legend 'Be good and you will be lonesome.'

To sum up: the book's a book, but with something in it. It is the diary of a skilled observer and writer, with originality and humor, but with too much of the reformer to find the world anything but a tragedy to those who think. If Jack Sprat were fond of sociology and his wife preferred humor, they might alternately enjoy reading Mark Twain's new book aloud.

65. Hiram M. Stanley: review, *Dial*

16 March 1898, xxiv, 186–7

Hiram M. Stanley (1857–1903) was the librarian of Lake Forest College near Chicago, where the *Dial* was published.

Mark Twain's recent account of his around-the-world lecture tour, which he entitles *Following the Equator*, is a first-rate specimen of that eminently sagacious mixture of sense and nonsense which is so characteristic of him. To many refined people he may seem the vulgar buffoon, entirely unrespectful, unconventional, irreverent; but this aspect is but his surface aspect. He reverences what is essentially worthy of reverence, as is evident from many a page in this volume. His remarks on reverence, indeed, show eminent sense and insight,—as when he says:

The reverence which is difficult, and which has personal merit in it, is the respect which you pay, without compulsion, to the political or religious attitude of a man whose beliefs are not yours. You cannot revere his gods or his politics, and no one expects you to do that, but you could respect his belief in them if you tried hard enough, and you could respect him, too, if you tried hard enough. But it is very difficult; it is next to impossible, and so we hardly ever try. If the man doesn't believe as we do, we say he is a crank, and that settles it. I mean it does nowadays, because we can't burn him.

In truth, the dominant note in his book is not jest but earnestness, moral and humane,—an earnest desire for sincerity and genuineness, but tearing sham to pieces and flinging it to the winds. If Mr. Clemens had not been Mark Twain, he might have been Carlyle.

But we have not space for exemplifying fully either the wisdom or the wit in this book. However, we mention the common Hindoo impression of the United States, as Mark Twain gives expression to it. When this country is named to the average Hindoo,—

Two torches flare up in the dark caverns of his mind, and he says, 'Ah, the country of the great man—Washington; and the Holy City—Chicago.' For he knows about the Congress of Religions, and this has enabled him to get an erroneous impression of Chicago.

Mark Twain's manner of writing is deliciously desultory; you never know on what continent the next page will land you. Altogether, we have a most brilliant and varied jumble of wit, humor, information, instruction, wisdom, poetry, irony, and jest. Mark Twain is continually stepping from the sublime to the ridiculous, and *vice versa*. As soon as he suspects he is getting eloquent, he at once jumps into outrageous farce. As Mark warns off the reviewer who shall attack him for padding, we will only say that his skill and brilliancy can almost redeem the plentiful padding in this book. As a book of travel, this work stands very high by reason of its incisiveness and vividness; and the inveterate travel-reader will mark the day he fell in with it with red-letter. Altogether, we find here that *rara avis*, a real book, full of thoroughly original characteristic impressions characteristically expressed, and thus intensely enjoyable to the real reader.

66. Theodore de Laguna: 'Mark Twain as a Prospective Classic', *Overland Monthly*

April 1898, xxxi, 364–7

In 1898 Theodore de Laguna (1876–1930) was a graduate student at the University of California, Berkeley. He subsequently became a professor of philosophy at Bryn Mawr College.

It was John Nichol (No. 27) who earlier had accused Mark Twain of debasing the English language.

It is an anomaly unprecedented in the history of criticism, that Mark Twain should live to receive even a doubtful recognition from the schoolmen of his time. For he has consistently despised prevailing canons of sound taste, and yet has reached the hearts of men. In the eyes of the few, he has been that most contemptible of creatures, a popular scribbler. With talents that might have justified a more select ambition, he has been willing to be popular.

His most enthusiastic admirers have been farthest from suspecting in him the elements of greatness. They can so thoroughly enjoy him without the least sense of intellectual inferiority, that he seems one of their own kind, no better than themselves. His humor is the national humor,—so wild and free and lawless in its adventures, that it seems to the uncultured mind too good to be literature. He writes in the living language, in 'modern English,' as he calls it,—the unaffected speech of men in general, the medium of intelligent conversation, 'the common drudge 'tween man and man.'

Those who have enjoyed him most, I repeat, have been the last to suspect him of greatness. The wonder is that within the century anyone should have awakened to the truth. How were we to respect a writer, who accumulates his 'and's' like an enthusiastic child, who trails out tag-end prepositions with unconventional freedom; who with exasperating complacency inserts the adverbial modifier between the infinitive and its sign; who says 'that much' and 'feel badly'? Such practices may be pardonable when committed in the privacy of home; but in literature are they not unclean and repulsive? The educated taste answers in the affirmative. In a language as old as ours, it is inevitable that the diction and idiom of culture should be widely differentiated from common speech and serenely elevated above its coarseness and vulgarity. But Mark Twain has persisted in his attachment to his mother tongue. It is hard for a college-bred man to forgive him.

When we consider that his treatment of language is of a piece with his conduct toward the traditional in general, we may not care to forgive him. For the irreverent Westerner has acted upon the principle, that the only memorial of the past worthy of respect is the inheritance of truth. The shams of the past and of the present are indiscriminately the subjects of his humor. Of all forms of falsehood, that which he has held up to most insulting ridicule is false sentimentality. In an age of effete romanticism, this is likely to hurt decent people's feelings.

His humor, like his language, is common clay. We have rightly called it the national humor; but to some minds, that is little to its credit. A constant feature is the adaptation of popular material. 'She resurrected nothing but the cat,' has been criticised as brutal violence perpetrated upon a word that is hallowed by a sacred connotation. We shall not deny the justice of the criticism; but Mark Twain is not to blame. He used the word as he found it. When the Western mother dives into an ancient clothes-chest and brings to the surface a faded relic of former years,—'resurrected' is the very word she uses and relishes. It is a piece of popular whimsicality like a thousand others that mold the vocabulary of a nation, and which are the national humorist's crude material.

It has for centuries been a commonplace of criticism, that laughter is equally degrading to the laughable object and to the man who laughs. That there could be innocent humor has been a childish superstition. But Mark Twain very evidently supposes that his humor degrades neither himself, nor his readers, nor, necessarily, the subject of his discourse. Chaucer, as we remember, assigned to himself the unappreciated 'Tale of Sir Thopas'—satirized the romantic craft in his own person. There was an assumption of moral greatness in this, which later Englishmen have not attempted to imitate. But with Mark Twain, self-satire is so frequent an artifice as altogether to escape comment.

We have observed that 'innocent humor' is a contradiction in terms. We might go farther and demonstrate upon infallible premises that the æsthetic worth of humor is strictly limited by its coarseness; not that the two are necessarily commensurate, but that the degree of coarseness measures the possibilities of humor. From this it would appear, that for the noblest humorous effects, sensual impurity is necessary. The science of rhetoric asserts no more certain principle; and no rhetorical law has been more carefully respected by genius of all times and nations. How then were we to recognize greatness in a humorist, whose writings contain not one unwholesome word or thought or suggestion?

It was a bitter commentary upon our narrow-mindedness, that Mark Twain should have conceived it necessary or advisable to publish his *Personal Memoirs of Joan of Arc* anonymously. He had been marked, apparently forever, as the 'prince of funny men,' and from such a character we could not be expected to tolerate so noble a romance— until, indeed, it had won its own fair fame. Just so, in the careless judgments passed upon his earlier works, the general conception of the American humorist had swallowed up all due appreciation of his magnificent abilities in serious art.

The charm of a few of his word pictures has at times been casually noticed. But he has never been celebrated for their worth. Yet scattered through his miscellaneous writings are not a few of the most sublime or beautiful natural descriptions in our literature. If we could name our favourite among them all, we might choose from *Tom Sawyer* an account of the wakening of nature, as the little runaway beheld it in the dawning of his first day of freedom,—a piece of exquisite simplicity and loveliness. Human scenes are pictured no less effectively. In *The Gilded Age*, the paragraphs upon the death of Laura Hawkins bear many signs of our author's technic; and they contain a description which is among the glories of American literature. Let us repeat the concluding sentences:—

When the spring morning dawned, the form still sat there, the elbows resting upon the table and the face upon the hands. All day long the figure sat there, the sunshine enriching its costly raiment and flashing from its jewels; twilight came, and presently the stars, but still the figure remained; the moon found it there still, and framed the picture with the shadow of the window sash, and flooded it with mellow light; by and by the darkness swallowed it up, and later the gray dawn revealed it again, and still the forlorn presence was undisturbed.

Mark Twain has not been generally acknowledged a narrative writer of the first ability. In the briefest form of narrative, the anecdote, he has, indeed, known few rivals; perhaps he may be said to have perfected the American variety as a literary type. But his powers of sustained narration have been seriously questioned. In the books of travel, nothing is sustained. And it has been unreservedly declared that in every one of his works where a plot is necessary, the plot is a failure. But the author of this criticism has evidently a narrow view of the possible merits of plot-construction. Mark Twain is assuredly not a novelist, and few would wish him one. He is a story-teller; let him be judged as such. Now it is commonly a high merit in a story to make the episode or incident an immediate object of pleasurable interest, not inferior to the narrative as a whole. For proof of this recall the story of *Aladdin*,—which must certainly take rank among the world's best half dozen,—or almost any one of Chaucer's tales, or *Robinson Crusoe*, or *Tom Sawyer*. In a pure story, the distinctly climacteric development of one dominant idea is a fault. As Mr. Lounsbury has pointed out in his *Studies of Chaucer*, the peculiar charm lies in the even distribution of interest. Story-telling is the simplest form of literary art, but not in the sense of being the least difficult. The curious history of *Pudd'n'-head Wilson* and 'Those Extraordinary Twins' well illustrates the difficulty of combining in one whole a host of equally interesting details. *Huckleberry Finn* certainly lacks artistic unity—not because almost any one of the episodes is in itself of equal æsthetic worth with the fortunes of the vagabond hero; but because it is a poor sequel and the connective tissue is flabby. *Tom Sawyer* is almost beyond criticism. In general, Mark Twain's plots appear to be excellent in their kind. The details are everywhere effectively presented, and they are not too diverse to be unified by the bonds of American humor.

Still less has he won distinction as a stylist, a master of the effects of tone and rhythm. In the might of his occasional eloquence, he shows a strength that cannot be denied, but his average style is said to have done more for the debasing of the English language than any other recent influence. It is the old story of the return to nature—or barbarism; it matters not which. It is a return to the living source of all inspiration and power,—the genius of the spoken language. Historically—as we believe—Mark Twain's style is of infinite import. Æsthetically, it has been seriously undervalued. Quite unpretentious, it is none the less admirably adapted to its peculiar content. 'The strangling hero sprang up with a relieving snort,' is no less a master-stroke than this (from a descriptive passage before mentioned): 'It was the cool gray dawn, and there was a delicious sense of repose and peace in the deep pervading calm and silence of the woods.' This quality of 'harmony,' as the rhetoricians call it, was once held to be the rare and distinguishing charm of the highest literary genius. Latterly it has fallen into less repute, as a Popish artificiality. With Mark Twain, the charm is unaffected, unostentatious, and irresistible.

Like several other writers of this century, he has given to the world one great character,—his own. How great the world has lately learned. It has been wisely said that no mere humorist can be great, even as a humorist; but it seems hard to believe that the intended victim of the aphorism was Mark Twain. Perhaps the critic's knowledge of our author was limited to a very few pages of *Innocents Abroad*. Surely he had never read *The Prince and the Pauper* or *Tom Sawyer*.

But perhaps he had read the latter; for it has met with some strange misappreciation. When that young scamp is brought face to face with darkness, loneliness, horror, agony, and death, with a timid, helpless child clinging to him alone for comfort in her utter despair,—his thoughtfulness, his patient kindness, his boyish soul's long-suffering endurance, must—it would seem—suffice to distinguish him from 'the thousands which anyone familiar with the commercial industry of writing books for boys can name only too readily.' We quote the words with a certain pleasure.

Huck is evidently the prose, as Tom is the poetry, of Mark Twain's younger self,—and no less a genuinely heroic spirit. 'The widow's been good friends to me sometimes, and I want to tell,' has long been to us the typical utterance of a stirring manliness.

'The world,' said a distinguished professor of literature, 'should be thankful for Mark Twain.' Could words better suggest the way in which the man and his books have been taken for granted? He has not taken himself for granted, but has striven toward ideals of his own clear judgment. And it is far from a misfortune, that the people have always so received him. No better foundation could be laid for an edifice of enduring fame, than such a popularity.

67. Anne E. Keeling: 'American Humour: Mark Twain', *London Quarterly Review*

July 1899, xcii, 154–62

This article is probably by the Annie E. Keeling who between 1881 and 1903 wrote more than a dozen inspirational novels and biographies, all published by the Book Stewards of the Wesleyan Methodist Book Room. One of these stewards, Charles H. Kelly, was the publisher of the *London Quarterly Review* in 1899.

The first part of this article, not included here, discusses works by Artemus Ward and Bret Harte.

Artemus Ward died and Mark Twain reigns in his stead; and there is sufficient spiritual kinship between the two to make the successorship quite appropriate and legitimate.

A change that might reasonably be deemed an improvement had declared itself in Charles Browne before his brief career closed. He had ceased to find it advisable to emphasise his wit by curiously phonetic spelling; this was typical of a more important alteration in his manner. His range of thought seemed wider, his wit had less of irresponsible schoolboy gaiety and more of serious intention. It was when he flung down the jester's bauble and laid aside the motley garb that Mark Twain—to give him the *nom de plume* he has made familiar wherever English is spoken—began to acquire a certain hold on the audience that had laughed so heartily with *Artemus*—scarcely at him. For a long time people of taste would turn their eyes from any book bearing the pseudonym that told of its writer's life on a Mississippi steamboat. 'He is so vulgar,' they alleged, 'how can you read such detestable stuff?' And the majestic *Revue des Deux Mondes*, reproducing in classically faultless French the *Jumping Frog*, that its writer had set forth in roughest dialect, bade its readers note the singular ineptitude of the stories which could be accepted as witty and amusing by our cousins in the States. Certainly there was little of Attic elegance in the English affected by the new humorist; and the record of a tour in

Europe in 1867, which became a popular favourite with English readers under the title of *The Innocents Abroad*, had something more than a note of aggressive provincialism—a sort of anxiety to depreciate, as far as possible, those Old World splendours in which the New World could claim neither part nor lot. It was supremely characteristic of this author in his earlier stage of development that, looking on the dreamlike beauty of the Italian lakeland with an eye that could take in no little of its loveliness, he must needs compare Como disparagingly with 'Lake Tahoe.' Lago di Como is placed at a lower altitude than its Transatlantic rival—unknown, we fear, despite its eulogist, to nine hundred out of every thousand who are familiar with the pictured charms of Como; 'Tahoe' is eighteen miles wide, Como but one. Charms measurable in miles of width and feet of altitude! is not here the old, old Transatlantic error of taking dimension as a test of grandeur? The 'lonely majesty' of Tahoe—'a sea whose royal seclusion is guarded by a cordon of sentinel peaks that lift their frosty fronts nine thousand feet above the level world'—this lonely majesty 'types the Deity'—and constitutes therefore superiority? Nay, but it is the human, historic, social element—the exquisite civilisation of centuries on centuries—which is the glory of the lovely accessible Italian lakes, and reminds us more aptly of divine wisdom as revealed in the Hebrew Scriptures, 'rejoicing in the habitable earth, and her delight with the sons of men.' Our writer, despite his predetermined intention to exalt things American above all others, betrays himself as subjugated by this very charm despite himself, as unconsciously raised and refined by it. No vulgarity is traceable in this scrap of vivid, eloquent description.

[quotes ch. 20 'From my window' to 'heaven itself'.]

So far, to show us that our jester has his share of the painter's eye and the poet's heart, and then the susceptible patriot and provincial must hark back to 'Tahoe,' and inform us with irritating exactitude of the depth—a hundred and eighty feet—at which in its 'strangely magnifying waters one may count the scales on a trout,' so wonderful the transparency of this 'noble sea reposing among the snow-peaks'—all very interesting to the writer and his compatriots; but the note struck is a discord notwithstanding.

It is much the same in the *New Pilgrim's Progress*—a joke elaborated through some hundreds of pages, and much concerned with the small acreage of Palestine, and the insignificant area of the 'kingdoms that

fell before the march of Israel; also with the sordidness, the unclean-
liness, and evil odours rife in Araby the Blest and the so long desecrated
Holy Land. We are dealing with a laughing iconoclast, who finds the
finest possible joke in the incongruousness between the dreamy,
gorgeous Orient as imaged in devout fancy by the pious Bible-readers
of the far West, and the poverty and ugliness blazed over by the
noonday sun in wasted, down-trodden Palestine, crushed under the
blighting rule of the Turk. The mood did not pass away rapidly. The
satirist ran less risk of wounding the religious feeling of his English
readers—whose numbers increased, notwithstanding what to many
seemed sheer irreverence on his part—when he applied his quaint
methods to the great cycle of Arthurian myths, dear for uncounted
generations to the fancy of us island-dwellers, and now better beloved
than ever because of the glory of new rich colouring and the heightened
significance of spiritual meaning with which the genius of our most
sovereign poet of the century had freshly invested them. *A Yankee at
the Court of King Arthur* displeased as many as it delighted. The story
goes that the daring author of that mad travesty, compact of crazy
incongruities and carefully contrived absurdities, being told that he
was held presumptuously irreverent, intimated that reverence was a
virtue he imperfectly appreciated. In some such fashion ran the tale;
if truly, the writer did himself injustice.

Many passages of his later works especially show him capable of
enthusiastic admirations, and rendering a delighted homage to qualities
which he can apprehend as really grand and worshipful. The boyish
buoyancy and frolic are obvious and delightful still; but under that
foam and sparkle some nobler qualities, always latent, are becoming
increasingly evident. Least familiar of any is the deep inward perception of the grimness and tragedy of life—which in his earlier books
seemed as conspicuously absent as it is from the quaint and queer
drolleries of Artemus Ward—of all the humorists with whom we have
dealt, the one whose story is the saddest and whose humour the most
incorrigibly cheerful.

In its unobtrusive way *Pudd'nhead Wilson*—almost the latest performance of its author—is a demonstration of the devilish mischief
done by that 'peculiar institution,' American slavery, as convincing as
Uncle Tom's Cabin. The indictment is dispassionate as indictment of so
monstrous an evil could be; there is little declamation, no exaggeration,
and such picturesqueness and grace of old-world dignity and kindliness as could be found among the better sort of slaveholders is touched

in with a kind of tender appreciation. But the injury to slave and slave-owner—the distorted morality on both sides, the hopeless degradation of the one, the cruel insolence of superiority in the other—are shown in action with a cogency that is something terrible. Humour there is in almost every scene and every page; but it is such humour as sheds a wild gleam on the greatest Shakespearian tragedies—on the deep melancholy of *Hamlet*, the heart-break of *Lear*.

The characters whose fortunes furnish forth the story are common-place enough, so is the motive of the action—an exchange of children in their cradles by a slave foster-mother, who, being 'only one-sixteenth black and that sixteenth didn't show,' could substitute her slave-born boy, thirty-one parts white, fair of face and hair and blue-eyed like his foster-brother, for the son and heir of the lordly master, and so, as she dreamed, ward off from her darling all the horrors of his heritage of woe. How her fraud results in evil such as her poor un-taught wit, however shrewd, could never have apprehended as possible, and how her son, thankless, heartless, faithless son to his real and his adoptive parent alike, is branded at last as perjured liar, thief, and murderer, and flung back into the thraldom she had tried to ward off from him—here is the originality in the plot, here the extraordinary power of the story, derived from the situation created for the otherwise insignificant personages and from the consequent evolutions of char-acter. It needs all the quaint inverted wisdom of the citations from 'Pudd'nhead Wilson's Kalendar' to waken the familiar laughter that used to convulse Mark Twain's readers in the older days; and even in these there is a note of bitter world-experience.

'Gratitude and treachery are merely the two extremities of the same procession. You have seen all of it that is worth staying for when the band and the gaudy officials have gone by,' is a sentiment that might have commended itself to Swift, though the English be not that of the great dean. 'Why is it that we rejoice at a birth and grieve at a funeral? It is because we are not the person involved;' and, 'Whoever has lived long enough to find out what life is, knows how deep a debt we owe to Adam, the first great benefactor of our race: he brought death into the world,' have the same stamp on them; the strong and gloomy fancy which conceived and the iron pen that elaborated in every detail the dreadful picture of the undying Struldbrugs in *Gulliver*, might very well have originated these two cruel little epigrams. But the humorist of our own day has a kindlier and more tolerant spirit than his forerunner. If he does not give us any of those enchantingly gracious pictures of the better side of slave-life which we owe to the creator of *Uncle Remus*, beloved of children, he will not blame the enthralled negroes for the moral defects due to their position; he refuses to see any hypocrisy in the noisy religion which could co-exist in them with a steady habit of larceny.

They had an unfair show in the battle of life, and they held it no sin to take military advantage of the enemy . . . in a small way, but not in a large one; . . . sure that in taking a trifle from the men who daily robbed them of an inestimable treasure—their liberty—they were not committing any sin that God would remember against them in the last great day. So, they would go to church and shout and pray their loudest and sincerest with their plunder in their pockets.

Piteous, humiliating fruit of injustice and oppression—'twice accursed,' hurtful to him who did and him who bore the wrong. Masters themselves had a double code of honour and compassion. 'He was a fairly humane man to slaves and other animals; he was an exceedingly humane man towards the erring of his own race.'

It might have been the writer's own father who sat for this thumbnail sketch of a slaveholder. In the much gayer and cheerier book put forth in 1897, *More Tramps Abroad*, Mark Twain shows us how intimate was his knowledge of the workings of slavery. He is in Bombay, and observing some authoritative German in the hotel dealing with a native servant guilty of some inadvertent error—

[quotes extracts from ch. 38 'Without *explaining*' to 'his cradle up'.]

Hence the brutality, which did not lie in the man's nature. Other masters punished awkwardness in murderous fashion; our author saw such a deed; the slaughter 'seemed a pitiful thing and somehow wrong'; but the man 'had a right to kill his slave if he wanted to.' In face of such possibilities, the argument, something too well worn, which the author of *Uncle Remus* advances, how the negro stood a better chance among white Christians than in his own dark heathen land, lacks convincing power. Better, one would say, that the negro should take his chance in Africa than help to demoralise a higher race than his own by his very helplessness, and infect with a taint of true savagery a civilisation achieved not without heroic effort prolonged over many generations. The evil system was not swept away a day too soon.

More Tramps Abroad, a record of a lecturing tour through British dependencies and of travelling and other experiences among populations keenly appreciative of the American guest, shows no falling off in the special qualities that won for this writer a really world-wide popularity. It sparkles with gay good humour, it is rich in vivid description, couched in unconventional graphic phrase, of the splendid variety of scenery in the Greater Britain of Africa, Asia, Australasia, and of sumptuous picturesqueness of humanity in the Far East. The satiric touch is sharp as ever; and as ever it is chiefly bestowed on things odious and evil, wheresoever found. Something there is however which at least has not been so patent before; an affectionate pride, a kind of loyal exultation, in the grandeur of British achievement, and the accumulated glories of the British name. 'If monuments,' says he, commenting on one to a stately memorial in Calcutta to 'one Ochterlony,' good, honourable serviceable, like 'seventy-five or a hundred other Englishmen' who lie in unmarked graves,

if monuments were always given in India for high achievement, duty straitly performed, and smirchless records, the landscape would be monotonous with them. The handful of English in India govern the Indian myriads with apparent ease, and without noticeable friction, through tact, training, and distinguished administrative ability, reinforced by just and liberal laws—and by keeping their word to the native whenever they give it.

With restrained but effective eloquence he tells again the dark tale of the Mutiny—not lengthily, yet with regret for his brevity; for 'there is not a dull place anywhere in the great story,' which his recapitulation will make a little familiar to the new generation of English who did not live in those tremendous days. 'The military history of England is old and great, but I think it must be granted that the crushing of the Mutiny is the greatest chapter in it'; and with such satisfaction as a near kinsman might take in telling the exploits of a mighty hero, he points out against what tremendous odds the sons of Britain 'fought the most unpromising fight that one may read of in fiction or out of it, and won it—thoroughly.' The same note of scarcely suppressed triumph thrills through the pages devoted to a vigorous description of thuggee, that elaborate religious murderer-conspiracy, which like a strongly rooted internal cancer lay 'embedded in the vitals of the empire,' and had so lain for generations, 'formidable with the sanction of age,' an unsuspected all-pervading evil. For a 'little handful of English officials in India set their sturdy and confident grip upon it and ripped it out, root and branch!' And proud is the blood-relation of those Englishmen as he writes of this 'most noble work,' and the modest, quiet way in which its achievers describe it. It is no blind advocate who speaks thus; where he sees a blot on our scutcheon he is not shy in pointing it out; but the voice is that of a faithful friend with a strong personal interest in our well doing, a legitimate pride in our justly earned honours.

We are justified surely in reckoning this distinctly novel tone and style in a widely popular American writer as a favourable sign of the times, especially when we remember the great vogue in his own country enjoyed by this sturdy foe of oppression and injustice, this lover of the heroic and the magnanimous.

Faulty style and easy irreverence may be condoned where such better qualities are conspicuous; and we may hail as no mean co-operator towards the 'Anglo-American alliance,' likeliest event to herald in universal peace by sea and land, the gay mocker who ministered so much to the mere mirth of young England some thirty years ago, and who still continues to provide clean, wholesome food for laughter, under the familiar style of Mark Twain.

68. Henry Harland: 'Mark Twain', London *Daily Chronicle*

11 December 1899

Henry Harland (1861–1905), an American novelist, wrote his early novels about Russian Jewish immigrants in New York under the pseudonym 'Sidney Luska'. He lived in London after 1890 and was associated with Aubrey Beardsley as an editor of *The Yellow Book* from 1894 to 1897.

What is the explanation of Mark Twain's great, continued, and very peculiar popularity? I say peculiar, because Mark Twain is not merely, like Mr. Hall Caine and Miss Marie Corelli, popular with the masses; he is popular also with the remnant; his works are enjoyed and esteemed by people of taste and cultivation—and that, in spite of faults, of vices, which, one would imagine antecedently, must render any work, to people of taste and cultivation, utterly abhorrent.

Let us be cruel (that we may be kind in due season), and give to a few of Mark Twain's more conspicuous and constant vices their common names. In re-reading *The Innocents Abroad*, for instance, I think one cannot help being struck by the vulgarity that mars the book, and by the illiteracy, by the ignorance and the inaccuracy, by the narrowness, the provincialism, above all by the perpetual, the colossal irreverence. And yet, one reads *The Innocents Abroad* with pleasure, even perhaps with some degree of profit; it is still, for all its vices, and much as they offend one, it is still a book one likes. Why? What is the explanation?

I'm afraid we shall never discover the explanation, unless we begin by considering the vices somewhat closely. It will only be by recognising and eliminating them, that we shall obtain, in the end, the residue of saving virtues. And we may eliminate at the outset, if you will, we may condone as venial, Mark Twain's illiteracy, ignorance, and inaccuracy. When he alludes to the grave-digger's discourse over the skull of Yorick, when he mentions that the signal for the fighting on St. Bartholomew's Day was rung from the towers of Notre Dame, when he translates 'Genova la Superba' 'Genoa the Superb'—it is easy to lift an eyebrow, shrug a shoulder, smile, and pass on. Even when he tells us that the 'pax hominibus bonæ voluntatis,' which he saw blazoned in gold on the walls of St. John Lateran, 'is not good scripture,' we can commend him, in charity, to the intercession of St. Jerome. But Mark Twain's vulgarity, his narrowness, his provincialism, his irreverence, are made of sterner stuff. They are in the very texture of his work, not merely on its surface—they are of its spirit, they inform it, they determine its savor; and they are all bound and mixed up together, they are inseparable; it is impossible to discuss one without connoting the others. They are different manifestations, as it were, of the same constitutional defect: a total inability, namely, to respect what he cannot understand; an instant conviction that what he cannot see does not exist, and that those who profess to see it are hypocrites—that what he does not believe is inevitably false, and that those who profess to believe it are either hypocrites or fools. As if a color-blind man were to condemn as fools or hypocrites those who profess to see blue in the Union Jack, or to admire the splendors of a sunset.

It is this constitutional defect, I fancy, which accounts for Mark Twain's most egregious solecisms, for his most unlovely blasphemies.

It is this which leads him to the perpetration of his numberless cheap and dreary jests about the 'Old Masters.' It is this which so deprives him of any sense of proportion as to enable him to write seriously of Raphael, Michael Angelo, and Canova in the same breath; to explain that the exterior of St. Peter's is 'not one-twentieth part as beautiful as the Capitol at Washington'; to suggest that it is the supreme mission of art to 'copy nature with faultless accuracy'; to prefer the marble millinery which has occasioned most of us a shudder in the Campo Santo at Genoa to the 'damaged and dingy statuary' of the Louvre; to declare that 'wherever you find a Raphael, a Rubens, a Michael Angelo, or a Da Vinci, you find artists copying them, and the copies are always the handsomer. Maybe the originals were handsome when they were new, but they are not now.'

It is this terrible inability to respect what he cannot understand, this fatal readiness to despise those whose opinions he does not share, which makes it possible for Mark Twain to crack his ghastly jokes about death, his dreadful jokes at the expense of things that to the majority of civilised mankind are sacrosanct, his jokes at the expense of the saints, and the pictures and relics of the saints—nay, at the expense of more sacred relics still, at the expense of the Crown of Thorns and the True Cross. 'They say St. Mark had a tame lion, and used to travel with him—and everywhere that St. Mark went the lion was sure to go.' 'When we see a party looking tranquilly up to heaven, unconscious that his body is shot through with arrows, we know that that is St. Sebastian.' 'I think we have seen as much as a keg of these nails.' What nails? Nails from the True Cross, if you can believe me. It is always, I suppose, the same inability to respect what he cannot understand which makes it possible for Mark Twain to write facetiously of his travels in Palestine, and to crack a final joke about the True Cross in the presence of the Holy Sepulchre.

All this is surely very shocking; to some of us it must be very repulsive. Why is it, then, that in spite of all this we can still read Mark Twain with pleasure, perhaps with profit, still esteem him, and acknowledge his good right to the popularity, even with the remnant, which he has won? Why must we still reckon *The Innocents Abroad* among the books we like?

Well, certainly not, at any rate, certainly not because of its humor. The humor of the book, one is surprised to find on re-reading it after a lapse of years, is by no means its most salient feature nor its brightest merit—is indeed, for the most part, extremely thin, flat, and inexpensive.

Sometimes, in our weaker moments, it may excite a pale flicker of a smile; never a laugh; never, never—*au grand jamais*—that deep internal glow which is our response to humor in its finer flower. But if it is not the humor of the book, what is it?

I wonder whether it isn't in some measure—no, in great measure— the downright barbarism of the book? The big, bluff, rough, honest barbarism of the book and of its writer? What Mark Twain cannot see, he cannot see at all; he cannot believe in it, he cannot allow for it; you and I are hypocrites (or fools) for professing to see it. But what he can see, he sees with the unwearied eyes of the barbarian, of one to whom the old world is new—of a shrewd, clear-headed barbarian, outspoken, fearless, sincere, who knows how to present his impressions lucidly, vividly. And it is necessarily interesting to get a clear-headed barbarian's impression of our old world, interesting and fascinating. He will gibe at our gods, mock at our sacred mysteries, profane our shrines, march booted and bare-headed upon our holy ground, he will outrage our sensibilities, trample upon our conventions, assault our prejudices and our fond illusions; but never mind. He cannot see what we can see, and we cannot hope to make him see it; but he will see much that we have not seen, and we (because the larger contains the less) shall be able, when he points it out, to see it with him. Fancy travelling through Europe with a keen-witted English-speaking pilgrim from the moon—visiting Paris and the Louvre with him, Rome and the Vatican, Naples, Constantinople, Athens, Como, and the Hellespont, and listening to his commentaries upon these familiar sights. Would it be instructive, suggestive, amusing, exhilarating? Well, Mark Twain, this pilgrim from the Mississippi valley, brings to Europe eyes very nearly as fresh as the moonman's. It is instructive, suggestive, amusing, exhilarating to travel with him. He speaks his own quaint manner of English with fluency and energy and picturesque eloquence; and he is good-humored and wholesome; and his heart is in the right place.

Of course, *The Innocents Abroad* is not the best of Mark Twain's books. *Roughing It*, I think, is a better book; I am sure *Tom Sawyer* and *Huckleberry Finn* are better books. But the qualities and the defects of *The Innocents Abroad* are the qualities and the defects of Mark Twain's temperament, and they are present in varying proportions in all his books: vulgarity, narrowness, irreverence, freshness of vision, honesty, good-humor, wholesomeness. Mr. Brander Matthews, in a 'Biographical Criticism' accompanying these volumes, says that Mark Twain 'must be classed with Molière and Cervantes.' But then Mr. Brander

Matthews, in the same article, brackets the late Mr. J. R. Lowell also with Molière and Cervantes, and that somehow shakes one's faith in Mr. Matthews's judgment. Time will show.

The present 'edition de luxe' of Mark Twain's works is handsomely printed upon good imitation hand-made paper, and ornamented by some of the worst wash-drawings (by a Mr. Peter Newell) that it has ever been my lot to see. 'Theatre' is spelled 'theater,' 'centre' 'center,' and 'traveller' is allowed but a single 'l.'

69. Harry Thurston Peck: 'As to Mark Twain', *Bookman* (New York)

January 1901, xii, 441–2.

Harry Thurston Peck (1856–1914), the author of this unsigned article, was professor of Latin at Columbia University (1882–1910) and editor of the *Bookman* (1895–1902).

The Washington *Times* (31 January 1901), in an article entitled 'A Little Man and a Great Subject', castigated Peck for this piece and praised Mark Twain extensively as the 'biggest, best and most human of our writer-folk'.

At a recent meeting of the Nineteenth Century Club Mark Twain delivered himself of some observations upon the subject of Sir Walter Scott as a novelist. He said that Scott can be read with interest by a boy of sixteen and can be re-read with interest by the same person after he has reached the age of ninety, but that between one's first and second childhood Scott is hardly to be reckoned with. It would have been well had Mr. Clemens extended his observations a little further in order to inform his audience at precisely what age his own historical novels may be regarded as interesting any human being. It is a subject on which we have ourselves endeavoured to secure some first-hand information

and have ingloriously failed. We know of one gentleman who succeeded in reading *Joan of Arc* to the end; but he was a book reviewer
and had to do it because he was a conscientious man. We tried it
several times, and then gave it up because of its egregious dulness. We
should like to know whether Mr. Clemens supposes that the various
beautiful editions of Scott's works that have lately been issued in
England and in this country have been issued solely for the benefit of
boys and dotards. Then there is the sumptuous reprint of Lockhart's
Life of Scott, published in five large volumes by the Macmillan Company. This appears to show that not only do very many persons
thoroughly enjoy the reading of what Scott wrote down himself, but
that they also like to read about him—a liking that has been further
gratified by the publication of a smaller life of the great romancer
composed by Mr. James Hay. There does not, therefore, seem to be
any reason for serious disquietude with regard to Scott; but we fear
that we cannot say as much for Mr. Clemens.

Mr. Clemens has of late and since his return to the country of his
birth been very conspicuously in what one of our magazines delights to
call 'the public eye.' He has succeeded in beating down a cabman's
charges to the extent of a quarter of a dollar—which, of course, was
a public-spirited thing for him to do. He has attended innumerable
dinners and other functions, and has made innumerable speeches at
them. He has said some things about the responsibility of our leading
citizens for the present condition of our municipal government, and
thus has pleased the city newspapers. The speakers who have introduced
him to his audiences have invariably beslavered him with praise, and
life has been to him of late what Mr. Grover Cleveland many years ago
described as just 'one grand sweet song.' Mr. Clemens himself, with
certain compunctions which we believe to have been sincere, has from
time to time requested these perfervid gentlemen to change their note
and to say something that should be an antidote to indiscriminate
eulogy. None of them complied; and, therefore, Mr. Clemens will no
doubt be doubly grateful that we are not possessed of a mind of such
obliquity as not to take him at his word. Putting aside all prejudice and
looking at his work in a purely achromatic way, a critical and truthful
judgment upon Mark Twain can be summed up in a very exiguous
space. Mark Twain is first and last and all the time, so far as he is anything, a humourist and nothing more. He wrote *The Jumping Frog*
and *Innocents Abroad* and *Roughing It*, and these are all the real books
that he ever wrote. He set forth the typically American characters of

Colonel Sellers and Tom Sawyer and Huckleberry Finn, and these are all the real characters that he ever drew. His later publications that are humorous in intention contain many gleams of the old Mark Twain; but, taken as entities, you cannot read them from beginning to end. Some unduly optimistic persons who are fond of literary cults grown under glass have tried very hard to make the world believe that Mr. Clemens has great gifts as a serious novelist and romancer. By dint of iteration the world, perhaps, has temporarily come to think that this is true; but all the same, it will not read these novels and romances, and it thereby shows that common sense and real discrimination may exist in practice even while they hold no place in theory. A hundred years from now it is very likely that *The Jumping Frog* alone will be remembered, just as out of all that Robert Louis Stevenson composed, the world will ultimately keep in memory the single tale of *Dr. Jekyll and Mr. Hyde*.

This spasmodic and ephemeral outburst of enthusiasm over Mr. Clemens emphasises for the thousandth time a melancholy truth about contemporary criticism. When a writer is doing good and forceful work and winning readers and laying the foundation and erecting the superstructure of an enviable reputation, our critics, even though they may admire him, have not the 'sand' to say so. They are poor dumb sheep that never dare to take the lead in anything; but they stand around with unintelligent and foolish bleatings until some one whom they are not afraid to follow shall tell them what they ought to say. When Kipling was doing his finest work, such as he has never equalled in these later years, the critics did not dare to take him seriously. He was so unconventional and rough and strong that he frightened them; and so they slunk timidly behind their ink-stands and said little feeble nothings and joked a little and called him a mere journalist, and then looked around to see if any one was going to hit them. After they found out that his work was instinct with true genius, and that he was in reality the one real literary phenomenon of the last quarter of our century, they all rushed in at once and spattered him with praise and daubed him over with their flattery, and did their very best to make him seem absurd. By this time, as it happened, Kipling's best had all been done, and he was entering upon a period of a decline which may or may not turn out to be temporary. But the critics were as blind to his decadence as they had been previously blind to his great power; and, therefore, all the things they should have said about his early work they said about his later, so that he has been going on for the last two years receiving praise and admiration that are clearly a misfit. The same thing is quite true concerning Mr. Clemens. In the speeches that he has lately made he has said some things that recalled his earlier humour, but in the majority of his utterances the humour has been forced and the laughter which it has evoked has been extremely hollow. Yet just because it was Mark Twain, and because Mark Twain was once a true, spontaneous and original humourist, the poor creatures who write about him believe that everything he says must be amusing and delightful. If they do not feel the fun of it themselves they think they ought to, and they write about it just as though they did.

70. R. E. Phillips: 'Mark Twain: More than Humorist', *Book Buyer*

April 1901, xxii, 196–201

The art of humorous story-telling is, according to Mark Twain, a distinctly American creation. 'The basis of this art,' he says, 'is to string incongruities and absurdities together in a wandering and sometimes purposeless way and seem innocently unaware that they are absurdities.' It is, it seems to me, with some such definition as this in mind that we have accustomed ourselves to refer to him as the 'great American humorist.' From the popular point of view he has defined his own work to a nicety. For nearly half a century we have accepted and approved the label. He is the great American humorist. But he is more than that. And so clearly is this the case that were the contrary true more than a good half of his work, at the least estimate, could never have been written.

It is a curious fact that for all time and almost without exception the world's greatest humorists have been among its keenest thinkers and observers. It was so with Cervantes and his *Don Quixote*, with Ben Jonson and the *Silent Woman*, with Addison and 'Sir Roger de Coverley', and it is so with Mark Twain. Moreover, the public has never admitted this serious basis of all the best humor without a struggle. It took more than a hundred years after the publication of *Don Quixote* for the world to see in it anything more than a tale of comic misadventures. Doubtless this spirit, summed up in two words in the old saw 'once a humorist always a humorist,' accounts in some measure for the present popular *précis* of Mark Twain. Yet, in the main, as already noted, with the exception of stories like the 'Jumping Frog,' and the like, which are purely humorous both in manner and conception, by far the largest part of Mark Twain's work is serious. One is bound to recall, for instance, that *Life on the Mississippi, Roughing It,* and parts of *Tom Sawyer,* and *Huck Finn,* are primarily records of actual experience; and that works like the *Innocents,* the *Tramp Abroad, Following the Equator,* etc., depend at least for their point of view upon this same underlying motive. It would be well, therefore, if one is to consider Mark Twain for the moment as something more than humorist to have in mind some clear idea of the main incidents in his early experience which has just been referred to as the underlying motive—the first cause, as it were—of a large part of his work.

The first few years of his life, then, Mark Twain spent in the little 'out-at-the-elbows, slave-holding' town of Hannibal, Missouri. There his family had moved from the town of Florida, also in Missouri, where, in 1835, Mark Twain was born. Previous to this the family had lived first in Lexington, Kentucky, and just before moving to Missouri, in Jameston, Tennessee. During the residence in Tennessee his father took up a large tract of land—some 80,000 acres—in the hope of providing for himself and himself by the expected rise in land values. But in this he was disappointed, and the incident is only noted here because years later it furnished the idea for the *Gilded Age,* which in 1873 the author wrote in collaboration with Charles Dudley Warner.

In 1847 his father died and Mark Twain was left with very little property, to shift for himself. He was then only twelve years old. He left school at once and went into a printing office with his brother. In 1853 began his 'wander years.' He came to New York, supporting himself by odd jobs of type-setting, and the like, and until 1857 lived the free life of a wanderer, first in New York, then in St. Louis, Muscatine, and finally in Keokuk, Iowa. In 1857 he met Horace Bixby and learned from him the difficulties of steamboat piloting along the Mississippi. Of this period he says:

I am to this day profiting by that experience; for in that brief, sharp schooling, I got personally and familiarly acquainted with about all the different types of human nature that are to be found in fiction, biography or history. The fact is daily borne in upon me that the average shore employment requires as much as forty years to equip a man with the same sort of education.

For nearly three years he served as cub-pilot on the Mississippi. With the advent of the Civil War his occupation was at once wiped out and he enlisted with the Confederates in the army. But he did not stay there long. He recently explained his sudden leave-taking by claiming that his plan of closing the rebellion by surrounding Grant and driving him into the ocean was not favorably received by his superior officers. At any rate, he soon left the army and is next heard from in Nevada as private secretary to his brother, who held a government position there. A year of fortune-hunting followed in the silver mines of the Humboldt and Esmeralda regions. His experiences here are told in *Roughing It*. Soon after, he became editor of the *Virginia City Territorial Enterprise*, and later, legislative correspondent at Carson City, where he first assumed the writing name of 'Mark Twain'—the Mississippi leadsman's call for two fathoms. Mr. Howells has recently said that Mark Twain writes English as if it were a 'primitive and not a derivative language;' and this is in large measure due to the influence of his Western newspaper training of that period.

But something more than the ability to write English as if it were a 'primitive language' came from that vigorous school of Western and Southwestern training. And first of all the short series of autobiographical sketches just mentioned. Here the stories are what they pretend to be—records of experience. They present a series of definite pictures of actual life. In *Roughing It*, for example, the author has given us the first and the only effectively true account we have of that 'free, disorderly, grotesque society of men—swarming hosts of stalwart men'—in whom was bound up the story of the rise, growth and culmination of the silver-mining fever in Nevada. The result is in some degree humorous, because such a society had its broadly humorous side. The episodes of Scotty Briggs in his interview with the clergyman about Buck Fanshaw's funeral, and that of Brigham Young who in his desire to make a small present to his favorite wife, to the value only of twenty-five dollars, is finally obliged to invest in several hundred at the same price in order to keep peace in the family, are examples of the best humor in the book. The first is the more effective because it grows out of the subject and so, while just as amusing as the other, adds to the understanding and appreciation of the picture as a whole. The latter is a return to the old method of incongruity of which the early sketches offer the best instances. But such episodes are rare. Fully half of the book is serious. One effective incident like that of the wife and the miners in whose eyes a woman in camp was a 'rare and blessed spectacle,' stands for more than the combined effect of all the purely humorous incidents in the book.

Similarly in *Life on the Mississippi*. Here again the real, actual and living predominates; the purely humorous or whimsical is secondary. The story goes that the author after the publication of the *Innocents*—his first considerable success—was besieged by publishers on all sides with the cry for more 'copy.' He had no more 'copy' to offer. He felt that he was written out. He confided his predicament to a friend and happened at the same time to relate some of his experiences as a cub-pilot along the Mississippi. The result was that the value of the material was at once recognized, and the author was urged to tell his experiences exactly as they had occurred, in book form. This he has done in *Life on the Mississippi*. The philosophy, point of view and ideas of the book are those of the river-men. It is a history of the motives, generosity, brutality, humor, even, of the life of that time along the Great River. All this is well told. Bits of description—such, for instance, as the race of the two steam-boats down the river ending in the unexpected explosion and conflagration—are particularly vivid. As an example of humor, the contest between the 'Child of Calamity' and the 'Corpse-maker of Arkansaw' is one of the best. It may, indeed, be taken as typical of all or of nearly all the humorous episodes in the book. The humor is on the order of the 'Scotty Briggs' rather than the 'Brigham Young' type. That is, it is in general based on the study and observation of character; and the characters whose whimsical traits are woven into incidents and episodes are more or less intimately connected with the idea of the narrative as a whole.

Here, from a purely humorous point of view, is a step in advance. But as yet the study and development of character results only in episode. In its further development it lies at the basis of the author's best humor, and of his success, in so far as he may be called successful, as a writer of romance. Meanwhile, the *Gilded Age* better, perhaps, than any other of the author's works, illustrates this imperfect method of introducing the study of character as a subsidiary interest, rather than as the main underlying idea. Here it is not enough to say that in the character of Colonel Sellers we have the best there is in the *Gilded Age*; nor that in the contrast between his irrepressible buoyancy—his 'millions in it'—and the actual failure of all his plans and ambitions we have the author's first development of the humorous and pathetic side by side in a single character; nor, finally, that the character is a masterpiece of observation, and the first man in the author's fiction. For while this is undoubtedly true it only emphasizes the main point that after all the character of the Colonel represents only an incidental part, and so fails to make the book as a whole effective.

The contrary is true, on the other hand, of what may be considered, with the possible exception of the *Prince and Pauper*, and the *Connecticut Yankee at the Court of King Arthur*, the best Mark Twain has done in the way of fiction. In *Tom Sawyer* and *Huck Finn*, for example, the characters of the two boys stand for everything. The main effect here is undeniably that of humor, and it is so primarily because 'Tom' and 'Huck' are humorous characters. They are real boys. One of them is Mark Twain. Naturally, the life of a boy in the Southwest, forty and more years ago, was different in many respects from what it is to-day. Then there was more freedom, more chance for adventure. But boys' logic and motives change but little. The desire to 'show off' is as strong to-day as it ever was with Tom Sawyer; and the efficacy of the 'sore toe' in getting a fence whitewashed is as sure. The only difficulty now a days is that we no longer have any fences to whitewash. Conditions have changed. The motive must be applied in a different way. But it still remains, and because this is so, and because this universal motive has been understood and applied in these two works, the humor of *Huck Finn* and *Tom Sawyer* is as effective now as it was then, and un-doubtedly always will be—a fact which could not have been the case had these two characters been developed merely as a secondary or subsidiary interest.

In both these books, however, there is something more than humor and the delineation of humorous character. In the character of Huck Finn, the outcast and son of the village drunkard, is summed up in some sort the entire spirit of justice and equality—democracy in its broadest sense—of the Southwest of half a century ago. He is more than the Lazarillo of the picaresque novel; more, even, than Hugo's Gavroche, the immortal ragamuffin of fiction. For they were only gamins, the outcasts of the lowest round of society. Huck Finn is the equal not only of all the characters in the book, but of all readers. In spite of his birth, he is human; he has our sympathy; we must own him brother. It is the consummate art of the author that has brought this result to bear. But it is the broad spirit of equality, the result of actual experience and long familiarity with the ideas and ideals of that early Southwestern life that, in the first instance, made the conception of such a character possible.

As a writer of romance, however, Mark Twain can never be wholly successful because he cares so little—practically not at all—for effective construction. Even in the two works just referred to there is no climax. The stories might be continued indefinitely. They end only with the end of the book. The most effective bit of construction in all its [his] works is seen in the short story of the 'Man that Corrupted Hadleyburg.' Here the construction is well-nigh perfect. In idea, too, and in conception and development of character within short story limits, the 'Hadleyburg' story is a masterpiece. It is conceived and worked out in the manner of Cervantes. And as a good-humored satire on the whims and foibles of one phase of our social life it stands, it seems to me, of all Mark Twain's writings, easily first.

But it is rather to the qualities that underlie his merits as a writer of romance and a humorist than to these merits in themselves that we wish here to call special attention. Mark Twain has so long been a cosmopolitan that we are in danger of forgetting, in speaking of him only as a humorist, how thoroughly American he is—especially in his point of view. Or, better still, how thoroughly Western he is. He has never been educated up—or down—to many of the false standards of Eastern and European culture. He still holds to the old ideas. Moreover, he is a Westerner of that time when the West had not yet come to borrow its ideas and so-called culture from its Eastern neighbors. He represents the West as it was forty years ago. His point of view is primitive, elemental, uneducated, perhaps, if reckoned by Eastern 'book-learning' standards of education. But he knows *men*. And his work has the sovereign merit of being honest, unaffected, vigorous and above everything, fearless. Of this point of view the best illustration is to be found, perhaps, in his first success—the *Innocents Abroad*. Here from the beginning we have the hard sense of the West set against the established customs and 'culture' of the East. Mark Twain was the first man to look upon the catacombs as a joke. Turner's *Slave Ship*, floundering about in that 'fierce conflagration of reds and yellows' reminded him of a 'tortoise-shell cat having a fit in a platter of tomatoes.' And as for the 'Old Masters,' he considered the modern copies in all respects superior to the originals. Twelve years later, in the *Tramp Abroad*, his judgment is somewhat modified. But, after all, his satire in both instances is directed not against one phase or another of art but against those who persist in seeing in art what from his point of view is not there. Both the *Innocents* and the *Tramp Abroad* are protests against affectation. In asking about the mummy 'Is it dead?' he directs his flings not so much at the mummy as at those who pretend to admire mummies because it is fashionable to do so, although they are really incapable of any such æsthetic enjoyment. The humorous description of Bassano's 'Hair Trunk' as the world's artistic masterpiece proves, moreover, that his point of view is still essentially American and Western however much it may have been modified by twelve years of 'cultivation;' and in its humorous application to the obvious absurdities of many phases of European life, of which the protest against the blind worship of 'art' is only one example, lies the main interest and significance both of the *Innocents* and of the *Tramp Abroad*. Their method is the method of *Don Quixote*—the application of the philosophy of common sense to social foibles.

But from this point of view—which we are wont to call 'thoroughly Western'—there is a much more significant result than this first protest against insincerity and affectation. And here we come to what seems to me the keynote of the character of Mark Twain as a serious writer. I refer to his sense of absolute fairness and justice, already noted in passing as one of the underlying motives in *Huck Finn*. In one of his early sketches called the 'Bloody Massacre,' Mark Twain satirizes quite mercilessly his own efforts toward becoming the champion of justice and right; and here he deplores the fact that in this sketch the public only read as far as the 'bloody' part, and passed over the underlying idea. That is the trouble today. The public forgets, or what is worse, will not admit that there is anything in Mark Twain beyond mere humor. They prefer to be amused. They read the 'bloody' part and skip the rest. But the fibre is none the less there. In *Joan of Arc* the character of the 'Maid' is based wholly upon the author's conception of what is just and right. It is his evident sympathy with her not as a romantic character in history, but as a human being forced to the highest sacrifice injustice can bring, that counts for most in the effectiveness of the book of which the 'Maid' is the central figure. Similarly, in the *Prince and Pauper*. Here the idea of justice is universalized. The old problem of class distinction, democracy based upon merit and equality, is written into a story for children. In a slightly different sense the same is true of the *Connecticut Yankee at the Court of King Arthur*; although here, of course, the more serious opinions are woven about a central motive which is purely whimsical. The chapter on 'Sixth Century Political Economy,' and repeated references throughout the book to the respect he has for any kind of 'unearned supremacy,' show in what direction these opinions tend. Moreover, this animating spirit of justice may be observed as the basis of a large part of his writing in which humor even as a secondary motive does not exist. In the essay on the 'Defence of Shelley,' the author criticizes Professor Dowden for upholding an unjust view of the poet's relations with Mary Godwin, for no other reason than that the blame for the separation should have been Shelley's and not his wife's. Again, with Mark Twain, to an unusual degree, the book is the man. The recent fortunate outcome of the relations between the author and his former publishers is only a concrete example of his spirit of justice applied to every-day life and conditions. Even in the recent humorous incident of the cab—humorous chiefly because the wrong motive has been attached to the unusual proceeding of a man constituting himself, of his own accord, a 'social' policeman—we have only a practical demonstration of the ideas already developed in the story called 'Traveling with a Reformer.'

In the last article Mark Twain has published—advice to the 'Person Sitting in Darkness'—his conception of justice and his ideas as an humanitarian are for the first time applied to world politics and questions of international importance. The conclusions reached in this article will doubtless appeal to all those who are opposed to the attitude of the present administration toward the 'savages' of the East. As a whole, however, it may be said that the article is rather a clever caricature upon the conditions, as they are supposed to exist, than a valid argument that wrong is being done by our present Eastern policy. But on one question raised in the article there can be no ground for dispute. It is evident that the 'Person Sitting in Darkness' has as much right to live and live without the interference of others for mere pecuniary gain as the most enlightened among us. And this, after all, is the broadly humanitarian view here taken by the author. In this respect Mark Twain is in exact opposition to the attitude of 'jingoism' of which, for instance, Mr. Kipling is so consistent an exponent. Upon Mr. Kipling it has been charged that he is more responsible, perhaps, than any other one man in England for the 'most diabolical development of the foul art of war.' Moreover, he urges taking up the white man's burden only where England stands to win and so to derive thereby added glory and commercial or pecuniary advantage. This is not to say that he has created the situations which have led to the troubles either in Africa or in the East. But, in treating of these situations as they exist, he has been the first to cry as Dick Heldar did: 'Give 'em hell! Oh, give 'em hell!'

Now Mark Twain in his way is just as patriotic as Kipling, but he is quieter about it. He goes at it in a different way. He is less of a 'jingo.' With Mark Twain the key-note is justice—not war and conquest for gain. He stands up for American standards because he believes that these standards are just. But he does not go so far as to say that we as Americans—or at least those set in high places over us—are infallible. The advice to the 'Person' proves this most abundantly. And yet he is not opposed to war as such when in its results it means progress and advancement of modern methods and civilization. 'The great bulk of the savages,' he says in one place, 'must go.' The white man needs their lands, but he objects to the manner of their taking-off. For instance, speaking of the reduction of population in South Africa by Mr. Rhodes' 'slow-misery and lingering-death' system he says, 'Rhodesia is a happy name for that land of piracy and pillage and puts the right stain upon it.' In general, however, the influence of Mark Twain is for peace rather than for war and conquest; and always—first, last and all the while—for justice, absolute democracy and humanity. This stands for more than humor, and more than success as a novelist. And it is largely through the recognition of the fact that underlying a great part of his work runs the undercurrent of seriousness of which justice, contempt for affectation and love of humanity are among the chief characteristics, that we shall eventually come to the best appreciation of Mark Twain as the 'great American humorist.'

71. T. M. Parrott: 'Mark Twain: Made in America', *Booklover's Magazine*

February 1904, iii, 145–54

Thomas Marc Parrott (1866–1960) joined the faculty of Princeton in 1896 and was professor of English there until his retirement. He published works on the Elizabethan dramatists, Victorian literature, and the poetry of the late nineteenth century.

The translations and criticism from *Revue des Deux Mondes* are discussed at some length by Henderson (No. 86). Lang's comment is from his article of February 1891 (No. 39). *Joan of Arc* appeared in *Harper's Magazine*, April 1895–April 1896, not in the *Century*.

The virgin soil of America has produced in the last century a rich harvest of humor. The first fruits of this harvest appeared even in Colonial times, when the genial warmth of the Quaker City's atmosphere dissolved the ice of Puritanism around the heart of Franklin and interfused his inborn Yankee shrewdness with the kindly charity of his adopted home. The wars and dissensions of the Revolutionary era stayed its growth, but with the opening of the nineteenth century it broke forth again in the delightful creations of Washington Irving, whose masterpieces of humor, *Knickerbocker's History*, *Rip Van Winkle*, and *The Legend of Sleepy Hollow*, in spite of their disguise of eighteenth-century English diction, are racy with the true flavor of the soil from which they sprang. And from Irving's day to our own this harvest, increasing alike in quantity, variety, and spontaneous charm, has been one of the staple products of our civilization. It has not been confined to any section of the country nor to any stratum of our varying levels of culture. The mining camp of the Rockies has borne fruit as well as the plantation of tidewater Virginia, the 'poor white' Mississippi river-town as well as the academic center of New England.

We are not, it must be frankly confessed, a witty nation; in American literature the 'wit' is a phenomenon, infrequent, and, as a rule, unappreciated. Wit, I fancy, is a plant that requires an older soil and more deliberate culture than American life can often afford. But humor, that kindly, democratic, half skeptical, half sentimental, attitude of mind toward the universe at large, is indigenous. Every good American is a humorist at heart; and humor in all its forms, from screaming farce to genial character-creation, finds in America what is accorded to no other form of literature or art, a general, intelligent, and sympathetic appreciation.

Of all our humorists, alive or dead, Mark Twain is the most widely popular and the most typically American. It is not too much, I think, to say that he is the most popular because he is the most typically American. This underlying source of his popularity has, however, been more generally realized abroad than at home, where the fastidious niceness of the professional critic has too often been unable to perceive in the creations of our greatest humorist anything more than the contortions of the professional buffoon. It was but a few years ago, for example, that a solemn critic in our most decorous periodical refused him admission to the sacred circle presided over by the Autocrat of the Breakfast Table, and declared that a circus-clown was as likely to attract the attention of the dramatic critic as Mark Twain that of the serious reviewer. And this a quarter of a century after the intelligent and sympathetic criticism of the *Revue des Deux Mondes* had introduced the author of the *Jumping Frog* and the *Innocents Abroad* to the delighted audience of Europe!

The autobiographic element in the work of Mark Twain has often been pointed out, but it is not perhaps generally realized that the interest of his books varies directly in proportion to the presence of this personal element. Where his work, to be successful, demands the exercise of the historic imagination, he fails lamentably, as in the luckless *Yankee at King Arthur's Court*. He is at his best when he is recording his own experiences; and in his happiest vein when he is transfusing them into a work of art, as in his crowning achievements of *Tom Sawyer* and *Huckleberry Finn*. And this is because his life itself has been typically—one might almost say, uniquely—American.

[gives biographical summary.]

Mr. Clemens' first printed article was, it appears, a fantastic burlesque of the paragraphs on river news contributed to the New Orleans *Picayune* by a patriarch of the piloting craft, over the signature of 'Mark Twain.' The parody so disgusted the old pilot that he entirely ceased to contribute to the press, and some years afterward departed this earthly life. 'At the time the telegraph brought the news of his death,' says Mr. Clemens,

I was a fresh, new journalist on the Pacific coast, and needed a *nom de guerre*; so I confiscated the ancient mariner's discarded one, and have done my best to make it remain what it was in his hands—a sign and symbol and warrant that whatever is found in its company may be gambled on as being the petrified truth. How I've succeeded, it would not be modest in me to say.

It was over this signature that a number of humorous sketches appeared in the California journals during the middle sixties, one of which soon travelled eastward and attracted considerable attention. This was the famous *Jumping Frog*, the best known, perhaps, of all Twain's shorter stories. It is a very admirable example of what he himself has defined as the American humorous story, which depends for its effect not upon its matter, but entirely upon the manner in which it is told. The fun of the story consists by no means in the climax, but far more in the wholly serious fashion in which the author—copying, he declares, the old miner from whom he first heard the tale—narrates the absurd history of Jim Smiley, with his passion for betting, his rat terriers, his fighting cocks, his bulldog, 'Andrew Jackson,' and his trained frog, 'Daniel Webster.' And this fashion of blending false and true, this sober narration of preposterous nonsense, has been from Franklin's time, as Professor Wendell has well pointed out, one of the distinguishing characteristics of American humor.

Mark Twain's first book, apart from a collection of his early sketches, was the *Innocents Abroad*, and the immense success of this work, one hundred and twenty-five thousand copies of which were sold within the first three years of its publication, established his reputation as a 'funny man,' a reputation which he has to this day found it very hard to live down. *Innocents Abroad* is not a great book; it is not one of those on which the author's fame will ultimately rest, but it is a very typical piece of work. Its fun depends upon its frank simplicity, its unflagging animal spirits, and its ludicrous contrast of civilizations. 'There are a good many things about this Italy which I do not understand,' the twenty-fifth chapter begins; and with a slight alteration—Old World for Italy—the words might serve as a motto for the whole book. No doubt if the author had understood more he would have laughed less, but the gaiety of nations would have been proportionately diminished. The excursion itself was the prototype of the thousand-and-one personally conducted parties which have since then started out to discover the Old World. Who that has encountered one of these queer collections, rushing through their predetermined round of sight-seeing, can fail to recognize the truth of the picture that the humorist drew?

[quotes ch. 61 ' "None of us" ' to ' "proud of it" ' and ' "We had cared" ' to ' "stores of America." ']

So long as the fruitful soil of our country continues to produce in bewildering multiplicity the counterparts of these travellers, the *Innocents Abroad* will remain a perennial fountain of laughter.

Some dozen years later, in 1880, Mr. Clemens published his second book of travel, *A Tramp Abroad*. This is, as might be expected, a somewhat riper book than the *Innocents*, and perhaps on that account it is hardly so amusing. It lacks something of the first, fine, careless rapture of the earlier work. And yet it is full of fun. One could spare, perhaps, the parodies of German legends and the prolonged farce of the ascent of the Riffelberg, but not the unforgetable sketches of Americans abroad. The embryo horse-doctor of Heidelberg, the innocent chatter-box of Lucerne, and 'somebody's grandson,' are types struck off with relentless accuracy, and yet with such sympathetic humor as to take all the sting out of the satire. No less delightful are the reminiscences of America—Jim Baker's story of the blue jay and the hole in the cabin, and Riley's tale of the man who put up at Gadsby's. Indeed, if it were not for one of the appendices, the opinion might almost be ventured that the best things in the *Tramp Abroad* were the tramp's meetings with his countrymen and his memories of his country. But this appendix contains the account of Mark Twain's epic combat with the 'awful German language,' and from its modest beginning, with the delusive scriptural quotation, to its triumphant close in the Fourth of July Oration in the German tongue, this extravaganza is a masterpiece. It is based, of course, upon a total ignorance of the laws of speech, and proceeds upon the absurd assumption that a language has been made, and therefore can be unmade, by the conscious volition of man. And yet the wild farce never wholly loses touch with reality. How true, for instance, the following description of the average style of a German newspaper is, only those can know who have lost time and temper in struggling to extract information from these ponderous and poly-syllabic sheets:

[quotes Appendix D 'An average sentence' to 'to a foreigner'.]

Roughing It, Mark Twain's first book of American life, appeared some eight years before *A Tramp Abroad*. It is, in the author's happy phrase, a 'record of several years of variegated vagabondizing,' covering the period of his departure for the mines until his first trip to Europe. The book, I suppose, has never been quite so popular as the *Innocents Abroad*, but it is distinctly more important. The description of the old stage-coach journey across the plains, two thousand miles or so in twenty days; the pictures of the 'flush times' in the mining camps, the incidental portraits, comic or tragic, of the 'bad man' of the West, are contributions of the highest value to our knowledge of a now vanished phase of American life. There is plenty of fun in the book, ranging from truly humorous character sketches to the broadest burlesque, and at times to the stalest sort of comic paper foolery; but there is something more than mere fun. As the author himself apologetically remarks, 'there is quite a good deal of information in the book.' And he goes on to say:

I regret this very much, but really it could not be helped. Information appears to stew out of me naturally like the precious ottar of roses out of the otter. Sometimes it has seemed to me that I would give worlds if I could retain my facts; but it cannot be. The more I calk up my sources and the tighter I get, the more I leak wisdom.

There is still another aspect in which *Roughing It* is a better book than the *Innocents*, and that is the side of the writer's character which it presents. Mark Twain's first book, it must be confessed, revealed in a strong light some of the most unpleasing traits which its author shared along with the average untutored American: his ignorance, his irreverence, his general self-satisfaction, and his occasional bumptiousness. But it is no uncommon phenomenon that the sort of American whom abroad one avoids like the plague is a very different character at home, and *Roughing It* shows plainly enough the presence in Mark Twain of certain qualities which one is glad to believe are typically American— unquenchable good humor even in the most trying situations, unfailing kindness towards one's fellow-man, unfaltering reverence for woman, versatility, energy, and honesty.

Life on the Mississippi, 1883, is a second work which may be ranked with *Roughing It* as a contribution to our knowledge of American life. Broadly speaking, the book falls into two parts, the first dealing with the writer's own experiences as a river pilot, the second being little more than newspaper 'copy' compiled during the course of an excursion twenty years later. There is some good stuff in the second part, but the first is gold without alloy. Here we have no brilliant set pieces of conscious joking, but a subtle humor of character, incident and situation, diffused throughout, and combined with a power of strong and sustained narrative such as no earlier work has shown, a power which even so severe a critic as the London *Athenæum* pronounced to be within the reach of few or no contemporary writers. If it were not too much like an Irish bull, one would say that Mark Twain's feet were nowhere planted so firmly upon the ground of remembered experience as when he is afloat upon the great river that washed the shores of his first home. Mention has been made somewhere of Mark Twain's tenacious memory for detail and his microscopic imagination; and it is no unfair assumption to suppose that these qualities are due, in part at least, to his long and arduous apprenticeship as a 'cub' pilot. In these pages he tells us repeatedly and elaborately how he was 'taught the river,' compelled by advice, warning, abuse, and mockery to remember all its varying marks and depths and bars in daylight and darkness, in fog and storm, at low water and in flood.

[quotes ch. 13 'I think' to 'pilots will not'.]

Mark Twain's first experiment in fiction was made some thirty years ago in company with Charles Dudley Warner. Their joint work, *The Gilded Age*, is an incoherent and sensational satire on the era of speculation and political corruption that followed the Civil War. Probably no living American was less fitted to pull in double harness than Mark Twain, and it would have been hard to find a more unsuitable mate for him than the gentle, bookish, and somewhat dreamy Warner. No wonder, then, that the book has failed to take rank among the masterpieces of either author. Yet it contains at least one episode, the steamboat race, and one character, Colonel Sellers, that are real additions to American literature. We are not likely to go wrong in assigning both of these to Mark Twain. The material for the episode he found, of course, in his own experience as a pilot, and Colonel Sellers had in all probability his origin in some of the genial liars with whom the author came in contact during his Western life; but both episode and character have been passed through the crucible of his imagination until they have been transformed into something far superior to mere accurate reporting or burlesque exaggeration. Listen for a moment to the Colonel as he expounds to a credulous hearer one of his schemes.

[quotes extracts ch. 8 'I have a small' to 'millions apiece!']

It is, I think, hardly too much to say that in such work as this we find for the first time distinct evidences of Mark Twain's real creative power.

The Adventures of Tom Sawyer, 1876, is the first in date of the trio of stories dealing with ante-bellum life in the slave-holding towns along the Mississippi, on which it now seems fairly evident that Mark Twain's fame will ultimately depend. Of these three it is the lightest, brightest, and most simply entertaining. The flood of animal spirits still runs bank-high through the book, breaking out at times into a foam of farce. There is, indeed, a bit of rather lurid melodrama woven into the texture of the story, a villainous half-breed, a bloody murder, buried treasure, and other stock properties of the penny dreadful. Though this matter is artfully arranged to give some striking scenes, it is to such a little masterpiece of pure comedy as Tom at the white-washing job, wherein the hero sells to his friends the privilege of doing the work for him, that we turn in grateful remembrance. The dialogue between Tom and his first victim, Ben Rogers, is inimitable:

[quotes ch. 2 ' "Say—*I'm* going" ' to 'in his heart'.]

We hardly need the author's assurance that most of the adventures in *Tom Sawyer* really occurred, for the story breathes conviction from every page. The scenes in the schoolroom, the Sunday-school, and the village church reproduce for us the atmosphere of the little inland town as persuasively as Mr. Aldrich's *Bad Boy* does that of old New England. And as a study in child-life, as a revelation of the soul of a boy, *Tom Sawyer* beats all rivals out of the field. One admirer has even gone so far as to declare it a very proper basis for a system of pedagogy. This, I fancy, would be an honor that the author never dreamed of.

Huckleberry Finn, 1885, shows a very distinct advance over *Tom Sawyer* in seriousness and power of composition. The real heart of the book, is of course, the narrative of Huck's flight down the Mississippi with the runaway nigger, Jim; and the successive incidents of this flight unroll for us a panorama of life on the great river in a series of pictures whose variety, reality, humor, and occasional tragic power, it is almost impossible to praise too highly. To quote Andrew Lang's apt words, it is 'a nearly flawless gem of romance and humor.' We feel that the author is standing on familiar ground, and dealing with the characters and scenes that surrounded his own youth. Consider, for example, this picture of daybreak on the Mississippi.

[quotes ch. 14 'Two or three' to 'just going it!']

Notable in this masterpiece, *Huckleberry Finn*, is the power of characterization. It is not too much, I think, to say that Jim is the best portrait of the negro slave in English literature, from Oroonoko to Uncle Remus. We need only compare him with the idealized figures in *Uncle Tom's Cabin*—white gentlemen with faces blackened for the occasion—to see the difference between work based upon understanding and that which is merely the product of the unaided imagination. The ignorance, superstition, humility, kind-heartedness, and grateful devotion of the slave have never been so vividly portrayed. Huck himself is an even more subtle study. It is no small task for the author of a book written throughout in the first person to keep himself out of the picture, to refrain from speaking in his own voice through the mouth of the supposed narrator. Even Thackeray has not wholly succeeded in disengaging himself from Henry Esmond. But Huck Finn is altogether objective; more objective, I think, and more individual than even his brother-in-arms, Tom Sawyer. Nothing in all the author's work shows so clearly his power of putting himself in another's place as this careful and loving portrait of a village outcast—dirty, idle, thievish, lying, and yet at heart so conscientious, so loving, and so true.

Pudd'nhead Wilson, the last of this group of stories, has an artistic unity which the others lack. Curiously enough this sombre story took shape in the author's mind as a farce, which turned into a tragedy under his very hands. In one of the most amusing glimpses of a literary workshop that an author has ever given us, Mr. Clemens tells of his trouble with the tangled story. The farce and the tragedy, he says, obstructed and interrupted each other at every turn, and created no end of confusion and annoyance, until he finally pulled the former up by the roots and left the other, 'a kind of literary Caesarean operation.'

The result of the operation, however, is by no means wholly gratifying. *Pudd'nhead Wilson* is a tragedy, but a very sordid one. There is no trace left of the light-hearted gaiety of *Tom Sawyer*, and very little of the genial humanity of *Huckleberry Finn*. On the contrary, the book is marked by a strong dash of ironical cynicism which finds utterance mainly in the *obiter dicta* of the titular hero, prefixed as mottoes to the various chapters. 'If you pick up a starving dog and make him prosperous, he will not bite you; that is the principal difference between a dog and a man,' says one of these. That is not the sort of thing that the Mark Twain of *Innocents Abroad* would have regarded as a joke, and it runs counter to the experiences of Tom with Muff Potter, and of Huck with 'nigger Jim.' It is, perhaps, a result of this bitter mood that there is no one figure in the book capable of arresting and retaining our sympathies. Tom Driscoll, the slave who takes his master's place, is a monster of meanness, cowardice, and ingratitude; the mulatto, Roxana, is a strongly conceived, but rather repellent character; and Pudd'nhead himself is, till the very close of the book, a mere lay figure on which to hang the author's own philosophizings. And yet the work is by no means devoid of power. It is a strong, direct, and simple piece of narrative; it has an ingeniously constructed plot and a startling climax; and like its predecessors it is a genuine and realistic picture of that phase of American life with which the author is most familiar. Had any one but Mark Twain written such a book it would no doubt have been more generally recognized as the grave and powerful piece of art it really is.

The Prince and the Pauper, 1880, is the first of a trio of stories dealing with medieval life. All of these, but especially the first, have a certain intellectual kinship with Innocents Abroad. In that book Mark Twain reported his discovery of Europe; in The Prince and the Pauper he proclaimed his discovery of the historic past. And apparently he was as much surprised to find that the past differed from his own age as he had once been to discover that they 'managed things better in France.' But he is by no means ready to admit that they managed things better under Henry the Eighth. Indeed his point of view is very much that of Charles Dickens, whose caricature of Henry as a cross between Blue Beard and Giant Blunderbore is probably responsible for the current misconception of that great king. It would, no doubt, be a somewhat harder task to point out such glaring inaccuracies in The Prince and the Pauper as occasionally disfigure the Innocents; but any one who has studied the social life of England under the Tudors, from contemporary sources, will feel before he is half way through the book that the colors are laid on too heavily. And the curious mingling in the diction of the stock phraseology of the historical novel—the gadzooks, by-my-fay style—with the fresh and racy vigor of Mark Twain's natural idiom, jars heavily upon the ear.

But after all The Prince and the Pauper, taken simply as a story, is a good story—simple, sweet, and interesting. And to those who care for something more than a mere story it will always have a peculiar charm as the fullest and frankest revelation of some of the author's noblest qualities, his sympathy with the poor and the rejected, his love of justice and mercy, and his hatred of cruelty and oppression in all their forms, whether in naked brutality, or cloaked under the delusive garb of law and established custom.

The *Yankee at the Court of King Arthur*, 1889, is to my mind the least successful of Mark Twain's novels. The conception on which it rests is, indeed, a capital one for a farce. But unfortunately the growing seriousness of the author's view of life did not permit him to handle his conception farcically. A great part of the book is occupied with a polemic, direct or veiled, against feudalism and chivalry—two very different institutions, by the way, although here perpetually confounded. And, after all, the age of feudalism and of chivalry is past and gone; there is no longer need of a Cervantes; why therefore beat the bones of the dead?

The *Personal Recollections of Joan of Arc*, 1896, is by all odds the most considerable work of this group. It is based upon more careful study, it holds closer to the truth of history, and it is a sincere attempt to re-draw without distortion or caricature the features of one of the most striking personalities of all times. One thing at least the shrewd Yankee found desirable at King Arthur's court—a good woman; and it is highly creditable to the Yankee's creator that the one thing which Mark Twain has found love-worthy in the despised Middle Ages is the pure and gracious figure of the Maid of Orleans. As every one knows, this story appeared anonymously in *The Century*, amid much debate as to its authorship. Really there was no question for debate; the first installment of the story contained at least one scene that no one but Mark Twain could have written; and several of the characters are familiar figures from his works, transplanted to the France of the fifteenth century—the Paladin, for example, is one of Mark Twain's genial braggarts, La Hire one of his golden-hearted ruffians. Yet it must be acknowledged that *Joan of Arc* is, perhaps, the least characteristic of Mark Twain's works. It is notably deficient in the fresh and vigorous dialogue which occupies so large a space in *Huckleberry Finn* and *Pudd'nhead Wilson*; it contains almost none of those superb bits of narrative which seem to bring a scene to life before our eyes; if the truth must be told, it is at times open to one charge that can be brought against none of his former works, the charge of dulness.

Since *Joan of Arc* Mark Twain has not produced any work that calls here for special consideration. *Following the Equator* is a relapse into the early manner of *Innocents Abroad*, without the fresh gaiety of that work; 'Tom Sawyer Detective,' and the 'Double-Barrelled Detective Story' continue a line of work first begun in *Pudd'nhead Wilson*, where the mere plot interest is superior to that in character or setting. 'The Man that Corrupted Hadleyburg' is a satire on Yankee hypocrisy and greed that would be wholly admirable, if it were not for the tragic catastrophe imposed so inaptly upon a climax of roaring farce. In addition to these we have a number of short stories, literary and critical essays, and impressions of travel. None of them is without the hallmark of Mark Twain's peculiar genius, but none of them constitutes any very distinct addition to his fame.

It is too soon to attempt any definitive estimate of Mark Twain's work. Mr. Clemens is still so far from old age that we may confidently look forward to fresh work which must be taken into account in any final summing up. But there are one or two points, touched on for the most part already in the course of this review, which may here be brought together with a view to obtaining at least a partial appreciation of his work. Enough has been said to show that Mark Twain is by no means the mere 'funny man' of popular conception, but a humorist of extraordinary powers, wide range, and deep human sympathies. He is a past master of farce, burlesque, and grotesque exaggeration; but he is also an inimitable story-teller, and at his best an unsurpassed delineator of character. His humor does not depend upon bad spelling or worse grammar, although he knows better than any man alive, perhaps, how to use dialect to heighten his effects. He is not, in the old sense of the word, a literary man. He does not connect with any of the established traditions of humor, but represents a new force, 'as simple in form,' to borrow Mr. Howells' fine comparison, 'and as direct as the statesmanship of Lincoln or the generalship of Grant.' And like these great Americans—both it may be noted, representatives of his own section—Mark Twain has devoted his great powers to the service of the right. His work is characterized by a sweet sunniness, across which no shadow of impurity ever falls. It is no small thing for us, as Americans, to be able to record that our greatest humorist has never written a page that can offend true modesty. His sympathy has always gone out to the poor, the despised, and the oppressed; and his unrivalled powers of ridicule have been steadily directed against conventionality, hypocrisy, affectation, and humbug. It is not, I think, too much to prophesy that, when the time comes for a final estimate of Mark Twain, he will be recognized as one of the most national of American authors, and one of the peculiar glories of American literature.

72. Harry Thurston Peck:
'Mark Twain at Ebb Tide', *Bookman*
(New York)

May 1904, xix, 235-6

This unsigned criticism was quite probably written by Harry Thurston Peck (see No. 69), who continued to contribute to the *Bookman* after relinquishing its editorship.

There is something unutterably pathetic about a book like Mark Twain's *Extracts from Adam's Diary*. It shows just how far a man who was once a great humourist can fall. We thought when we read 'A Double-Barrelled Detective Story' that Mark Twain could do no worse. But we were wrong. The other book may have been more ridiculous; but this one is more pitiable. We glance at the paper wrapper; we see the advertisement of the 'Complete Works of Mark Twain'; we read the titles: *The Adventures of Huckleberry Finn*, *The Jumping Frog of Calaveras*, *Life on the Mississippi*, *The Gilded Age*, *The Innocents Abroad*, *The Adventures of Tom Sawyer*, and we remember a man who through the sheer strength and originality of his genius won the world's laughter. Then we read *Extracts from Adam's Diary*. Had these Extracts been written by a man without a great name, no amount of 'pull' or adroit argument would have enabled him to palm them off on a first-class metropolitan daily as 'Sunday Special' matter.

73. Hammond Lamont:
'Mark Twain at Seventy', *Nation*

14 December 1905, lxxxi, 478–9

Hammond Lamont (1864–1909), the author of this unsigned article, was managing editor of the New York *Evening Post* from 1900 to 1909 and editor of the *Nation* from 1906 to 1909.

The most significant thing about the dinner to Mark Twain on December 5 was the greeting from forty of the leading men of letters of England. No other American author, we are confident, could receive such a tribute. In the opinion of foreigners, Mark Twain is the greatest of living American writers. An interesting side-light is thrown on his fame by an incident in Kipling's first visit to America, some fifteen years ago. Mark Twain was the man of whom Kipling had heard, and whom, above others, he wished to see. In the interval since then his reputation has grown, both at home and abroad. Bret Harte, whose name was often coupled with his, is dead. No one is left to dispute his preëminence, or even to compare with him.

He did not, however, come into his own at once. People were suspicious of him because he was not born and bred to the literary traditions of Boston, New York, or Philadelphia. Nor did he, when at last he had fairly started on his career, accept the conventions of his generation and conform to the standards of either of these three centres of culture. He was not reared with Hawthorne, Lowell, Longfellow, and Holmes; and consequently New England pitied him. He never attended the so-called 'Knickerbocker School'; and New York saw at once that he suffered much from lack of early advantages. True, his essays and sketches used to appear in the staid pages of the *Atlantic*, but they were a horrible shock to the dowager duchesses of Boston. The *Atlantic*, however, was erratic. It not only tolerated Mark Twain, but for a time it was edited by a man named Thomas Bailey Aldrich, who had not graduated from Harvard, indeed had never attended college, and who was therefore not a member of the Brahmin caste. These literary pariahs, however, occasionally get on in spite of deficiencies in taste and education. Mr. Aldrich, for example, managed to write some things that people have condescended to read. Indeed, one of his stories, 'Marjorie Daw,' so took the fancy of a budding author that, changing the name of the personages of the tale, he kindly offered to sell it to the *Evening Post*. What is worth stealing must have some merit. Mark Twain's success has been more dazzling than Mr. Aldrich's—and with good reason.

He knows America and knows it whole. Born in Missouri seventy years ago, he saw every type of man, woman, and child, white and black, that lived in the vast Mississippi Valley. As pilot on a Mississippi steamboat he made the acquaintance of the pioneers from New England, New York, Pennsylvania, and the Western Reserve, who pushed across the prairies and filled the vacant lands of Illinois, Iowa, Wisconsin, Minnesota, Nebraska, and Kansas. He was scarcely less at home in the Gulf States, for which the Mississippi was the great highway. As Territorial secretary of Nevada and editor of the Virginia City *Enterprise*, he knew at first hand the mining camps of the Pacific Coast, the gamblers, the railway builders, and the politicians. He has dwelt for many years in the East. He has travelled extensively. He has read widely. With some native talent to start with, he has in the slow course of time picked up almost as good an equipment for literary work as a man will get in four years at Harvard or Columbia.

He has not devoted himself to carving cherry-stones according to academic rules, but to the best of his ability he has written books to read. Delicate questions of usage have not troubled him any more than they troubled Shakspere or Defoe; he has had larger problems on his mind. We do not, we trust, undervalue choice, exact, and even academic English. A careless, sloppy style is not virtue. Misusing words and taking the edge off their meaning is the favorite amusement of fools. But Mark Twain has had stories to tell—big ones and good ones. His swift, racy style—words of the people as the people understand them—smelling of the soil, is as excellent in its kind as the classic sentences of Hawthorne. In *Huckleberry Finn* and *Tom Sawyer* he had matter enough to last an ordinary novelist a lifetime. That, after all, is the essential. The manner, we admit, is not that of the late Walter Pater in *Marius the Epicurean*. It is—if the two writers be at all commensurable—far better.

Yet it is the bulk of Mark Twain's work, rather than the admirable handling of details, that gives it power. To say nothing of his ventures into historical romance—he has shown us on an extensive scale surpassingly vivid pictures of many phases of our life. 'Here,' cry his European eulogists, 'is America as it is or was.' They are right. *Huckleberry Finn* is a cross-section of Missouri and lower Illinois. You may rise from the perusal, feeling that you have actually lived there, that you know intimately a whole social stratum of ante-bellum days, and that you have enjoyed one of the most entertaining and moving tales in our language. The episode of that feud between the Grangerfords and the Shepherdsons, with the men running along the river-bank, shooting at the swimming boys, and shouting 'Kill them! kill them!' grips the memory like those stirring scenes where Crusoe came upon the footprints of the savages and the outlaws stormed the castle of Front de Bœuf.

In saying this we mean that Mark Twain is a much greater man than the humorist of *The Jumping Frog*. That he is a humorist of the first rank no discriminating person has dreamed of denying for the last thirty years. But he is a humanist as well, if we accept the term in its broader sense—one versed in human affairs. His humor has served to keep clear and steady his vision of human relations, has helped him to pierce the sophistries of politicians, and to test the fleeting fashions of a day by eternal principles, has closed his ears to the passing cries of party, and enabled him to stand with courage, and to lift a voice that carries far, for justice and mercy to all men, of all colors, in all lands.

74. Unsigned article, 'Mark Twain', *Spectator*

25 May 1907, xcviii, 825–6

The *Spectator's* commentary about the honorary degree from Oxford catalogues Clemens' virtues and accomplishments in the most naive manner of an exultant empire in an imperialistic age. The 'youthful journalist' referred to in this article was Rudyard Kipling, who included an animated description of his interview with Mark Twain in *From Sea to Sea* (New York, 1899).

Some thirty-five years ago Mr. Samuel Clemens—or Mark Twain as it is pleasanter to call him—was deputed by his fellow-passengers to ask for recognition from the Royal Humane Society for the captain and the lifeboat crew of the steamer *Batavia* for saving life at sea. Quite characteristically, he asked for no reward for himself. He was satisfied if he had been of any service 'standing around the deck in a furious storm, without any umbrella, keeping an eye on things and seeing that they were done right, and yelling whenever a cheer seemed the important thing.' That was enough for him; but what he asked for was recognition for the captain and the crew from the Humane Society, who, he wrote, would 'in so remembering them increase the high honour and esteem in which the Society is held all over the civilised world.' Perhaps we may reapply the words to the position of the author at the present moment. Another 'humane society' is proposing to confer a distinction upon an honoured personage. The University of Oxford has offered an honorary degree to Mark Twain, which will be conferred upon him at the forthcoming Commemoration, and it is certainly true that in honouring the great American writer Oxford honours herself. To the majority of her sons, perhaps, it falls to 'stand around the deck' and to cheer whenever a cheer seems necessary, while the distinguished few occupy the attention of countries and continents. But it is the privilege of all, as owning the same motherhood, to bestow fraternal honours and compliments. Such a distinction as an honorary degree is offered in hearty recognition of the name, not only of a man of letters, but one who has set an example of upright, brave, and strenuous living.

For the record of Mark Twain's life, apart from its aspect as belonging to a distinguished writer, is one of fine energy, undaunted resolution, and the widest experience of men and manners. He was born seventy-one years ago, in 1835, and his work begins with his decision, at the not very mature age of thirteen, to become a printer. Besides his printing work, he was engaged, according to his own account, to scribble on a paper belonging to his uncle, 'the *Weekly Hannibal Journal*, two dollars a year in advance—five hundred subscribers, and they paid in cordwood, cabbages, and unmarketable turnips.' A year or two later he was travelling, still as a journalist, picking up what work he could, and it was perhaps at this stage that he came in for the quaint adventures which he has described in that admirable little piece of satire, 'How I Edited an Agricultural Paper.' In this interesting journal, it may be remembered, the temporary editor gave the valuable advice that 'turnips should never be pulled, it injures them. It is much better to send a boy up and let him shake the tree'; also, that 'the guano is a fine bird, but great care is necessary in rearing it.' But these journalistic experiences, although they doubtless involved some hard knocks, and probably on occasion that lack of food which is salutary to the soul of a young writer, were not the hardest part of his schooling. It was as a pilot on the Mississippi River that he gained the experience which enabled him eventually to give the world a real book. As a pilot, indeed, he literally 'made his name' as no other living writer has made it; he was casting about for a pseudonym by which to sign a squib he had written on the captain of his steamboat, and the name was suddenly called to him by a deck-hand heaving the lead '*mark twain.*' After that, as private secretary to his brother, 'Treasurer, Comptroller, Secretary of State, and Acting Governor in the Governor's absence' of Nevada Territory, seeing all that a young man could wish to see of Indians, highwaymen of the Rocky Mountains, Mormons, and silver-miners; later, again, as professed journalist, author, and successful lecturer; later still, when his reputation as writer and humourist had spread through the English-speaking inhabitants of five continents, compelled through the failure of a publishing firm to work as hard as ever to rehabilitate his fortunes,—in all these changes and chances preserving the same courage, independence, and health of vision, he has earned the title of a good deal more than a man of letters; he has been a man of action. 'Compelled' to work, indeed, is hardly the right word to use in reference to his position when the publishing firm with whom he was connected in later years became bankrupt. He was sixty years old in 1896 when the firm came to grief, even as Scott was fifty-six when the house of Ballantyne fell seventy years before; and, like Scott, he set himself at once to mend the shattered pieces. 'Compelled' to work he was, but only by the vigour and bravery of his own character.

Mark Twain will always be remembered first and foremost as a humourist; but it is only because his claims as a humourist are overwhelming that he has not been acclaimed as a serious student of character, a novelist, and a charming writer of whimsical historical romance. His 'output' has been large and continuous; but if out of the many volumes filled with his writings we were to select as typical of his best work *Tom Sawyer*, *A Tramp Abroad*, and that most delightful of fantasies for children, *The Prince and the Pauper*, he would take his stand as the author of three books which are classical of their kind, and we should still be leaving out of account such admirable work as *Life on the Mississippi*, *Huckleberry Finn*, *The Innocents Abroad*, and the extremely clever and imaginative *tour de force*, *A Yankee at the Court of King Arthur*. As for *Tom Sawyer*, Mark Twain once described it to a youthful journalist on whom he did not think he was wasting a two hours' interview as 'all the boy that I have known or recollect.' But *Tom Sawyer* contains a good deal more than a mere study of irresponsible boyhood, admirably as such a study is presented, not only in the wild escapades of that honest and engaging scapegrace, but in the childish tenderness of such passages as the scribbling of the message 'We ain't dead—we are only off being pirates,' on the sycamore-bark left to console the sorrowing Aunt Polly. There are two or three scenes in the book which grip the heart: Tom and Huck hiding in the churchyard, the stealthy digging of the bodysnatchers, the moon suddenly shining on the poor pallid thing taken from the grave, and Injun Joe, the half-breed, creeping with his knife round the doctor wrestling with his drunken 'pard'; Tom and Becky Thatcher with the bats flying round their heads in the depths of the cave, and the horror of darkness as their only candle goes out; and last, the hideous end of the half-breed, walled up in the cave and hacking away at the door with his broken bowie-knife, not because he hopes to get out, but for something to do. Those three scenes must always haunt any reader who has taken up the book as boy or man. *Tom Sawyer*, of course, pairs with *Huckleberry Finn*. Out of the two chief books of travel, it would be more difficult to select three, and three only, characteristic passages. If three are to be chosen, perhaps the *Tramp Abroad* contains them in the immortal Gambetta-Fourtou duel, with the 'postage-stamp containing several cartridges,' and the lamentable consequences to M. Gambetta's second; Mark Twain's search in the dark for his odd slipper, during which the pedometer marked forty-seven miles; and, of course, the wonderful ascent of the Riffelberg, with the mule that ate the nitro-glycerine, the paregoricking of the corps of guides, the boiling of the thermometer, and the descent by the glacier. It is all, surely, the most admirable fun and light-heartedness. But fun, light-heartedness, and an unrivalled sense of humour are by no means Mark Twain's only, nor even, perhaps, his most commanding, characteristics. He has a peculiar power of presenting pathetic situations without 'slush,' as could be proved by a dozen charming scenes from that daintiest of children's stories, *The Prince and the Pauper*. But he is, above all, the fearless upholder of all that is clean, noble, straightforward, innocent, and manly. If there is a certain meaning to the phrase 'American journalism' which is distasteful to Englishmen, Mark Twain, of American writers, stands for all that Englishmen like best. He has his extravagances; some of his public, indeed, would insist on them. But if he is a jester, he jests with the mirth of the happiest of Puritans; he has read much of English knighthood, and translated the best of it into his living pages; and he has assuredly already won a high degree in letters in having added more than any writer since Dickens to the gaiety of the Empire of the English language.

75. William Lyon Phelps:
'Mark Twain', *North American Review*

5 July 1907, clxxxv, 540–8

William Lyon Phelps (1865–1943) taught English literature at
Yale from 1893 to 1933. An enthusiastic teacher and critic of wide
interests, he wrote many books, mostly on modern English and
European literature, and contributed a monthly column, 'As I
Like It', to *Scribner's Magazine* from 1922 to 1943.

This *North American Review* article is apparently the text Phelps
used for a talk on Mark Twain in Hartford in January 1907. See
Introduction (p. 6) for Clemens' reaction to a newspaper report
of the talk.

H. L. Mencken first saw this article when it was published in
1910 as a chapter of Phelps' *Essays on Modern Novelists*. Mencken
observed that it was 'the first honest and hearty praise of *Huckleberry Finn* by a college professor in good standing' that he had ever
seen, 'and the first faint, trembling admission, by the same sort of
professor, that Mark Twain was a greater artist than Oliver
Wendell Holmes'. (*Smart Set*, June 1910, xxxi, 153. See also
Nos. 77 and 88.)

The author of *Initial Studies in American Letters* was Henry A.
Beers, professor of history at Yale and a friend and mentor of
Phelps. The passage from Charles Francis Richardson's *American
Literature: 1607–1885* appears in a chapter entitled 'Borderlands of
American Literature'. The other reference to Clemens listed in the
index of that book contrasts him with Charles Dudley Warner,
whose work Richardson praises for 'truth and wholesomeness, a
genuine local flavor without coarseness' and for 'delicacy of touch'.

During the last twenty years, a profound change has taken place in the
attitude of the reading public toward Mark Twain. I can remember
very well when he was regarded merely as a humorist, and one opened
his books with an anticipatory grin. Very few supposed that he
belonged to literature; and a complete, uniform edition of his 'Works'

would perhaps have been received with something of the mockery that greeted Ben Jonson's folio in 1616. Professor Richardson's *American Literature*, which is still a standard work, appeared originally in 1886. My copy, which bears the date 1892, contains only two references in the index to Mark Twain, while Mr. Cable, for example, receives ten; and the whole volume fills exactly 990 pages. Looking up one of the two references, we find the following opinion:

But there is a class of writers, authors ranking below Irving or Lowell, and lacking the higher artistic or moral purpose of the greater humorists, who amuse a generation and then pass from sight. Every period demands a new manner of jest, after the current fashion. . . . The reigning favorites of the day are Frank R. Stockton, Joel Chandler Harris, the various newspaper jokers, and 'Mark Twain.' But the creators of *Pomona* and *Rudder Grange* of *Uncle Remus and his Folk-lore Stories*, and *Innocents Abroad*, clever as they are, must make hay while the sun shines. Twenty years hence, unless they chance to enshrine their wit in some higher literary achievement, their unknown successors will be the privileged comedians of the republic. Humor alone never gives its masters a place in literature; it must co-exist with literary qualities, and must usually be joined with such pathos as one finds in Lamb, Hood, Irving or Holmes.

It is interesting to remember that before this pronouncement was published, *Tom Sawyer* and *Huckleberry Finn* had been read by thousands. Professor Richardson continued: 'Two or three divisions of American humor deserve somewhat more respectful treatment,' and he proceeds to give a full page to Petroleum V. Nasby, another page to Artemus Ward and two and one-half pages to Josh Billings, while Mark Twain had received less than four lines. After stating that, in the case of authors like Mark Twain, 'temporary amusement, not literary product, is the thing sought and given,' Professor Richardson announces that the department of fiction will be considered later. In this 'department,' Mark Twain is not mentioned at all, although Julian Hawthorne receives over three pages!

I have quoted Professor Richardson at length, because he represents an attitude toward Mark Twain that was common all during the eighties. Another college professor, who is to-day one of the best living American critics, says, in his *Initial Studies in American Letters* (1895), 'Though it would be ridiculous to maintain that either of these writers [Artemus Ward and Mark Twain] takes rank with Lowell and Holmes, . . . still it will not do to ignore them as mere buffoons, or even to predict that their humors will soon be forgotten.' There is no allusion in his book to *Tom Sawyer* or *Huckleberry Finn*, nor does the critic seem to regard their creator as in any sense a novelist. Still another writer, in a passing allusion to Mark Twain, says, 'Only a very small portion of his writing has any place as literature.'

Literary opinions change as time progresses; and no one could have observed the remarkable demonstration at the seventieth birthday of our great national humorist without feeling that most of his contemporaries regarded him, not as their peer, but as their Chief. Without wishing to make any invidious comparisons, I cannot refrain from commenting on the statement that it would be 'ridiculous' to maintain that Mark Twain takes rank with Oliver Wendell Holmes. It is, of course, absolutely impossible to predict the future; the only real test of the value of a book is Time. Who now reads Cowley? Time has laughed at so many contemporary judgments that it would be foolhardy to make positive assertions about literary stock quotations one hundred years from now. Still, guesses are not prohibited; and I think it not unlikely that the name of Mark Twain will outlast the name of Holmes. American Literature would surely be the poorer if the great Boston Brahmin had not enlivened it with his rich humor, his lambent wit and his sincere pathos; but the whole content of his work seems slighter than the big American prose epics of the man of our day.

Indeed, it seems to me that Mark Twain is our foremost living American writer. He has not the subtlety of Henry James or the wonderful charm of Mr. Howells; he could not have written *Daisy Miller*, or *A Modern Instance*, or *Indian Summer*, or *The Kentons*—books of which every American should be proud, for they exhibit literary quality of an exceedingly high order. I have read these books over and over again, with constantly increasing profit and delight. I wish that Mr. Howells might live forever, and give to every generation the pure intellectual joy that he has given to ours. But the natural endowment of Mark Twain is still greater. Mr. Howells has made the most of himself; God has done it all for Mark Twain. If there be a living American writer touched with true genius, whose books glow with the divine fire, it is he. He has always been a conscientious artist; but no amount of industry could ever have produced a *Huckleberry Finn*.

When I was a child at the West Middle Grammar School of Hartford, on one memorable April day, Mark Twain addressed the graduating-class. I was thirteen years old, but I have found it impossible to forget what he said. The subject of his 'remarks' was Methuselah. He informed us that Methuselah lived to the ripe old age of nine hundred and sixty-nine. But he might as well have lived to be several thousand—nothing happened. The speaker told us that we should all live longer than Methuselah. Fifty years of Europe are better than a cycle of Cathay, and twenty years of modern American life are longer and richer in content than the old patriarch's thousand. Ours will be the true age in which to live, when more will happen in a day than in a year of the flat existence of our ancestors. I cannot remember his words; but what a fine thing it is to hear a speech, and carry away an idea!

I have since observed that this idea runs through much of his literary work. His philosophy of life underlies his broadest burlesque —for *A Connecticut Yankee in King Arthur's Court* is simply an exposure of the 'good old times.' Mark Twain believes in the Present, in human progress. Too often do we apprehend the Middle Ages through the glowing pages of Spenser and Walter Scott; we see only glittering processions of 'ladies dead and lovely knights.' Mark Twain shows us the wretched condition of the common people, their utter ignorance and degradation, the coarseness and immorality of technical chivalry, the cruel and unscrupulous ecclesiastical tyranny and the capricious insolence of the barons. One may regret that he has reversed the dynamics in so glorious a book as Malory's *Morte d'Arthur*, but, through all the buffoonery and roaring mirth with which the knights in armor are buried, the artistic and moral purpose of the satirist is clear. If I understand him rightly, he would have us believe that *our* age, not theirs, is the 'good time'; nay, ours is the age of magic and wonder. We need not regret in melancholy sentimentality the picturesqueness of bygone days, for we ourselves live, not in a material and common-place generation, but in the very midst of miracles and romance. Merlin and the Fay Morgana would have given all their petty skill to have been able to use a telephone or a phonograph, or to see a moving picture. The sleeping princess and her castle were awakened by a kiss; but in the twentieth century a man in Washington touches a button, and hundreds of miles away tons of machinery begin to move, fountains begin to play and the air resounds with the whir of wheels. In comparison with to-day, the age of chivalry seems dull and poor. Even in chivalry itself our author is more knightly than Lancelot; for was there ever a more truly chivalrous performance than Mark Twain's essay on Harriet Shelley, or his literary monument to Joan of Arc? In these earnest pages, our national humorist appears as the true knight.

Mark Twain's humor is purely American. It is not the humor of Washington Irving, which resembles that of Addison and Thackeray;

it is not delicate and indirect. It is genial, sometimes outrageous, mirth —laughter holding both his sides. I have found it difficult to read him in a library or on a street-car, for explosions of pent-up mirth or a distorted face are apt to attract unpleasant attention in such public places. Mark Twain's humor is boisterous, uproarious, colossal, overwhelming. As has often been remarked, the Americans are not naturally a gay people, like the French; nor are we light-hearted and careless, like the Irish and the Negro. At heart, we are intensely serious, nervous, melancholy. For humor, therefore, we naturally turn to buffoonery and burlesque, as a reaction against the strain and tension of life. Our attitude is something like that of the lonely author of the *Anatomy of Melancholy*, who used to lean over the parapet of Magdalen Bridge, and shake with mirth at the horrible jokes of the bargemen. We like Mark Twain's humor, not because we are frivolous, but because we are just the reverse. I have never known a frivolous person who really enjoyed or appreciated Mark Twain.

The essence of Mark Twain's humor is Incongruity. The jumping frog is named Daniel Webster; and, indeed, the intense gravity of a frog's face, with the droop at the corners of the mouth, might well be envied by many an American Senator. When the shotted frog vainly attempted to leave the earth, he shrugged his shoulders 'like a Frenchman.' Bilgewater and the Dolphin on the raft are grotesquely incongruous figures. The rescuing of Jim from his prison cell is full of the most incongruous ideas, his common-sense attitude toward the whole transaction contrasting strangely with that of the romantic Tom. Along with the constant incongruity goes the element of surprise— which Professor Beers has well pointed out. When one begins a sentence, in an apparently serious discussion, one never knows how it will end. In discussing the peace that accompanies religious faith, Mark Twain says that he has often been impressed with the calm confidence of a Christian with four aces. Exaggeration—deliberate, enormous hyperbole—is another feature. Rudyard Kipling, who has been profoundly influenced by Mark Twain, and has learned much from him, often employs the same device, as in 'Brugglesmith.' Irreverence is also a noteworthy quality. In his travel-books, we are given the attitude of the typical American Philistine toward the wonders and sacred relics of the Old World, the whole thing being a gigantic burlesque on the sentimental guide-books which were so much in vogue before the era of Baedeker. With so much continuous fun and mirth, satire and burlesque, it is no wonder that Mark Twain should not always be at his best. He is doubtless sometimes flat, sometimes coarse, as all humorists since Rabelais have been. The wonder is that his level has been so high. I remember, just before the appearance of *Following the Equator*, I had been told that Mark Twain's inspiration was finally gone, and that he could not be funny if he tried. To test this, I opened the new book, and this is what I found on the first page:

We sailed for America, and there made certain preparations. This took but little time. Two members of my family elected to go with me. Also a carbuncle. The dictionary says a carbuncle is a kind of jewel. Humor is out of place in a dictionary.

Although Mark Twain has the great qualities of the true humorist —common sense, human sympathy and an accurate eye for proportion —he is much more than a humorist. His work shows very high literary quality, the quality that appears in first-rate novels. He has shown himself to be a genuine artist. He has done something which many popular novelists have signally failed to accomplish—he has created real characters. His two wonderful boys, Tom Sawyer and Huckleberry Finn, are wonderful in quite different ways. The creator of Tom exhibited remarkable observation; the creator of Huck showed the divine touch of imagination. Tom is the American boy—he is 'smart.' In having his fence whitewashed, in controlling a pool of Sabbath-school tickets at the precise psychological moment, he displays abundant promise of future success in business. Huck, on the other hand, is the child of nature, harmless, sincere and crudely imaginative. His reasonings with Jim about nature and God belong to the same department of natural theology as that illustrated in Browning's 'Caliban.' The night on the raft with Jim, when these two creatures look aloft at the stars, and Jim reckons the moon laid them, is a case in point.

We had the sky up there, all speckled with stars, and we used to lay on our backs and look up at them, and discuss about whether they was made or just happened. Jim he allowed they was made, but I allowed they happened; I judged it would have took too long to *make* so many. Jim said the moon could a *laid* them; well, that looked kind of reasonable, so I didn't say nothing against it, because I've seen a frog lay most as many, so of course it could be done. We used to watch the stars that fell, too, and see them streak down. Jim allowed they'd got spoiled and was hove out of the nest.

Again, Mark Twain has so much dramatic power that, were his literary career beginning instead of closing, he might write for us the great American play that we are still awaiting. The story of the feud between the Grangerfords and the Shepherdsons is thrillingly dramatic, and the tragic climax grips one by the heart. The shooting of the drunken Boggs, the gathering of the mob and its control by one masterful personality, belong essentially to true drama, and are written with power and insight. The pathos of these scenes is never false, never mawkish or overdone; it is the pathos of life itself. Mark Twain's extraordinary skill in descriptive passages shows, not merely keen observation, but the instinct for the specific word—the one word that is always better than any of its synonyms, for it makes the picture real —it creates the illusion, which is the essence of all literary art. The storm, for example:

[quotes ch. 20 'It was my watch' to 'and miss them'.]

Tom Sawyer and *Huckleberry Finn* are prose epics of American life. The former is one of those books—of which *The Pilgrim's Progress*, *Gulliver's Travels* and *Robinson Crusoe* are supreme examples—that are read at different periods of one's life from very different points of view; so that it is not easy to say when one enjoys them the most—before one understands their real significance or after. Nearly all healthy boys enjoy reading *Tom Sawyer*, because the intrinsic interest of the story is so great, and the various adventures of the hero are portrayed with such gusto. Yet it is impossible to outgrow the book. The eternal Boy is there, and one cannot appreciate the nature of boyhood properly until one has ceased to be a boy. The other masterpiece, *Huckleberry Finn*, is really not a child's book at all. Children devour it, but they do not digest it. It is a permanent picture of a certain period of American history, and this picture is made complete, not so much by the striking portraits of individuals placed on the huge canvas, as by the vital unity of the whole composition. If one wishes to know what life on the Mississippi really was, to know and understand the peculiar social conditions of that highly exciting time, one has merely to read through this powerful narrative, and a definite, coherent, vivid impression remains.

By those who have lived there, and whose minds are comparatively free from prejudice, Mark Twain's pictures of life in the South before the war are regarded as, on the whole, nearer the truth than those supplied by any other artist. One reason for this is the aim of the author; he was not trying to support or to defend any particular theory—no, his aim was purely and wholly artistic. In *Uncle Tom's Cabin*, a book by no means devoid of literary art, the red-hot indignation of the author largely nullified her evident desire to tell the truth. If one succeeds in telling the truth about anything whatever, one must have something more than the *desire* to tell the truth; one must know how to do it. False impressions do not always, probably do not commonly, come from deliberate liars. Mrs. Stowe's astonishing work is not really the history of slavery; it is the history of abolition sentiment. On the other hand, writers so graceful, talented and clever as Mr. Page and Mr. Hopkinson Smith do not always give us pictures that correctly represent, except locally, the actual situation before the war; for these gentlemen seem to have *Uncle Tom's Cabin* in mind. Mark Twain gives us both points of view; he shows us the beautiful side of slavery—for it had a wonderfully beautiful, patriarchal side—and he also shows us the horror of it. The living dread of the negro that he would be sold down the river, has never been more vividly represented than when the poor woman in *Pudd'nhead Wilson* sees the water swirling against the snag, and realizes that she is bound the wrong way. That one scene makes an indelible impression on the reader's mind, and counteracts tons of polemics. The peculiar harmlessness of Jim is beautiful to contemplate. Although he and Huck really own the raft, and have taken all the risk, they obey implicitly the orders of the two tramps who call themselves Duke and King. Had that been a raft on the Connecticut River, and had Huck and Jim been Yankees, they would have said to the intruders, 'Whose raft is this, anyway?'

Mark Twain may be trusted to tell the truth; for the eye of the born caricature artist always sees the salient point. Caricatures often give us a better idea of their object than a photograph; for the things that are exaggerated, be it a large nose, or a long neck, are, after all, the things that differentiate this particular individual from the mass. Everybody remembers how Tweed was caught by one of Nast's cartoons.

Mark Twain is through and through American. If foreigners really wish to know the American spirit, let them read Mark Twain. He is far more American than their favorite specimen, Walt Whitman. The essentially American qualities of common sense, energy, enterprise, good humor and Philistinism fairly shriek from his pages. He reveals us in our limitations, in our lack of appreciation of certain beautiful things, fully as well as he pictures us in coarser but more triumphant aspects. It is, of course, preposterous to say that Americans are totally different from other humans; we have no monopoly of common sense and good humor, nor are we all hide-bound Philistines. But there is something pronounced in the American character, and the books of

Mark Twain reveal it. He has also more than once been a valuable and efficient champion. Without being an offensive and blatant Jingo, I think he is well satisfied to be an American.

Mark Twain is our great Democrat. Democracy is his political, social and moral creed. His hatred of snobbery, affectation and assumed superiority is total. His democracy has no limits; it is bottomless and far-reaching. Nothing seems really sacred to him except the sacred right of every individual to do exactly as he pleases; which means, of course, that no one can interfere with another's right, for then democracy would be the privilege of a few, and would stultify itself. Not only does the spirit of democracy breathe out from all his greater books, but it is shown in specific instances, such as 'Travelling with a Reformer'; and Mark Twain has more than once given testimony for his creed, without recourse to the pen.

At the head of all American novelists, living and dead, stands Nathaniel Hawthorne, unapproached, possibly unapproachable. His fine and subtle art is an altogether different thing from the art of our mighty, democratic, national humorist. But Literature is wonderfully diverse in its content; and the historian of American Letters, in the far future, will probably find it impossible to omit the name of Mark Twain, whose books have warmed human hearts all over the world.

76. Charles Whibley: column, *Blackwood's Magazine*

August 1907, clxxxii, 279–86

Charles Whibley (1859–1930), scholar, critic and journalist, was a close friend and disciple of W. E. Henley. He wrote successively for the *Scots Observer*, the *Pall Mall Gazette*, and the *New Review*. From 1897 to the end of his life he contributed a monthly column, 'Musings without Method', to *Blackwood's Magazine*.

For the last month London has suffered from a violent attack of hilarity. Painfully she has held her poor sides. So fiercely has she rocked with noisy laughter that her public monuments have been in danger of destruction. For Mark Twain has been in her midst, and has transmitted, through the voices of obsequious journalists, his messages of mirth. And Mark Twain is a humourist, a simple truth which nobody is permitted to forget. He is a humourist who cannot open his mouth without provoking the wonder of the world, and, thanks to the industry of energetic reporters, we have not lost one single pearl of his speech.

It is not Mark's fault,—Mark they call him, to prove their familiarity,—nor the fault of the reporters, if a word spoken by the humourist has escaped us. All the world knows that the sublime heights of fun were climbed when Mark Twain referred happily to his own funeral. The compositors who set up this brilliant sally were so keenly conscious of their privilege that they fitted the master's incongruity with a bold series of misprints. Mark Twain designing his own funeral! Isn't it funny? Lives there a curmudgeon who will refrain from laughter when he hears of it? Still gayer was the phantasy which accused Mark Twain of stealing the Ascot Gold Cup. There's imagination for you! There's a pretty invention! Fleet Street accepted the joke as one man, and it will be surprising if the great man's luggage is not ransacked for the lost treasure by the Customs officers of his free and independent fatherland.

At last the humourist has left these shores. The echo of his last joke has died away, though the throats of his admirers are still husky with appreciative laughter. And so well did London play her part that if he rang his bell or asked for a lucifer match, the neighbourhood of Dover Street palpitated with excitement. Unhappily, upon this enthusiasm, as upon most others, time has and will have a chastening effect. Our exhausted capital is beginning to understand that it can have too much of a good joke, and that nothing stales so rapidly as the thing called 'humour.'

Humour as a solid quality and a lucrative trade is of modern invention. The ancients knew well that its effect was an effect of light and shade. They were humorous in flashes, and their humour was infinitely enhanced, because it was set against a background of gravity. To be funny at all hours and in all places is as vile a sin against taste as it would be to dissolve in floods of tears before strangers. The great men who dared to laugh in an earlier age than ours laughed in moderation and with a wise purpose. Aristophanes and Lucian, Chaucer and Rabelais, Shakespeare and Fielding, are the true humourists of the world. They did not jest and jibe out of season. They held up folly to ridicule, not to amuse the groundlings, but to reveal, in a sudden blaze of light, the eternal truths of wisdom and justice. Their humour is precious on account of its parsimony. They do not at every turn slap their reader on the back and assure him that there is nothing congruous in the visible world. Of the irreverence that turns whatever is beautiful or noble into a stupid jest they knew nothing. They kept their humour in its proper place; they used it for a wise purpose; they did not degrade it to catch an easy round of applause; and, fortunately for them, they are to-day refused the august title of humourist, which sits so appositely upon the shoulders of Mark Twain.

The essence of humour is that it should be unexpected. The modern humourist is never unexpected. He beats the drum from the moment at which he appears upon the stage. He does not cease to beat it until he quits the stage for the last time. His mouth is always awry, as though he fed upon sour apples, and he demands that his auditors also should twist their lips. From morning till night he grins through a horse-collar, and is surprised if all the world does not applaud his grimaces. To the rash fellow who confesses that he does not understand his fun, the professional humourist has a ready answer. He tells the wretch, with a shrug of pity, that he has no sense of humour, and has no right to criticise wholesome ribaldry. The boot, of course, is on the other leg.

The professional humourist is the one person to whom the proper exercise of humour is forbidden, and he does but add insult to injury when he dares to criticise his victim's understanding.

Yet the professional humourist to-day inherits the earth. He is the most popular of God's creatures. He has his own 'organs,' in which he makes a desperate attempt to look at all things from a ridiculous point of view. He assures you, with a sentimental leer, that his fun is always amiable, as though amiability were a sufficient atonement for an imbecile lack of taste. He is prepared to tickle you with his jokes from early morn to nightfall, and he has been so grossly flattered that he believes there is a positive virtue in his antics. He is perfectly convinced that he is doing good, and he needs very little persuasion to believe that he is the only regenerator of mankind. Gradually, too, he is encroaching upon all the professions which are not legitimately his own. The pulpit knows him, and the senate. Worse still, he has invaded the Courts of Law, and sits grinning upon the bench at his own ineptitude, which appears to the obsequious barristers, who hope some day to wear his cap and bells, to sparkle with the brilliance of true Attic wit.

The secret of modern humour is revealed to all. Its basis is an obvious incongruity. Not the subtle παρὰ προσδοκίαν of the ancients, not a whimsical turn of phrase or twist of idea, which surprises us in the masters, but a coarse, crass confusion of past with present or of grave with gay.

[Whibley here traces the evolution of 'modern humour' through the writings of Motteux, D'Urfey, Tom Brown, Ned Ward, Charles Cotton and Thomas Bridges, who 'sowed the seeds of the easy incongruity which has debauched the humour of to-day'.]

The end and aim of Mark Twain, then, are the end and aim of Cotton and Bridges. For him the art of Europe and the chivalry of King Arthur serve the purpose of Virgil and Homer. He travesties them with a kind of malignant joy. He brings whatever time has honoured down to the level of a Yankee drummer, In *The Innocents Abroad* he sets a slur of commonness upon beauty and splendour. With the vanity of a crude civilisation he finds every custom ridiculous that does not conform with the standard of the United States. The restraints of honour are food for his mirth. He holds his sides when he thinks of the old masters. They are not brought down to this our date. Nor does he understand that there are certain institutions, certain manifestations of genius, which should be sacred even for the jester. Newness is not the only virtue known to the world, and he who laughs at what is old, merely because it is old, proves a lack of intelligence which no whimsicality can excuse.

In other words, Mark Twain the humourist is a bull in the china-shop of ideas. He attempts to destroy what he could never build up, and assumes that his experiment is eminently meritorious. When, as in *A Yankee at the Court of King Arthur*, he gave full rein to his fancy, he achieved such a masterpiece of vulgarity as the world has never seen. His book gives you the same sort of impression which you might receive from a beautiful picture over which a poisonous slug had crawled. The hint of magnificence is there, pitilessly deformed and defaced. That Mark Twain is in perfect sympathy with his creature is perfectly evident. He frankly prefers Hartford, Conn., to Camelot. He believes that in all respects his native land is superior to the wisest and noblest society that the eye of Arthur saw or any other eye has seen. He is sure that refinement and 'gentility' were unknown before his own time. The Knights of the Round Table, he declares, used words which would have made a Comanche blush. 'Indelicacy is too mild a term to convey the idea.' In our own nineteenth century, he informs us, 'the earliest samples of the real lady and real gentleman discoverable in English history—or in European history, for that matter—may be said to have made their appearance.' That is what it is to be a humourist. But even if we permit the humour we must still question the historical accuracy of the statement, and regret that Mark Twain ever thought it necessary to comment upon the ancients, against whom he cherishes a fierce antipathy.

His verbal humour, if less reckless than his history, is far more dismally deplorable. Here is his comment upon Merlin: 'He is always blethering around in my way, everywhere I go; he makes me tired. He don't amount to shucks as a magician.' Who can resist this amazing humour? And again, who, save a churl, would refuse the tribute of a laugh to the following exquisite criticism of the same wonder-worker? 'Merlin's stock was flat,' writes Mark Twain, 'the King wanted to stop his wages: he even wanted to banish him; but I interfered. I said he would be useful to work the weather, and attend to small matters like that, and I would give him a lift now and then when his poor little parlour-magic soured on him.' Isn't there a snigger in every word of it? And before this brilliancy must we not confess that humour, like delicacy and all the other virtues, made its first appearance in the nineteenth century and in America?

This monstrous incongruity demands two qualities for its indulgence: a perfect self-esteem, and an exaggerated common-sense. No one who is not confident that he engrosses the graces can affect to find pleasure in thus insulting the past. No one whose sense is not common in all respects can apply all the resources of a vulgar logic to the creations of fancy and emotion. That Mark Twain is fully equipped for his purpose is only too clear. His humour and his talk alike proclaim it. And it is the more pitiful, because he has a talent which stands in need of no folly for its embellishment. Had he never cut a joke, had he refrained always from grinning at grave and beautiful things, how brilliant a fame would have been his! When you are tired of his irreverence, when you have deplored his noisy jibes, when his funeral and his theft of the cup alike pall upon your spirit, take down his *Life on the Mississippi,* and see what perfect sincerity and a fine sympathy can accomplish. Mark Twain writes of the noble river as one who knows its every change and chance. Yet he writes of it with an austere restraint and without any desire to humanise it out of its proper character. And there is humour, too, in his descriptions,—not the tortured humour of a later day, but humour sufficient to play, like light upon shade, in the grave places of his history. As he says himself, he loved the pilot's profession far better than any he has followed since, and his love and understanding shine in every page of his masterpiece. As the river kept no secrets from him, so his quick memory enabled him to recover the impressions of his youth. To cite his own expressive words,

The face of the water, in time, became a wonderful book—a book which was a dead language to the uneducated passenger, but which told its mind to me without reserve, delivering its most cherished secrets as clearly as if it uttered them with a voice. And it was not a book to be read once and thrown aside, for it had a new story to tell every day. . . . There was never so wonderful a book written by man.

In this passage Mark Twain strikes the real note of his life and experience. With equal truth he tells us at what cost he acquired this deep knowledge of the river and its moods.

[quotes ch. 9 'Now, when I' to 'new to me' and 'But, as I' to 'to note them'.]

Yet the very fact that Mark Twain recognised the change which had come over his vision is the best proof that he submitted willingly to the marvellous spell of the river. His mental process was the reverse of Wordsworth's. Wordsworth learned

> To look on nature, not as in the hour
> Of thoughtless youth; but hearing oftentimes
> The still, sad music of humanity,
> Not harsh nor grating, though of ample power
> To chasten and subdue.

Mark Twain, on the other hand, heard 'the still, sad music of humanity' when he but half knew the river. A profounder knowledge silenced the music, and persuaded him to own, with sincerity, that he gazed upon the sunset scene without rapture, but with the understanding of an intimate.

The author of *Life on the Mississippi* was also the creator of Tom Sawyer and Huck Finn, two boys who will survive to cast shame upon all the humour of America. And it is for the sake of a genuine talent that we deplore Mark Twain's studied antics. It should not have been for him to light the thorns which crackle under the pot. It should not have been for him to encourage the gross stupidity of his fellows. The moderation of one who has known men and rivers should have been revealed to all the world. But Mark Twain, in submitting to the common demand, shares the general love of exaggeration. 'Govern a great country as you would cook a small fish,' said the Chinese philosopher; 'that is, do not overdo it.' The tendency of to-day is to overdo all things. Humour, which should be a relief, and nothing more, is now an end in itself.

[Whibley comments upon the meaningless proliferation of pageants and the degeneration of the idea of the Henley regatta from a sport engaged in for its own sake to a symbolic contest between nations.]

Some day there will be a reaction, and then it will be recognised that pleasure counts in life as much as success, and that solid blocks of humour are as blatant an outrage upon good sense as a daily pageant, or as games played with no other aim than by hook or by crook to snatch a victory.

77. H. L. Mencken: review, *Smart Set*

August 1909, xxviii, 157

H[enry] L[ouis] Mencken (1880–1956), critic and journalist, became literary editor of *Smart Set* in 1908 and was co-editor from 1914 to 1923. He was a founder and editor of *American Mercury* (1924–33).

This selection is the conclusion of a brief review of *Is Shakespeare Dead?* in which Mencken dismisses the book as inaccurate and says, 'All that [Mark Twain] proves, indeed, is that the majority of Shakespeare's contemporaries were densely blind to his enormous genius.' Mencken restated and amplified his views on *Huckleberry Finn* in 1910 (*Smart Set*, June 1910, xxxi, 153–4) and again in 1913 (No. 88).

Mr. Clemens's book, indeed, makes sorry reading for those who hold him in reverence. He is, by great odds, the most noble figure America has ever given to English literature. Having him, we may hold up our heads when Spaniards boast of Cervantes and Frenchmen of Molière. His one book, *Huckleberry Finn*, is worth, I believe, the complete works of Poe, Hawthorne, Cooper, Holmes, Howells and James, with the entire literary output to date of Indiana, Pennsylvania and all the States south of the Potomac thrown in as makeweight. But since *Following the Equator*, his decline has been almost pathetic. Once a great artist, he is now merely a public character. He has gone the road of Wycherley: the old humanity and insight have given place to the smartness of the town wit. Let us try to forget this latter-day Mark Twain, with his pot boilers and his wheezes, and remember only the incomparable Mark Twain that was—and will be through the ages—just as we try to forget that the Thackeray who wrote *Barry Lyndon* also wrote *Lovell the Widower*, and that the Shakespeare who wrote *Much Ado About Nothing* wrote also *Cymbeline*.

78. Unsigned notice,
Saturday Review

23 April 1910, cix, 516

The word to fit Mark Twain is not easily found. To say of him that he was a humourist is to pervert language. Comic—at times irresistibly so—perhaps; but not humorous. The comic mood is nowhere near to humour. His best work is a mere overflow of mental good spirits; and, unless the reader be equally full-bodied, he may find himself depressed from sheer reaction. He was first among the funny men of America—a country which can never become seriously minded or reflective enough to produce a humourist. His spirit and tone were very near to those of our own comic press. This is not the time for humour. People want to be amused boisterously, and pay their funny men to that end, just as the mediaeval baron paid his fool.

Mark Twain was the best of them all. The secret of his success was this: to please his fellows he had simply to be himself—to give himself the rein. His vein was the vein of Elizabethan farce. However crude the absurdity it went down with his readers, because it was forced down. Literally he made his readers laugh. That is why he bored so many of them. With his faults he had the supreme excuse that condones many of the artistic blemishes in Shakespeare's early farces—he was vital.

79. Frank Jewett Mather:
'Two Frontiersmen', *Nation*

28 April 1910, xc, 422-3

Frank Jewett Mather (1869–1953), the writer of this unsigned article on Henry James and Mark Twain, was an author and art critic. He was an assistant editor of the *Nation* from 1901 to 1906 and professor of art and archaeology at Princeton from 1910 to 1933.

It is an odd reflection that the future literary historian who seeks the greatest American writer of the end of the nineteenth century will pretty surely have to choose between Mark Twain and Henry James. None of their contemporaries, we feel, has so fully realized his native gift. Mark Twain and Henry James have apparently gone as far as it is possible to go in diametrically opposite directions. Yet there is a point at which their talents meet. Both are essentially frontiersmen. Mark Twain is the chronicler *par excellence* of the palpable frontier of robust America; Henry James is the scrupulous analyst of that spiritual frontier which unrobust and nostalgic America established in the old country. Each has brought to his chosen material a singular expertness and fidelity. If Mark Twain has stretched his muscles and spent his sympathy from the Mississippi to the Sierras, Henry James has no less lived strenuously through the more sombre spiritual adventure of the American in Europe.

Sooner or later, sociologists will take account of a significant reciprocal movement. Just as America has attracted the alert, muscular, and hopeful hordes of Europe who seek material prosperity, so Europe has obsessed the gentler, more discursive, and brooding imaginations of a certain type of Americans. It is easy to dismiss them, once for all, as bad Americans. A careful reading of Henry James's novels would prompt a more pitying judgment. Through their lack of simplicity and of constructive energy these people are aliens in their own land. They long for certain fruits of leisure and joys of reflection that it supplies in rather short measure. They are oppressed by the sense of a relentless activity the value of which they are forced to question. Whether they go to Europe or stay, they are in a manner outlanders, and where they settle in numbers there is a spiritual frontier.

It is needless to say that Henry James is their prophet. That he is their advocate, it would be hazardous to assert. With them he shares the habit of suspending judgment in favor of simple observation. Their minds and his are possibly never made up. A kindred destiny forces them to seek a lodging-place amid the graceful forms and complicated allurements of relatively finished civilizations.

Now, the characteristic of Mark Twain's people is that their minds are made up on all main issues. They laugh at themselves and their neighbors, but they never ask the paralyzing question *cui bono?* For them anything and everything is worth while. Their extreme exemplar is the Yankee at King Arthur's Court. It never occurs to them to see the other side. Why is *Innocents Abroad* an infinitely diverting book? Partly, we think, because the innocents are so supremely unconscious of the fact that the gods are laughing not with them, but at them. No other writer has created so many forth-right efficient persons; no one so fully grasped the stalwart *insouciance* which is the very genius of outward America.

How exterior Mark Twain was, it is difficult to imagine. It was at once his superiority and his limitation. One may say that the philosopher in the man almost never slopped over into his books. His concern was with action, and it is significant that when he essayed what he probably regarded as higher flights, not the novel but sheer romance was the result—*Joan of Arc*. He is akin to the great impersonal geniuses who have made the picaresque tale classic—the Le Sages, the Defoes, the Smolletts. His manner grew inevitably out of his matter. It was plain, forceful, with the effective inelegant flexibility of life itself. In a high degree, he was creative. He set forth in flesh and blood pretty much all that Whitman intimated in nebulous and rhythmical metaphysic. A great figure who knew his bent and followed it to culmination with instinctive and unperturbed consistency.

An equal fidelity to his vision distinguishes Henry James. Being complicated, he has disdained to make it simpler than it is. Every phase of the soul yearning for orderliness amid the tumult of mere deeds—all the pathos of the temperament vainly seeking congenial forms—he has fathomed and exemplified. Is Europe a home, a casual inspiration, a mere narcotic? Such problems he never settles. Enough that it draws those pioneers who at home find no space for dreams. As Mark Twain was predestined to be a clear writer, Henry James was fated to be a difficult and obscure one. Mark Twain's material has bounds—is as apparent as a pack train on a sky line. Henry James's material leads him to deeper mental involutions, border-line stuff, where the landmarks are matter of conjecture.

Of these two great writers whose stars have led them to antipodal frontiers, which will the future choose? We are not in a position to answer. Possibly the future will perceive the value of Mark Twain's four-square pioneers, whereas, when America has absorbed her nostalgics, Henry James's people may look like odd and incredible figments. We rather think that some place may be found for them beside other exemplars of disillusion—Pater's Marius and Byron's melancholy Childe. And obviously the ultimate preference will depend largely upon whether the choice is by life or by art. On either score, Mark Twain's chances seem pretty good, while the fate of Mr. James's delicate art seems to be involved in the hesitancy that afflicts his own heroes.

80. Unsigned notice, *Dial*

1 May 1910, xlviii, 305-7

The report of Mark Twain's death on the 21st of April, this time not 'greatly exaggerated' but sadly and literally true, was the occasion of heart-felt grief to the entire nation, we may almost say to the whole world. No American of our time was more widely known; no other American writer lately among the living had endeared himself to so large and cosmopolitan an audience. His life, ended midway in its seventy-fifth year, had been rich in human experience, had fulfilled the season of mellow fruitfulness, and had given literary expression, as few other lives have done, to the qualities of buoyancy and independence so characteristic of the typical American temperament. It was also a life which, in its personal aspects, revealed the qualities of manliness and sympathy, was admirable in its public and private relations, and bore with fortitude the buffets of ill-fortune. There are tests of character which few men can suffer without some show of weakness; his character they served only to sweeten and strengthen.

Mark Twain's life may be divided into two nearly equal parts. Of the first part, which includes his boyhood days, his experiences as a journeyman printer and editor, his brief career as a Mississippi pilot, his briefer career as a Confederate soldier, and his adventures in the mining-camps and rude settlements of the West, we have the most vivid of records in his books—in *Tom Sawyer* and *Huckleberry Finn* and *Roughing It*, and in the countless short stories and sketches which began with 'The Jumping Frog' and are probably not yet at an end, for only a part of the work which he humorously styles his *Autobiography* has been put into print. Those early days left him with a fund of recollections upon which his drafts were honored—as was similarly the case with Bret Harte—for long years after the experiences themselves had become old (although not unhappy) far off things. As the recorder of these phases of pioneer life which he knew at first hand, and of which he almost alone has preserved for us the very form and pressure, we are immeasurably in his debt. There are few things that we know as well as what it was to be a boy in a Missouri country town, a futile skirmisher in the early days of the Civil War, and a traveller on the lower Mississippi, few bygone types that are as real to us as the miners and stage-coach drivers and politicians and bar-room loafers of the untutored West of the mid-century. The writings in which these things have been preserved for us are Mark Twain's best, because they are his raciest and least self-conscious.

The next best group of his books is provided by *The Innocents Abroad*, *A Tramp Abroad*, and *Following the Equator*, the three extensive records of unconventional travel. Yet in these the touch of sophistication is seen, and becomes progressively pronounced with each succeeding narrative. The second is not as good as the first, and the third is distinctly weaker than the second, more artificial in its conception and more forced in its humor. When the author transplanted himself to the East for permanent residence in the seventies, he abandoned the primal sources of his inspiration, and never developed others of comparable importance. Going farther and farther afield in search of fresh material, he illustrated anew the myth of Antæus, and displayed a pitiable weakness. Over some of his later flounderings in the alien elements of literary criticism, history, and metaphysics, it were best discreetly to draw a veil. There was in him a streak of the Philistine which might have remained undetected had he 'kept to his last,' but which was sharply revealed when he infringed upon the domain of intellectual and scholarly concerns.

The present is not, however, the best occasion for dwelling upon Mark Twain's limitations, or for emphasizing the ephemeral character of a considerable part of his work. A fair share of that work, at least, stands upon a level so high as to be in no danger of passing out of sight. Up to an advanced point in his career, he grew steadily in power and wisdom; his sympathies became ever broader and deeper, and his expressive faculty kept pace with the larger demands that were made upon it. From the exuberant journalist who gave us entertainment in his earlier days he developed into something like a sage to whom we came to look no less for counsel than for amusement. We learned to detect in his homely speech the movings of a fine spirit, instinct with the nobler promptings of democracy, hating shams and ostentatious vulgarity, gentle and gracious in its quieter moods, but fanned to burning indignation when facing some monstrous wickedness, such as the corruption of our political life, or the dastardly act of the American soldier in the Philippines who betrayed his rescuer and shamelessly boasted of the shameful deed, or the infamy of the royal libertine who distilled a fortune from the blood of the miserable natives of the Congo. Even more than by his strictly literary work, he earned our gratitude for the brave words which he spoke upon such themes as these, words that cleared the moral atmosphere and made us see things in the light of naked truth.

Nor should we, in our tribute to the man, forget the silent heroism with which he endured loss of fortune in his advancing years, and shouldered the burden of a debt incurred by the rascality of his associates, a debt for which he was only indirectly responsible, and which he might have evaded without serious impairment of his reputation. The strenuous labors of the years of lecturing and writing which enabled him to discharge in full the shadowy obligations which he then assumed took their toll of his vitality, but won for him an esteem higher than is ever the reward of the artist alone. This action ranks with the similar examples set by Scott and Curtis; it is one of those shining deeds that reveal the man himself, in contradistinction to the works by which most men of creative genius are contented to be known.

The attitude of criticism toward Mark Twain as a writer has undergone a slow but complete change during the past thirty years. From being thought of simply as a 'funny man,' of the kin of Josh Billings and Artemus Ward, he has gradually come to be recognized as one of our foremost men of letters. This is a profoundly significant transformation of opinion, and to account for it fully would require a more careful analysis than we here have space to undertake. The recognition has been unduly delayed, partly because so much of his output has been utterly unworthy of his best self, and partly because his work in its totality is of so nondescript a character. The conventional way to distinction in literature is by the fourfold path of the poem, the play, the novel, and the essay. Occasionally, also, an historian compels literary recognition. But Mark Twain was neither a poet nor a playwright nor an historian. He was hardly a novelist, either, for his share in *The Gilded Age* does not seriously count, and his work in the form of fiction is not remarkable as story-telling pure and simple. If we are to group him at all, it must be with the essayist, using that term elastically enough to include with him our own Irving, and such Englishmen as Swift and Carlyle. We must either do this, or fall back upon the *sui generis* solution of the problem. Again, if we make a subdivision of the essayist class for the humorists alone, we encounter the difficulty offered by our obstinate association of that term with mere fun-making and the appeal to the lighter interests of human nature. Obviously, our subdivision must take yet another step, and admit that, on the one hand, there are humorists who make us laugh and have hardly any other influence over us, and humorists who are also creative artists, and critics of life in the deeper sense, and social philosophers whose judgments are of weight and import. If we are to classify Mark Twain at all, it must be with the latter distinguished company; and his title to kinship with the three English writers above mentioned, and even with such alien prototypes as Aristophanes and Rabelais and Cervantes, is at least not scornfully to be put aside.

81. Arnold Bennett: comment, *Bookman* (London)

June 1910, xxxviii, 118

Arnold Bennett (1867–1913), the novelist, was one of a group of British authors, including Barry Pain, Walter Jerrold, Jerome K. Jerome, E. V. Lucas, and others, who contributed to this 'Mark Twain Number' of the *Bookman*.

I never saw Mark Twain. Personally I am convinced that his best work is to be found in the first half of *Life on the Mississippi*. The second half is not on the same plane. Episodically, both *Huckleberry Finn* and *Tom Sawyer* are magnificent, but as complete works of art they are of quite inferior quality. Mark Twain was always a divine amateur, and he never would or never could appreciate the fact (to which nearly all Anglo-Saxon writers are half or totally blind), that the most important thing in any work of art is its construction. He had no notion of construction, and very little power of self-criticism. He was great in the subordinate business of decoration, as distinguished from construction; but he would mingle together the very best and the very worst decorations. The praise poured out on his novels seems to me exceedingly exaggerated. I like his travel-sketches; by their direct, disdainful naïveté they remind me of Stendhal's. I should be disposed to argue that he has left stuff which will live for a long time among us Anglo-Saxons, but not that he was complete enough to capture Europe.

82. Sydney Brooks:
'England and Mark Twain',
North American Review

June 1910, cxci, 822–6

Sydney Brooks (1872–1937) was a journalist and frequent contributor to English and American periodicals. In 1907, as London correspondent for *Harper's Weekly*, he described Clemens' visit to England to receive an honorary degree from Oxford (*Harper's Weekly*, 20 July 1907, li, 1053–4; 27 July, 1086–9).

This *North American Review* article was signed simply 'Britannicus'. The reliance on the sensibilities of the 'average reader of Mark Twain's works' echoes Clemens' own statement to Andrew Lang (Introduction, p. 15) that he wrote for 'the masses' rather than the 'cultivated classes'.

Englishmen for forty years and more have loved Mark Twain with an ardor very little below that of his own countrymen. Ever since the 'Jumping Frog' made its appearance he has been to them the supreme example of humor in its most piquant, most American form, and the unrivalled guardian, since Charles Dickens died, of the sources of deep, human, elemental laughter. It is possible, indeed, that Englishmen have profited by just the shade of mental difference that separates the two peoples to extract from Mark Twain's humor a more exquisite relish than even the Americans themselves, for whom its flavor can scarcely have the charm of an exotic. The tussle with the German language, the duel in the *Tramp Abroad*, the trials of an urban editor of an agricultural paper, the forty-seven-mile search in the dark for the lost bedroom slipper, the ascent of the Riffelberg with the mule that ate the nitroglycerine; these and a hundred other inimitable passages that leap to the mind when Mark Twain's name is breathed have won in England an appreciation as keen and diffused as in America. Tom Sawyer and Huck Finn are as much the friends of English as of American boyhood. Humor has as many styles and fashions as dress, and it would be almost an impertinence to predict for Mark Twain the immortality of a Cervantes; but this much may at least be said, that forty shifting and convulsive years instead of impairing have enhanced Mark Twain's popularity with his English readers. There is that in his writings which draws one as much to the man as to the author, and it is not merely for his books, but for the spirit and character revealed in them and for all they have heard of his life and its trials and triumphs that Englishmen feel in Mark Twain a tender and semi-proprietary pride. We have long been used to looking upon him as the national author of America. In England we have had for a generation or more no national author. Tennyson, perhaps, came nearer to being one than any other writer, but even Tennyson never commanded the devotion that the Scotch showered on Sir Walter, the English of fifty years ago on Dickens and the Americans on Mark Twain. And having no national author of our own, we have perforce claimed Mark Twain as *the* representative 'racial' author of his day and have felt for him only a little less admiration, gratitude and affection than his own country-men. To writers alone is it given to win and hold a sentiment of this quality—to writers and occasionally, by the oddness of the human mind, to generals. The 'popularity' of statesmen is a poor and flickering light by the side of this full flame of personal affection. It has gone out to Mark Twain from all the English-speaking peoples not only for what he has written, for the clean, irresistible extravagance of his humor and his unfailing command of the primal feelings, for his tenderness, his jollity and his power to read the heart of boy and man and woman; not only for the tragedies and afflictions of his life so unconquerably borne; not only for his brave and fiery dashes against tyranny, humbug and corruption at home and abroad, but also because, beyond any other man of his time, he incarnated and universalized the American spirit. His humor, while wholly and distinctively American, has the large human qualities, the sense of the fundamental contrasts of life, that overflows all national boundaries. His freshness of heart and emotion beneath a show of merry cynicism, his indomitable common sense, his spiritual hardiness, his touch of misanthropy, his idealizing faith in women and democracy—all that is American too; but it is American-ism carried by genius to a point where it appeals to the whole of human-ity. More than any man of our generation has Mark Twain made the world laugh. But his humor has always been on the side of the angels. He has jibed at much, but never at anything that made for nobility.

No doubt there are some Englishmen who still regard him as a mere *farceur*, who find his 'irreverence' an insuperable stumbling-block and who cannot reconcile themselves to a famous man of letters being so precisely the opposite of a literary man. 'Culture,' literary priggishness and the academic type of criticism will always find it hard to accept Mark Twain at his true value. One English critic some years ago summed him up, or thought he did, in the word 'barbarian,' declaring that the essence of his talent was merely the spirit of vandalism; and the reproach of not being an 'artist' will, no doubt, long be hurled at him by the men who are all sensitiveness and little sense. But the average reader of Mark Twain's works, which is much the same as saying the average man or woman throughout the English-speaking world, is wiser than the most acute of critics in trusting his own instincts and discarding the foot-rule of formalism. He came stark into the world of letters; there is no precedent for him; and he brought with him the spirit of the Mississippi Valley as it was fifty or sixty years ago, a spirit scarcely congenial to the pedants of æstheticism. 'It is becoming difficult already,' wrote an Englishman the day after Mark Twain's death,

to conceive the conditions amid which he grew up in the Mississippi Valley—a frontier settlement where life was hard, happy-go-lucky and self-reliant, and the men and women who lived it were fraternal and kindly; where an absolute irreverence of speech and manner went hand in hand with a real Puritanism of outlook and conduct; where the atmosphere was charged with courage, a reckless surplusage of cheerfulness, spontaneous vigor, comradeship, profanity, homespun idealism, and a total innocence of the conventions, the arts, the standards and the boredom of civilization. That was the school in which Mark Twain graduated. It formed him in the decisive years when the lines of character are unalterably laid down, and he repaid its wholesome discipline by portraying it with the intimacy of a lover and the touch of a reporter of genius. As journeyman printer, prospector, miner, pilot, soldier and journalist he saw it from all sides. Its spirit became his spirit.

That I believe to be true; but one can understand how often a writer of such upbringing, standpoint and instincts must have shocked the measured delicacy of English 'culture.' To appreciate Mark Twain the less one has in one's composition of the professional critic and the more of the elemental qualities of humanity the better. Happily, most of us are human beings before we are critics; and Mark Twain, if the supercilious few grudge his title to fame, will always carry with him the devoted responsiveness of warm-hearted many. A few lapses from the highest taste, a few things one might wish had been said differently —what are they against that brimming treasure of wholesomeness, masculinity and exuberant mirth?

It is, of course, as a humorist that Mark Twain has conquered the world and fairly enslaved the English-speaking peoples. No one on either side of the Atlantic has arisen in the past thirty years to challenge his incontestable supremacy as the dispenser of joyousness and mirth— of mirth now mocking, now tender, now whirling through a riot of extravagance, now vital with the sense of tears in mortal things, now tipped with a ferocity of sarcasm, but always clean, fresh, whimsical and fortifying. The obituary notices that have appeared in the English papers do full justice to this side of his genius. But they are, happily, not less insistent on the absurdity of looking upon Mark Twain as a humorist merely. He never sank into the tiresomeness of 'the funny man.' 'It takes,' says one English writer,

a man of courage, of sympathy, of experience, a man with a heart and a sense of the pathos and tragedy of life, to be a great humorist. Mark Twain was all this; an irreclaimable jester like Artemus Ward was precisely what he could never have been. He was too big a man and too responsible, and kept with him too constant a vision of life's broadest and most fundamental contrasts to sink into an habitual fun-maker. It is true, perhaps, that at the mention of his name the mind leaps first of all to the passages in which he gave fancy the freest rein. But these are not the passages, admirable as they are in flow, light-heartedness and abandon, that give the full measure of the man. Indeed, if you were to leave out from his works everything in which Mark Twain set out to be deliberately, wantonly, irresistibly side-splitting, I am not sure that his highest merits as a writer would not stand out more clearly. He was the very Homer of boyhood; he wove some historical romances of an extraordinary imagina- tive delicacy; he depicted life on the Mississippi with a force and picturesqueness and fidelity that in years to come will make men turn to him as the social his- torian of his place and time; he had encountered men and women under a unique diversity of conditions and at the closest range; he saw into them with the penetration of a man of the widest human sympathies and of a genuine dramatist; and he drew them, and drew their surroundings, with the direct, telling, vigorous and, at the same time, elaborated impressionism that with him was a gift of nature.

Three years ago England showed Mark Twain how much she loved him, how high a place he held as a writer and a man in the heart of the nation. I was with him frequently in those memorable weeks. He invited me to study him at leisure and completely, in order that I might know 'what a real American college boy looks like.' The impression I gathered was that 'a real American college boy,' in the seventy-second year of his youth, would rather stand than sit, rather walk than stand, rather smoke than sleep and rather talk than do anything. The welcome he received was one continuous ovation. His humor was never happier nor his zest in life more abounding; the interest in all he did and said reached literally through all classes of society. At the Royal garden-party at Windsor, where the guests included with hardly an exception all the most famous men and women in England, Mark Twain admittedly was the most popular man present. As he drove from the station to the castle he was kept incessantly bowing in response to the delighted cheers of the crowds that lined the streets—a purely popular crowd of sight-seers and holiday-makers, who recognized Mark Twain as easily as they recognized the Prime Minister, and considerably more easily than they recognized the Archbishop of Canterbury, and gave him a greeting that must have touched his heart. Half the notable men and women of the land hurried across the lawns to welcome him, and the King and Queen honored him with a far larger portion of their time and conversation than they spared for any of their other guests. At the House of Commons, at the dinner given in his honor by the American Ambassador and attended by much of what is best in the world of English letters, at the luncheon in his honor given by the Pilgrim's Club when his health was proposed by Mr. Birrell in one of the happiest, wittiest and most graceful and feeling speeches I have ever listened to, at Oxford where the degree of D.Litt. was conferred upon him to the uproarious delight of the undergraduates who formed a cheering bodyguard around him whenever he appeared in the streets —it was just the same: by every possible means in their power the English people made of his visit a demonstration of their affection and regard. Nor are they a people whose affection and regard are lightly given. Mark Twain had won them as a great writer, a great citizen and a great gentleman; and his passing leaves a vacancy in the hearts of a world-scattered race that will not soon or easily be filled.

83. Harry Thurston Peck: article, *Bookman* (New York)

June 1910, xxxi, 387–93

In the first part of this article, not included here, Peck discusses the difference between wit and humour, citing the works of Juvenal, Martial and Horace as examples. Then before dealing with Mark Twain he considers briefly many earlier American humorists whose work lost its appeal very quickly. Peck's appreciation of Mme Blanc's French translation of 'The Jumping Frog' is ironically at variance with the small satisfaction which the translator herself took in it (see No. 86).

The moral of these reminiscences is that while humour of a sort is always abundant, the humour which lives throughout the ages is very rare indeed—rarer than the noblest poetry, the most profound essays, the most brilliant wit, and the dramatic expression of poignant tragedy. We are to-day noting the death of one who for more than thirty years has been regarded as a humourist of the highest order, occupying indeed a unique position, since his humour seems even to have stood the searching test of translation into other languages. Mark Twain was as well known in England and Australia and the other British colonies as in his own country. The greatest university of the English-speaking race honoured him with a degree—the first ever given by Oxford to a humourist as such. In translation he has been read in Germany and France and other foreign countries. During his lifetime a sort of legend has sprung up regarding him as there has concerning Miguel Cervantes. Men who are usually sane have tried to see in Mark Twain's jokes and off-hand comic skits a deep philosophy, just as they have tried to find in *Don Quixote* a melancholy idealism. During the last years of his life he seems to have taken this adulation seriously; for his later writings—irrelevant, eccentric, void of either wit or humour—were poured forth by him as though he really felt himself inspired, so that he could not perpetrate a piece of drivel or by any chance be guilty of a *sottise*. However, we must remember that Mr. Clemens lived long and wrote much. Only the very greatest of authors can expect to have their works endure, especially if most of them be works of humour. In some few books will be found the *fine fleur*, the cream, the golden nugget by which we are to judge the writer. In his other books there may be grains of gold, but not enough to make them precious, and this especially is true of Mark Twain. His humour was only in part the humour of Juvenal and Aristophanes. It was quite as irreverent and often quite as full of sharply unexpected contrasts. But it had a quality of its own which you can find nowhere else.

Going over the entire list of the many volumes to which this author set his name, there are only four or five at the most that are likely to last for a great length of time. I am certain that not more than three of them will be read a century from now. Perhaps it may be well to name the books under their respective categories, and then to give the reason for their comparative longevity. Therefore, I should say that the first two books—*The Jumping Frog* (1867) and *The Innocents Abroad* (1869) —are never likely go out of print or out of favour. *Roughing It* (1872) will be valued both for its humour and for its history throughout many years. *The Adventures of Tom Sawyer* (1876) and *Huckleberry Finn* (1885) will remain for perhaps two decades. All the rest of Mr. Clemens's books may perhaps be sold by subscription agents among his 'complete works' for a certain time, but they will not be read. *A Tramp Abroad* marks the beginning of a first decline. *A Yankee at the Court of King Arthur* makes one feel sorry for its author. *Joan of Arc* is distinctly dull; and *The Autobiography of Mark Twain*, which has been dragging its slow way along for many months, is formless and in places without any meaning whatsoever. His best friends have regretted that he ever began to write it. It is to be hoped that his heirs and executors will suppress it.

We must, therefore, judge Mark Twain as a humourist by the very best of all he wrote rather than by the more dubious productions in which we fail to see at every moment the winning qualities and the characteristic form of this very interesting American. As one would not judge of Tennyson by his dramas, nor Thackeray by his journalistic chit-chat, nor Sir Walter Scott by those romances which he wrote after his fecundity had been exhausted, so we must not judge Mark Twain by the dozen or more specimens which belong to the later period, when he was ill at ease and growing old. Let us rather go back with a sort of joy to what he wrote when he did so with spontaneity, when his fun was as natural to him as breathing, and when his humour was all American humour—not like that of Juvenal or Hierocles—acrid, or devoid of anything individual—but brimming over with exactly the same rich irresponsibility which belonged to Steele and Lamb and Irving. It may seem odd to group a son of the New World and of the great West with those earlier classic figures who have been mentioned here; yet upon analysis it will be discovered that the humour of Mark Twain is at least first cousin to that which produced Sir Roger de Coverley and Rip Van Winkle and The Stout Gentleman. In other words, there is really no such thing as American humour, but rather all humour is of the same vintage. Its essence lies, first in the projection of an attractive personality; second, in the assumption by that personality of a sort of appealing ignorance; and finally a genuine understanding of things as they really are.

Now when Mark Twain wrote *The Jumping Frog* and a little later his greatest book, *The Innocents Abroad*, he was (perhaps unconsciously) creating for a million readers a human being who never had any real existence, but who was so delicately depicted and with so many little touches of verisimilitude as to make him more real than his own creator. He was a visitant from the West, professing to know nothing, pleased, just as a child is pleased, with everything that is unknown to him; and, like a child, opening his eyes wonderingly and with intense enjoyment upon a new world. His innocence is like the innocence of Partridge in Fielding's great romance; yet there are twinkles and glints of shrewdness which makes one feel that here is a child who will some day put away childish things. But in the meantime, you enjoy his *naïveté* and are glad that he is not yet quite 'grown up.' When he tells a story he tells it as though unconscious of its humour. His *insouciance* and gravity form such a delightful background for the intensely comic and beautifully irrational actions that are narrated! Hear Mark Twain tell of his old friend Smiley, who owned the Jumping Frog:

[quotes 'He ketched a frog' to 'ever *they* see'.]

The richness of this and of what follows might well have tempted, as it did, translators over all the world. One would hardly think it possible for a Frenchman to Gallicise such a piece of native humour; yet in the *Revue des Deux Mondes* for July 15, 1872, *The Jumping Frog* appears in French as *La Grenouille Sauteuse Du Comté De Calaveras.*

It must be said that even without the dialect the humour holds its own.
As a matter of curiosity, let us reproduce just a bit of this daring
experiment.

[quotes '*Il attrapa un jour*' to ' "*Daniel, des mouches!*" ']

This is almost as good as the original. It shows that its humour is
not local and limited, but that it contains the element of the Universal,
for has not some one said that the judgment of foreign nations is
practically the judgment of posterity?

But in *The Innocents Abroad* there is larger scope and sway for this
born genius. He is as *naif* and innocent and ignorant as the friend of
the apocryphal Smiley; but he has a myriad of subjects to present to
us. Here indeed he resembles Horace because he is *vafer*, and because
when admitted to our confidence he plays around our heart-strings.
It is not his companions alone upon whom he throws the warm glow
of his humour. If he tells us of the Poet Lariat and the Oracle and
Blücher and Dan, so almost with the confidence of a babe does he
tell us of himself, of the mistakes that he made and of the ridiculous
things that he did. Thus he will narrate the conspiracy against the
captain of the ship for the poor tea that was served out. Mark takes
a cup of it and boldly goes up to the captain and asks him whether he
expects people accustomed to good living to live upon such slops as
that. And the captain blandly tastes the liquid and quietly remarks that
it isn't particularly good tea, but that he considers it a very fair specimen of coffee! Thus Mark recounts his first supper in France:

[quotes ch. 10 'We stopped' to ' "plagued French!" ']

Thus, again, the assumption of ignorance—a dense, dull, idiotic
ignorance in the presence of all the foreign guides, every one of whom
was invariably called Ferguson. Here is a passage concerning one of
them that is worth transcribing by way of reminiscence:

[quotes ch. 27 'He had reserved' to 'guide to say'.]

The Innocents Abroad was published forty-one years ago, and yet
one could go on quoting from it indefinitely with an absolute certainty
that every quotation would hit the mark and evoke Homeric laughter
just as it did when the pages were fresh from the press. Dan buying
gloves from a girl in Gibraltar; Mark Twain's first experience with a
Turkish bath; Mark Twain weeping at the grave of Adam—these and
a score of episodes are already classic, and they will remain so. This

is true of *The Innocents Abroad*. It is not true of any other volume to which the author set his name. In *Roughing It*, perhaps the account of Buck Fanshawe's funeral may hold its own, though the dialect will possibly in time be obsolete and cease to have the peculiar effectiveness which it has even to-day; though it will be a long time before we forget the courtly question asked by Scotty Briggs the gambler of the new minister from the East:

'Are you the duck that runs the gospel mill?'

This is essentially Juvenalian. Again, most persons would have said that in *The Gilded Age*, Mark Twain had created an absolutely new character in fiction when he drew Colonel Sellers; yet somehow Colonel Sellers is remembered to-day only by people who belong to Bookland. Therefore, if Mark Twain's reputation stands—and it certainly will stand—it will be upon *The Jumping Frog* and *The Innocents Abroad*. It is only short-sighted persons who talk of Mark Twain's profound 'philosophy of life.' He had no philosophy of life, any more than Fielding had or Steele or Harte. But like them he had an instinct for pure humour, which was most effective when it was most unconscious. There was the irreverence of Juvenal and his unexpectedness; but more than all else was that wonderful gift of projecting an absolutely humorous and winning character. Addison has given us Sir Roger, and Dickens has given us a whole portrait gallery; but Mark Twain created just one personage with whom we laugh or wonder or are indignant, and this personage is Mark Twain himself—Mark Twain, be it understood, and not Mr. Samuel L. Clemens. A century hence, or two centuries hence, the dross will be separated from the gold, and men and women will still take infinite delight in Smiley and Dan'l Webster, but most of all in the man who was essentially American, right-minded, telling truths in the spirit of one who jests, and giving to those who choose his earliest books a pure and wholesome and natural enjoyment.

84. William Lyon Phelps:
'Mark Twain, Artist', *Review of Reviews*
(New York)

June 1910, xli, 702–3

Clemens' 'essay on "The Meaning of Life"' was presumably *What Is Man?* which had been published anonymously in 1906. The piece first appeared in the United States over Mark Twain's name in 1917.

If necessity is the mother of invention, misfortune is the mother of literature. When Nathaniel Hawthorne was ejected from the Custom-House at Salem he went home in a despondent frame of mind, only to be greeted by his wonderful wife's pertinent remark, 'Now you can write your book.' He responded to this stimulus by writing the best book ever written in the Western Hemisphere, *The Scarlet Letter.* We learn from a famous chapter in *Roughing It* that if Samuel L. Clemens had not gone to help a sick friend, or if his partner had received the note he left for him before starting on this charitable expedition, Samuel L. Clemens would have been a millionaire. This episode has since his death been printed in a list of the misfortunes that marked his romantic and tragic career. But if at that time Mr. Clemens had become a millionaire, and he missed it by the narrowest possible margin, he never would have become Mark Twain. He struggled against his destiny with all the physical and mental force he possessed. He tried to make a living by every means except literature, and nothing but steady misfortune and dire necessity made him walk in the fore-ordained path. Mark Twain always regarded himself as the plaything of chance; professing no belief in God, he never thanked Him for his amazing successes, nor rebelled against Him for his sufferings. But if ever there was a man whose times were in His hand, that man was Mark Twain.

Mark Twain was a greater artist than he was humorist; a greater humorist than he was philosopher; a greater philosopher than he was thinker. Goethe's well-known remark about Byron, 'The moment he thinks, he is a child,' would in some respects be applicable to Mark Twain. The least valuable part of his work is found among his efforts to rewrite history, his critical essays on men and on institutions, and his contributions to introspective thought. His long book on Joan of Arc is valuable only for its style; his short book ont he Shakespeare-Bacon controversy shows appalling ignorance; his defense of Harriet Shelley is praiseworthy only in its chivalry; his attack on Fenimore Cooper is of no consequence except as a humorous document; his labored volume on Christian Science has little significance; and when his posthumous essay on the 'Meaning of Life' is published, as I am afraid it will be before long, it will surprise and depress more readers than it will convince.

As a philosopher, Mark Twain was a pessimist as to the value of the individual life and an optimist concerning human progress. He agreed with Schopenhauer that non-existence was preferable to existence; that sorrow was out of all proportion to happiness. On the other hand, he had absolutely nothing of Carlyle's peculiar pessimism, who regarded the human soul as something noble and divine, but insisted that modern progress was entirely in the wrong direction, and that things in general were steadily growing worse. Carlyle believed in God and man, but he had hated democracy as a political principle; Mark Twain apparently believed in neither God nor man, but his faith in democracy was so great that he almost made a religion out of it. He was never tired of exposing the tyranny of superstition and of unmasking the romantic splendor of medieval life.

Mark Twain was one of the foremost humorists of modern times; and there are not wanting good critics, who already dare to place him with Rabelais, Cervantes, and Molière. Others would regard such an estimate as mere hyperbole, born of transient enthusiasm. But we all know now that he was more than a funmaker; we know that his humor, while purely American, had the note of universality. He tested historical institutions, the social life of past ages, political and religious creeds, and the future abode of the saints by the practical touchstone of humor. Nothing sharpens the eyes of a traveler more than a sense of humor; nothing enables him better to make the subsequent story of his journey pictorially impressive. *The Innocents Abroad* is a great book, because it represents the wonders of Europe as seen by an unawed Philistine with no background; he has his limitations, but at any rate

> of things are formed *after* he sees them, and not before.
> with his own eyes, not through the colored spectacles of
> n. *Roughing It* is a still greater book, because in the writing
> no background was necessary, no limitations are felt; we know
> testimony is true. The humor of Mark Twain is American in
its point of view, in its love of the incongruous, in its fondness for
colossal exaggeration; but it is universal in that it deals not with passing
phenomena, or with matters of temporary interest, but with essential
and permanent aspects of human nature.

As an artist Mark Twain already seems great. The funniest man in
the world, he was at the same time a profoundly serious artist, a
faithful servant of his literary ideals. The environment, the characterization, and the humanity in *Tom Sawyer* remind us of the great
novelists, whose characters remain in our memory as sharply defined
individuals simply because they have the touch of nature that makes
the whole world kin. In other words, *Tom Sawyer* resembles the
masterpieces of fiction in being intensely local and at the same time
universal. Tom Sawyer is a definite personality; but he is also eternal
boyhood. In *Huckleberry Finn* we have three characters who are so
different that they live in different worlds, and really speak different
languages, Tom, Huck, and Jim; we have an amazingly clear presentation of life in the days of slavery; we have a marvelous moving picture
of the Father of Waters; but, above all, we have a vital drama of
humanity, in its nobility and baseness, its strength and weakness, its
love of truth and its love of fraud, its utter pathos and its side-splitting
mirth. Like nearly all faithful pictures of the world, it is a vast tragi-
comedy. What does it matter if our great American had his limitations
and his excrescences? To borrow his own phrase, 'There is that about
the sun that makes us forget his spots.'

85. Simeon Strunsky: unsigned article, *Nation*

Simeon Strunsky (1879–1948), journalist, essayist and novelist, served on the staff of the New York *Evening Post* from 1906 to 1924 and then on that of the New York *Times* from 1924 to 1948. Beginning in 1932 he contributed the anonymous column 'Topics of the Times' to the editorial page of that newspaper.

The passages by W. D. Howells are from 'My Memories of Mark Twain' (*Harper's Magazine*, July 1910, cxxxi, 174 and 178), the first of three articles in a series which was completed in the August and September issues of *Harper's*. These, together with a collection of his own reviews of Mark Twain's works, Howells then issued as *My Mark Twain* (New York, 1910).

Mark Twain's memory may suffer from a certain paradoxical habit we have fallen into when passing judgment on the illustrious dead. The habit consists in picking out for particular commendation in the man what one least expects. If the world thinks of him as a great humorist, the point to make is that at bottom he was really a philosopher. If his shafts struck at everybody and everything, the thing to say is that he liked best what he hit hardest. If one of his books sold five thousand copies, the attempt is made to base his future fame on the comparatively unknown book. The motive behind such reasoning is commendable enough. It is the desire not to judge superficially, the desire to get at the 'real' man behind the mask which all of us, according to tradition, wear in life. It is a praiseworthy purpose, but, in the hands of the unskilled or the careless, a perilous one. And worse than either in the intellectual snob whose business it is constitutionally to disagree with the obvious. We make no attempt to classify the writer who has declared that Mark Twain, when he wrote *Innocents Abroad*, was terribly in earnest; that he set out to satirize and was funny only because he could not help it. This represents the extreme of a tendency that is made manifest on every side, to turn Mark Twain into everything but what he was—a great compeller of laughter.

One gets dreadfully weary of such topsy-turvy criticism. There are times when one would like to believe that Napoleon will be remembered because he won Austerlitz and Marengo, and not because he divided up France into a vast number of small peasant holdings; that Lincoln was a great man because he signed the Proclamation of Emancipation and wrote the Gettysburg address, and not because he kept his temper under criticism and in adversity. It is well to try to pierce behind the veil of Maya, but no amount of analysis can do away with the popularly accepted beliefs that mothers are primarily maternal, that actresses' talents lie in the direction of the stage, that joyful people laugh, and that people who make wry faces are either pessimists or dyspeptics. What use is there in trying to make a serious book out of the *Innocents Abroad*, when we know well that the Mark Twain who wrote it was primarily a fun-maker? For ourselves, we confess that we have been unable to find any grave purpose in the 'Jumping Frog of Calaveras.' We recall the Hawaiian stranger whom Mark Twain kissed for his mother's sake before robbing him of his small change. We recall the horse he rode in Honolulu; it had many fine points, and our traveller hung his hat upon one of them. We recall that other horse behind which he went driving one Sunday with the lady of his choice; it was a milk-dealer's horse on week-days, and it persisted in travelling diagonally across the street and stopping before every gate. These adventures are easy to recall, but the hidden serious purpose within them remains hidden from us.

The serious element in Mark Twain the man and the writer, it would, of course, be futile to deny. His hatred of sham, his hatred of cruelty, his hatred of oppression, appear in the *Innocents Abroad*, as they do in his *Connecticut Yankee* and in his bitter assaults on the Christian Scientists and the American missionaries in China of the Boxer days. But to say that Mark Twain was a great humorist because he was an intensely serious man is not true, whatever truth there may be in the formula that humorists are humorists because they are men of sorrow. We would reverse the formula. We would say that humorists are often sad because they are humorists, and that from much laughing the rebound must necessarily be towards much grief. If it is commonly asserted that the humorist laughs because of the incongruities of life, it is, nevertheless, just as safe to maintain that the man born to laughter will be driven by his instincts to search out incongruities. There was no fundamental pessimism in Mark Twain. As Mr. Howells brings out in his chapter of reminiscences in the last *Harper's*, Mr. Clemens had the soul of untamed boyishness. He was boyish in his exuberance of manner, in his taste for extraordinary clothes, and in his glee at earning a great deal of money:

The postals [announcing his share of the daily profits from the *Gilded Age*] used to come about dinner-time, and Clemens would read them aloud to us in wild triumph. $150—$200—$300 were the gay figures which they bore, and which he flaunted in the air before he sat down at table, or rose from it to brandish, and then, flinging his napkin into his chair, walked up and down to exult in.

One thing there was in Mark Twain that was not apparently boyish or simple. Mr. Howells asserts positively that in his later years Twain believed neither in the Christian theology, in God, nor in immortality:

All his expressions to me were of a courageous renunciation of any hope of living again, or elsewhere seeing those he had lost. He suffered terribly in their loss, and he was not fool enough to try ignoring his grief. He knew that for that there were but two medicines; that it would wear itself out with the years, and that meanwhile there was nothing for it but those respites in which the mourner forgets himself in slumber. I remember that in a black hour of my own when I was called down to see him, as he thought from sleep, he said, with an infinite, an exquisite compassion, 'Oh, did I wake you, did I *wake* you?' Nothing more, but the look, the voice, were everything; and while I live they cannot pass from my sense.

Here at last we have the disillusion that is said to dwell in the innermost soul of the great humorist. But here, too, we seem to feel that the gray vision of the future was with him not a cause, but a result. When the buoyant soul sinks back upon itself it is apt to feel the riddle of life very keenly indeed.

86. Archibald Henderson:
'The International Fame of Mark Twain',
North American Review

December 1910, cxcii, 805–15

Archibald Henderson (1877–1963) was a professor of mathematics (1908–48) at the University of North Carolina and head of the mathematics department from 1920 until his retirement. He wrote scholarly works on history and literature as well as on mathematics. Besides books on Einstein (whose pupil he had been) and G. B. Shaw, he wrote *Mark Twain* (New York, 1912) and 'Mark Twain: His Unique Position in the Republic of Letters' (*Harper's Magazine*, May 1909, cxviii, 948–55).

Simboli's article, 'Mark Twain from an Italian Point of View', appeared in the *Critic* (June 1904, xliv, 518–24). Howells had written 'Mark Twain: An Inquiry' for the *North American Review* (5 February 1901, clxxii, 306–21), where it was reprinted in the issue for June 1910.

Art transmitting the simplest feelings of common life, but such always as are accessible to all men in the whole world—the art of common life—the art of a people—universal art.—TOLSTOY: *What is Art?*

It is a mark of the democratic independence of America that she has betrayed a singular indifference to the appraisal of her literature at the hands of foreign criticism. Upon her writers who have exhibited derivative genius—Irving, Hawthorne, Emerson, Longfellow—American criticism has lavished the most extravagant eulogiums. The three geniuses who have made permanent contributions to world literature, who have either embodied in the completest degree the spirit of American democracy or who have won the widest following of imitators and admirers in foreign countries, still await their final and just deserts at the hands of critical opinion in their own land. The genius of Edgar Allan Poe gave rise to schools of literature in France and on the continent of Europe; yet in America his name remained until now debarred from inclusion in a so-called Hall of Fame! Walt Whitman and Mark Twain, the two great interpreters and embodiments of America, represent the supreme contribution of democracy to universal literature. In so far as it is legitimate for any one to be denominated a 'self-made man' in literature, these two men are justly entitled to that characterization. They owe nothing to European literature—their genius is transcendently original, native, democratic. The case of Mark Twain is a literary phenomenon which imposes upon criticism, peculiarly upon American criticism, the distinct obligation of tracing the steps in his unhalting climb to an eminence completely international in character. Mark Twain achieved that eminence by the sole power of brain and personality. In this sense his career is unprecedented and unparalleled in the history of American literature. Criticism must define those signal qualities, traits, characteristics—individual, literary, social, racial, national—which encompassed his world-wide fame. For if it be true that the judgment of foreign nations is virtually the judgment of posterity, then is Mark Twain already a classic.

Upon the continent of Europe, Mark Twain first received notable critical recognition in France at the hands of that brilliant woman, Mme. Blanc ('Th. Bentzon'), who devoted her energies in such great measure to the popularization of American literature in Europe. The essay on Mark Twain, in the series which she wrote, under the general title 'The American Humorists,' appeared in the *Revue des Deux Mondes* in 1872 (July 15th). In addition to a remarkably accurate translation of 'The Jumping Frog' into faultless French, this essay contained a minute analysis of *The Innocents Abroad*; and at this time Mme. Blanc was contemplating a translation of *The Innocents Abroad* into French. There is no cause for surprise in the discovery that a scholarly Frenchwoman, reared on classic models and confined by rigid canons of art, should stand aghast at this boisterous, barbaric, irreverent jester from the Western wilds of America. When one reflects that Mark Twain began his career as one of the sage-brush writers and gave free play to his democratic disregard of the traditional and the classic as such, it is not to be wondered at that Mme. Blanc, while honoring him with elaborate interpretation in the most authoritative literary journal in the world, could not conceal an expression of amazement over his enthusiastic acceptance in English-speaking countries:

Mark Twain's 'Jumping Frog' should be mentioned, in the first place, as one of his most popular little stories—almost a type of the rest. It is, nevertheless, rather difficult for us to understand, while reading the story, the 'roars of laughter' that it excited in Australia and in India, in New York and in London; the numerous editions of it which appeared; the epithet of 'inimitable' that the critics of the English press have unanimously awarded to it. . . .

We may remark that a Persian of Montesquieu, a Huron of Voltaire, even a simple Peruvian woman of Madame de Graffigny, reasons much more wisely about European civilization than an American of San Francisco. The fact is that it is not sufficient to have wit or even natural taste in order to appreciate works of art.

It is the right of humorists to be extravagant; but still common sense, although carefully hidden, ought *sometimes* to make itself apparent. . . . In Mark Twain the Protestant is enraged against the pagan worship of broken marble statues—the democrat denies that there was any poetic feeling in the Middle Ages. . . .

In the course of this voyage with Mark Twain (*The Innocents Abroad*), we at length discover, under his good-fellowship and apparent ingenuousness, faults which we should never have expected. He has in the highest degree that fault of appearing astonished at nothing—common, we may say, to all savages. He confesses himself that one of his great pleasures is to horrify the guides by his indifference and stupidity. He is, too, decidedly envious. . . . We could willingly pardon him his patriotic self-love, often wounded by the ignorance of Europeans, above all, in what concerns the New World, if only that national pride were without mixture of personal vanity. . . .

Taking the 'Pleasure Trip on the Continent' altogether, does it merit the success it enjoys? In spite of the indulgence that we cannot but show to the judgments of a foreigner; while recollecting that those amongst us who have visited America have fallen, doubtless, under the influence of prejudices almost as dangerous as ignorance, into errors quite as bad—in spite of the wit with which certain pages sparkle—we must say that this voyage is very far below the less celebrated excursions of the same author in his own country.

It is only too patent that the humor of Mark Twain, the very qualities which won him his immense and sudden popularity, make no appeal to Mme. Blanc. She conscientiously and painstakingly upbraids him *au grand sérieux* for those features of his work most thoroughly surcharged with *vis comica*. Three years later Mme. Blanc returns to the criticism of Mark Twain, in an essay in the *Revue des Deux Mondes* (March 15th, 1875), entitled 'L'Age Doré en Amérique' —an exhaustive review and analysis of *The Gilded Age*. The Savage charm and genuine simplicity of Mark Twain are not devoid of attraction even to her sophisticated intelligence; and she is inclined to infer that jovial irony and animal spirits are qualities sufficient for the amusement of a young nation of people such as are the Americans, since they do not pique themselves upon being *blasés*. According to her judgment, Mark Twain and Charles Dudley Warner are lacking in the requisite mental grasp for the 'stupendous task of interpreting the great tableau of the American scene.' Nor does she regard their effort at collaboration as a success from the standpoint of art:

From this association of two very dissimilar minds arises a work very difficult to read; at every moment we see the pen pass from one hand to the other and the romancer call the humorist to order, only too often call him in vain. . . . Do not expect of Mark Twain either tact or delicacy, but count upon him for honest and outspoken shrewdness. . . .

The charm of Colonel Sellers wholly escapes her, for she cannot understand the truly loving appreciation with which this genial burlesque of the later American industrial brigand was greeted by the American people. The remarkable talents of Mark Twain as a reporter impress her most favorably; but she is repelled by 'that mixture of good sense with mad folly—disorder,' the wilful exaggeration of the characters, and the jests which are so elaborately constructed that 'the very theme itself disappears under the mass of embroidery which overlays it.' 'The audacities of a Bret Harte, the temerities of a Mark Twain still astonish us,' she concludes; 'but soon we shall become accustomed to an American language whose savory freshness is not to be disdained in lieu of still more delicate and refined qualities that time will doubtless bring.'

In translating 'The Jumping Frog' (giving Mark Twain the opportunity for re-translating it—'clawing it back'—into English which furnished amusement for thousands), in elaborately reviewing, with long citations, *The Innocents Abroad* and *The Gilded Age*, Mme. Blanc rendered a genuine service to Mark Twain, introducing him to the literary world of France and Europe. In 1881 Émile Blémont still further enhanced the fame of Mark Twain in France by publishing in free French translation a number of his slighter sketches, under the title *Esquisses Américaines de Mark Twain*. In 1884 and again in 1886 appeared editions of *Les Aventures de Tom Sawyer*, translated by W. L. Hughes. In 1886 Eugène Forgues published in the *Revue des Deux Mondes* (February 15th) an exhaustive review, with lengthy citations, of *Life on the Mississippi*, under the title 'Les Caravanes d'un Humoriste.' His prefatory remarks in regard to Mark Twain's fame in France at this time may be accepted as authoritative. He called attention to the commendable efforts of French scholars to popularize these 'transatlantic gayeties.' But the result of all the efforts to import into France a new mode of comic entertainment was an almost complete check. There was one notable exception; for *The Adventures of Tom Sawyer* was really appreciated and praised as—an 'exquisite idyll'! The peculiar twist of national character, the specialized conception of the *vis comica* revealed in Mark Twain's works, tended to confine them to a restricted *milieu*. To the French taste, Mark Twain's pleasantry appeared *macabre*, his wit brutal, his temperament dry to excess. By some, indeed, his exaggerations were regarded as 'symptoms of mental alienation'; and the originality of his verve did not conceal from French eyes the 'incoherence of his conceptions.'

It has been said [remarks M. Forgues] that an academician slumbers in the depths of every Frenchman; and this it was which militated against the success of Mark Twain in France. Humor, with us, has its laws and its restrictions. So the French public saw in Mark Twain a gross jester, incessantly beating upon a tom-tom to attract the attention of the crowd. They were tenacious in resisting all such blandishments.... *As a humorist* Mark Twain has never been appreciated in France. The appreciation he has ultimately secured—an appreciation by no means inconsiderable, but in no sense comparable to that won in Anglo-Saxon and Germanic countries—was due to his shrewdness and penetration as an observer, and to his marvellous faculty for evoking scenes and situations by the clever use of the novel and the *imprévu*. There was, even to the French, a certain lively appeal in an intelligence absolutely free of convention, sophistication or reverence for traditional views *qua* traditionary.

Although at first the salt of Mark Twain's humor seemed to be lacking in the Attic flavor, the leisurely exposition of the genially naïve American in time won its way with the *blasé* Parisians. It is needless to cite those works of his which were subsequently translated into the French language. It has been recorded that tourists who could find no copy of the Bible in the street book-stalls of Paris were confronted on every hand with copies of *Roughing It*! When the English edition of Mark Twain's collected works appeared (Chatto and Windus: London), that authoritative French journal, the *Mercure de France* (December, 1899), paid him this distinguished tribute:

His public is as varied as possible, because of the versatility and suppleness of his talent which addresses itself successively to all classes of readers. He has been called the greatest humorist in the world, and that is doubtless the truth; but he is also a charming and attractive storyteller, an alert romancer, a clever and penetrating observer, a philosopher without pretensions and, therefore, all the more profound, and finally a brilliant essayist.

Perhaps the present writer may be pardoned for mentioning that when an essay of his on Mark Twain appeared in *Harper's Magazine*, in 1909, M. Lux, reviewing it in *L'Indépendence Belge*, says:

In Mark Twain's writings are to be distinguished, exalted and sublimated by his genius, the typically American qualities of youth and of gayety, of force and of faith. His countrymen love his philosophy, at once practical and high-minded. They are fond of his simple style, animated with verve and spice, thanks to which his work is accessible to all classes of readers. . . . He describes his contemporaries with such an art of distinguishing their essential traits, that he manages to evoke, to *create* even, characters and types of eternal verity. The Americans profess for Mark Twain the same sort of vehement admiration that we have in France for Balzac.

In Italy, as in France, Mark Twain was regarded as a remarkable impressionist; and *The Innocents Abroad* had wide popularity in Rome. But with the peculiar *timbre* of Mark Twain's humor his Italian audience was not wholly sympathetic; they never felt themselves thoroughly *au courant* with the spirit of his humor.

Translation, however accurate and conscientious [as the Italian critic, Raffaele Simboli, has pointed out] fails to render the special flavor of his work. And then in Italy, where humorous writing generally either rests on a political basis or depends on *risqué* phrases, Mark Twain's *Sketches* are not appreciated because the spirit which breathes in them is not always understood. The story of the 'Jumping Frog,' for instance, famous as it is in America and England, has made little impression in France and Italy.

It was rather among the Germanic peoples and those most closely allied to them racially and temperamentally, the Scandinavians, that Mark Twain found most complete and ready response in Europe. At first sight, it seems almost incredible that the writings of Mark Twain, with their occasional slang, their not infrequent colloquialisms, and their local peculiarities of dialect, should have borne translation into other languages, especially into so complex a language as the German. It must, however, be borne in mind that, despite these peculiar features of his writings, they are couched in a style of most marked directness, simplicity and native English purity.

He writes English [says Mr. Howells] as if it were a primitive and not a derivative language, without Gothic or Latin or Greek behind it or German and French beside it. The result is the English in which the most vital works of English literature are cast. . . .

The ease with which Mark Twain's works were translated into foreign, especially the German and allied tongues, and the eager delight with which they were read and comprehended by all classes, high and low, constitute perhaps the most signal conceivable tribute not only to the humanity of his spirit, but to the genuine art of his natural and forthright style. 'The Jumping Frog' one would imagine to be very recalcitrant to translation. But I was amazed to discover the naturalness and accuracy of both the French and German translations; not only was the spirit of the original preserved: the universality of the anecdote appeared in yet clearer light. Take a brief passage —that in which Smiley and the stranger touch their respective frogs in order to make them jump. First read M. Blémont's translation into French:

Maintenant, dit-il, êtes-vous prêt? Bon! Mettez votre bête à coté de Daniel, leurs pattes de devant bien alignées. Y êtes-vous? je donne le signal.
L'alignement établi, il cria:—Un, deux, trois! Sautez!
Et chacun d'eux pressa au même instant sa grenouille par derrière. La nouvelle grenouille sauta. Daniel voulut sauter aussi, Daniel fit un effort, haussa les épaules, tenez! comme ça, à la français. Mais, bah! Daniel ne pouvait plus bouger! La pauvre bête semblait plantée là aussi solidement qu'une enclume. On eût dit qu'elle était ancrée sur place. Smiley n'en fut pas médiocrement écœuré. Mais il n'eut pas la moindre idée de ce qui s'était passé en son absence. Naturellement!

The translation is apt and clever, for M. Blémont has preserved the spirit—the *ton goguenard*—of the original—lacking in the translation of Mme. Blanc. Equally satisfactory, in catching the *tone* of the story, is the German translation of Herr Moritz Busch:

Na, wenn Sie jetst parat sind, so setzen Sie ihn neben Daniel'n hin, seine Vorderpfoten ganz in derselben Linie wie Daniel'n seine, und ich werde das Signal geben. Dann sagte er: 'Eins—zwei—drei—hopps!' und er und der Bursche gaben den Fröschen hinten einen Tipps, und der neue Frosch hüpfte fort. Aber Daniel that einen Säufzer und hob die Schultern—so—wie'n Franzose—aber's half nichts, er konnte sich nicht rippeln noch rappeln, er sass so fast wie ein Ambos, und er war nicht mehr im Stande, sich zu regen, als wenn er mit einem Anker festgekettet wäre. Smiley war sehr überrascht davon und sehr böse darüber, aber er hatte natürlich keine Ahnung, an was es lag.

One reason—by no means an insignificant reason—why Mark Twain is regarded in Germany almost as if he were a native German writer is that no other English or American author has had so many translators and editors. *Mark Twain's Ausgewählte Humoristische Schriften*, in twelve volumes (Lutz: Stuttgart), as the Viennese philologist, Dr. Leon Kellner, has pointed out, read 'precisely like a German original'—a truly remarkable circumstance. And almost more remarkable still—Mark Twain's *Jugendschriften* have already, some years gone, passed into the fixed repertory of German school literature!

As early as 1872, Mark Twain had secured Tauchnitz, of Leipzig, for his Continental agent. German translations soon appeared of *The Jumping Frog and Other Stories* (1874), *The Gilded Age* (1874), *The Innocents Abroad* (1875), *The Adventures of Tom Sawyer* (1876). Numerous translations soon followed in Germany—published by Mann (Leipzig), Freytag (Leipzig), Lutz (Stuttgart), Reclam's *Universal-bibliothek*, etc. A few years later his sketches, many of them, were translated into virtually all printed languages, notably into Russian and modern Greek. His more extended works rapidly came to be translated into German, French, Italian, Dutch and the languages of Denmark and the Scandinavian peninsula.

The elements of the colossally grotesque, the wildly primitive, in the works of Mark Twain—the underlying note of melancholy, the strain of persistent idealism, not less than the bohemianism—awake a responsive chord in the Germanic consciousness. Mark Twain's stories of the Argonauts, the miners, and the desperadoes; his narratives of the wild freedom of the life on the Mississippi, the lawless and barbaric encounters—all appealed to the Germanic passion for the grotesque. To the Europeans, this wild genius of the Pacific Slope (strange misnomer!) seemed to function in a sort of unexplored fourth-dimension of humor—vast and novel—of which they had never dreamed. In his *Psychopathik des Humors*, Schleich reserved for American humor, with Mark Twain as its leading exponent, a distinct and unique category which he denominated '*phantastisch,*' '*grossdimensional.*' In commenting upon the works of Mark Twain and his popularity in German Europe, Carl von Thaler unhesitatingly affirms that Mark Twain was entertained with absolutely unprecedented hospitality in Vienna—an honor hitherto paid to no German author! In Berlin the young Kaiser bestowed upon him the most distinguished marks of his esteem. He praised Mark Twain's work, notably *Life on the Mississippi*, with the intensest enthusiasm; the passages in *A Tramp Abroad* dealing with German student life were also singled out for commendation. After hearing the Kaiser's eulogy on *Life on the Mississippi*, Mark Twain was astounded and touched to receive a similar tribute, the same evening, from the *portier* of his lodging-house.

That a crowned head and a *portier*, the very top of an Empire and the very bottom of it, should pass the very same criticism and deliver the very same verdict upon a book of mine—and almost in the same hour and the same breath—

this, Mark Twain confessed, was the most extraordinary coincidence of his life.

By German critics Mark Twain was hailed as the leading exponent of American humor, not only in the United States, but, in Herr Ludwig Salomon's phrase, 'everywhere that culture rules.' *Robinson Crusoe* was held to exhibit a limited power of imagination in comparison with the ingenuity and resourcefulness of *Tom Sawyer*. At times the German critics confessed their inability to discover the dividing-line between astounding actuality and humorously fantastic exaggeration. The description of the barbaric state of western America possessed an indescribable fascination for the Europeans. At times Mark Twain's bloody jests froze the laughter on their lips; and his 'revolver humor' made their hair stand on end. 'Such adventures,' one bold critic observes, 'are possible only in America—perhaps only in the fancy of an American!'

Mark Twain's greatest strength [says von Thaler] lies in his little sketches, the literary snapshots. The shorter his work, the more striking it is. He draws directly from life. No other writer has learned to know so many different varieties of men and circumstances, so many strange examples of the *Genus Homo*, as he; no other has taken so strange a course of development.

The deeper elements of Mark Twain's humor did not escape the attention of the Germans, nor fail of appreciation at their hands. In his aphorisms, embodying at once genuine wit and experience of life, they discovered the universal human being; and it is chiefly for this reason that they found these aphorisms worthy of profound and lasting admiration. Franz Sintenis saw in Mark Twain a 'living symptom of the youthful joy in existence'—a genius capable at will, 'despite this boyish extravagance,' of the virile formulation of fertile and suggestive ideas. On the occasion of Mark Twain's seventieth birthday, German Europe united in honoring the man and writer. Able critical reviews of his life and work were published in Germany and Austria—more in German Europe than in America! From these various essays—in such authoritative publications as the *Neue Freie Presse* (Vienna),

Tägliche Rundschau (Leipzig), *Allgemeine Zeitung* (Munich), *Gymnasium* (Paderborn), and the *Illustrirte Zeitung* (Leipzig)—I select one short passage from the pen of the able critic, Dr. Leon Kellner, of Vienna:

A bohemian fellow, who is full of mischief without the slightest trace of malice in it, an imaginative story-teller who is always ready to make himself and others ridiculous without coming anywhere near the truth, a fantastic and Johnny-look-in-air who nevertheless never loses the solid ground from under his feet, a vagabond and adventurer, who from crown to sole remains a gentleman and with the grand manner of a Walter Scott keeps his commercial honor unsoiled—that is the writer Mark Twain and the citizen Samuel Langhorne Clemens in one person.

He hails Mark Twain as 'the king of humorists'—who understood how to transmute all earthly stuff, such as the negro Jim and the street Arab, Huckleberry Finn, into 'the gold of pure literature.' At the time of Mark Twain's death, when so many tributes were paid him all over the world, one of his German critics wrote, with genuine insight into the deeper significance of his work:

Although Mark Twain's humor moves us to irresistible laughter, this is not the main feature in his works; like all true humorists, *ist der Witz mit dem Weltschmerz verbunden,* he is a witness to higher thoughts and higher emotions, and his purpose is to expose bad morals and evil circumstances in order to improve and ennoble mankind.

Mark Twain is loved in Germany, the critics pointed out, more than all other humorists, English or French, because his humor 'turns fundamentally upon serious and earnest conceptions of life.' It is a tremendously significant fact that the works of American literature most widely read to-day in Germany are the works of—striking conjunction!—Ralph Waldom Eerson and Mark Twain.

'The Jumping Frog' fired the laugh heard round the world; it initiated Mark Twain's international fame. *The Innocents Abroad* won the thoughtful attention of the English people. Since that day Mark Twain has been the adored author of England and the colonies; in lieu of a national author, the English chose Mark Twain for the national author of the English-speaking world. His popularity in England was as great as in America or Germany; all classes read his works with unfeigned delight; critics of the highest authority praised his works in the most glowing terms. The personal ovation to him in 1907, which I witnessed, was the greatest ovation ever given by an English public to a foreign visitor not a crowned head; and Oxford University honored him with her degree.

At that time the oldest of England's periodicals, The *Spectator*, paid Mark Twain this significant and comprehensive tribute:

[quotes extracts No. 74 'It is all' to 'English language'.]

It is gratifying to citizens of all nationalities to recall and recapture the pleasure and delight Mark Twain's works have given the world for decades. It is peculiarly gratifying to Americans to rest confident in the belief that, in Mark Twain, America has contributed to the world an international and universal genius—sealed of the tribe of Molière, a congener of Defoe, of Fielding, of Le Sage—a man who will be remembered, as Mr. Howells has said, 'with the great humorists of all time, with Cervantes, with Swift, or with any other worthy his company; none of them was his equal in humanity.'

87. John Macy on Mark Twain

1913

Chapter from *The Spirit of American Literature* (New York, 1913), pp. 248–77.

John Albert Macy (1877–1932), author and critic, edited Helen Keller's *The Story of My Life* (1903) and wrote a life of Edgar Allan Poe (1907). *The Spirit of American Literature* established him as an important critic. He was subsequently literary editor of the Boston *Herald* (1913–14) and the *Nation* (1922–3). Among his other books are *Socialism in America* (1915), *The Critical Game* (1922), and *The Story of the World's Literature* (1925).

As a footnote to his comment that Mark Twain, 'the unshakeable realist', was always the enemy of 'sentimentality and pretension', Macy observed, 'Be it noted, as is proper in a consideration of a master of irony and hater of sham, that Mark Twain was himself a sentimentalist at least once, in "*A Dog's Tale*." ' Macy concludes his chapter on Mark Twain with a brief 'Biographical Note' and bibliography, here omitted.

It was *A Manual of American Literature* (G. P. Putnam's Sons: New York and London, 1909), edited by Theodore Stanton, which called *Connecticut Yankee* 'a cruel parody' of Malory. This volume was prepared as No. 4000 of the Tauchnitz *Collection of British Authors*, in which Mark Twain and many other American authors had been published. Elmer J. Bailey, the author of the chapter on 'The Essayists and the Humourists', concludes his remarks on Mark Twain with the observation that 'it is not impossible that future critics may come to regard *The Prince and the Pauper* (1882) and *The Personal Recollections of Joan of Arc* (1896), two serious and dignified pieces of writing, as Mr. Clemens's best work' (p. 358).

Gulliver's Travels is to be found in two editions, one for adult minds, the other for adventurous immaturity. The texts differ but little, if at all; differences are mainly differences in the reader. For one audience

Gulliver's Travels is a story book like *Robinson Crusoe* and *Treasure Island*. For the other audience it is a tremendous satire on human nature, a vast portrait of man, the nakedly simple narrative uttering profundities before which the sentimental quail and hypocrites wear an unhappy smile. The boy who follows the strange fortunes of Doctor Gulliver does not know that Swift is talking over his head to the parents who gave the boy the wonder book. All satire is dual in its nature. It speaks in parable, saying one thing and meaning a deeper parallelism. It is a preacher in cap and bells.

To the holiday mood of the world and the wholesomely childish popular mind Mark Twain's books, like *Gulliver's Travels*, appeal instantly. For forty years he has been a favourite comedian, a beloved jester, picturesque, histrionic in all his public attitudes. His books have been sold by hundreds of thousands. Of *Joan of Arc*, one of his least popular books ('I wrote it for love,' he says, 'and never expected it to sell'), sixteen thousand copies were sold in the years from 1904 to 1908. Mark Twain was the most successful man of letters of his time; in the duration and variety of his powers, in the number and enthusiasm of his audience he has no rival in English literature after Dickens.

To say in the face of that towering popularity that he is greater than his reputation may seem praise beyond reason, and it may be presumptuous to suggest that the millions who admire him do not all know how great a man they admire or what in him is most admirable. Nevertheless it is true that this incorrigible and prolific joker has kept the world chuckling so continuously that it has not sobered down to comprehend what a powerful, original thinker he is. If you mention his name, some one says, 'Oh, yes! do you remember what he said when it was reported that he was dead?' You smile appreciatively and insist, 'Yes, but have you read *Joan of Arc*? Have you really read, since you grew up, the greatest piece of American fiction, *Huckleberry Finn*?' The response is apt to be more willing than intelligent. Some men of letters, like Mr. Bernard Shaw, and some critics, such as Professor W. L. Phelps and Professor Brander Matthews, have measured his significance. Mr. Howells, after warning us not to forget the joker in the gravity of our admiration, said it all in a few words, 'Clemens, the sole and incomparable, the Lincoln of our literature.' Other critics remain truer to the critic type by condescending to contemporary greatness and reserving highest praise for Mark Twain's equals who lived long ago, Swift, Molière, Cervantes, Fielding. As an example of the timid ineptitude of critics in the presence of living greatness, I quote from a handbook of American literature published five or six years ago. In it *A Connecticut Yankee in King Arthur's Court* is called a 'cruel parody of Malory's *Morte d'Arthur.*' It is not cruel and it is not a parody; in other respects the criticism is profoundly true. 'It is unfortunate'—says the same handbook—'it is unfortunate for Mr. Clemens that he is a humorist; no one can ever take such a man seriously.' It is unfortunate; just as it is a burning shame that Lamb was not an epic poet and that Swift was not a church historian.

To take humorists seriously is superficially incongruous. We should approach all satirists from Aristophanes to George Meredith in a spirit of gay delight. If we talk too solemnly about them, their spirits will wink us out of countenance. However, it is a well-established custom to discuss masters of humour, who have been dead a long time, as if they were really important in the history of human thought; and, without a too ponderous solemnity, one may seriously praise and expound the wisdom of the great laugh-maker who died two years ago.

Mark Twain began as a newspaper reporter, a 'funny-column' man. He was a natural story-teller; his delightful, flexible voice was a melancholy vehicle for outrageous absurdities, and the mask of a grieved and puzzled countenance was a gift of the gods to a platform humorist. His natural talents of mind and manner made him successful on the Pacific Coast before he thought of himself as a professional man of letters. As he grew older, he cultivated the gifts which he had discovered by accident, came in time to a perfect and conscious command of his art, and by much reading and writing and experience made himself a very great master of prose.

His first book of sketches, printed in 1867, is of no better quality than the work of hundreds of newspaper men who put a little fun into their day's scribbling and so get a little fun out of it. The sketches had given Clemens a local reputation before they were printed as a book, and prompted the proprietors of the *Alta California* to send him on the famous voyage of the steamer *Quaker City*. The report of that voyage is *Innocents Abroad*, a first-rate book of travel, which revealed at once an accomplished writer of sincere, vigorous English. As if the spirit of incongruities had conspired to make fun doubly funny, *Innocents Abroad* has been regarded, by those who read with any part of their organism except their intellect, as an expression of American irreverence grinning at the august beauties of Europe. So far as it is disrespectful, its satire is aimed at the dishonest American tourist, at the gaping pretender who feigns to see beauty where it is not, or where he does not see it, and misses beauty where it is. Upon the 'pilgrims' with their fraudulent enthusiasms, their vandal thefts of 'souvenirs' from places that they call sacred, the clerk of the party pours his scornful ridicule. To swindlers who exploit art and antiquity for the sake of the tourist's dollar he gives no quarter. Romances that thoughtless people accept as lovely but which are essentially base, like the story of Abelard, he tears to shreds. The unshakable realist here begins to deal those blows to sentimentality and pretension which ring through all his work to the last. Disingenuous books of travel he piles in a heap, sets fire to them and dances round the pyre.

[quotes ch. 48 'Nearly every book' to 'with his tongue'.]

The passage expresses Mark Twain's lifelong attitude toward books and men. He looked on the world with a serious, candid and penetrating eye, analyzing the human fool, affectionately tolerant of his folly except when it is mixed with meanness and cruelty. In a letter he wrote shortly before his death he said, referring to his book on Shakespeare:

In that booklet I courteously hinted at the long-ago well established fact that even the most gifted human being is merely an ass, & always an ass, when his forbears have furnished him an idol to worship. Reasoning cannot convert him, facts cannot influence him. I wrote the booklet for pleasure—*not* in the expectation of convincing anybody that Shakespeare did not write Shakespeare. And don't *you* write with any such expectation. Such labors are not worth the ink & the paper—except when you do them for the pleasure of it. Shakespeare the Stratford tradesman will still be the divine Shakespeare to our posterity a thousand years hence.

In *Innocents Abroad*, the self-deceptions and pious buncombe of the pilgrims, the mendacious guides, the 'tall' traditional stories told for money to tourists by vergers and ciceroni (stories beside which 'American exaggeration' is shrinking understatement)—all these impositions move the recording Innocent to cut capers, to play the vacant idiot, and then to pour out one of his level streams of deadly accurate and demolishing irony. It is a pleasure to read him in his abusive moods, and it was a greater pleasure to hear him in one of his coolly passionate tirades, speaking sentences amazingly finished and constructed as if a prose style were as natural to him as breathing, in a voice even, deliberate, modulated and sweet with rage.

Besides much excellent fooling and vigorous destruction of what is revered but not reverend, there is in *Innocents Abroad* a good deal of fine, clear description of things seen. Indeed the book is on the whole a serious report of sights and events. The characterization of the pilgrims reveals the gift that was later to draw shrewd portraits of human beings, real and fictitious. Mark Twain shows in this book, as in much of his writing, the deep enthusiasm for natural beauty which is impossible to people who can harbour dishonest admirations. The description of Vesuvius is powerful, graphic, as fresh as if no other man had seen and described it.

Clemens's next book, *Roughing It*, is 'merely a personal narrative' describing 'the rise, growth and culmination of the silver mining fever in Nevada.' It appeared at the time when Bret Harte was capturing the fancy of unsophisticated readers with his delightful, disingenuous tales of the Wild West. 'O. Henry,' in some respects a better story-teller than Bret Harte, has said that the editors of New York magazines (and their Eastern readers) are so naïvely ignorant that in a cowboy yarn the author can stab a man with a lariat and they will not know the difference. To this romantic ignorance Bret Harte appealed with pictures of a theatric California and portraits of miners such as never dug in the real earth. His tales are skilfully written, humorous, quaisi-pathetic and engagingly readable, but they are made 'for export' to people who do not know the flavour of better native wines. In his book, *Is Shakespeare Dead?* Mark Twain says:

I know the argot of the quartz-mining and milling industry familiarly; and so whenever Bret Harte introduces that industry into a story, the first time one of his miners opens his mouth I recognize from his phrasing that Harte got the phrasing by listening—like Shakespeare—I mean the Stratford one—not by experience. No one can talk the quartz dialect correctly without learning it with pick and shovel and drill and fuse.

Harte's unreality is deeper than that; he is a sentimentalist, who makes untrustworthy assays of man and society. He mistakes the iron pyrites of melodrama and farce for the gold-bearing quartz of human nature. This is not to deny Bret Harte's merits, which are genuine if not of a high order. He is not exceptional in his attitude toward life and toward fiction. Too many American story-tellers of considerable literary skill are thinly romantic; they move in regions of artificial adventure and moonlit emotion. Only in the last quarter of the nineteenth century did the spirit of realism find itself at home among a people reputed to be sensible and practical, but really sentimental and foolish and content with a conduct of private and public affairs that fills an intelligent business man with despair. Their thinking is childish, and they swallow with delight any silly story, whether it is presented as a work of fiction or a fact of history and government.

The first strong voice of realism in the western part of America is Mark Twain, and *Roughing It* is its first expression—a statement that some Americans would probably meet by pointing out that Mark Twain changes the names of Nevada people and invents things that really did not happen! Imagination is wasted on a people who hug Mark Twain's jokes as a child hugs a jumping-jack and do not know that *Roughing It* is an important social study, reconstructing in its own unmethodical fashion a phase of American history, a section of the national life. Under the touch of a great instinctive humourist, whose vision is sharp and undeluded, whose lively caricature plays over a cold sense of fact, the silver boom-town, its comedy and tragedy, takes permanent and accurate shape for the benefit of an inquisitive posterity that will wish to study our social history.

In *The Gilded Age* Mark Twain and Charles Dudley Warner worked together two claims, only one of which shows real metal. The story is of two sets of characters brought together in a forced and unconvincing unity. The young people from the east with their commonplace love affairs figure in one plot, which crosses the fortunes and misfortunes of Colonel Sellers and his family. Everything in the book except Colonel Sellers may be sacrificed without great loss to literature. Sellers is a colossal comic creation, the embodied spirit of western mushroom hopes and bubble enterprise. The type is so true to human nature, and especially to American human nature in a land of rapid haphazard exploitation, sudden wealth and disastrous 'progress,' that the authors were besieged with claimants for the honour of having sat as model. There was a real person, a kinsman of Clemens, who suggested the character, but there was no model except perennial humanity. The book as a whole is amateurish and lacking in cohesion. One suspects that Colonel Sellers kept the two humourists gayly interested in the work, and that they made up the rest of the book in a perfunctory way at a low pitch of creative enthusiasm. Some years later in *The American Claimant* Mark Twain brought Colonel Sellers on the stage again. In this book, as in *The Gilded Age*, the story is nothing (unless it is a 'cruel parody' of *Little Lord Fauntleroy*). But Sellers is himself, generous and pathetically lovable, for all his sham wisdom and magniloquent inflation. He is, like Don Quixote and some of Dickens's characters, drawn taller than life-size, but he is true to the outlines of humanity, a pantographic enlargement of man.

The delight with which the public received Colonel Sellers encouraged Clemens to try another work of fiction. He wrote one of the best of boys' books, *Tom Sawyer*. The adventure in the cave and the finding of gold are the good old-fashioned stuff of dime novels. Mark Twain, like that other wise man with the heart of a boy, Stevenson, has taken the traditional boy romance and made it literature. Except for its one affluent adventure in treasure-trove, the book is all actual boy life, a masterly biography of the universal youngster. The adult novel in America is not yet adult, but four men of letters, Aldrich, Warner, Mr. Howells and Mark Twain, have limned us immortally as we all were in the golden age. It may be that *Tom Sawyer* and *Huckleberry Finn*, Aldrich's *Story of a Bad Boy*, Howells's *Flight of Pony Baker*, and Warner's *Being a Boy* are the reaction of humour and naturalism against the era of St. Rollo.

Like all true books about boys, *Tom Sawyer* gives glimpses of the social conditions and habits of the older generation. There are wider glimpses in *Huckleberry Finn*. Indeed this is more than a boy's book or a book about boys. It is a study of many kinds of society seen through eyes at once innocent and prematurely sage. Those who are fond of classifying books may see in *Huckleberry Finn* a new specimen of the picaresque novel of adventure; some classifiers, going back further for analogies, have called it the 'Odyssey of the Mississippi,' which is strikingly inept. It is a piece of modern realism, original, deep and broad, and it is in American literature deplorably solitary. It is one of the unaccountable triumphs of creative power that seem to happen now and again, as *Robinson Crusoe* happened, and the surrounding intellectual territory has not its comrade.

Huck's dialect is a marvel of artistry. As Clemens says in a significant preface, the shadings in the dialects reported by Huck 'have not been done in a haphazard fashion, or by guesswork; but painstakingly, and with the trustworthy guidance and support of personal familiarity with these several forms of speech.' To maintain Huck's idiom and through it to describe a storm on the Mississippi with intense vividness; through the same dialect to narrate the tragic feud between the Grangerfords and the Shepherdsons; to hint profound social facts through the mouth of a boy and not violate his point of view—this is the work of a very great imagination. Huck's reflection on Tom Sawyer's proposal to 'steal a nigger out of slavery' is a more dramatic revelation of the slaveholder's state of mind than *Uncle Tom's Cabin*, and expresses more powerfully than a thousand treatises the fact that 'morality' is based on economic and social conditions.

Well, one thing was dead sure, and that was that Tom Sawyer was in earnest, and was actually going to help steal that nigger out of slavery. That was the thing that was too many for me. Here was a boy that was respectable and well brung up; and had a character to lose; and folks at home that had characters; and he was bright and not leather-headed; and knowing and not ignorant; and not mean, but kind; and yet here he was, without any more pride, or rightness, or feeling, than to stoop to this business, and make himself a shame, before everybody.

Colonel Sherburn's speech to the crowd that came to lynch him is a sermon on cowardice and valour delivered to the American bully. It is Mark Twain uttering one of his favourite ideas through the Colonel. (Perhaps Huck would not have reported the Colonel's words so accurately.)

[quotes ch. 22 'They swarmed up in front' to 'I didn't want to'.]

The Prince and the Pauper, which like *Huckleberry Finn*, is read with delight by children, is a parable in democracy. Lazarus and Dives, in the figures of two pretty boys, change places, and for once the mighty learn by experience how the other half lives. The same idea is dramatized in *A Connecticut Yankee in King Arthur's Court*, where the king, incognito, goes out among the people. Mark Twain hated the lords of the earth. In 'The Czar's Soliloquy' his hatred is at a white heat. In the course of one of those enchanting monologues with which he entertained his guests he said that every Russian child should drink in with his mother's milk the resolution to kill a czar, 'until every Romanoff would rather sit on a stool in his back yard than on a throne of crime.' He laughed also at the hypocrisy of false republicanism and proved that every democrat loves a lord and why. Humanity, ridiculous, pathetic and pretentious, is all divided into castes, each caste merciless and snobbish. Its portrait is drawn in this passage from *A Connecticut Yankee*:

Toward the shaven monk who trudged along with his cowl tilted back and the sweat washing his fat jowls, the coal-burner was deeply reverent; to the gentleman he was abject; with the small farmer and the free mechanic he was cordial and gossipy; and when a slave passed by with a countenance respectfully lowered, this chap's nose was in the air—he couldn't even see him. Well, there are times when one would like to hang the whole human race and finish the farce.

That is written not about a mythical England of the dark ages, but about *us*. The book is a satire on society. Two conditions of uncivilization are thrown into grotesque contrast primarily for the fun of it all, and also for the sake of flaying priesthood and kingship. The book is not a 'parody' of *Morte d'Arthur*, and it is not cruel. Mark Twain would not have been so witless as to parody a harmless old book; he is not interested in Malory, but in man, and especially in the conflict between man's intelligence and his superstitions.

It is, however, worth noting that like all wise men who chance to give their opinions about books Mark Twain is a good critic. He touches unerringly on Malory's weaknesses, his lack of humour and his inability to characterize. In Malory Sir Dinadan is represented as having delivered a convulsing ballad, but Malory cannot give the ballad, or furnish his humourist with anything to say. Mark Twain seizes this chance to make Sir Dinadan the court bore. Sandy tells the Yankee a story which is taken from Malory, and the Yankee makes a comment which is a just and compact criticism of that inchoate bundle of legends.

When you come to figure up results, you can't tell one fight from another, nor who whipped; and as a picture of living, raging, roaring battle, sho! why, it's pale and noiseless—just ghosts scuffling in a fog. Dear me, what would this barren vocabulary get out of the mightiest spectacle?—the burning of Rome in Nero's time, for instance? Why, it would merely say, 'Town burned down; no insurance; boy brast a window; fireman brake his neck!' Why, that ain't a picture!

Clemens was a shrewd critic of books because he was a shrewd critic of men. He was not hypnotized by what other people thought of the good and the great; he thought for himself. The essays on Cooper and Shelley and Mr. Howells are better than most of the work of professional critics. Some of his casual remarks about books and authors are memorable. He disliked *The Vicar of Wakefield*, because the misadventure of Moses at the fair is represented as funny, whereas it is a pathetic and touching thing when a boy is deceived. Clemens had no admiration for Jane Austen and used to argue with Mr. Howells, who adores her. Most people will agree with Mr. Howells, but nobody can forget, once he has heard it, Mark Twain's way of putting his disapproval: 'A very good library can be started by leaving Jane Austen out.'

A Connecticut Yankee in King Arthur's Court has obvious kinship to

Don Quixote. Both books satirize the ideals of a spurious chivalry. Don Quixote, an idealist, tilts with facts and is beaten, until finally his mind is 'freed from the dark clouds of ignorance with which the continual reading of those detestable books of chivalry had obscured it.' The Yankee, the incarnation of facts, tilts with childish idealism and religious credulity and is beaten! It has been often said that 'Don Quixote gave the death blow to chivalry'—a statement which carelessly overlooks the fact that chivalry never existed. The state of society of which it is the legendary picture had passed before Cervantes; and if by chivalry is meant the literary ideal, that ideal Cervantes did not kill, for it survived lustily to the nineteenth century. The Knight of La Mancha was product of a library of romance which was never read by greater numbers of people than in the past hundred years.

It may be that Cervantes *ought* to have laughed 'Amadis de Gaul and all his generation' off the stage. Then we should have been spared those poor modern imitations of a genuine old literature, those legends of paper kings and tinsel knights which Tennyson and other men of our world, having no real feeling for them, except in a half-hearted anachronistic way, could not make convincing. That Tennyson should have devoted a lifetime to a masterpiece of such flimsy stuff as the *Idyls of the King*, which are not of the spirit of the age and therefore not vital, and that people should take seriously as a kingly ideal his insufferable prig of a hero, show that unfortunately Cervantes did not succeed in clarifying the English mind, whatever medicinal effect he may have had on the Spanish. Wagner used legends akin to the Arthurian for operatic purposes, and in his *Ring* he turned the stories into parables on modern society. One English poet, Swinburne, tried to make the Arthurian story truly tragic by adding to it, or imputing to it, a Greek fate-motive of which the old legends are quite innocent. In the hands of most other modern poets the ideals of chivalry, not being native and intensely felt, but merely admired through a misty literary haze, are both confused and feeble.

A Connecticut Yankee is a humourist's jest, not at any true ancient manner of thought or at any class of fairy tale, but at the falsification of history and at idiotic moonshine held up to admiration as serious story and clothed in the grave beauty of poetry. Not that Mark Twain was a conscious critic of nineteenth-century imitation romance, but like all realists he was filled with the spirit of his time, and quite without intention of making romantic poets and other sentimentalists uncomfortable, he sends the world of terrific and really interesting facts crashing into the stage world of false moonlight and tin armour. The knights of legend, as their modern poetic champions portray them, are garrulous boobies and bullies. Their chivalric attitude toward women is a fraud that disgusts a truly chivalrous man. The sentimentalist who admires Arthur as 'perfectly lovely' and who thinks it philistine to laugh at him, will never understand, of course, that Tennyson's *Idyls* are commonplace and the laureate himself a tedious philistine; nor will they ever understand the great realists, Molière, Fielding, Cervantes, Mark Twain. True chivalry is possible only in those who detest false chivalry. Mark Twain was a supremely chivalrous man, a man of exquisite courtesy and of beautiful loyalty to all ancient and contemporary idealisms. I have read somewhere the opinion that he was vulgar, but the unique cannot be vulgar; moreover, as Pudd'nhead Wilson says, 'There are no people who are quite so vulgar as the over-refined.' Clemens has also been called irreverent. He *was* disrespectful of all superstitions, including his own. Says Pudd'nhead Wilson, 'Let me make the superstitions of a nation, and I care not who makes its laws or its songs either.'

Mark Twain was a globe-trotter; he knew all grades and conditions of man, and he was a reader of history and biography; he was early cured of the grossest of superstitions, abject patriotism, with which all peoples are drenched and with which Americans, especially, seem to be afflicted.

That is the Mark Twain who 'jokingly' said that the only distinct native criminal class in America is congressmen, the Mark Twain who despairingly predicted that America, having proved that it was not capable of being truly democratic, would probably set up a monarchy in the course of another century, and who uttered as blasting an arraignment of American plutocracy as ever fell from a man's lips. Americans, complaisant and sentimental, do not yet know the power of Mark Twain's Swiftian attacks on our flimsy-minded patriotism and religiosity. After his death he was slandered by nice critics who purvey optimism and water to the multitude; they spoke of his 'kindly wit and humour which never hurt any one.' From such libel may he be defended! Some missionaries, politicians, soldiers, and priests of several churches from Rome to Huntington Avenue, Boston, will, if they have read his works, tell a different story.

Only a man whose heart is purged of counterfeit idealism can be the lofty idealist that Mark Twain was. He worshipped truth and worthy individuals dead and living. His *Personal Recollections of Joan of Arc* is a tribute to a heroine whose nobility is authentic, whose good head and good heart are proved by documents. It is an eloquent book, instinct with such reverence and passion for beauty as are possible in a soul that is not moved by hazy pieties or tricked by too easy credulity. The tone of the book is sustainedly perfect, the style excellently managed by the same imagination that holds unbrokenly true the character and diction of Huckleberry Finn. After he acknowledged the book everybody saw that he must have written it, and pointed to the obvious Mark-Twain-isms, but when the story was first published anonymously, many wise critics failed to guess the authorship. In one character Mark Twain is enjoying himself in his everyday manner—in the Paladin, the comic foil, the picturesque liar whom Mark Twain likes to introduce into all human company. The episode in the Fifteenth Chapter of the Second Book, laughter in the lap of tragedy, is one of those wrenching contrasts of human feelings such as only the Shakespeares can draw unfalteringly.

In the work of no modern prose writer is there wider range than in the work of Mark Twain—from *Huckleberry Finn* to *Joan of Arc*. He had wonderful breadth of knowledge and interest; whatever he encountered he pondered. And he seems to have turned almost every experience into a written page. When, at the end of his life, he came to write what was to be 'the best and truest autobiography ever written,' he confessed in whimsical desperation that he could not tell the truth and never had told the truth, that as Pudd'nhead Wilson says, the very ink with which history is written is prejudice. He must also have found that he had already written in his other books as much of his autobiography as it was possible for him to write. His books are a record of his career from his memories of boyhood to his last travels round the world.

He wrote three more books of the desultory type of *Innocents Abroad*, and *Roughing It*—namely, *A Tramp Abroad*, *Life on the Mississippi*, and *Following the Equator*. His sketches of travel are first-rate examples of that informal sort of tourists' essay to which in their way belong Thackeray's *Cornhill to Cairo* and Kinglake's *Eothen*. Of travel books there are many; of vital ones there are all too few. Those few are made by great original talkers who find something more or less apropos to say in any scene they chance to visit. *Life on the Mississippi* is the record in 'the King's English' of the country and types of life made even more surely immortal in the dialect of *Huckleberry Finn*. *Pudd'nhead Wilson*, a fantastic tale, is laid on the lower Mississippi before the war. Like

Mark Twain's other attempts to write a novel in conventional form, *Pudd'nhead Wilson* is not well-constructed; it succeeds by virtue of one comic character, whose 'calendar' became the vehicle of Mark Twain's epigrams. As he confesses in the introduction to 'Those Extraordinary Twins,' he is not a born novelist; his account of his difficulty in managing a story will make any one chuckle who has ever tried to write fiction.

[quotes 'the book was finished' to 'any more anyway'.]

Among Clemens's miscellanies are several little masterpieces, 'The Man That Corrupted Hadleyburg,' *Eve's Diary*, and *Captain Stormfield's Visit to Heaven*. 'The Man That Corrupted Hadleyburg' condenses human avarice and human mendacity into a fable that says, 'There you are numbered,' and leaves you laughing and morally naked. Hadleyburg is a town lying on the east bank of the Mississippi River; it extends eastward to the west bank of the river.

Eve's Diary is a beautiful piece of poetic prose. It is a joke, of course; the absent-minded brontosaurus is there to prove it, and the respectable American librarians and library trustees, who (owing to their lack of historical knowledge) objected to Eve's costume and ruled the book off the shelves, made the joke a perfect torture of hilarity. Nevertheless it is poetry. Eve's effort to gather the stars in a basket is such a conception as only genius is blessed with. The comedy of the sketch appeals immediately to that national calamity, American humour, which never was on earth until after the voyages of Columbus. Many Americans no doubt curl up in convulsed delight at the excruciating fun of the passage which closes the book; but a civilized man will appreciate its tender beauty.

[quotes 'Forty Years Later' to '*there* was Eden'.]

Captain Stormfield's Visit to Heaven completes the work which satire, science, and intellectual honesty have been engaged in for over a century—it makes ultimate nonsense of the sentimentalist's Heaven.

Mark Twain's mind was of universal proportions; he meditated on all the deep problems, and somewhere in his work he touches upon most of the vital things that men commonly think about and wonder about. As he once quaintly said: 'I am the only man living who understands human nature; God has put me in charge of this branch office; when I retire, there will be no one to take my place, I shall keep on doing my duty, for when I get over on the other side, I shall use my influence to have the human race drowned again, and this time drowned good, no omissions, no Ark.' His was the veracity of an accurately controlled extravagance. A destroyer of false idols, he was an idolator of beauty, especially of beautiful women. He was a man of exquisite dignity, very sensitive and fine, and yet capable at seventy of fooling like a boy.

The final philosophy of this lover of boys and men and women and cats is, as he says, 'a desolating doctrine.' That is, it is desolating to timidity, but very brave for those who can square their shoulders and look things straight in the eye. It teaches that we have an interior Master whom our conduct must satisfy and whom nothing but good conduct will leave in peace. It eliminates all extraneous bribes to be good. It is like the religion which is preached in a work by another austere moralist—in Mr. Bernard Shaw's *The Showing-Up of Blanco Posnet*. And it bears some resemblance to the humane scepticism of Mr. Thomas Hardy. Without studying or caring at all for official philosophy (and all the wiser for the omission), Mark Twain came to a position of ethical and materialistic determinism which is rife in the thought of our time and is in one aspect as old as the Greek who said: 'Character is fate.' For his philosophy most readers quite properly care nothing. They care for his portrait of Mankind. And that is the greatest canvas that any American has painted.

88. H. L. Mencken: 'The Burden of Humor', *Smart Set*

February 1913, xxxviii, 151–4

Mencken's demand in 1913 for the release of all of Mark Twain's unpublished writings is now being belatedly met by the edition of 'The Mark Twain Papers' published by the University of California Press. The unfinished condition and irresolute development of many of these literary pieces exonerates Olivia Clemens from the burden of Mencken's charge, often repeated by others, that she had 'suppressed' parts of Mark Twain's work.

What is the origin of the prejudice against humor? Why is it so dangerous, if you would keep the public confidence, to make the public laugh?

Is it because humor and sound sense are essentially antagonistic? Has humanity found by experience that the man who sees the fun of life is unfitted to deal sanely with its problems? I think not. No man had more of the comic spirit in him than William Shakespeare, and yet his serious reflections, by the sheer force of their sublime obviousness, have pushed their way into the race's arsenal of immortal platitudes. So, too, with Æsop, and with Lincoln and Johnson, to come down the scale. All of these men were humorists, and yet all of them performed prodigies of indubitable wisdom. And contrariwise, many an undeniable pundit has had his guffaw. Huxley, if he had not been the greatest intellectual duellist of his age, might have been its greatest wit. And Beethoven, after soaring to the heights of tragedy in the first movement of the Fifth Symphony, turned to the divine fooling, the irresistible bull-fiddling of the *scherzo*.

No, there is not the slightest disharmony between sense and nonsense, humor and respectability, despite the almost universal tendency to assume that there is. But, why, then, that widespread error? What actual fact of life lies behind it, giving it a specious appearance of reasonableness? None other, I am convinced, than the fact that the average man is far too stupid to make a joke.

He may *see* a joke and love a *joke*, particularly when it floors and flabbergasts some person he dislikes, but the only way he can himself take part in the priming and pointing of a new one is by acting as its target. In brief, his personal contact with humor tends to fill him with an accumulated sense of disadvantage, of pricked complacency, of sudden and crushing defeat; and so, by an easy psychological process, he is led into the idea that the thing itself is incompatible with true dignity of character and intellect. Hence his deep suspicion of jokers, however their thrusts. 'What a damphool!'—this same half-pitying tribute he pays to wit and butt alike. He cannot separate the virtuoso of comedy from his general concept of comedy itself, and that concept is inextricably mixed with memories of foul ambuscades and mortifying hurts. And so it is not often that he is willing to admit any wisdom in a humorist, or to condone frivolity in a sage.

In all this, I believe, there is a plausible explanation of the popular, and even of the critical attitude toward the late Samuel Langhorne Clemens (Mark Twain). Unless I am so wholly mistaken that my only expiation lies in suicide, Mark was the noblest literary artist, who ever set pen to paper on American soil, and not only the noblest artist, but also one of the most profound and sagacious philosophers. From the beginning of his maturity down to his old age he dealt constantly and earnestly with the deepest problems of life and living, and to his consideration of them he brought a truly amazing instinct for the truth, an almost uncanny talent for ridding the essential thing of its deceptive husks of tradition, prejudice, flubdub and balderdash. No man, not even Nietzsche, ever did greater execution against those puerilities of fancy which so many men mistake for religion, and over which they are so eager to dispute and break heads. No man had a keener eye for that element of pretense which is bound to intrude itself into all human thinking, however serious, however painstaking, however honest in intent. And yet, because the man had humor as well as acumen, because he laughed at human weakness instead of weeping over it, because he turned now and then from the riddle of life to the joy of life—because of this habit of mind it is the custom to regard him lightly and somewhat apologetically, as one debarred from greatness by unfortunate infirmities.

William Dean Howells probably knew him better than any other human being, but in all that Howells has written about him one is conscious of a conditioned admiration, of a subtle fear of allowing him too much merit, of an ineradicable disinclination to take him quite seriously. The Mark that Howells draws is not so much a great artist as a glorious *enfant terrible*. And even William Lyon Phelps, a hospitable and penetrating critic, wholly loose of orthodox shackles—even Phelps hems and haws a bit before putting Mark above Oliver Wendell Holmes, and is still convinced that *The Scarlet Letter* is an incomparably finer work of art than *Huckleberry Finn*.

Well, such notions will die hard, but soon or late, I am sure, they will inevitably die. So certain am I, indeed, of their dying that I now formally announce their death in advance, and prepare to wait in patience for the delayed applause. In one of his essays Dr. Phelps shows how critical opinion of Mark has gradually evolved from scorn into indifference, and from indifference into toleration, and from toleration into apologetic praise, and from apologetic praise into hearty praise. The stage of unqualified enthusiasm is coming—it has already cast its lights before England—and I am very glad to join the lodge as a charter member. Let me now set down my faith, for the literary archeologists of day after tomorrow:

I believe that *Huckleberry Finn* is one of the great masterpieces of the world, that it is the full equal of *Don Quixote* and *Robinson Crusoe*, that it is vastly better than *Gil Blas*, *Tristram Shandy*, *Nicholas Nickleby* or *Tom Jones*. I believe that it will be read by human beings of all ages, not as a solemn duty but for the honest love of it, and over and over again, long after every book written in America between the years 1800 and 1860, with perhaps three exceptions, has disappeared entirely save as a classroom fossil. I believe that Mark Twain had a clearer vision of life, that he came nearer to its elementals and was less deceived by its false appearances, than any other American who has ever presumed to manufacture generalizations, not excepting Emerson. I believe that, admitting all his defects, he wrote better English, in the sense of cleaner, straighter, vivider, saner English, than either Irving or Hawthorne. I believe that four of his books—*Huck*, *Life on the Mississippi*, *Captain Stormfield's Visit to Heaven*, and *A Connecticut Yankee*—are alone worth more, as works of art and as criticisms of life, than the whole output of Cooper, Irving, Holmes, Mitchell, Stedman, Whittier and Bryant. I believe that he ranks well above Whitman and certainly not below Poe. I believe that he was the true father of our national literature, the first genuinely American artist of the blood royal.

Such is my feeling at the moment, and such has been my feeling for many a moon. If any gentleman in the audience shares it, either wholly or with qualifications, then I advise him to buy and read the biography of Mark lately published by Albert Bigelow Paine (*Harper*), for therein he will find an elaborate, painstaking and immensely interesting portrait of the man, and sundry shrewd observations upon the writer.

Not that I agree with Paine in all his judgments. Far from it, indeed. It seems to me that he gets bogged hopelessly when he tries to prove that *The Innocents Abroad* is a better book than *A Tramp Abroad*, that he commits a crime when he puts *Joan of Arc* above *Huck Finn*, and that he is too willing to join Howells and other such literary sacristans in frowning down upon Mark's clowning, his weakness for vulgarity, his irrepressible maleness. In brief, Paine is disposed, at times, to yield to current critical opinion against what must be his own good sense. But when you have allowed for all this—and it is not obtrusive—the thing that remains is a vivid and sympathetic biography, a book with sound merit in every chapter of it, a mountain of difficulties triumphantly surmounted, a fluent and excellent piece of writing. Paine tells everything that is worth hearing, whether favorable to Mark or the reverse, and leaves out all that is not worth hearing. One closes the third volume with unbounded admiration for the industry of the biographer, and with no less admiration for his frankness and sagacity. He has given us a rich and colorful book, presenting coherently a wise selection from a perfect chaos of materials. The Mark Twain that emerges from it is almost as real as Huckleberry Finn.

And what a man that Mark Twain was! How he stood above and apart from the world, like Rabelais come to life again, observing the human comedy, chuckling over the eternal fraudulence of man! What a sharp eye he had for the bogus, in religion, politics, art, literature, patriotism, virtue! What contempt he emptied upon shams of all sorts—and what pity! Mr. Paine reveals for us very clearly, by quotation and exposition, his habitual attitude of mind. He regarded all men as humbugs, but as humbugs to be dealt with gently, as humbugs too often taken in and swindled by their own humbuggery. He saw how false reasoning, false assumptions, false gods had entered into the very warp and woof of their thinking; how impossible it was for them to attack honestly the problems of being; how helpless they were in the face of life's emergencies. And seeing all this, he laughed at them, but not often with malice. What genuine indignation he was capable of was leveled at life itself and not at its victims. Through all his later years the riddle of existence was ever before him. He thought about it constantly; he discussed it with everyone he knew; he made copious notes of his speculations. But he never came to any soothing custom made conclusion. The more he examined life, the more it appeared to him to be without meaning, and even without direction; the more he pondered upon the idea of God, the more a definite idea of God eluded him. In the end, as Mr. Paine tells us, he verged toward a hopeless pessimism. Death seemed to him a glad release, an inestimable boon. When his daughter Jean died, suddenly, tragically, he wrote to her sister: 'I am so glad she is out of it and safe—safe!'

It is this reflective, philosophizing Clemens who stands out most clearly in Mr. Paine's book. In his own works, our glimpses of him are all too brief. His wife and his friends opposed his speculations, perhaps wisely, for the artist might have been swallowed up in the sage. But he wrote much to please himself and left a vast mass of unpublished manuscript behind him. Certainly it is to be hoped that these writings will see the light, and before long. One book described by Mr. Paine, *Three Thousand Years Among the Microbes*, would appear to be a satire so mordant and so large in scale that his admirers have a plain right to demand its publication. And there should be a new edition, too, of his confession of doubt, *What is Man?* of which a few copies were printed for private distribution in 1905. Yet again we have a right to ask for most if not all of his unpublished stories and sketches, many of which were suppressed at the behest of Mrs. Clemens, for reasons no longer worth considering. There is good ground for believing that his reputation will gain rather than suffer by the publication of these things, and in any case it can withstand the experiment, for *Huck Finn* and *Life on the Mississippi* and the *Connecticut Yankee* will remain, and so long as they remain there can be no question of the man's literary stature. He was one of the great artists of all time. He was the full equal of Cervantes and Molière, Swift and Defoe. He was and is the one authentic giant of our national literature.

APPENDIX A: TWO MARK TWAIN LETTERS

Letter to Andrew Chatto

16 July 1889

Andrew Chatto (died 1913) of Chatto & Windus was Clemens' English publisher at this time. James Ripley Osgood (1836–92) had been Clemens' publisher in the United States. When his publishing firm failed in 1885, he became the London representative of Harper & Brothers.

The text of this letter is taken from an unsigned typescript on Charles L. Webster & Co. letterhead in the Mark Twain Papers.

July, 16th. 1889

Dear Mr. Chatto;—

Your statements and drafts came yesterday, for $364.00, for which I thank you and endorse your opinion that it's a very good return for an off year.

I have revised the *Yankee* twice; Stedman has critically read it and pointed out to me some needed emendations; Mrs. Clemens has read it and made me strike out many passages and soften others; I have read chapters of it in public several times where Englishmen were present, and have profited by their suggestions. Next week I shall make a *final* revision. After that, if it still isn't blemishless I can't help it, and ain't going to try.

Now mind you, I have taken all this pains because I wanted to say a Yankee mechanic's say against monarchy and its several natural props, and yet make a book which you would be willing to print exactly as it comes to you, without altering a word.

We are spoken of, (by Englishmen) as a thin-skinned people. It is you that are thin skinned. An Englishman may write with the most brutal frankness about any man or any institution among us, and we re-publish him without dreaming of altering a line or a word. But England cannot stand that kind of a book, written about herself. It is England that is thin-skinned. It causeth me to smile, when I read the modifications of my language which have been made in my English Editions to fit them for the sensitive English palate.

Now as I say, I have taken laborious pains to so trim this book of offence that you'll not lack the nerve to print it just as it stands. I'm going to get the proofs to you just as early as I can. I want you to read it carefully.

If you can publish it without altering a single word, or omitting one, go ahead. Otherwise, please hand it to J. R. Osgood in time for him to have it published at my expense.

This is important, for the reason that the book was not written for America, it was written for England. So many Englishmen have done their sincerest best to teach us something for our betterment, that it seems to me high time that some of us should substantially recognize the good intent by trying to pry up the English nation to a little higher level of manhood in turn.

Sincerely yours

Mess. Chatto & Windus,
   London.

Letter to Andrew Lang

1890(?)

This letter, which lacks both salutation and signature, apparently was part of a draft of the letter Clemens actually sent. Lang's 1891 article in the *Illustrated London News* (No. 39) appears to be a response to some of the arguments presented here.

They vote, but do not print. The head tells you pretty promptly whether the food is satisfactory or not; and everybody hears, and thinks the whole man has spoken. It is a delusion. Only his taste and his smell have been heard from—important, both, in a way, but these do not build up the man, and preserve his life and fortify it.

The little child is permitted to label its drawings 'This is a cow—this is a horse,' and so on. This protects the child. It saves it from the sorrow and wrong of hearing its cows and its horses criticised as Kangaroos and work-benches. A man who is whitewashing a fence is doing a useful thing, so also is the man who is adorning a rich man's house with costly frescoes; and all of us are sane enough to judge these performances by standards proper to each. Now, then, to be fair, an author ought to be allowed to put upon his book an explanatory line: 'This is written for the Head;' 'This is written for the Belly and the Members.' And the critic ought to hold himself in honor bound to put away from him his ancient habit of judging all books by one standard, and thenceforth follow a fairer course.

The critic assumes, every time, that if a book doesn't meet the cultivated-class standard, it isn't valuable. Let us apply his law all around: for if it is sound in the case of novels, narratives, pictures, and such things, it is certainly sound and applicable to all the steps which lead up to culture and make culture possible. It condemns the spelling book, for a spelling book is of no use to a person of culture; it condemns all school books and all schools which lie between the child's primer and Greek, and between the infant school and the university; it condemns all the rounds of art which lie between the cheap terra cotta groups and the Venus de Medici, and between the Chromo and the Transfiguration; it requires Whitcomb Riley to sing no more till he can sing like Shakespeare, and it forbids all amateur music and will grant its sanction to nothing below the 'classic.'

Is this an extravagant statement? No, it is a mere statement of fact. It is the fact itself that is extravagant and grotesque. And what is the result? This—and it is sufficiently curious: the critic has actually imposed upon the world the superstition that a painting by Raphael is more valuable to the civilizations of the earth than is a Chromo; and the august opera than the hurdy-gurdy and the villagers' singing society; and Homer than the little everybody's-poet whose rhymes are in all mouths to-day and will be in nobody's mouth next generation; and the Latin classics than Kipling's far-reaching bugle-note; and Jonathan Edwards than the Salvation Army; and the Venus di Medici than the plaster-cast peddler; the superstition, in a word, that the vast and awful comet that trails its cold lustre through the remote abysses of space once a century and interests and instructs a cultivated handful of astronomers is worth more to the world than the sun which warms and cheers all the nations every day and makes the crops to grow.

If a critic should start a religion it would not have any object but to convert angels; and they wouldn't need it. The thin top crust of humanity—the cultivated—are worth pacifying, worth pleasing, worth coddling, worth nourishing and preserving with dainties and delicacies, it is true; but to be caterer to that little faction is no very dignified or valuable occupation, it seems to me; it is merely feeding the over-fed, and there must be small satisfaction in that. It is not that little minority who are already saved that are best worth lifting at, I should think, but the mighty mass of the uncultivated who are underneath. That mass will never see the Old Masters—that sight is for the few; but the chromo maker can lift them all one step upward toward appreciation of art; they cannot have the opera, but the hurdy-gurdy and the singing class lift them a little way toward that far height; they will never know Homer, but the passing rhymester of their day leaves them higher than he found them; they may never even hear of the Latin classics, but they will strike step with Kipling's drum-beat, and they will march; for all Jonathan Edwards's help they would die in their slums, but the Salvation Army will beguile some of them up to pure air and a cleaner life; they know no sculpture, the Venus is not even a name to them, but they are a grade higher in the scale of civilization by its ministrations of the plaster-cast than they were before it took its place upon their mantel and made it beautiful to their unexacting eyes.

Indeed I have been misjudged, from the very first. I have never tried in even one single little instance, to help cultivate the cultivated classes. I was not equipped for it, either by native gifts or training. And I never had any ambition in that direction, but always hunted for bigger game—the masses. I have seldom deliberately tried to instruct them, but have done my best to entertain them. To simply amuse them would have satisfied my dearest ambition at any time; for they could get instruction elsewhere, and I had two chances to help to the teacher's one: for amusement is a good preparation for study and a good healer of fatigue after it. My audience is dumb, it has no voice in print, and so I cannot know whether I have won its approbation or only got its censure.

Yes, you see, I have always catered for the Belly and the Members, but have been served like the others—criticised from the culture-standard—to my sorrow and pain; because, honestly, I never cared what became of the cultured classes; they could go to the theatre and the opera, they had no use for me and the melodeon.

And now at last I arrive at my object and tender my petition, making supplication to this effect: that the critics adopt a rule recognizing the Belly and the Members, and formulate a standard whereby work done for them shall be judged. Help me, Mr. Lang; no voice can reach further than yours in a case of this kind, or carry greater weight of authority.

APPENDIX B: THE SUBSCRIPTION BOOK

George Ade:
'Mark Twain and the Old Time Subscription Book', *Review of Reviews* (New York)

June 1910, xli, 703–4

George Ade (1866–1944), journalist, author and humorist, was known at the turn of the century for his 'fables in slang' and for his stage comedies. On 22 July 1908 Clemens wrote to Howells about *Pink Marsh*, a collection of stories by George Ade first published in 1897, 'Thank you once more for introducing me to the incomparable Pink Marsh. I have been reading him again after this long interval, & my admiration of the book has over-flowed all limits, all frontiers' (*Mark Twain–Howells Letters*, p. 832).

Mark Twain should be doubly blessed for saving the center table from utter dullness. Do you remember that center table of the seventies? The marble top showed glossy in the subdued light that filtered through the lace curtains, and it was clammy cold even on hot days. The heavy mahogany legs were chiseled into writhing curves from which depended stern geometrical designs or possibly bunches of grapes. The Bible had the place of honor and was flanked by subscription books. In those days the house never became cluttered with the ephemeral six best sellers. The new books came a year apart, and each was meant for the center table, and it had to be so thick and heavy and emblazoned with gold that it could keep company with the bulky and high-priced Bible.

Books were bought by the pound. Sometimes the agent was a ministerial person in black clothes and a stove-pipe hat. Maiden ladies and widows, who supplemented their specious arguments with private tales of woe, moved from one small town to another feeding upon prominent citizens. Occasionally the prospectus was unfurled by an undergraduate of a freshwater college working for the money to carry him another year.

The book-agents varied, but the book was always the same,—many pages, numerous steel engravings, curly-cue tail-pieces, platitudes, patriotism, poetry, sentimental mush. One of the most popular, still resting in many a dim sanctuary, was known as *Mother, Home, and Heaven*. A ponderous collection of *Poetical Gems* did not involve the publishers in any royalty entanglements. Even the *Lives of the Presidents* and *Noble Deeds of the Great and Brave* gave every evidence of having been turned out as piece-work by needy persons temporarily lacking employment on newspapers. Let us not forget the *Manual of Deportment and Social Usages*, from which the wife of any agriculturist could learn the meaning of R.S.V.P. and the form to be employed in acknowledging an invitation to a levee.

Nobody really wanted these books. They were purchased because the agents knew how to sell them, and they seemed large for the price, and, besides, every well-furnished home had to keep something on the center table.

Subscription books were dry picking for boys. Also they were accessible only on the Sabbath after the weekly scouring. On weekdays the boys favored an underground circulating library, named after Mr. Beadle, and the hay-mow was the chosen reading room. Let one glorious exception be made in the case of *Dr. Livingstone's Travels in Africa*, a subscription book of forbidding size, but containing many pictures of darkies with rings in their noses.

Just when front-room literature seemed at its lowest ebb, so far as the American boy was concerned, along came Mark Twain. His books looked, at a distance, just like the other distended, diluted, and altogether tasteless volumes that had been used for several decades to balance the ends of the center table. The publisher knew his public, so he gave a pound of book for every fifty cents, and crowded in plenty of wood-cuts and stamped the outside with golden bouquets and put in a steel engraving of the author, with a tissue paper veil over it, and 'sicked' his multitude of broken-down clergymen, maiden ladies, grass widows, and college students on to the great American public.

Can you see the boy, a Sunday morning prisoner, approach the new book with a dull sense of foreboding, expecting a dose of Tupper's *Proverbial Philosophy*? Can you see him a few minutes later when he finds himself linked arm-in-arm with Mulberry Sellers or Buck Fanshaw or the convulsing idiot who wanted to know if Christopher Columbus was sure-enough dead? No wonder he curled up on the hair-cloth sofa and hugged the thing to his bosom and lost all interest in Sunday-school. *Innocents Abroad* was the most enthralling book ever printed until *Roughing It* appeared. Then along came *The Gilded Age*, *Life on the Mississippi*, and *Tom Sawyer*, one cap sheaf after another. While waiting for a new one we read the old ones all over again.

The new uniform edition with the polite little pages, high-art bindings and all the boisterous wood-cuts carefully expurgated can never take the place of those lumbering subscription books. They were the early friends and helped us to get acquainted with the most amazing story-teller that ever captivated the country boys and small-town boys all over America.

While we are honoring Mark Twain as a great literary artist, a philosopher, and a teacher, let the boys of the seventies add their tribute. They knew him for his miracle of making the subscription book something to be read and not merely looked at. He converted the Front Room from a Mausoleum into a Temple of Mirth.

Bibliography

The following is a list of bibliographies, collections of critical articles and twentieth-century commentaries on Mark Twain's writing.

ASSELINEAU, ROGER, *The Literary Reputation of Mark Twain from 1910 to 1950* (1955): 'a critical bibliography of Mark Twain criticism in the United States as well as in Great Britain, France, Germany, Italy, Spain and Latin America'.

KAPLAN, JUSTIN, *Mark Twain: A Profile* (1967): a concise survey of material written since 1910 with emphasis on historical studies.

LEARY, LEWIS, *Articles on American Literature 1900–1950* (1954): an index of popular as well as scholarly writings, unannotated.

LEARY, LEWIS, *Index to Articles on American Literature, 1951–1959* (1960).

LEARY, LEWIS, *Mark Twain's Wound* (1962): an excellent group of essays which 'speak, not only of Mark Twain and his wound, but of the vagaries and progress of American literary criticism during the past forty years'.

SCOTT, ARTHUR L., *Mark Twain: Selected Criticism* (1955): contains some nineteenth- as well as twentieth-century reviews.

SMITH, HENRY NASH, *Mark Twain: A Collection of Critical Essays* (1963): 'Asselineau . . . has so thoroughly documented the development of critical opinion about Mark Twain during the first half of this century that the present collection may appropriately concentrate on the period since 1950.'

STOVALL, FLOYD, *Eight American Authors, A Review of Research and Criticism* (1956): includes a chapter on Mark Twain; a *Bibliographical Supplement* was issued in 1963.

WAGENKNECHT, EDWARD, *Mark Twain, The Man and His Work* (1935, 1961, 1967): all three editions publish extensive bibliographies of Mark Twain criticism with idiosyncratic commentary.

WOODRESS, JAMES, *American Literary Scholarship 1963* [with annual continuations] (1965–): each issue contains a thorough and thoughtful discussion of publications of Mark Twain's works as well as of biographical and critical studies.

Index

II MARK TWAIN: CHARACTERISTICS

III GENERAL